THE DEVIL, DISEASE, AND DELIVERANCE
ORIGINS OF ILLNESS IN NEW TESTAMENT THOUGHT

THE
DEVIL, DISEASE
AND DELIVERANCE

ORIGINS OF ILLNESS IN NEW TESTAMENT THOUGHT

JOHN CHRISTOPHER THOMAS

CPT Press
Cleveland, Tennessee

The Devil, Disease, and Deliverance
Origins of Illness in New Testament Thought

Published by CPT Press
900 Walker ST NE
Cleveland, TN 37311
USA
email: cptpress@pentecostaltheology.org
website: www.cptpress.com

Library of Congress Control Number: 2010940275

ISBN-10: 1935931032
ISBN-13: 9781935931034

The Graeca font used to print this work is available from Linguist's Software, Inc., PO Box 580, Edmonds, WA 98020-0580 USA tel (425) 775-1130 www.linguistsoftware.com.

BWHEBB, BWHEBL, BWTRANSH [Hebrew], BWGRKL, BWGRKN, and BWGRKI [Greek] Postscript® Type 1 and TrueTypeT fonts Copyright © 1994-2009 BibleWorks, LLC. All rights reserved. These Biblical Greek and Hebrew fonts are used with permission and are from BibleWorks, software for Biblical exegesis and research.

For my parents, Wayne and Betty Fritts, who first taught me to love the biblical text, to search for its meaning, and to struggle with its implications.

CONTENTS

PREFACE

Upon the completion and publication of my PhD thesis on Foot-washing in John 13 and the Johannine Community, I began to spend a good deal of time in prayer and reflection with regard to the nature and purpose of my next major research project. Those who have invested the required time and energy on a PhD thesis know well how one's life tends to be defined by the periods before and after completion of this post-graduate journey. In my own case, it was not too long until I began to sense that my next project should be devoted to a topic that in many ways is one of the most troublesome issues currently facing those working and ministering within the Pentecostal and charismatic traditions. This leading did not come as a bolt out of the blue but emerged as a result of the confusion within the tradition over the role of the demonic in illness. Somewhat to my surprise, there was no readily available comprehensive study of New Testament texts which focuses on the origins of illness. Thus, my own interpretive journey began with an examination of Jas 5.14-16, which in turn led to a study of the many other relevant New Testament texts.

The method of the study will be discussed in the Introduction. With regard to the scope of the research, I have attempted to read everything I could locate on the various texts examined. Inevitably, some sources have been overlooked. I fear this is particularly true with the earlier portions of the book. Unfortunately there comes a time when one must simply stop looking at the secondary literature and finish the project. I apologize in advance for the inevitable lacunae.

This research, which has taken place over the course of the last seven years, has been aided by many, and I am happy to acknowledge my indebtedness to a number of those who have facilitated its completion. The Church of God School of Theology has provided periodic study leaves over the course of the last few years and graciously granted a sabbatical leave to bring the project to completion. The Woodward Ave. Church of God and the Church of God Executive Committee generously underwrote much of this research when other sources of funding became unavailable owing, in part, to the subject matter of the research. At a time when many Pentecostal scholars continue to be ignored by funding agencies, I was blessed to have such benefaction. My good friends, William and Peggy Bridges, continue to include the support of Pentecostal scholarship as part of their faithful stewardship.

Aside from brief periods of research at Emory University and St John's Theological College (Nottingham), the bulk of this book was written at Tyndale House, Cambridge. The warm environment provided by this residential library is surely one of the best places in the world to conduct biblical research. My sincere thanks to all those who have made a place for and welcomed me there over the years.

My thanks also go to many friends, students, and colleagues who have listened to me, critiqued the work, discerned its meaning, and prayed for me during the process of writing. Special mention should be made of colleagues who have encouraged me often in this journey: Steve Land, Cheryl Bridges Johns, Corky and Kimberly Alexander, Rick Waldrop, Jackie Johns, Bob Crick, Lee Roy Martin, and Hollis Gause. Heartfelt thanks are due my friend and colleague, Rick Moore, who not only suggested the title for this monograph, but carefully read and edited the whole of the manuscript. A succession of graduate assistants have each made contributions toward the publication of this volume. They include: Marcia Anderson, Daniel Chatham, Jerry Ingram, Everett Franklin, and Scott Ingram. The prayer group at Woodward (Ronnie Davis, Jerry Stephens, Merville Weerasekera, and many others) provided much needed spiritual support. As usual, the people who have sacrificed most for the completion of this and many other research projects are my wife, Barbara, and my daughters, Paige and Lori. Their love, energy, consistency, companionship, and faith contribute more to me than any of them can know. Thanks for bearing with all those (transatlantic) separations!

My parents, Wayne and Betty Fritts, who each encountered more than one serious illness during the course of this project, have taught me much about this topic and life. From very early in my life their love for the biblical text nurtured my own. Without their spiritual, financial, and emotional support, I would never have had the opportunity to pursue the academic study of the New Testament and certainly would not have been able to bring any of the many programs or projects to completion. My love and gratitude for them cannot be adequately expressed. This book is dedicated to them as a small token of my love, admiration, respect, and thanks.

It is my prayer that this work will contribute in a small way to a better understanding of an aspect of Pentecostal thought and ministry which is controversial and, at the same time, extraordinarily important.

PREFACE TO CPT PRESS EDITION

Little did I realize when this study first appeared some thirteen years ago that it would be met by a number of very positive reviews or that its publication would result in several invitations to discuss the book and its contents at a variety of educational institutions and three ecumenical dialogues in seven countries on five continents. These venues included the International School of Theology-Asia (Queson City, Philippines), Mattersey Hall (UK), North Park Seminary (Chicago, IL, USA), Oral Roberts University (Tulsa, OK, USA), Tyndale Seminary (Toronto, Canada), the University of Birmingham (UK), as well as the Lausanne Consultation on Theology entitled 'Deliver Us from Evil' (Nairobi, Kenya), and two World Council of Churches Consultations on Healing (Accra, Ghana and Santiago, Chile). Not only was I highly honored by such invitations, but these and other times of dialogue and engagement were also occasions on which I learned immensely from a variety of dialogue partners including both academics and practitioners. For these opportunities I am extremely grateful.

Nor did I anticipate that this academic monograph would find the place in the market that it has, going through several printings, even as the price of the book doubled and almost tripled when its rights passed from one publisher to another. For all those who purchased copies of the work I offer my heartfelt thanks, especially to those who purchased copies after the price began to skyrocket. Surprisingly (to me at any rate), despite such price increases there continues to be an interest in the work and for this I am humbled.

When this volume first appeared I had no idea that within a decade it would find a place amongst a variety of other Pentecostal titles with a press dedicated to just such scholarship, CPT Press, which was created, in part, to support the work of the Centre for Pentecostal Theology which I direct along with my esteemed colleague and good friend Lee Roy Martin. To this point the press has had great success in publishing quality Pentecostal scholarship at reasonable prices. It is with a great deal of joy that I celebrate the appearance of this CPT Press edition of *The Devil, Disease, and Deliverance.*

It should perhaps be noted that the CPT Press edition of *The Devil, Disease, and Deliverance* is similar in most respects to its earlier counterpart, with a few small changes. The most obvious difference is that the text has been reset entirely, meaning that there are some differences in pagination between the Sheffield Academic Press/ Continuum edition and the current one. I trust that this inconvenience will not be too taxing for the reader. Errors in the original that have been brought to my attention have been corrected, though no doubt others have been introduced (!). On a couple of occasions slight interpretive corrections or clarifications have been made, which I leave for the reader to discern. The indices for this edition have been prepared by Reverend Larry Flickner, my graduate assistant and MDiv student at the Pentecostal Theological Seminary. I also wish to thank my former graduate assistant Shawn Hitt for his assistance in preparing the manuscript. Another graduate assistant, Vickie Williams, is thanked for reading the manuscript at proof stage.

As in the preface to the first edition it is my prayer that this work will contribute in a small way to a better understanding of an aspect of Pentecostal thought and ministry which is controversial and, at the same time, extraordinarily important.

ABBREVIATIONS

AusBR	*Australian Biblical Review*
BAG	Walter Bauer, William F. Arndt, and F. William Gingrich, *A Greek-English Lexicon of the New Testament and Other Early Christian Literature* (Chicago: University of Chicago Press, 2nd edition, 1958)
BDF	Friedrich Blass, A. DeBrunner, and Robert W. Funk, *A Greek Grammar of the New Testament and Other Early Christian Literature* (Cambridge: Cambridge University Press, 1961)
Bib	*Biblica*
BibSac	*Bibliotheca Sacra*
BJRL	*Bulletin of the John Rylands Library of Manchester*
CBQ	*Catholic Biblical Quarterly*
CTR	*Criswell Theological Review*
DNTT	*New International Dictionary of New Testament Theology*
DPCM	S.M. Burgess and G.B. McGee, *Dictionary of the Pentecostal and Charismatic Movements* (Grand Rapids: Zondervan, 1988)
EDNT	*Exegetical Dictionary of the New Testament*
EPTA	*European Pentecostal Theological Association Bulletin*
EstBíb	*Estudios Bíblicos*
ETL	*Ephemerides Theologicae Lovanienses*
ETR	*Études Theologiques et Religieuses*
EvQ	*Evangelical Quarterly*
Exp	*Expositor*
ExpT	*Expository Times*
Int	*Interpretation*
HTR	*Harvard Theological Review*
JBL	*Journal of Biblical Literature*
JETS	*Journal of the Evangelical Theological Society*
JPT	*Journal of Pentecostal Theology*
JSNT	*Journal for the Study of the New Testament*
JTS	*Journal of Theological Studies*

NeoT	*Neotestimentica*
NovT	*Novum Testamentum*
NRT	*La nouvelle revue théologique*
NTS	*New Testament Studies*
PTR	*Princeton Theological Review*
RB	*Revue biblique*
RevExp	*Review and Expositor*
RHR	*Revue de l'historie des religions*
RSR	*Recherches de science religieuse*
RTP	*Revue de Théologie et de Philosophie*
SJT	*Scottish Journal of Theology*
TDNT	Gerhard Kittel and Gerhard Friedrich (eds.), *Theological Dictionary of the New Testament* (trans. Geoffrey W. Bromiley; 10 vols; Grand Rapids: Eerdmans, 1964-)
TynB	*Tyndale Bulletin*
ZNW	*Zeitschrift für die neutestamentliche Wissenschaft*

INTRODUCTION

The relationship between the Devil and disease, sickness and sin, healing and forgiveness, and exorcism and deliverance is an intriguing and controversial issue. Biblical scholars have long debated the exact understanding of Christians, Jews, and pagans about such matters.[1] Pastoral psychologists,[2] pastoral counselors,[3] and social scientists[4] have made several attempts to integrate the psychic, physiological, and spiritual dimensions of mental and physical health.

But such scholarly interests pale in comparison to the attention this topic has received at the popular level within the Pentecostal and Charismatic traditions. While I do not have at my disposal the data that would enable me to make hard and fast claims concerning the specific ways in which individuals within the tradition line up on this issue, since so much of the data exists in oral instead of published form, it does seem to me that Pentecostals and Charismatics can generally be divided into the following three categories.

---

[1] O. Bücher, *Dämonenfurcht und Dämonenabwehr* (Stuttgart: Kohlhammer, 1970); idem., *Das Neue Testament und die dämonischen Machte* (Stuttgart: Katholisches Bibelwerk, 1972); idem, *Christus Exorcista* (Stuttgart: Kohlhammer, 1972); J.M. Hull, *Hellenistic Magic and the Synoptic Tradition* (Naperville, IL: SCM Press, 1974); M. Smith, *Jesus the Magician* (San Francisco: Harper & Row, 1978); D. Aune, 'Magic in Early Christianity', in *Aufstieg und Niedergang der römischen Welt* (Berlin: Walter de Gruyter, 1980) II.23.2, pp. 1507-57; and E. Yamauchi, 'Magic or Miracle? Diseases, Demons, and Exorcisms', in *Gospel Perspectives: The Miracles of Jesus* VI (ed. by D. Wenham and C. Blomberg; Sheffield: JSOT Press, 1986), pp. 89-183.

[2] S. Southard, 'Demonizing and Mental Illness (2): The Problem of Assessment: Los Angeles', *Pastoral Psychology* 34 (1986), pp. 264-87.

[3] R.L. Hudson, 'Sin and Sickness', *Journal of Pastoral Care* 13 (1956), pp. 65-75; S.B. Page, 'Some further Observations on Sin and Sickness', *Journal of Pastoral Care* 13 (1959), pp. 144-54; and S. Southard, 'Sin or Sickness?' *Pastoral Psychology* 11 (May, 1960), pp. 31-34.

[4] D.C. O'Connell, 'Is Mental Illness a Result of Sin?' *Lumen Vitae* 15 (1960), pp. 233-43.

2 The Devil, Disease, and Deliverance

First, there are those who see lurking behind every illness or misfortune demonic activity. For these believers there is a clear line of demarcation between the Devil (illness) and God (healing). In each circumstance the believer is to rebuke Satan, curse the demonic oppression, and utilize the authority God has bestowed upon him/her through Jesus Christ. Generally, those who take this position attribute any failure to receive healing to a deficiency on the part of those who pray. A lack of faith or the presence of sin might prevent healing, but it is never God's will for a believer to continue in such suffering. God's will is for all to be healed.

A second group within the tradition would maintain that while ultimately all disease is from the Devil, not every individual sick person is ill as the direct result of Satanic attack. In other words, while there may be instances of believers suffering disease at the hands of Satan, many Christians may become sick from 'natural causes'. Such a position is advocated for a couple of reasons. First, many of these believers hold that since sin and sickness entered the world through the Fall of Adam and will not finally be removed until the parousia, individual Christians are just as likely to suffer physically as an unbeliever. Such is the fate of those who live in a fallen world. Second, the idea that demons can possess and/or oppress Christians is viewed, at best, as resting upon very meager biblical support and, at worst, as an unbiblical heresy. The bottom line is these individuals believe that not every illness can be attributed directly to the Devil. The implication of this assessment is that God might sometimes use suffering for his glory. Prayer for the sick is always legitimate, but it might not always be God's will to bring physical healing.

A final group is comprised of what might be called 'functional deists'. These believers genuinely believe in God's power to heal and the Devil's ability to inflict suffering, but they have become rather disengaged and detached from the whole business. On the one hand, this apathy is, in part, the result of reaction to outlandish (and sometimes embarrassing) claims made by some proponents of divine healing. In addition, when healing does not occur, these individuals are faced with the dilemma of seeking to reconcile this failure to receive healing with claims that it is always God's will to heal. On the other hand, many of these believers are so frustrated by the inability to know whether or not it is God's will to heal in a specific situation that they choose simply to become onlookers rather than participants. It would be wrong to assume that such individuals never pray for healing, but if and when healings occur these believers are ordinarily astounded by their occurrence. At the very least, such individuals bring a somewhat skeptical attitude to the enterprise and do not usually offer fervent prayers for healing.

As one who serves both in the seminary (as a Professor of Biblical Studies) and in the parish (as an Associate Pastor) I must admit that I am both troubled and perplexed by this state of affairs. Two aspects are most disconcerting. First, the confusion over the relationship between sin and sickness has caused many in our tradition to be less certain about God's ability and desire to intervene in this world to bring healing. Such uncertainty serves to undermine one of the five foundational beliefs which characterized early Pentecostalism.[5] Second, such confusion regarding divine healing suggests that biblical scholars working within the tradition have not done their homework on this topic, at least in a form that is readily accessible. Therefore, the following study seeks to be an exegetical and interpretive journey to discover what the New Testament says about the Devil, Disease, and Deliverance.

The general approach of this study is informed by James D.G. Dunn's *Unity and Diversity in the New Testament* and Gordon D. Fee's *The Empowering Presence of God*. Like Dunn's work, this study seeks to allow the diverse voices of the New Testament to be heard before attempting to construct a New Testament Theology on the topic. Similar to Fee's work, this study attempts to offer an in-depth examination of each relevant text.

The methodological approach employed in this investigation is primarily that of literary analysis, with some utilization of historical studies at points where such seems appropriate. The rationale for this approach is twofold. First, much historical critical study of New Testament texts has resulted in artificial hypothetical reconstructions of the *Sitz-im-Leben* of a given work which often predetermine the meaning of a text despite hints in the text itself that such constructs ignore or obscure some of its rather obvious di-

---

[5] S.J. Land has shown that the early Pentecostal view of Jesus included five primary dimensions: Jesus as Savior, Sanctifier, Holy Ghost Baptizer, Healer, and Coming King. Cf. S.J. Land, *Pentecostal Spirituality: A Passion for the Kingdom* (JPTSup 1; Sheffield: Sheffield Academic Press, 1993).

mensions. Thus, this study begins with a reading of the text, not with an exploration of that which stands behind the text. Second, my own research endeavors have convinced me that literary approaches have much to contribute to historical enquiries. Therefore, a careful reading of the text on its own terms can, I believe, often give fresh insight into the complex historical questions which have dominated much scholarly activity. In this case the methodological decision to begin with the text has significant interpretive implications.

Specifically, many scholars have attempted to approach the issue of demons in the New Testament by constructing a first-century view of the demonic and then reading the New Testament texts against this backdrop. Because the backdrop is usually one which sees demons behind nearly every illness, most every New Testament illness is taken as implicit evidence that a similar viewpoint is shared by the individual author in question. However, when a literary approach is employed it is amazing how little evidence the texts themselves offer for such a construct. No doubt this approach will result in not a few disagreements with other interpreters, but such are probably inevitable in this day of methodological diversity.

What follows, then, is an examination of the Devil, disease, and deliverance in New Testament thought.

1

JAMES 5.14-16

With so much terrain to cover one might legitimately ask, why begin with James 5? Several reasons may be offered in support of this strategy. First of all, Jas 5.14-16 gives a glimpse, be it ever so slight, into how one early Christian church ministered to believers who were suffering physically. In fact, of the many New Testament passages which advocate divine healing, this is the only text which describes a procedure to be followed. Second, this passage makes explicit the fact that sin and sickness are sometimes related. Third, James appears to assume that healing from physical infirmities is an expected and ongoing part of the community's life. Fourth, in view of the fact that the church represented by the Epistle of James appears to be distinctively non-Pauline in theological perspective and focus,[1] it may prove helpful, therefore, to begin this journey with a less prominent form of early Christian thought in order to appreciate more fully the diversity which is to be found in the early church and to gain leverage on this complex topic.

A final reason for choosing James 5 as the first point of inquiry is related to the place of this passage within early Pentecostalism. In the *Theological Roots of Pentecostalism* Donald Dayton has shown that the rise of the divine healing movement is an indispensable backdrop for viewing the emergence of Pentecostalism.[2] By the end of the nineteenth century healing ministries were quite common.[3] Understandably, Jas 5.14-16 became one of the more significant texts

---

[1] Whether this epistle assumes some knowledge of the Pauline mission or not, it certainly represents a distinct approach to the Christian life.

[2] D.W. Dayton, *Theological Roots of Pentecostalism* (Grand Rapids: Zondervan, 1987), pp. 115-41.

[3] Cf. P.G. Chappell, 'Healing Movements', *DPCM*, pp. 353-74.

for this practice and its accompanying doctrine.[4] The relationship
between sin and sickness, suggested in Jas 5.14-16, raised many
questions and caused not a little disagreement and division among
advocates and antagonists alike.[5] Therefore, to begin this examination with a study of Jas 5.14-16 is most appropriate.

The issues of authorship, provenance, and date of the Epistle of
James are all very much in dispute.[6] Although an extensive examination of these issues is well beyond the scope of this study, a few
things are assumed about the Epistle of James in this chapter. Very
few scholars would dispute the claim that James comes from a Jew-
ish-Christian milieu.[7] Although the process of assigning a date of
composition to most New Testament documents is a rather tenuous
affair,[8] and despite the arguments offered in favour of a late date
for James,[9] the Epistle shows signs of coming from a primitive
community.[10] The attention to grace and works notwithstanding, it
is not altogether certain that James was composed in reaction to the

---

[4] Dayton, *Theological Roots of Pentecostalism*, pp. 124-25.

[5] Compare the attitude of C. Cullis (*Faith Cures; or, Answers to Prayer in the Healing of the Sick* [Boston: Willard Tract Repository, 1879]), an early proponent of
divine healing, with that of W.P. Harrison ('Faith-cure in the Light of Scripture',
Methodist Quarterly Review 28 [1889], pp. 402-405), an early critic of divine healing.

[6] For recent discussions of these issues cf. R.P. Martin, *James* (Waco: Word,
1988), pp. lxi-lxxvii; D. Guthrie, *New Testament Introduction* (Downers Grove: IVP,
1990), pp. 722-53; and L.T. Johnson, *The Letter of James* (New York: Doubleday,
1995), pp. 89-121.

[7] Some scholars have gone so far as to insist that James was originally a Jewish
(non-Christian) document. Cf. L. Massebieau, 'L'Épitre de Jacques, est-elle
l'oeuvre d'un Chrétien?' *RHR* 32 (1895), pp. 249-83; F. Spitta, 'Der Brief des Jacobus untersucht', *Zur Geschichte und Litteratur des Urchristentums* 2 (1896), pp. 1-
239; A. Meyer, *Das Rätsel des Jacobusbriefes* (Giessen: Töpelmann 1930); B.S.
Easton, *The Epistle of James* (Nashville: Abingdon, 1957), pp. 10-11; H. Thyen, *Der
Stil der Jüdisch-Hellenistichen Homile* (Göttingen: Vandenhoeck und Ruprecht, 1935),
p. 16; and R. Bultmann, *Theology of the New Testament* II (trans. K. Grobel; New
York: Scribner's Sons, 1955), p. 143.

[8] As J.A.T. Robinson (*Redating the New Testament* [Philadelphia: Westminster,
1976]) has demonstrated.

[9] P.H. Davids (*The Epistle of James* [Grand Rapids: Eerdmans, 1982], p. 4) provides a helpful chart of twentieth-century commentators and their positions regarding the date of James.

[10] Both Davids (*The Epistle of James*, pp. 20-21, 28-34) and Martin (*James*, pp.
xix-lxxvii) conclude that the materials in James point to a Palestinian milieu. They
also suggest that the book is based upon the teaching of James the Just and was
completed later by another hand. Cf. Johnson, *James*, pp. 118-21, who argues co-
gently for an early date.

Pauline mission. Indeed, one would expect much more attention would have been given to issues such as circumcision if James were written as a polemic against Paul.[11] If these assumptions are anywhere near the mark, the implication for this study is that the document to be examined preserves testimony regarding early Christian practice that emerged in some isolation from the Pauline mission.

An Examination of James 5.14-16

James 5.14-16 occurs near the end of the epistle in a context which delineates the appropriate responses to various situations in life. After directing those in trouble to pray and those who are happy to sing praises to God, James turns his attention to those in the community who are sick.

> Is anyone sick among you? Let that one call for the elders of the church and let them anoint him with oil and pray in the name of the Lord. And the prayer of faith will save the sick and the Lord will raise him up. And if sin has been committed, it will be forgiven him. Therefore, confess sins one to another and pray for one another that you might be healed. The powerful strong prayer of the righteous accomplishes much.

Verse 14

James begins this verse with the question, 'Are there any sick among you?' ($\dot{\alpha}\sigma\theta\epsilon\nu\epsilon\hat{\iota}$ $\tau\iota\varsigma$ $\dot{\epsilon}\nu$ $\dot{\nu}\mu\hat{\iota}\nu$). An overwhelming majority of scholars understand James to be addressing those who are physically sick when he uses the term $\dot{\alpha}\sigma\theta\epsilon\nu\dot{\epsilon}\omega$.[12] Only a handful of writers main-

---

[11] It should be noted that the relationship of James to the Pauline communities is greatly debated.

[12] Cf. J. Calvin, *Commentaries on the Catholic Epistles* (Grand Rapids: Eerdmans, 1948), pp. 355-56; J.B. Mayor *The Epistle of James* (Minneapolis: Klock & Klock, 1977), p. 169; E.M. Wilson, 'The Anointing of the Sick in the Epistle of James, and its Bearing on the Use of Means in Sickness', *PTR* (1921), pp. 65-66; J. Chaine, *L'Épître de Saint Jacques* (Paris: J. Gabalda, 1927), p. 208; J. Marty, *L'Épître de Jacques* (Paris: Librairie Felix Alcan, 1935), p. 126; C. Pickar, 'Is anyone Sick among you?' *CBQ* 7 (1945), pp. 166-67; R.V.G. Tasker, *The General Epistle of James* (Grand Rapids: Eerdmans, 1957), p. 129; A. Hamman, 'Prière et Culte chez S. Jacques', *ETL* 34 (1958), p. 41; K. Condon, 'The Sacrament of Healing', *Scripture*

tain that James is referring to those who are emotionally or spiritually discouraged.[13] Ordinarily this latter interpretation appears to be offered for dogmatic reasons.[14] That ἀσθενέω here means physical illness is borne out by several facts. First, ἀσθενέω and its cognates '… are the most common New Testament expressions for sickness.…'[15] Second, κακοπαθέω in v. 13 almost certainly refers to personal distress produced by physical circumstances or personal situations other than sickness.[16] The appearance of ἀσθενέω on the heels of κακοπαθέω would suggest a change of topic, from those who are distressed or discouraged to those who are physically sick.[17] In the light of such evidence it seems best to conclude that here James is addressing those in the community who are physically ill.[18]

In contrast to his instructions in v. 14 for individual (and/or private) prayer, James admonishes those who are sick to 'call for the elders of the church'. Such a directive may imply that the sick person was too ill to attend the community's corporate worship but had to request a visit to his or her home from the leaders of the

---

11.14 (April, 1959), pp. 35-36; E. Thurneysen, *La Foi et les Oeuvres* (trans. C. Pittet; Paris: Delachaux & Niestlé, 1959), pp. 158-59; C.L. Mitton, *The Epistle of James* (Grand Rapids: Eerdmans, 1966), p. 197; J. Wilkinson, 'Healing in the Epistle of James', *SJT* 24 (1971), p. 328; J. Cantinat, *De Saint Jacques et de Saint Jude* (Paris: J. Gabalda, 1973), p. 247; R. Béraudy, 'Le sacrement des malades. Etude historique et théologiques', *NRT* 96 (1974), pp. 600-605; M. Dibelius, *James* (ed. H. Koester; trans. M.A. Williams; Philadelphia: Fortress Press, 1976), p. 252; M.P.V. Barrett, 'Lessons in Patience and Prayer', *Biblical Viewpoint* 14 (1980), pp. 52-58; R. Kugelman, *James* (Wilmington: Michael Glazier, 1980), p. 63; S. Laws, *The Epistle of James* (New York: Harper & Row, 1980), pp. 225-26; Davids, *Epistle of James*, p. 192; D.P. Scaer, *James the Apostle of Faith* (St. Louis: Concordia, 1983), p. 131; F. Vouga, *L'Épitres de Saint Jacques* (Genève: Labor et Fides, 1984), pp. 140-41; C. Brown, *That You May Believe* (Grand Rapids: Eerdmans, 1985), p. 196; A. Motyer, *The Message of James* (Downers Grove: IVP, 1985), pp.193-94; Martin, *James*, p. 206; G.S. Shogren, 'Will God Heal Us – A Re-examination of James 5.14-16a', *EQ* 61 (1989), p. 100; K. Warrington, 'Some Observations on James 5.13-18', *EPTA* 8 (1989), pp. 161-63; and Johnson, *James*, p. 330.

[13] C. Armerding, ' "Is Any Among You Afflicted" ', *BibSac* 95 (1938), pp. 195-201; H.J. Blair, 'Spiritual Healing: An Enquiry', *EQ* 30 (1958), pp. 149-50; R. Hayden, 'Calling the Elders to Pray', *BibSac* 138 (1981), p. 260; and C.R. Wells, 'Theology of Prayer in James', *CTR* 1 (1986), pp. 101-103.

[14] One of the few exceptions is P.H. Alexander, 'James', *DPCM,* pp. 477-78.

[15] G. Stählin, 'ἀσθενής', *TDNT*, I, p. 492.

[16] Davids, *Epistle of James,* p. 191.

[17] Vouga, *L'Épitre de Saint Jacques,* p. 140.

[18] Warrington ('Observations', p. 163) suggests that James' use of ἀσθενέω is deliberately ambiguous so as '… to allow for the widest possible healing process'.

church.[19] However, such a conclusion may be a bit premature. For as Condon cautions, ἀσθενέω does not necessarily imply a grave illness,[20] and a number of places where προσκαλέω occurs in the New Testament depict a summoning of individuals or groups in close proximity to the one who calls.[21] Consequently, it is not clear whether the believer was to receive prayer from the elders in a context of public worship or at his or her home. What is clear is that the sick person was to call for prayer by the elders.

The appearance of groups of elders in the New Testament is remarkably widespread. They are mentioned in connection with the Jerusalem church (Acts 11.30; 15.2, 4, 6, 22-23; 16.4; 21.18), the Pauline mission (Acts 14.23 and 20.17-38), the Pauline circle (1 Tim. 4.14; 5.17-19; Tit. 1.5), and the Petrine churches (1 Pet. 5.1). In addition to these occurrences of elder, the author of 2 John and 3 John refers to himself as *the* Elder. It may be concluded that the term elder designates a position of leadership in the early church, perhaps modeled after the practice of the synagogue.[22]

As has often been noted, James does not advocate calling for those who possess the charism of healing, which would have been likely in the Pauline community (as 1 Corinthians 12 might imply). Why, if James knows of the charismata, does he not instruct the sick person to call for those in the community known to possess the gift of healing? Could it be that James' directive is a put down of such claims? Or does this verse suggest that the charismata were unknown to James and/or his church? Several explanations have been offered to untie this mysterious knot.

One way to approach this issue is to assume that the leaders of the early local churches would most certainly have possessed the

---

[19] Marty, *L'Epitre de Jacques*, pp. 126-27; Cantinat, *De Saint Jacques*, p. 247; Mitton, *Epistle of James*, p. 197; Kugelman, *James*, p. 63; Davids, *Epistle of James,* p. 192; Scaer, *James the Apostle*, p. 131; Brown, *That You May Believe*, p. 196; Motyer, *Message of James*, p. 194; and Martin, *James*, p. 206.

[20] Condon, 'Sacrament', pp. 35-36. Cf. also Cantinat, *De Saint Jacques*, p. 247 and L.P. Rogge, 'The Relationship between the Sacrament of Anointing the Sick and the Charism of Healing within the Catholic Charismatic Renewal', (PhD Dissertation, Union Theological Seminary, 1984), p. 165.

[21] Cf. Matthew 10.1; 15.10, 32; 18.2; 20.25; Mk 3.13; 7.14; 8.1, 34; 10.42; 12.43; Lk. 7.18; 18.10.

[22] For an excellent overview of the role of elders in both Jewish and Graeco-Roman contexts cf. G. Bornkamm, 'πρεσβύτης', *TDNT*, VI, pp. 651-83.

gift of healing.[23] To put it in the form of a question, does it not seem likely that individuals who possessed the gift of healing would naturally become leaders within their particular local Christian community?[24] Such an understanding clearly assumes that James' community is familiar with the charismata and it seeks to harmonize the experience of the Pauline communities with that of James.

Another way to explain James' words is to connect the power to heal with the office of elder itself.[25] This proposal has the advantage of being able to explain why the elders are called for without bringing the charismata into the discussion. It does, however, necessitate the attribution of a rather over-developed and institutional definition to the office of elder.

It is also possible to read the directive of James in 5.14 to call the elders of the church as a way of circumventing charismatic healers.[26] However, such a view is difficult to defend. For while assuming the widespread existence of the gift of healing in early Christianity may be safe, concluding that the instruction to call for the elders of the church is some sort of polemic against charismatic healers is a weight that the argument from silence may not be able to bear.

Finally, it is possible to discuss the role of the elder without bringing in the matter of a healing gift at all.[27] However, this approach does not do justice to the issue of healing in early Christianity, nor the reason for specifically requesting the elders to minister in such situations.

---

[23] Calvin, *Commentaries*, p. 356; Mayor, *Epistle of James*, p. 169; F. Mussner, *Der Jakobusbrief* (Freiburg: Herder, 1964), p. 219; B. Reicke, 'L'onction des malades d'apres Saint Jacques', *La Maison-Dieu* 113 (1973), p. 59; and Rogge, 'Relationship', p. 168.

[24] The action of ordaining as an elder one who possessed the gift of healing is found ca. 500 CE in the *Canons of Hippolytus* (8).

[25] J. Coppens ('Jacq v, 13-15 et l'onction des malades', *ETL* 53 [1977], p. 205) argues, 'Il n'est donc pas question d'un recours à un quelconque charisme même pas au charisme de guérison, le χάρισμα ἰαμᾶτων mentionné dans 1 Cor., XII, 28. L'épître envisage, au contraire, nous l'avons déjà souligné, l'action d'un ministère institué.' Cf. also the comments by Condon ('Sarament', p. 38), Dibelius (*James*, pp. 252-53) and E. Schweizer, *Church Order in the New Testament* (trans. F. Clarke; London: SCM Press, 1961), p. 201.

[26] Cf. Shogren, 'Will God Heal Us?', p. 100.

[27] Cf. Cantinat, *De Saint Jacques*, p. 248 and Brown, *That You May Believe*, p. 196.

It appears safest to conclude that the elders were to be called because they were recognized leaders in the church. As such they represent the community and its ability to minister to those who are physically ill. That a healing ministry is not restricted to the elders is made clear in v. 16, where the body of believers is encouraged to pray for one another in order that healings might occur. Whether James and his church were familiar with the gifts of the Spirit as defined in the Pauline literature or not, it is likely that at least one or more of the elders was recognized as having been used by God to facilitate the healing of individuals.

This assessment is based in part on the prominence of healing miracles in the New Testament accounts. The Gospels describe the empowerment of and mandates given to the disciples, and through them the readers of the gospels, to heal the sick, among other things (Mt. 10.1, 8; Mk 6.13; Lk. 9.2, 6, 11; 10.9). Acts narrates extraordinary healings through a variety of individuals (3.7; 5.16; 8.7; 9.34; 14.8-10; 19.12; 28.8-9). Several of the epistles also assume that healings were part and parcel of the church's proclamation (e.g. 1 Cor. 12.9 and 1 Pet. 2.24). If, on the one hand, James is working with a conception of the gift of healing anything like that of Paul,[28] then in all likelihood one or more of the elders and perhaps one or more of the congregation at large were known for their healing gifts.[29] On the other hand, if James is writing before the Pauline idea of the gift of healing has emerged, or if James and his community pursue a distinctively non-Pauline approach in this regard, it is still likely that members of both the group of elders and the congregation would have been involved in healings such as those described in the Gospels and Acts.[30]

---

[28] That the Petrine community had such an exposure is at least suggested by 1 Pet. 4.10-11.

[29] One of the points upon which James and Paul are in agreement is that healings are to take place *within* the Christian community, the body of Christ.

[30] For evidence that healings continued in the early church long beyond the first century CE, cf. R.A.N. Kydd, *Charismatic Gifts in the Early Church* (Peabody: Hendrickson, 1984), esp. pp. 26, 44, 49, 54, 59, and 61. In addition, cf. Kydd's 'Jesus, Saints, and Relics: Approaching the Early Church through Healing', *JPT* 2 (1993), pp. 91-104. Cf. also R. MacMullen, *Christianizing the Roman Empire A. D. 100-400* (New Haven: Yale University Press, 1984).

The specific duties of the elders in these situations involve three elements: 1) offering prayer, 2) while anointing the sick person with oil, 3) in the name of the Lord.

Just before the prayer is offered,[31] the elders are to anoint the sick person with oil. Despite the questions surrounding the origin and meaning of this act, it should be noted that its mention by James gives the impression that he is not instituting something new but is describing an action with which his readers would have been familiar.[32] But having made this observation, what exactly is the purpose of anointing with oil?

In the Old Testament, anointing with oil is found in a variety of contexts. It could be used in conjunction with the coronation of kings (1 Sam 9.16), the consecration of priests (Exod. 29.7), the calling of a prophet (1 Kgs 19.16), the consecration of sacred objects (Exod. 30.22-29), and the treatment of wounds (Isa. 1.6) and/or disease (Lev. 14.15-18).[33] In later rabbinic thought (Mishnah *Sabbath* 23.5) anointing with oil could even be used as part of the preparation of the dead for burial.

However, the nearest parallel to the admonition given in James 5.14 is found in Mk 6.13. Here the Twelve, having been sent out by Jesus, are described as 'casting out many demons and anointing many sick people with oil'. In this Marcan passage there is a clear distinction drawn between exorcisms and healings, with oil being used in the case of the latter.[34] While most commentators acknowledge that oil had medicinal associations in antiquity, there appears to be unanimity of opinion that the anointing with oil described in Mk 6.13 served as a symbol of God's healing power.[35] Reicke goes

---

[31] Since the participle ἀλείψαντες is in the aorist tense it probably denotes action prior to that of the leading verb, which in this case is προσεύχομαι. Cf. Johnson, *James*, p. 331. However, the aorist participle does not always denote action prior to the leading verb. Cf. *BDF*, pp. 174-75.

[32] Wilkinson, 'Healing', p. 338.

[33] Cf. the helpful summary in B. Reicke, 'L'onction des malades d'après Saint Jacques', pp. 51-54. Cf. also D. Lys, 'L'onction dans la Bible', *ETR* 29 (1954), pp. 3-54 and F. Vouga, 'Jacques 5/13-18', *ETR* 53 (1977), pp. 104-105.

[34] W.L. Lane, *The Gospel of Mark* (Grand Rapids: Eerdmans, 1974), pp. 209-10.

[35] Cf. the discussions in the following: E.P. Gould, *The Gospel according to Mark* (Edinburgh: T. & T. Clark, 1896), p. 108; M.-J. Lagrange, *Évangile selon Saint Marc* (Paris: Gabalda, 1947), pp. 154-55; C.E.B. Cranfield, *The Gospel according to St Mark* (Cambridge: Cambridge University Press, 1959), p. 201; D.E. Nineham, *Saint*

so far as to say that the disciples had received a mandate from Jesus to anoint with oil.[36] Owing to the similarities between the practice in Mk 6.13 and Jas 5.14 it may not be going beyond the evidence to conclude that the action advocated by James was based upon and/or in the directive of Jesus and/or the action of his disciples.[37]

Although many scholars define the use of oil in Jas 5.14 in medicinal terms,[38] the similarities to Mk 6.13, as well as the context of healing as an answer to the prayers of the elders and people, appear to rule out such an option.[39] The argument that the oil is an indication that James is describing an exorcism seems even further from the mark,[40] since James, who exhibits a knowledge of demons, could certainly have given his instructions in exorcism terminology if he had chosen and since Mk 6.13 clearly differentiates between exorcisms and healings. Least likely is the idea that when James mentions anointing with oil he has in mind the institution of Extreme Unction, since the purpose for the anointing he describes is

---

Mark (Baltimore: Penguin Books, 1963), p. 171; V. Taylor, *The Gospel According to St. Mark* (Grand Rapids: Baker, 1981), p. 306; E. Schweizer, *The Good News according to Mark* (Richmond: John Knox Press, 1970), p. 131; W. Hendricksen, *The Gospel of Mark* (Grand Rapids: Baker, 1975), p. 232; H. Anderson, *The Gospel of Mark* (London: Oliphants, 1976), p. 165; L.W. Hurtado, *Mark* (New York: Harper & Row, 1983), p. 84; C.S. Mann, *Mark* (Garden City: Doubleday, 1986), p. 293; R.A. Cole, *Mark* (Grand Rapids: Eerdmans, 1989), p. 171; and R. Guelich, *Mark 1-8.26* (Waco: Word, 1989), p. 323.

[36] Reicke, 'L'onction des malades d'après Saint Jacques', p. 51.

[37] Reicke, 'L'onction des malades d'après Saint Jacques', p. 51. Cf. also Condon, *Sacrament*, p. 38; Dibelius, *James*, p. 252; and Johnson, *James*, p. 331.

[38] Cf. Mayor, *Epistle of James*, p. 170; W.H. Bennett, *The General Epistles* (New York: Henry Frowde. 1900), p. 55; J.H. Ropes, *The Epistle of James* (Edinburgh: T. & T. Clark, 1961), pp. 305-306; Chaine, *L'Épître de Saint Jacques*, p. 211; Hamman, 'Prière et culte', p. 42; Condon, 'Sacrament', p. 38; Thurnegsen, 'La foi', pp. 164-65; Wilkinson, 'Healing', pp. 338-39; Kugelman, *James*, p. 64; Laws, *Epistle of James*, p. 227; and T. Powell, 'Anointing with Oil', in *DPCM*, p. 11.

[39] The medicinal interpretation of oil was rejected as early as Calvin (*Commentaries*, pp. 355-56). Cf. also the critiques of this position offered by E.M. Wilson, 'The Anointing of the Sick', pp. 64-95 and Shogren, 'Will God Heal Us?', pp. 101-104.

[40] Cf. the comments of E.C. Blackman, *The Epistle of James* (New York: Macmillan, 1957), p. 152; Hamman, 'Prière et culte', p. 42; Condon, 'Sacrament', p. 39; Bornkamm, 'πρεσβύτης', p. 664 n. 83; Dibelius, *James*, pp. 252-53; Martin, *James*, p. 48; and Powell, 'Anointing with Oil', p. 11.

to bring healing and preserve life, not to prepare for death.[41]

If such explanations of the significance of anointing with oil fail to explain the text in a satisfactory manner, then how ought this anointing be understood? It is of course possible, on the one hand, to understand the anointing as an aid to or help with healing,[42] or, on the other hand, to use sacramental language to describe its significance.[43] But while the former suggestion does not seem to account sufficiently for the fact that both Mark and James specifically mention oil, not some other aid, the latter proposal appears to force the Spirit's operation into an overly defined sacramental system. Since there is no indication that James worked within such a 'sacramental' framework, this latter suggestion is especially difficult to demonstrate.

Inasmuch as the anointing is to function alongside of prayer and as healing is not dependent upon the anointing with oil, as v. 16 makes clear, it is likely that the anointing with oil serves as some kind of sign.[44] Since the significance of the act is not made specific in either Mark or James, it is probable that the use of oil as a sign would have incorporated some of the meaning it had come to have generally. In other words, given its many associations with medicine it would only seem natural that oil would come to serve as a sign of

---

[41] The comments of G. Beasley-Murray (*The General Epistles* [London: Lutterworth Press, 1965], p. 39) on the doctrine of Extreme Unction being based on James 5.14 are not uncommon, 'Therein is a sad commentary on the way in which the Church became more concerned with burying humanity than with saving it.' At Vatican II, the Roman Catholic Church officially removed the terminology of Extreme Unction, renaming it 'the sacrament of anointing the sick'. This change was a recognition that its purpose was not primarily a spiritual aid to the dying. I would like to thank Father Peter Hocken for pointing this out to me in correspondence.

[42] As A. Plummer, (*The General Epistles of St. James, St. Jude and St. Peter* [New York: Funk and Wagnell, 1900], p. 327), Mitton (*Epistle of James*, p. 199), Tasker (*The General Epistle*, p.131), and Stevenson (*James Speaks for Today* [London: Marshall, Morgan & Scott, 1986], pp. 96-97) suggest.

[43] As do Calvin (*Commentaries*, p. 356), Scaer (*James the Apostle*, p. 132), and Davids (*Epistle of James*, p. 193).

[44] Although not agreeing on its precise nature, several scholars believe that anointing with oil is best understood as a sign. Cf. T. Manton, *An Exposition on the Epistle of James* (London: Banner of Truth Trust, 1962), p 447; Wilson, 'The Anointing of the Sick', p. 75; Blair, 'Spiritual Healing', p. 150; Shogren, 'Will God Heal Us?', pp. 105-106; Warrington, 'Observations', p. 107; Motyer, *Message of James*, p. 196; D.J. Moo, *James* (Grand Rapids: Eerdmans, 1985), pp. 178-81; and Martin, *James*, p. 209.

healing. Only in this case, the healing would not be the direct result of the oil but would be of supernatural origin.

But such general associations with healing do not exhaust the richness of this sign nor fully explain the rationale behind the choice of oil as the sign. There is some evidence that by the first century CE, oil had come to have much more powerful associations with healing. Several ancient sources express the idea that oil obtained from the tree in paradise had healing virtues. An example from the *Life of Adam and Eve* (9.3), a document which is roughly contemporary with much of the New Testament, demonstrates this point:

> But Adam said to Eve, 'Rise and go with our son, Seth, near to Paradise, and place earth on your heads and weep, beseeching God so that he might have mercy on me, and send his angel into Paradise and give me from the tree out of which the oil flows, and bring it to me, and I will anoint myself and rest.'[45]

This same story line is found two to three centuries later in the *Gospel of Nicodemus*, also known as the *Acts of Pilate* (19), where Seth is quoted as saying:

> Prophets and patriarchs, listen. My father Adam, the first created, when he fell into mortal sickness, sent me to the very gate of paradise to pray to God that he might lead me by an angel to the tree of mercy, that I might take oil and anoint my father, and he arise from his sickness. This also I did. And after my prayer an angel of the Lord came and asked me: What do you desire, Seth? Do you desire because of the sickness of your father, the oil that raises up the sick, or the tree from which flows such oil? This cannot be found now. Therefore go and tell your father that after the completion of 5,500 years from the creation of the world, the only-begotten Son of Man shall become man and descend below the earth. And he shall anoint him with oil. And he

---

[45] Cited according to the translation of M.D. Johnson in J.H. Charlesworth, *The Old Testament Pseudepigrapha*, II (Garden City: Doubleday, 1985), p. 273. Cf. also the *Apocalypse of Moses 13.1-3*.

shall arise and wash him and his descendants with water and the Holy Spirit. And then he shall be healed of every disease.[46]

Similar ideas concerning oil are expressed in the *Apocalypse of Moses* (9) and 4 *Ezra* (2.12).

These texts suggest that oil from a tree in paradise had come to have healing virtues associated with it, the implication being that such oil would again become available in the messianic age. Obviously, James does not regard the oil as having healing virtues in and of itself. However, the associations which oil had come to have with healing generally and eschatological healing in particular suggest that its presence in Jesus' ministry and in the practice of the early church signified the power of God to heal, which was one implication of the inauguration of the Kingdom of God. Consequently, oil was a powerful reminder to the church that God was able to heal and that his healing powers were already being made manifest. Such an eschatological emphasis fits the use of oil in the context of Mk 6.13 nicely, for the Twelve were sent to preach conversion (Mk 6.12) owing to the nearness of the Kingdom of God. The eschatological emphasis also fits well in James, for in the previous passage (Jas 5.1-11), the writer exhorts his readers to be patient in the face of suffering and persecution ἕως τῆς παρουσίας τοῦ κυρίου.[47] Neither would the associations between oil and the Spirit found in the Old Testament (esp. Zechariah 4) be lost on the hearers.

This anointing is to be done 'in the name of the Lord'. At the very least, this qualification clearly designates this action as a religious anointing[48] and distinguishes it from magical rites of the day. But how should 'in the name of the Lord' be understood? Does the use of the name carry a potent efficacy on its own?[49] Does its use verify that the individual who uses the name is a representative of

[46] Cited according to the translation of A.J.B. Higgins in E. Hennecke, *New Testament Apocrypha*, I (ed. W. Schneemelcher; Philadelphia: Westminster, 1963), p. 472.

[47] Cf. Béraudy, 'Le sacrement', p. 604. For a helpful overview of eschatology in the epistle of James cf. the discussion in Davids, *Epistle of James*, pp. 38-39.

[48] Ropes, *Epistle of James*, p. 307.

[49] For this position cf. W. Heitmüller, *Im Namen Jesus* (Göttingen: Vandenhoeck und Ruprecht, 1903), p. 86; J. Moffatt, *The General Episles James, Peter and Jude* (London: Harper and Brothers, 1928), p. 79; Mussner, *Der Jakobusbrief*, pp. 220-21; and Dibelius, *James*, p. 252.

the Lord?[50] Or, does the phrase 'in the name of the Lord' specify the one who is to anoint (priests)[51] or the kind of oil that is to be used (consecrated)?[52]

In attempting to answer these questions, it should perhaps be remembered that the words of Jesus in the Johannine tradition include directives to make requests 'in my name' (Jn 14.13-14 and 16.23).[53] Such a tradition prompts Bietenhard to conclude:

> It is obedience to Jesus (ἐν τῷ ὀνόματι τοῦ κυρίου) that the sick in the church are healed by anointing with oil (Jm. 5.14f.), for Jesus has pledged his disciples to mutual assistance. Healing does not take place by pronouncing a set formula, but through the Lord in answer to the prayer which calls upon Him in faith.[54]

A variety of other things in early Christianity are also either done or commanded to be done in Jesus' name. These include: baptism (Acts 2.38; 8.16; 10.48; 1 Cor. 1.15), exorcism (Mt. 7.22; Mk 9.38; Lk. 10.17; Acts 16.19), healing (Acts 3.6; 4.10), speaking boldly (Acts 9.28), assembling (1 Cor. 5.4), giving thanks (Eph. 5.20), being justified (1 Cor. 6.11), and giving commands (2 Thess. 3.6). In fact, Paul goes so far as to say whatever one does should be done in the name of the Lord Jesus (Col. 3.17).

The phrase 'in my name' is also found in Jas 5.10, where those upon whom suffering has been inflicted are exhorted to follow the example of the prophets who, despite such afflictions, 'spoke in the name of the Lord'. This use of the phrase seems to convey the idea of speaking with the authority of the Lord or in his behalf.[55] The close proximity of these phrases in James, the implication of Mk 6.13 that Jesus himself had instructed the disciples to anoint with oil, the role of the elders as representatives of the community, and the significance of the anointing itself all suggest that to anoint 'in the name of the Lord' meant to act in conformity to the Lord's di-

---

[50] Cf. Reicke, *The Epistles of James, Peter, and Jude*, p. 57 and Davids, *Epistle of James,* p. 193.

[51] Pickar, 'Is Anyone Sick Among You?', p. 170.

[52] The Venerable Bede, *Commentary on the Seven Catholic Epistles* (trans. D. Hurst; Kalamazoo: Cistercian Pub., 1985), p. 62.

[53] Barrett ('Lessons', p. 56) is one of the few writers to make this connection.

[54] H. Bietenhard, 'ὄνομα', *TDNT*, V, p. 278.

[55] Johnson, *James*, p. 331.

rectives and on his behalf as eschatological agents. It is possible that the words of Jesus in the Fourth Gospel concerning prayer may serve as a secondary reason for this action.

Verse 15

Following the anointing with oil, but in close conjunction with it, the elders are to offer prayer. More specifically, they are to offer 'the prayer of faith'. Several aspects of this verse are worthy of comment.

First, reference to the prayer of faith seems to indicate that it is the prayer and not the oil that brings about the healing.[56] Second, as it is the prayer offered by the elders which is demanded, it appears as though *their* faith is being emphasized.[57] Third, only here in the New Testament does the word εὐχή mean prayer.[58]

The prayer of faith may be defined in terms of the epistle itself. James makes clear that when someone in need makes a request of the Lord, such a petition should be made with the confident expectation that God will hear and answer the prayer (1.5-8). To doubt that God will respond to the prayer is to be double-minded. A person who doubts will not receive anything from God. Therefore, to offer the prayer of faith is the opposite of doubting and/or being double-minded. Such a bold statement might be taken to imply that prayer offered without doubt must certainly result in receiving that which is requested. However, James elsewhere indicates that the prayer of faith must be accompanied by proper motives. Selfish prayers or those offered for other wrong motives will result in the petitioner not receiving that which was requested (4.3).

In this particular case, 'the prayer of faith will save the sick and the Lord will raise him up'. While it is true that in its other four occurrences in James (1.21; 2.14; 4.12; 5.20) σώζω has a soteriological

---

[56] Calvin, *Commentaries*, p. 357; Reicke, *The Epistles of James, Peter, and Jude*, p. 59; Scaer, *James the Apostle*, p. 131; and R.P. Martin, *James*, p. 209.

[57] R.P. Martin, *James*, p. 209.

[58] In its other two occurrences it means a vow (Acts 18.18 and 21.23), although εὐχή is used for prayer in classical Greek. Cf. J.C. Thomas, 'εὐχή', *The Complete Bible Library: The New Testament Greek-English Dictionary – Delta-Epsilon* (ed. by T. Gilbrant; Springfield: Complete Biblical Library, 1990), pp. 658-59.

or eschatological meaning,[59] most scholars rightly conclude that, owing to its meaning in other New Testament passages,[60] its use in the papyri,[61] and its context in Jas 5.15, σῴζω must here at least include physical healing.[62] Similarly, while ἐγείρω often can be used in reference to the resurrection,[63] it is commonly used to describe the effects of a physical healing in the New Testament,[64] and most scholars take it in that sense here.[65] Clearly then, one aspect of the elders' prayer is for the physical healing of those who call for prayer.

It addition to healing for the body, the sick person will receive forgiveness of sin if needed, a thought that may extend the meaning of σῴζω in this context. The background to this verse appears to be a belief common in Judaism that there was often a direct connection between sin and sickness. The evidence for this connection is plentiful. Not only is this idea found in the Torah (Deut. 28.22-27), the Psalms (38), the Prophets (Isa. 38.17), and the Wisdom Literature (numerous places in Job), but it is also found in literature nearer to the time of the New Testament (Sir. 18.19-21; Testament of the Twelve Patriarchs: *T. Reub.* 1.7; *T. Sim.* 2.12; *T Zeb.* 5.4; and *T. Gad* 5.9-10). However, claims that the Jews always made

---

[59] Only a handful of scholars argue for such a definition of σῴζω here. Cf. Vouga, *L'Épître de Saint Jacques*, p. 142; Scaer, *James the Apostle*, pp. 132-33; and Pickar ('Is Anyone Sick Among You?', p. 171), who argues that σῴζω refers to the spiritual effects of Extreme Unction.

[60] Cf. its meaning in Mt. 9.21; Mk 5.28, 34; 6.56; 12.52; and Lk. 8.48.

[61] Cf. A. Deissmann, *Light from the Ancient East* (Grand Rapids: Baker, 1978), p. 181 n. 8.

[62] Manton, *Exposition*, p. 454; Mayor, *Epistle of James*, p. 173; Ropes, *Epistle of James*, p. 328; Chaine, *L'Épître de Saint Jacques*, p. 212; Marty, *L'Épître de Jacques,* pp. 127-28; Tasker, *The General Epistle*, p. 132; Hamman, 'Prière et culte', p. 43; Mitton, *Epistle of James*, p. 200; E.M. Sidebottom, *James, Jude, 2 Peter* (Grand Rapids: Eerdmans, 1971), p. 62; Wilkinson, 'Healing', p. 334; Cantinat, *De Saint Jacques*, p. 251; Dibelius, *James*, p. 254; Kugelman, *James*, p. 65; Davids, *Epistle of James*, p. 194; Moo, *James*, p. 181; R.L. Omanson, 'The Certainty of Judgment and the Power of Prayer', *RevExp* 83 (1986), p. 433; and Martin, *James*, p. 211.

[63] Cf. 1 Cor. 15.15-16, 29, 32, 35, 42-44, 52; 2 Cor. 1.9; 4.14. Vouga (*L'Épître de Saint Jacques*, p. 142) and Scaer (*James the Apostle*, pp. 132-33) take ἐγείρω in this way here.

[64] Cf. Mt. 9.5-7, 25; Mk 1.31; 2.9, 11-12; 5.41; 9.27; and Acts 3.7.

[65] Ropes, *Epistle of James*, p. 308; Tasker, *The General Epistle,* p. 132; Mitton, *Epistle of James*, p. 201; Wilkinson, 'Healing', p. 334; Cantinat, *De Saint Jacques*, p. 251; Dibelius, *James*, p. 254; Davids, *Epistle of James*, p. 194; Moo, *James*, p. 181; and Martin, *James*, p. 211.

such a connection are not well-founded.[66] For as H.H. Rowley concludes, while there may be innocent suffering in the Old Testament, not all suffering is innocent. 'The Bible never tries to reduce the facts of experience to the simplicity the theorist seeks.'[67] James makes clear, through the use of a future more probable clause,[68] that while sin may very well be the reason for sickness, sin is not always the reason for it.[69] The implication of this statement is that one cannot assume that sickness is the direct result of sin. Apparently, the sick person is the one who would know whether or not an illness was the result of sin, as James advocates confession of sin to one another in order to receive healing. Neither a private confession to the elders nor an expectation that the elders should discern the sin is implied. It would appear that the sin would not be something about which the sick person would have any doubts, but rather would be apparent.[70] There is no hint that those whose illness is not the direct result of sin are presumed guilty of sin until proven innocent, nor are they under pressure to conjure up some fault.

However, the question remains, in those cases where sin is the direct cause of sickness, what is the precise nature of the causal relationship? Although a number of passages in the New Testament attribute some illnesses to the effects of demon possession, there is absolutely no evidence that this is what James has in mind. While his knowledge of demons (2.19) and the Devil's activity (4.7) makes it theoretically possible that James might know of individuals who, as a result of the Devil, were bound by disease, he gives not the slightest hint about such a possibility here. If it is assumed for the moment that James does attribute such sickness to demons, it is odd that he is not explicit about this matter in the one place in the

---

[66] For statements to this effect cf. the comments of Condon, 'Sacrament', p. 41 and W. Barclay, *The Letters of James and Peter* (Philadelphia: Westminster, 1960), p. 154.

[67] H.H. Rowley, *The Faith of Israel* (London: SCM Press, 1956) p. 114. Cf. also his comments on pp. 115-16 and those of Wilkinson, 'Healing', p. 333.

[68] The future more probable clause implies considerable probability of fulfillment. Cf. H.E. Dana and J.R. Mantey, *A Manual of the Greek New Testament* (Toronto: Macmillan, 1957), p. 287.

[69] Scaer (*James the Apostle*, p. 133) is virtually alone when he claims that in Jas 5.15, 'There is no necessary connection between sin and sickness'.

[70] Cf. Marty, *L'Épître de Jacques*, p. 128.

whole New Testament where one finds the clearest directives given concerning healing and the resulting forgiveness.

Another explanation of the causal relationship between sin and sickness that does not prove convincing is the idea that sin has inherent power which results in illness. If James does not attribute healing qualities to the oil itself, it is difficult to believe that he would attribute inherent power to sin.

Rather, it appears that James' words are best understood against the backdrop of the Old Testament and its affirmations about the relationship between sin and sickness. For not only is the Old Testament clear in identifying God himself as the author of the punishment for sin generally,[71] but in those passages where there is an explicit connection made between sin and sickness God is also invariably the one responsible for the illness (cf. Lev. 26.16; Num. 12.9-10; 2 Kgs 5.27; 2 Chron. 21.14-15; Psalm 38). Given the Jewish orientation of the Epistle of James and the extent to which sickness resulting from sin was attributed to God in the first century, the most plausible explanation regarding the relationship between sin and sickness in Jas 5.15 is that God is responsible for certain illnesses. Such an interpretation is in line with the way in which God is acknowledged to afflict as well as bring relief in vv 17-18, where through the prayer of Elijah God first withholds rain and later sends it.[72]

That the sickness is the result of sin might be implied in that πεποιηκώς appears in the perfect tense: 'if (κἄν plus the subjunctive) he has comitted sins (in the past with the effects still felt) it will be forgiven him'.

---

[71] Cf. A. Lods, 'Les idées des Israélites sur la maladie', in *Vom Alten Testament* (ed. K. Budde; Giessen: Alfred Töpelmann, 1925), pp. 181-93; L. Morris, 'The Punishment of Sin in the Old Testament', *AusBR* 6 (1958), pp. 63-83; H. Mowvley, 'Health and Salvation in the Old Testament', *The Baptist Quarterly* 22 (1967), pp. 100-13; and M.L. Brown, *Israel's Divine Healer* (Grand Rapids: Zondervan, 1995). P.D. Miller (*Sin and Judgment in the Prophets* [Chico: Scholars Press, 1982], pp. 132-37) concludes that in the prophets the correspondence between sin and judgment is articulated in three ways: 1) judgment is sometimes the natural consequence of certain sinful deeds; 2) judgment is sometimes seen as the retribution of God; and 3) judgment can also be seen as having a purifying, reclaiming, and renewing effect.

[72] I am indebted to Dr Blaine Charette for this insight.

Verse 16

In the light of the fact that sometimes illness is the direct result of sin and that the prayer of faith is instrumental in both healing and forgiveness, James asserts, '(οὖν) confess your sins to one another and pray for one another'.[73] Confession of sin is well-known in the Old Testament both for the individual (cf. Lev. 5.5; Num. 5.7; Pss. 32.5; 38.3-4; 40.12; 50; 106; 51.3-5; Prov. 20.9; 28.13; and Job 33.26-28) and for the community (Lev, 16.21; 26.40; Dan. 9.4-10; and Ezek. 10.1). According to Gerhard von Rad, there are two elements involved in confession: (1) the confession (or acknowledgement) of sin and (2) the praise of God.

> In accepting a justly imposed judgment, the man confesses transgression, and he clothes what he says in the mantle of an avowal giving God the glory. The essence of this and of every act of praise is that in all circumstances it declares God to be in the right.[74]

Confession of sin is remarkably widespread in early Christianity as well (cf. Mk 1.5; Mt. 3.6; Acts 19.18; 1 Jn 1.9; 1 Clem. 51.3; 52.1; Did. 4.14; 14.1; Barn. 19.12; Hermas, *Vis.* 1.1.3; 3.1.5-6; *Sim.* 9.23.4).

It is likely that the confession of sin advocated by James is not simply a general confession,[75] but rather a confession of those sins which were thought to have resulted in illness.[76] At the very least, such confession would function as 'preventive medicine'.[77] While some commentators have attempted to interpret the confession of

---

[73] The appearance of οὖν in v. 16 has convinced several scholars that a close connection is to be made between the content of vv. 15 and 16. Cf. Mayor, *Epistle of James,* p. 175; Chaine, *L'Épître de Saint Jacques,* p. 215; Moo, *James,* pp. 182-83; and Martin, *James,* p. 210.

[74] G. von Rad, *Old Testament Theology,* I (trans. D.M.G. Stalker; New York: Harper & Row, 1962), p. 359.

[75] An interpretation advocated by Tasker, *The General Epistle,* pp. 134-35; Mitton, *Epistle of James,* pp. 202-203; Kugelman, *James,* p. 68; Hamman, 'Prière et culte', p. 43; Laws, *Epistle of James,* p. 232; and F. Manns, 'Confessez vos péchés les uns aux Autres', RSR 58 (1984), p. 235.

[76] Ropes, *Epistle of James,* p. 309; Chaine, *L'Épître de Saint Jacques,* p. 217; and Blackman, *James,* p. 155.

[77] Davids, *Epistle of James,* p. 195.

sin as a private act either to elders[78] or to fellow believers who had been wronged by a brother or sister,[79] in all likelihood James is calling for a public confession of particular sins not unlike that implied in other early Christian documents.[80] The mutual and fraternal confession of sin is for the specific purpose of intercession. While Marty goes too far in affirming that, 'L'idée semble bien être que le pouvoir de remettre les péchés a été confié à des hommes', James does seem to imply that individual believers are spiritually accountable for one another. This idea is similar to the way in which the Elder admonishes his readers in 1 Jn (5.16-17).[81]

Upon hearing the specific sins and needs of a brother or sister, the believer is to petition God on behalf of the confessor. Such prayers should result in healing. Although some commentators argue that a 'spiritual' healing is described in v. 16,[82] noting that ἰά-ομαι is sometimes used metaphorically for healing in the New Testament, this interpretation does not do justice to the evidence for several reasons. First, v. 16 is closely connected to the preceding discussion about physical healing by the use of οὖν. Second, ἰάομαι appears frequently in the papyri in contexts which describe physical healing.[83] In addition, ἰάομαι takes on a spiritual application in the New Testament *only* when it appears in quotations from the Old Testament.[84] Therefore, it is better to take ἰάομαι as having reference to physical healing.

James ends this verse with the exhortation that the prayer of a righteous person accomplishes much. Instead of taking δίκιαος as

---

[78] Sidebottom (*James, Jude*, p. 62) takes the confession as having reference to the elders of v 14.

[79] Motyer, *Message of James*, pp. 201-202. Cf. also the comments of the Venerable Bede (*Commentary*, p. 62), who calls for the confession of minor faults to one another while confessing the major sins to the priests.

[80] On the nature of public confession in early Christianity cf. the discussion in R.E. Brown, *The Epistles of John* (Garden City: Doubleday, 1982), p. 208 and J.C. Thomas, *Footwashing in John 13 and the Johannine Community* (JSNTSup 61; Sheffield: Sheffield Academic Press, 1991), p. 185. For this interpretation cf. also Johnson, *James*, pp. 134-35.

[81] Cf. Augustine's remarks in his *Homilies on John* 59.5.

[82] Cf. the comments of Marty (*L'Épître de Jacques*, p. 131), Mussner (*Jakobusbrief*, p. 227), Cantinat (*De Saint Jacques*, p. 254), Scaer (*James the Apostle*, pp. 133-34), and Laws (*Epistle of James*, p. 238).

[83] Chaine, *L'Épître de Saint Jacques*, p. 217.

[84] Cf. Moo (*James*, p. 183) and Davids (*Epistle of James*, p. 193).

having reference to individuals of extraordinary faith, it seems as though James is emphasizing the ordinariness of those who offer prayer,[85] as is clear from the qualifying statement made regarding Elijah (ἄνθρωπος ἦν ὁμοιοπαθὴς ἡμῖν). Instead of importing a definition of δίκαιος into Jas 5.16, the most reasonable course of action is to allow James' use of δίκαιος in other contexts to inform its meaning here. As Vouga points out, in the epistle of James δίκαιος and its cognates designate belief, as in the case of Abraham or Rahab, which is not simply faith, but faith which is manifest by its works (cf. Jas 2.21, 24, 25; and 1.20; 2.23; 3.18 respectively).[86] The righteous person here described is one who - does those things which are pleasing to God and in conformity to his will - something which is no small order to be sure, but which James implies is within the reach of every believer. The description of Joseph offered in Mt. 1.19 is perhaps as good an example of this understanding of δίκαιος as one finds in the New Testament.

James makes clear that prayer offered by such believers is very powerful and effective. Chaine goes so far as to say that the prayer of the just is endowed with an extremely powerful and incomparable virtue.[87] The author communicates the potency of prayer by the combination of πολὺ, ἰσχύει, and ἐνεργουμένη. Whether one takes ἐνεργουμένη as a middle or passive participle, it is difficult to avoid the conclusion that James regards prayer as a very powerful resource for the believer and the church when faced with illnesses.[88] The admonition about prayer and faith in Jas 1.6-8 dovetails nicely with this strong affirmation concerning the power of prayer.

James closes this pericope by pointing to Elijah's success in prayer as an example to encourage his readers.

---

[85] Cf. Davids, *Epistle of James*, p. 196; Moo, *James*, p. 187; K. Warrington, 'The Significance of Elijah in James', *EvQ* 66 (1994), p. 224; and Johnson, *James*, p. 336.

[86] Vouga, *L'Épître de Saint Jacques*, p. 144.

[87] Chaine, *L'Épître de Saint Jacques*, p. 217.

[88] The thought is not unlike that of Mk 11.22-24. For a treatment of this text cf. S.E. Dowd, *Prayer, Power, and the Problem of Suffering: Mark 11.22-25 in the Context of Markan Theology* (Atlanta: Scholars Press, 1988).

Conclusions and Implications

Several conclusions and implications for the purposes of this enquiry emerge from this chapter.

First, Jas 5.14-16 makes very clear that James regarded some illnesses as being the direct result of sin. While he offers some qualification of this statement, the fact that sin and sickness are connected so explicitly should not be ignored nor softened.

Second, in those cases where sickness is the direct result of sin, confession of that sin is required. Such confession is to be made at least to fellow believers for the specific purpose of intercession. There is no indication that the sick believer is to be preoccupied with discovering some secret sin that may have been committed, rather the implication is that the sick believer would know full well the nature of the sin. There is also the impression left that confession should be a normal part of the worshipping community's life.

Third, James advocates a continuing ministry of healing, which would incorporate anointing with oil at the hands of the elders and fervent praying with the expectation that healing will result. James does not appear to consider the possibility that healing might not be attained.[89]

Fourth, it is also remarkably clear that James does not consider all illness to be the direct result of sin, which might imply that certain illnesses are simply the consequence of living in a sinful world. It may be deduced that in such cases the sick believers are not presumed to be guilty of sin until proven innocent.

Fifth, in keeping with much Old Testament thought, James seems to imply that sickness which accompanies sin is the direct result of God's own activity.

---

[89] M. Turner's conclusion at this point (*The Holy Spirit and Spiritual Gifts: Then and Now* [Carlisle: Paternoster Press, 1996], pp. 253-54) seems at variance with the text of James itself.

2

THE PAULINE LITERATURE

The investigation of Jas 5.14-16 revealed a number of significant points concerning the Devil, disease, and deliverance. But much more may be gleaned concerning this topic from other New Testament writers.

Although not offering as clear a statement regarding the relationship between sin and sickness as does James, the Pauline literature is examined next for several reasons. The extent of the Pauline literature is one reason to take it up at this point. As is well known, more letters are attributed to Paul than any other writer in the New Testament.[1] But more than sheer numbers, since the Reformation the Pauline literature has been considered by many to be the heart of the New Testament. Any thematic enquiry into New Testament theology must soon come to the Pauline corpus, if not begin with it. Not only are the Pauline epistles important for this examination owing to their number, but they are also significant because their intended audiences range from several congregations, if Paul's directive to exchange letters is taken into account (cf. Col. 4.16), to specific individuals. Such diversity of audience allows for the discernment of the various nuances of Paul's thought on this topic as his theological position is concretized in different situations.

A final reason offered for examining the Pauline epistles next is the significant amount of relevant data found there. Such material includes Paul's teaching regarding the gifts of healings, texts which

---

[1] Although the authenticity of several letters attributed to Paul are widely disputed, on any reckoning there are more letters in the New Testament from Paul's hand than from any other author. Fortunately, the vast majority of the relevant Pauline texts for this enquiry comes from those epistles where there has been little dispute over the issue of authorship. The exceptions are the Pastorals, which will receive separate attention.

reveal Paul's attitude toward illness (his own and that of others), and passages which suggest a relationship between sin and sickness (even death).

The Gifts of Healings

From the outset it should be observed that Paul and his communities appear to have been quite familiar with healings and mighty works. By his own admission Paul's preaching was characterized not so much by wise and persuasive words but rather by 'a demonstration of the Spirit and Power'. Paul's purpose for such reliance upon the Spirit was in order that the Corinthians' faith 'might not be in the wisdom of men but in the power of God'. In point of fact, 'signs and wonders and mighty acts' appear to have occurred with such a degree of regularity in his ministry among the Corinthians that Paul could point to them as signs of his own apostolic status (2 Cor. 12.12). Lest it be concluded that such a dynamic ministry was confined to the Corinthian church one should note Paul's testimony to the Romans (15.18-19) that what Christ had accomplished through him 'in word (λόγῳ) and deed (ἔργῳ)' was 'by the power of signs and wonders, by the power of the Spirit'.

Therefore, it should come as no surprise to find in one of the Pauline lists of the charismata (1 Cor. 12.4-11) an entry related to healing, the gifts of healings (χαρίσματα ἰαμάτων). It should be sufficiently clear from the face of it that when Paul speaks of these gifts he is not describing individuals adept in the 'powers of suggestion'[2] nor those with 'a natural gift of sympathy or empathy combined with a capacity of knowing the right thing to do in any individual situation and with any individual patient'.[3] Rather, the healings here described would appear to be on the order of those attributed to Jesus and the Apostles in the Gospels and Acts.[4] Specifically, the Pauline epistles offer evidence of 'cures and healings experienced in the Pauline communities for which no natural or rational

---

[2] A possibility suggested by A.T. Robertson and A. Plummer, *First Epistle of St. Paul to the Corinthians* (Edinburgh: T. & T. Clark, 1929), p. 266.

[3] J. Wilkinson, *Health and Healing: Studies in New Testament Principles and Practice* (Edinburgh: Handsel, 1980), p. 109.

[4] D.A. Carson, *Showing the Spirit* (Grand Rapids: Baker, 1987), p. 39.

explanation would suffice – they could only be put down to the action of God'.[5]

What is a bit unclear is Paul's rationale both for using the word 'gifts' to describe this particular gift, when it does not occur with the other gifts named in this listing, and for placing both terms in the plural (χαρίσματα ἰαμάτων). It could be argued that this construction was necessary 'because each cure was a special and fresh gift from God',[6] in other words because the gift is 'the actual healing itself'.[7] The plural can also be taken to mean that a member of the community would receive the gift to heal a particular kind of illness or a group of illnesses but not all.[8] However, it is going too far to demand that the plurals exclude the possibility that one member may receive many gifts of healings. After all, Paul does say 'and to another gifts of healings in one Spirit' (ἄλλῳ δὲ χαρίσματα ἰαμάτων ἐν τῷ ἑνὶ πνεύματι). Perhaps Siegfried Schatzmann is closer to the mark in concluding that '… the gifts of healing are sovereignly bestowed upon some believers commensurate with the illnesses present, either in number or kind.'[9] Such an understanding preserves the continuity of this gift with the others, that is the ability to heal through the Spirit,[10] and respects the variety of the healing gifts involved.

The import of this brief discussion of the gifts of healings is to note that there were those within the Pauline communities who possessed the ability to perform healings through the Spirit. As with the other charismata, the purpose of such activity was for the edification of the body. Although specific instructions with regard to the function of the healing gifts are lacking, in contrast to the situation described in James 5, something may still be deduced about its

---

[5] J.D.G. Dunn, *Jesus and the Spirit* (Philadelphia: Westminster, 1975), p. 210. Cf. also the comments by D. Baker, 'The Interpretation of 1 Corinthians 12-14,' *EQ* 46 (1974), p. 231.

[6] J.A. Beet, *A Commentary on St. Paul's Epistle to the Corinthians* (London: Hodder and Stoughton, 1882), p. 216.

[7] Dunn, *Jesus and the Spirit*, p. 211.

[8] Cf. Robertson and Plummer, *First Corinthians*, p. 266 and Carson, *Showing the Spirit*, pp. 39-40.

[9] S. Schatzmann, *A Pauline Theology of the Charismata* (Peabody: Hendrickson, 1987), p. 37.

[10] As opposed to taking each healing as the gift(s). Cf. G.D. Fee, *The First Epistle to the Corinthians* (Grand Rapids: Eerdmans, 1987), p. 594.

practice. Given the spontaneous nature of Corinthian worship it may be that the gifts of healings functioned rather like the other gifts operated (cf. 1 Cor. 14.26). If so, the individual endowed with the gifts of healings would offer prayer for a sick member (with the laying on of hands?) whenever he or she was moved upon by the Spirit. Of course, such a scenario assumes that those with healing gifts acted when the Spirit prompted them to do so. However, in the light of Paul's admonitions regarding orderly worship, it is not difficult to imagine the emergence of a 'somewhat' fixed order of worship in which prayer for the sick formed a part. Even so, it is likely that there were times when healings took place 'spontaneously' as well.

Before leaving this brief discussion of the gifts of healings it is advantageous to explore its relationship to the gift which follows it in 1 Cor. 12.10, miraculous works (ἐνεργήματα δυνάμεων). Although puzzling to many Western readers, it is obvious that Paul makes a distinction between healings and miracles.[11] But what sort of distinction is being made and how are miraculous works to be defined? It would seem safe to assume that while such miraculous works might possibly include healings, clearly this meaning is not its primary one here.[12] As was noted earlier, Paul uses the term δύναμις in making reference to the manifestation of the power of God which accompanied his preaching (Rom. 15.19; 1 Cor. 2.4-5) and which the Corinthians themselves had witnessed (2 Cor. 12.12). Unfortunately, these Pauline texts do not make explicit the exact nature of such miraculous works. Based primarily on the evidence of the Gospels and Acts, scholars define these works as nature miracles,[13] chastisements inflicted upon evildoers such as Elymas

---

[11] U. Brockhaus, *Charisma und Amt* (Wuppertal: Theologischer Verlag Rolf Brockhaus, 1972), pp. 191-92.

[12] Cf. Fee, *First Corinthians*, p. 594.

[13] C.K. Barrett, *A Commentary on the First Epistle to the Corinthians* (London: A. & C. Black, 1968), p. 286; A. Bittlinger, *Gifts and Graces* (trans. H. Klassen; London: Hodder and Stroughton, 1967), pp. 40-42; Dunn, *Jesus and the Spirit*, p. 210; Carson, *Showing the Spirit*, p. 286; and Schatzmann, *A Pauline Theology of the Charismata*, p. 38.

the sorcerer,[14] raising the dead,[15] but most frequently exorcisms.[16] In an extended footnote on the meaning of miraculous works, Hans Conzelmann offers some philological support for this last option:

> Or is Paul thinking specially of exorcisms, which of course are consciously distinguished from healing of the sick, not only in the synoptics (indirectly also in John, where no exorcisms are recounted; nor in Epidaurus either)? ἐνέργεια/ἐνεργεῖν in the OT and NT almost always denote the working of divine (or demonic) powers.[17]

While it is difficult to be certain about the meaning of miraculous works in this passage, the possibility that it has reference to exorcism must be considered one of the leading options, despite the fact that 'demon possession as such does not feature prominently in Paul's thought'.[18]

Two questions may be raised in concluding this section: 1) what is the relationship between gifts of healings and miraculous works and 2) what is its significance for this investigation as a whole? In attempting to answer the first question it should be noted that while the gift of faith would be of great value to those with gifts of healings or those who performed miraculous works, it might be going too far to define the gift of faith primarily in this way.[19] Might not the gift of faith be crucial to the community, and various members

---

[14] Robertson and Plummer, *First Corinthians*, p. 266.

[15] Bittlinger, *Gifts and Graces*, pp. 40-42.

[16] Robertson and Plummer, *First Corinthians*, p. 266; J. Weiss, *Der Erste Korintherbrief* (Göttingen: Vandenhoeck & Ruprecht, 1910), p. 301. E.-B. Allo, *Première Épitre aux Corinthiens* (Paris: Gabalda, 1956), p. 337; J. Héring, *The First Epistle of Saint Paul to the Corinthians* (trans. A.W. Heathcote and P. J. Allrock; London: Epworth Press, 1962), p. 126; H. Berkhof, *The Doctrine of the Holy Spirit* (London: Epworth Press, 1965), p. 86; Bittlinger, *Gifts and Graces*, pp. 40-42; M. Green, *I Believe in the Holy Spirit* (London: Hodder and Stoughton, 1975), p. 180; Carson, *Showing the Spirit*, p. 40; and Schatzmann, *A Pauline Theology of the Charismata*, p. 38.

[17] H. Conzelmann, *1 Corinthians* (trans. J.W. Leitch; Philadelphia: Fortress, 1975), p. 209 n. 29.

[18] Dunn, *Jesus and the Spirit*, p. 210.

[19] As R. P. Martin appears to suggest in *The Spirit and the Congregation: Studies in 1 Corinthians 12-15* (Grand Rapids: Eerdmans, 1984), p. 14. Cf. also C. Senft, *La première épitre de Saint Paul aux Corinthiens* (Paris: Delachaux & Niestlé, 1979), p. 158.

within it, in numerous other ways?[20] Undoubtedly there is some degree of overlap between the gifts of faith, healings, and miraculous works;[21] perhaps one or more members in the Pauline communities were endowed with all three, but it does seem that Paul wishes a distinction to be made between them, so it is perhaps best to honor his intention. If the distinction between healing gifts and miraculous works was intended by Paul and if miraculous works include exorcisms, then the implication for the broader concerns of this study is that healings within the Pauline communities seem to have had little to do with exorcism or, it would appear, with the Devil in general. Such a conclusion suggests that Paul saw the gifts of healings less in terms of power and more in terms of comfort and relief. But if this analysis is correct, what is Paul's view about the origin of sickness? To this topic the next section is devoted.

The Origins of Sickness in Pauline Thought

1 Corinthians 11.27-34 – 'Some of You Are Sick and Dying'
Contrary to what may commonly be assumed, with the possible exception of the passage devoted to the thorn in the flesh (a topic to be taken up later in this chapter) Paul does not attribute sickness or disease to the Devil and/or demons. While it is true that Paul is very careful to make clear the connection in Rom. 5.12-21 between sin and death, he shows no interest whatsoever in exploring the relationship between sin and sickness in this passage. In point of fact, 1 Cor. 11.27-34 appears to be Paul's most explicit statement about the origin of certain illnesses.

The letter known as 1 Corinthians was written by Paul to the church in Corinth ca. 53-54 CE. Among the many issues Paul addresses in this epistle are the following: rivalry and division within the church, sexual immorality, association with pagan feasts, improper beliefs and attitudes regarding the sacraments, problems

---

[20] Allo (*Première Épitre aux Corinthiens*, p. 326) comes to a similar conclusion when he observes, 'Il est possible que les "guérisons" surnaturelles et "les énergies" (c'est-a-dire tous les autres genres du prodiges) soient données comme les effets spéciaux de cette "foi"; cependant celle-ci paraît plutôt être une première espèce distinguée des deux autres; ce serait donc plutôt le don de grandes intiatures que ne sont pas spécifiquement surnaturelles'.

[21] As Carson (*Showing the Spirit*, p. 40) rightly observes.

with spiritual gifts, and uncertainty about the resurrection. Located within the second half of the letter (1 Corinthians 7-15), which contains Paul's responses to various issues raised by some in the Corinthian church via a letter to him (1 Cor 7.1), is a section devoted to the Lord's Supper.

After chiding the readers for their divisions and other shameful behavior at the Lord's table (11.17-22), Paul cites 'received' Jesus tradition which had been transmitted to him (11.23-26), placing the death of Jesus and the celebration of the Lord's Supper within an eschatological context. At this point, Paul delivers an extremely stern warning to the Corinthians (11.27-34), with the hope that such an admonition would result in producing proper attitudes and behavior.

> Therefore, whoever eats the bread or drinks the cup of the Lord in an unworthy manner, shall be guilty (of sinning against) the body and the blood of the Lord. A man should examine himself, and then eat of the bread and drink of the cup. For the one who eats and drinks judgment to oneself eats and drinks not discerning the body. For this reason many among you are weak and sick and many are asleep. But if we were judging ourselves, we would not have been judged. And when judged by the Lord we are being disciplined, in order that we might not be condemned with this world. Therefore, my brothers, when coming together for the purpose of eating wait for one another. If any one is hungry, let that one eat at home, in order that you do not come together into judgment.

The interpretation of 1 Cor. 11.27-34 is complicated by the fact that its central purpose is a bit unclear. Is Paul primarily interested in discussing the Lord's Supper, a meal which has been abused through the Corinthians' shameful behavior, or is his main purpose to address, once again, the divisive nature of the Corinthian church life, an attitude which is concretized on this occasion by their behavior at the table of the Lord? It should be observed that both emphases can claim support from other texts in 1 Corinthians. On the one hand, the Lord's Supper earlier received extensive attention in 1 Cor. 10.1-22,[22] while on the other hand the issue of divisions in the church is addressed on several occasions before and after 11.27-34 (1.10-17; 3.1-23; 6.1-11; 12.12-31; 14.26-40).

A number of additional questions arise somewhat naturally from the reading of this text. What does it mean to eat and drink the body and blood of the Lord in an unworthy manner, to be guilty of the body and blood of the Lord, to examine oneself before eating and drinking, to fail to discern the body? More important for this study, what is the connection between failure to discern the body and the presence of illness and death in the community? Where does such illness and death come from and what are their purposes? What is God's role in all this and what exactly does this text tell us about the Devil, disease, and deliverence? With these questions in mind, the text of 1 Cor. 11.27-34 is now explored.

Verse 27

By using the term Ὥστε, Paul makes clear that the section which follows (11.27-34) is loosely connected with that which precedes it (11.17-26). Owing in part to this connection with the preceding verses it is also evident that 'eating the bread and drinking the cup' have reference to the eucharistic elements. Paul states that it is possible to partake of these elements 'in an unworthy manner'. Exactly what it means to participate in the Lord's Supper 'in an unworthy manner' is unclear. It could be that the Corinthians were somehow misusing the symbols of the supper,[23] or that they were approaching the table in an irreverent fashion.[24] It is also possible that their unworthy manner had to do with their conduct at the Lord's table (cf. 1 Cor. 11.21-22), where they went on with private meals while

---

[22] For the suggestion that additional reference is made to the Lord's Supper in 1 Cor. 5.11 and 1 Cor. 16.20b-24 cf. C.H. Talbert, *Reading Corinthians* (London: SPCK, 1987), p. 80.

[23] Cf. J. Calvin, *Commentary on the Epistles of Paul the Apostle to the Corinthians* (Edinburgh: Calvin Translation Society, 1843), pp. 385-86; Beet, *Corinthians*, p. 196; and E. Käsemann, *Essays on New Testament Themes* (trans. W. J. Montague; London: SCM Press, 1964), pp. 122-23.

[24] Cf. J. Wesley, *Explanatory Notes upon the New Testament* (Salem, OH: Schmul, n.d.), p. 432 and I.H. Marshall, *Last Supper and Lord's Supper* (Exeter: Paternoster Press, 1980), pp. 113-14.

the poorer brothers and sisters were being mistreated.[25] Whatever the precise nature of the offence, the consequences were very grave. For to participate in the Lord's Supper in an 'unworthy manner' is to be guilty of, or responsible for, the body and blood of the Lord.

Paul does two things to ensure that the readers understand the severity of their actions. First, he uses a term, ἔνοχος, which, understood forensically, means 'guilty' or 'liable'.[26] Second, Paul shifts from language which describes the eucharistic elements, 'bread and cup', to language which describes the Lord's physical body, 'body and blood'. While maintaining a sense of continuity between the eucharistic elements and the Lord's physical body, there can be little doubt that Paul seeks to place emphasis upon the death of Jesus.[27] In other words, the Corinthians are being told that when they participate in the Lord's Supper in an unworthy manner, they identify not with the recipients of the salvation which comes from Jesus' death, but rather with those who were responsible for crucifying him.[28] A most serious charge indeed!

Verse 28

Seeing that participation at the Lord's table in an unworthy manner produces such ghastly results, Paul calls for a cautious approach to the Lord's table. In particular, the Corinthians are urged to examine themselves before participating in the Lord's Supper. It should be noted that the object of the examination or test is self. Such a statement might convey the idea of an introspective examination[29] by which one seeks to arrive at an honest accounting of oneself[30] so

---

[25] Cf. Barrett, *First Corinthians*, p. 273; F.F. Bruce, *1 and 2 Corinthians* (London: Oliphants, 1971), p. 115; W.F. Orr and J.A. Walther, *1 Corinthians* (Garden City: Doubleday, 1976), pp. 273-74; Fee, *First Corinthians*, p. 561; and N. Watson, *The First Epistle to the Corinthians* (London: Epworth Press, 1992), pp. 124-25.

[26] Cf. H. Harse, 'ἔνοχος,' *TDNT*, II, p. 828; F. Thiele, 'ἔνοχος,' *DNTT*, II, pp. 142-43; and R. Kratz, 'ἔνοχος,' *EDNT*, I, p. 457.

[27] Käsemann, *Essays on New Testament Themes*, p. 123.

[28] Scholars who make this identification include: Käsemann, *Essays on New Testament Themes*, p. 123; Barrett, *First Corinthians*, p. 273; J. Ruef, *Paul's First Letter to Corinth* (Baltimore: Penguin, 1971), p. 121; D. Prior, *The Message of 1 Corinthians* (Leicester: IVP, 1985), p. 189; Fee, *First Corinthians*, p. 561; and Watson, *First Corinthians*, p. 125.

[29] A.N. Bogle, '1 Corinthians 11.23-34,' *ExpT* 12 (1900-1901), p. 479.

[30] Prior, *1 Corinthians*, p. 189.

that the meal is understood for what it is and approached appropriately.[31] While introspection was no doubt part of this examination, in all likelihood the specific backdrop of the Corinthian situation, with its particular problems, is what Paul has in mind here. While theoretically the self-examination would involve whether one had 'betrayed Christ by fornication (Ch. 5), or by sharing in demonic meals (Ch. 10)',[32] it most likely would center on the nature of one's relationship with others in the body[33] and the way in which one treats others at the meal itself. The eschatological context, that the meal is a proclamation of Jesus' death until the parousia, as well as the realization that such examination takes place in the very presence of God serve to heighten the importance of this self-examination.[34]

Yet, despite such a stern warning, Paul does not suggest that this self-examination would lead to a withdrawal from the Lord's table.[35] Rather, his words seem to imply that this period would be a time to rectify any troubling attitudes or actions, especially if reconciliation or restitution were needed with a fellow believer. Such an approach, perhaps based on the Jesus tradition (Mt. 5.23-24), is documented in the Didache (14).[36]

Verse 29

In this verse Paul continues his emphasis on the need for self-examination by saying, 'For the one who eats and drinks [the bread and cup] without discerning the body, eats and drinks judgment to oneself'. Earlier it was noted that one who eats and drinks in an unworthy manner is implicated in the death of Jesus. This situation called for self-examination. Now Paul says that one can actually bring judgment upon oneself by not discerning the body. Whatever

---

[31] Wesley, *Explanatory Notes*, p. 432.

[32] So Héring (*First Corinthians*, pp. 120-21), citing Theodoret of Cyr.

[33] Bruce, *1 and 2 Corinthians*, p. 115.

[34] Cf. the relevant comments of Käsemann, *Essays on New Testament Themes*, p. 126; Barrett, *First Corinthians*, p. 273; X. Léon-Dufour, *Le partage du pain eucharistique selon le Nouveau Testament* (Paris: Éditions du Sevil, 1982), p. 254; and Fee, *First Corinthians*, p. 562.

[35] In fact, the opposite is suggested in that καὶ οὕτως immediatley follows the admonition regarding self-examination.

[36] Cf. Thomas, *Footwashing in John 13 and the Johannine Community* for similar developments within the Johannine community.

this latter phrase may mean, it is important to note that for Paul the very act of eating and drinking can bring judgment. But of course the meaning of 'eating and drinking judgment upon oneself' is determined in part by the meaning of discerning the body. For on the one hand, it is likely that the issue of not discerning the body is linked to eating and drinking in an unworthy manner and to the issue of self-examination. On the other hand, an understanding of what 'not discerning the body' means may also illumine the specific way in which one can eat and drink judgment to oneself.

The traditional way of understanding σῶμα in v. 29 is to identify it with the eucharistic elements.[37] Support for this interpretation comes from the immediate context where bread and cup, body and blood are used in a closely connected, some would say, interconnected, way. In addition, as σῶμα occurs in v. 27 with reference to the physical body of Jesus, it is likely to have that meaning here.[38] It is also sometimes claimed that διακρίνω fits better with σῶμα when it is understood in this way.[39] When body is interpreted in this fashion, not to discern the body means to misunderstand its significance[40] or not to distinguish it from common or ordinary meals.[41] Consequently, one eats and drinks in an unworthy fashion when the body is not discerned, i.e. treated with sufficient dignity and respect.

The second major option is to take σῶμα as having reference to the church.[42] Several reasons may be offered in support of this in-

---

[37] So Calvin, *Corinthians*, p. 385; Wesley, *Explanatory Notes*, p. 432; Beet, *Corinthians*, p. 196; Allo, *Première Épitre aux Corinthiens*, pp. 282-83; Käsemann, *Essays on New Testament Themes*, p. 127; Barrett, *First Corinthians*, p. 275; Conzelmann, *First Corinthians*, p. 202; Senft, *La première épitre de Saint Paul aux Corinthiens*, p. 153; Marshall, *Last Supper and Lord's Supper*, p. 114; Léon-Dufour, *Le partage du pain eucharistique selon le Nouveau Testamant*, p. 254; and G. Dautzenberg, 'διακρίνω,' *EDNT*, I, p. 305.

[38] Cf. Marshall, *Last Supper and Lord's Supper*, p. 114.

[39] Barrett, *First Corinthians*, p. 275.

[40] Allo, *Première Épitre aux Corinthiens*, p. 283.

[41] Weiss, *Der Erste Korintherbrief*, p. 291; Héring, *First Corinthians*, p. 120; and L. Morris, *1 Corinthians* (Leicester: IVP, 1985), p. 161.

[42] Cf. A.J.B. Higgins, *The Lord's Supper in the New Testament* (London: SCM Press, 1952), pp. 72-73; Bruce, *1 and 2 Corintians*, p. 115; Ruef, *First Corinthians*, p. 122; Orr and Walther, *I Corinthains*, p. 274; F.L. Arrington, *Divine Order in the Church* (Grand Rapids: Baker, 1981), p. 116; Fee, *First Corinthians*, pp. 563-64; C.L. Porter, 'An Interpretation of Paul's Lord's Supper Text in 1 Corinthians 10.14-22 and 11.17-34', *Encounter* 50 (1989), pp. 43-44; and Watson, *First Corinthians*, pp. 124-25.

terpretation. First, already in 1 Cor. 10.17 Paul makes a direct equation between the one (eucharistic) loaf and the one body (of the church).[43] Second, in 1 Cor. 12.12-26 Paul speaks at length about the body (of the church).[44] Third, while the immediate context is the Lord's Supper, the broader context concerns the divisions within the community that manifest themselves at the Lord's table in particular.[45] Finally, it is observed that the problem at Corinth was not a failure to distinguish consecrated elements from common ones,[46] but rather a failure to acknowledge one another. On this interpretation, to eat and drink in an unworthy fashion is to be guilty of not discerning who the church really is and to disregard its essential unity, thus eating and drinking judgment to oneself, owing not so much to the violation of the eucharistic elements, as to the violation of the body (church).[47]

However, to see these two interpretive options (i.e. body = bread, body = church) as mutually exclusive may be going too far,[48] for as G.W.H. Lampe rightly notes, 'the two are so closely intertwined as to be indistinguishable from each other in this context'.[49] In point of fact, there appears to be an extremely tight interplay in this entire section between the bread and cup, the body and blood of Jesus, and the church as the body of Christ. Moreover, it is difficult to believe that the Corinthians themselves would have made the

---

[43] Cf. Orr and Walther, *1 Corinthians*, p. 274 and Fee, *First Corinthians*, p. 564.

[44] Fee, *First Corinthians*, p. 564.

[45] Fee, *First Corinthians*, p. 564.

[46] Cf. Higgins, *The Lord's Supper in the New Testament*, p. 72 and Watson, *First Corinthians*, p. 124.

[47] Not everyone is convinced by this relatively new line of approach. For example, cf. the remarks of Leon-Dufour (*Le partage du pain eucharistique selon le Nouveau Testamant*, p. 254 n. 52), 'Le term *sôma* ("corps"), objet du discernment requis, peut sans doute se rapporter au corps du Seigneur dont il vient d'être question; par contre, rien n'autorise ici le sens de "corps ecclesial"'. Cf. also the stronger and earlier remarks of Allo (*Première Épitre aux Corinthiens*, p. 283), 'Comprendre "le Corps" au sens du corps des fidèles, dont le mauvais communiant ne saurait pas reconnaître les droits et la dignité dans le pain qui les représente, c'est une exégèse aussi plate que tirée par les chereux'.

[48] Cf. F. Chenderlin, *Do This as My Memorial* (Rome: Biblical Institution Press, 1982), p. 178; Prior, *1 Corinthians*, p. 190; and Watson, *First Corinthians*, p. 125.

[49] G.W.H. Lampe, 'Church Discipline in the Epistle to the Corinthians,' in *Christian History and Interpretation: Studies Presented to John Knox* (ed. W.R. Farmer, C.F.D. Moule, and R.R. Niebuhr; Cambridge: Cambridge University Press, 1967), p. 346.

kinds of airtight distinctions that are often seen in contemporary exegetical and theological argumentation. Rather, given the hints Paul had offered them earlier about the bread and body (1Cor. 10.17) and their own predisposition toward an extremely high (perhaps somewhat magical?) view of the sacraments, it seems likely that they would have seen a fair amount of overlap and interplay among these concepts.[50] In particular, Paul seems to be saying that the bread and cup are powerful signs of the body and blood (the death) of Jesus, which is the basis of salvation for the believing community. The church is, at the same time, closely connected with both the sign (one loaf, one body) and with Jesus (as his body). Charles Talbert nicely brings out the implications of this interpretation for the meaning of v. 29 when he concludes, 'Given the context, failure to discern the body can mean only an inability to perceive the Christian unity rooted in the sacrifice of Christ and actualized in the sacred meal'.[51]

Verse 30

Having warned his readers that they eat and drink judgment to themselves when they do not discern the body and therefore eat and drink in an unworthy manner, Paul now identifies some of the results of such actions; many of them are ill and a number of them have died. If, as this verse says, many of the Corinthians are ill and dying as a result of their grievous behavior, and such is the most natural reading of the text, then the question must be raised, is it possible to establish the precise nature of the relationship between their actions and their sufferings?

---

[50] A. Farrer ['The Eucharist in 1 Corinthians,' in *Eucharistic Theology Then and Now* (London: SPCK, 1968), p. 26] agrees, 'We moderns can ask, if we wish, whether the offence is sacrilege or uncharity, but we can be certain that the alternatives we pose were no alternatives for St. Paul'.

[51] Talbert, *Reading Corinthians*, p. 79. Cf. also the comments of M.E. Thrall [*I and II Corinthians* (Cambridge: Cambridge University Press, 1965), p. 85], 'The image [of the body] signifies, among other things, that the community is united (12.12, 13, 25, 26). This sense of unity is created and expressed at the Lord's Supper. "Because there is one loaf, we, many as we are, are one body; for it is one loaf of which we all partake" (10.17). By splitting up into *sharply divided groups* (verse 18) the Corinthians were denying the meaning of the rite and destroying what should have been the essential and distinguishing characteristic of their community. They had therefore become wilfully blind to the fact that as Christians they were members of Christ's Body.'

One can argue that illness and death are related to the eucharistic elements in a causal way.[52] That is to say, illness and death are metaphysical results of abusing the elements themselves.[53] This would mean, in the famous words of Hans Lietzmann, that the medicine of immortality (φάρμακον ἀθανασιας) has become the poison (medicine) of death (φάρμακον θανάτου).[54] However, while the Corinthians may have had a somewhat magical view of the sacraments, there is no indication that Paul did.[55]

On the basis of the Corinthians' possible association with demons mentioned in 1 Cor. 10.20-21, C.K. Barrett concludes that demons were the probable cause of the physical disease present in the congregation.[56] However, this suggestion fails to convince for a couple of reasons. First, while it is true that Paul warns the Corinthians to avoid fellowship with demons, and it is theoretically possible that he could attribute disease to them, Paul neither identifies them as a possible cause of disease nor does he give any hints as to the presence of demons in 11.30. Second, nowhere in the Pauline corpus, with the possible exception of 2 Cor. 12.7-10, is disease or illness attributed to demons. Consequently, to infer such here would appear to outdistance the evidence.

In addition to the weaknesses mentioned with each of these suggestions, the text itself undercuts them both, for in v. 32 Paul makes clear that such calamities come from God himself.[57] This should come as no surprise given Paul's previous description of the fate of the Israelites in the wilderness (1 Cor. 10.1-13).[58] But such a conclusion has proven unsettling to more than one scholar and sev-

---

[52] Cf. Weiss, *Der Erste Korintherbrief*, pp. 290-91; M. Goguel, *L'Euchuristie: Des Origins a Justin Martyr* (Paris: Librairie Fischbacher, 1910), pp. 177-78; and A.D. Nock, *Early Gentile Christianity and Its Hellenistic Background* (New York: Harper Torch Books, 1964), pp. 130-31.

[53] Héring, *First Corinthians*, p. 120.

[54] D.H. Lietzmann, *Korinther I-II* (Tübingen: J.C.B. Mohr, 1923), p. 61.

[55] Cf. Conzelmann, *1 Corinthians*, p. 203 and Senft, *La première épitre de Saint Paul aux Corinthiens*, p. 154.

[56] Barrett, *First Corinthians*, p. 275.

[57] Beet, *Corinthians*, p. 197; Higgins, *The Lord's Supper in the New Testament*, p. 73; Orr and Walther, *1 Corinthians*, p. 274; R.H. Gundry, *Soma in Biblical Theology* (Cambridge: Cambridge University Press, 1976), p. 67; Senft, *La première épitre de Saint Paul aux Corinthiens*, p. 154; Morris, *First Corinthians*, p. 161; and Harrisville, *First Corinthians*, p. 202.

[58] Talbert, *Reading Corinthians*, p. 79.

eral have felt compelled to modify or soften it. For example, Gordon Fee observes:

> Most likely Paul does not see the judgment as a kind of 'one for one,' that is, the person who has abused another is the one who gets sick. Rather, the whole community is affected by the actions of some, who are creating 'divisions' within the one body of Christ. Probably the rash of illnesses and deaths that have recently overtaken them is here being viewed as an expression of divine judgment on the whole community.[59]

Of course, there is no way to know with any degree of certainty whether Fee's assessment at this point is accurate or not. Yet, when 1 Cor. 11.30 is compared with what might be called its closest New Testament counterparts (Jn 5.14; Acts 5.1-11; and esp. Jas 5.15-16), it would appear to be closer to a 'one for one' situation than Fee wants to allow.

Hans Conzelmann also feels compelled to modify Paul's words. In a footnote to his comments on 11.30, Conzelmann writes:

> The statement cannot be reversed. It is not an abstract principle. We cannot go on to infer that where illnesses appear, there wrong conditions prevail. What Paul here holds against the Corinthians can be said only in a unique situation. He does not accuse the individual sick people, but the community: it is sick.[60]

Obviously, Conzelmann is correct in cautioning against making the statement of 1 Cor. 11.30 into a principle. Yet to dismiss the one text in the entire Pauline corpus where Paul goes out of his way to identify the cause of illness would appear to be a bit arbitrary and does not facilitate the attempt to come to grips with Paul's thought as a whole on this topic.

I. Howard Marshall goes beyond Fee and Conzelmann in concluding that while Paul may have believed what he said, his statement simply cannot be true.

> Where Paul does enter into an area that is hard for us to comprehend is when he warns those who partake unworthily of the danger of divine judgment upon their action. He regards the

---

[59] Fee, *First Corinthians*, p. 565.

[60] Conzelmann, *1 Corinthians*, p. 203 n. 115.

bodily weakness and sickness of many in the church and the fact that some have fallen asleep in death as evidence of the Lord's judgment. A connection of this kind between sin and disease or death was certainly made in the first century (John 9.2; Jas. 5.15) and Paul probably shared this view. We may observe that in Paul's view the judgment was intended for the good of those who were thus disciplined.... The moral purpose of the judgment can accordingly be defended. What is more difficult is the direct causal relationship between a sinful act and a physical penalty inflicted by the Lord: can calamities be directly associated with specific acts of sin? What Paul was doing was to give an explanation of actual events in the church; the facts were that some people were ill and some had died, and Paul interprets these calamities as judgments upon sin. It is, therefore, Paul's *interpretation* of those events which raises questions. All that we can say is that he believed that divine judgment could overtake those who participated unworthily in the sacraments; it is not a view that is generally shared in most western Christendom which holds that, whatever may have happened in the first century, this kind of connection cannot be drawn today.[61]

The problem here is that although Marshall is uncomfortable with such an association, Paul is not reluctant to attribute disease and death to God, and it would appear in this context to be on a 'one to one' basis. In his comments Marshall moves from Paul's worldview to that of his own, and such an interpretive move is quite a proper one to make. But in so doing he misses an opportunity to reflect upon how this equation made sense to Paul, for this *specific* relationship between sin and sickness does not seem to be reflected in all of Paul's thought regarding illness.

So, how could Paul make the equation between sin and sickness on *this* occasion? In a footnote to this discussion Marshall pushes the issue forward by suggesting that, 'Paul could probably claim prophetic powers to discern that a specific event was an act of judgment....'[62] In a similar vein Fee proposes, 'Most likely Paul is

---

[61] Marshall, *Last Supper and Lord's Supper*, p. 115.

[62] Marshall, *Last Supper and Lord's Supper*, p. 172 n. 14. He then goes on to note, '... but it would be foolhardy for modern Christians to claim similar prophetic powers'.

here stepping into the prophetic role; by the Spirit he has seen a divine cause and effect between two otherwise independent realities.... [63]

Verse 31

The idea that prophetic discernment is the criteria by which Paul determines which illnesses are the result of judgment from those that are not may help in understanding Paul's approach in this area, but it does not relieve the community from its responsibility of discernment in such matters. For if they had been discerning of their sinful behavior and took the appropriate action, they would not have been inflicted with such calamities. Is it going too far to think that Paul would have expected his readers, given their prophetic gifts, also to have made the connection between suffering and sin?

Verse 32

Paul refuses to conclude this discussion without attempting to make some sense of these calamities for his readers, so in this verse he equates the Corinthians' suffering with divine discipline. Therefore, the believers should not despair, for their calamities have a redemptive purpose. These sufferings are in reality 'pedagogical works of grace',[64] for they are meant to discipline and teach these believers. By using the term παιδευόμεθα Paul implies that the readers should learn to act in a manner which is in keeping with their true identity, the body of Christ. This learning should lead to a lifestyle with which the Lord is pleased. However, the ultimate goal of such discipline, which is expressed by a purpose (ἵνα) clause, is that they not be condemned with the world. F.F. Bruce sums up nicely, '... so here the judgment of *the Lord* is a disciplinary chastisement to preserve believers from being overwhelmed in the condemnation pronounced on the godless world'.[65]

Paul closes this section (vv. 33-34) by offering specific suggestions regarding the improvement of the Corinthians' conduct. By

---

[63] Fee, *First Corinthians*, p. 565.

[64] Watson, *First Corinthians*, p. 126. Senft (*La première épitre de Saint Paul aux Corinthiens*, p. 154) refers to these illnesses as 'des signes de l'amour et la fidélité de Dieu'.

[65] Bruce, *1 and 2 Corinthians*, p. 115.

awaiting the arrival of everyone when they gather to eat and by satisfying their hunger at home, they will not gather into judgment.

There are at least four implications of the examination of 1 Cor. 11.27-34 for the primary purpose of this study. 1) It is clear that, at least in this context, Paul sees a connection between sinful behavior and illness or death. That this is the case is quite difficult to deny. 2) Paul has no qualms about attributing illness and death to God. The experience and fate of the Israelites (described in 1 Corinthians 10), who died in the wilderness because God was not pleased with them, in some ways prepares the reader for the attribution in 1 Cor. 11.30-32. 3) The purpose of such affliction is pedagogical/disciplinary. The implication is that God uses illness and death as a means of correction in order that the believer might avoid the coming judgment/condemnation of the world. 4) Paul says that if the Corinthians were discerning of the body, they would not have been judged in this way. This statement implies, at the very least, that if they examine themselves, the Corinthians would avoid such divine afflictions in the future. It perhaps also suggests that those who are ill might be healed after such self-examination.

Thus, 1 Cor. 11.27-34 bears witness to one aspect of Paul's thought regarding the Devil, disease, and deliverance. But did he always make a connection between illness and sin? The next section of this chapter seeks to reveal other dimensions of his thought by examining Paul's attitude to those who were sick, including himself.

Paul's Attitude Toward Illness

Galatians 4.13-16 – Paul's Illness

One of the passages that reveals something of Paul's attitude toward illness is Gal. 4.13-15. Located near the middle of the epistle, these verses are part of a transitional section of the letter (4.12-20), the purpose of which many scholars have been hard-pressed to understand. Although it has been labeled as 'an afterthought'[66] and as an 'erratic train of thought',[67] the place of 4.13-16 in the epistle is

---

[66] E.D. Burton, *The Epistle to the Galatians* (Edinburgh: T & T Clark, 1921), p. 325.

[67] H. Schilier, *Der Brief an die Galater* (Göttingen: Vandenhoeck & Ruprecht, 1949), p. 208.

far from pedestrian.[68] Rather, this passage yields an example of correspondence which, for one reason or another, includes a section devoted to renewal of friendship.[69] Often such a device is utilized when the writer has been particularly stern at an earlier point in the epistle.[70] Consequently, the tone of Galatians to this point explains this section in which Paul calls upon the Galatians to remember their friendship. He writes:

> And you know that on account of weakness of the flesh I preached to you previously, and you neither despised nor rejected your temptation in my flesh, but as an angel of the Lord you received me, as Christ Jesus. Therefore, where is your happiness? For I testify to you that if possible you would have gouged out your eyes and given them to me.

Verse 13

In this verse Paul appeals to the memory of the Galatians regarding how they received the gospel from him at the first. He reveals that his preaching was δι᾽ ἀσθένειαν τῆς σαρκὸς. Two things should be noted about this phrase. First, since the force of διά with the accusative is causal, the phrase can scarcely mean anything other than Paul preached to them *because of* weakness of the flesh,[71] not *while suffering from* weakness of the flesh.[72] Second, despite the various meanings of ἀσθένεια and its cognates, it is almost certain to mean physical illness in this context.[73] Alternative interpretations,

---

R.N. Longenecker, *Galatians* (Dallas: Word, 1990), p. 188.

[69] H.D. Betz, *Galatians* (Philadelphia: Fortress, 1979), p. 221 and E. Krentz *Galatians* (Minneapolis: Augsburg, 1985), p. 63.

[70] W. Hansen, *Galatians* (Leicester: IVP, 1994), pp. 130-31.

[71] Cf. J.B. Lightfoot, *Saint Paul's Epistle to the Galatians* (London: MacMillan, 1896), p. 174; A. Loisy, *L'Epitre aux Galates* (Paris: Nourry, 1916), p. 169; Burton, *Galatians*, p. 238; D.H. Lietzmann, *An die Galater* (Tübingen: J.C.B. Mohr, 1923), p. 27; *BDF*, §223 (3); P. Bonnard, *L'Epitre de Saint Paul aux Galates* (Paris: Delachux et Niestlé, 1972), p. 92; F.F. Bruce, *The Epistle to the Galatians* (Grand Rapids: Eerdmans, 1982), p. 208; R.Y.K. Fung, *The Epistle to the Galatians* (Grand Rapids: Eerdmans, 1988), p. 196; and Longenecker, *Galatians*, p. 190.

[72] As H.N. Ridderbos proposes in *The Epistle of Paul to the Churches of Galatia* (Grand Rapids: Eerdmans, 1956), p. 166.

[73] Despite R.H. Cole's (*Galatians* [Grand Rapids: Eerdmans, 1989], p. 168 n. 1) protest that 'to assume physical illness is a little unfair'.

which take ἀσθένεια as having reference to physical exhaustion,[74] weakness in outward appearance,[75] the results of having been stoned,[76] or as a symbol of his persecutions generally,[77] simply fail to convince. Perhaps the closest verbal parallel to this phrase is found in Rom. 6.19 where Paul says, 'I spoke to you in familiar language on account of the weakness of your flesh' (ἀνθρώπινον λέγω διὰ τὴν ἀσθένεια τῆς σαρκὸς ὑμῶν). Since in the Romans passage the phrase does not mean illness, but rather the Romans' inability to understand the gospel (because of their sinful nature?), is it not possible that in Gal. 4.13 the phrase has reference to some inability of Paul's? While theoretically such is possible, at least three things argue against this understanding in Gal. 4.13. 1) In Rom. 6.19 it is clear that Paul does not refer to illness, owing in part to his use of ἀνθρώπινον. Such a qualifier is not part of the Galatian text. 2) If the phrase were to mean the same in Galatians as in Romans, a virtual contradiction would be created in Gal. 4.13: namely, the reason why Paul preached to the Galatians was his inability to preach. 3) In v. 14 Paul makes clear that the weakness is in *his* flesh, not in *their* flesh as is recorded in Rom. 6.19. Therefore, despite the frequent use of ἀσθένεια in the Pauline corpus to mean weakness generally, it is more likely that in Gal. 4.13 'weakness of the flesh' means infirmity.[78] In addition to the reasons offered above for this interpretation it should not go unnoticed that ἀσθένεια and its cognates are the most frequently used terms for illness in the New Testament generally and in the Pauline literature in particular. Besides, if Paul were ill, what other way could he have described his illness than in the way the text of Gal. 4.13 reads? Therefore, in this verse Paul

---

[74] Ridderbos, *Galatians*, p. 166.

[75] Cf. J. Calvin, *Commentaries on the Epistles of Paul to the Galatians and Ephesians* (trans. W. Pringle; Edinburgh: Calvin Translation Society, 1864), p. 127 and J. Zmijewski, 'ἀσθένεια', *EDNT*, I, p. 170.

[76] J. Bligh, *Galatians* (London: St. Paul's Publications, 1969), p. 384.

[77] C.H. Cosgrove, *The Cross and the Spirit: A Study in the Argument and Theolgy of Galatians* (Macon: Mercer University Press, 1988), pp. 78-79. J.A. Beet, *A Commentary on St. Paul's Epistle to the Galatians* (London: Hodder and Stoughton, 1885), p. 124.

[78] For a similar conclusion cf. Burton, *Galatians*, p. 238; G. Stählin, 'ἀσθενής', *TDNT*, I, p. 493; Betz, *Galatians*, p. 224; Bruce, *Galatians*, p. 208; Krentz, *Galatians*, p. 63; J.R.W. Stott, *The Message of Galatians* (Leicester: IVP, 1986), p. 113; and Longenecker, *Galatians*, p. 190.

reminds the Galatians that his initial preaching to them was a result of his own illness.

As to the nature of the illness, there have been several guesses. Malaria,[79] epilepsy,[80] and eye disease,[81] all have their advocates. The infirmity has also been connected in one way or another to the thorn in the flesh by several scholars.[82] If the infirmity is to be understood in this way, it is odd that Paul does not describe his illness as being from Satan, as he does when referring to the thorn in the flesh. Unfortunately, there is simply too little evidence available to make an assessment concerning either this possible association or the identification of the illness generally.[83] Perhaps the most that can be said concerning the nature of the illness is that it appears to have been temporary, in that Paul eventually left Galatia, and some aspect of it appears to have had the potential to invite the disgust and rejection of the Galatians.

Verse 14

Whatever the identity of Paul's illness, it proved to be a temptation to the Galatians. But the precise nature of the temptation is uncertain. Even Paul's own words (οὐκ ἐξουθενήσατε οὐδὲ ἐξεπτύσατε), which might help to qualify the temptation, are open to several interpretations.

One line of approach argues that the temptation which the Galatians faced was to reject Paul owing to the commonly held belief that demons were responsible for illnesses.[84] This interpretation draws upon a literal understanding of ἐκπτύω ('to spit') for sup-

---

[79] W.M. Ramsay, *Historical Commentary on the Galatians* (London: Hodder & Stoughton, 1900), p. 425 and W. Neil, *The Letter of Paul to the Galatians* (Cambridge: Cambridge Univeristy Press, 1967), p. 69.

[80] J. Klausner, *From Jesus to Paul* (London: George Allen & Unwin, 1944), pp. 325-30 and P.R. Jones, 'Exegesis of Galatians 3 and 4,' *RevExp* 69 (1972), p. 482.

[81] D. Guthrie, *Galatians* (London: Nelson, 1969), p. 125.

[82] Wesley, *Explanntory Notes*, p. 482; Ramsay, *Galatians*, p. 425; Klausner, *From Jesus to Paul*, p. 325; Bonnard, *Galates*, p. 92; Stott, *Galatians*, p. 113; Cole, *Galatians*, p. 169; and apparently Beet, *Galatians*, p. 126 and Burton, *Galatians*, p. 239.

[83] For the idea that the infirmity is not identifiable cf. Beet, *Galatians*, p. 125; Burton, *Galatians*, p. 239; Bonnard, *Galates*, p. 93; Bruce, *Galatians*, p. 229; Cole, *Galatians*, p. 168; and Longenecker, *Galatians*, p. 191.

[84] J. de Zwaan, 'Gal 4, 14 aus dem Neugriechischen erklärt,' *ZNW* 10 (1909), pp. 246-50; Lietzmann, *Galater*, p. 27; Bonnard, *Galates*, p. 92; Betz, *Galatians*, p. 225; Longenecker, *Galatians*, p. 191.

port. It is argued that one of the ways to avoid the demon(s) that afflicted certain individuals was to spit upon the sick person.[85] This action, so it is alleged, would serve to protect the passerby.

Others suggest that the Galatians' temptation to reject Paul was owing to the belief that such infirmity was a sign of divine displeasure.[86] This interpretation is not only supported by appeal to the general attitudes of the day (i.e. Jn. 9.2 and Acts 28.3,4), but also by the fact that it fits in with Paul's own attitude in 1 Cor. 11.30-31. The fact that ἐκπτύω likely has a figurative rather than a literal meaning is circumstantial evidence in favor of this position.

Alternative interpretations of the temptation include the natural reluctance one might have in believing 'a gospel proclaimed by a sick man,'[87] the responsibility of having a sick man among them and caring for him,[88] and the idea that Paul was repulsive in appearance[89] (perhaps due to stoning).[90]

Whatever the origin of the temptation, Paul feared that it would result in the Galatians despising him. Both ἐξουθενέω and ἐκπτύω carry this meaning. The first of these terms clearly means 'despise' in the Pauline literature (Rom. 14.3,10; 1 Cor. 1.28; 6.4; 16.11; 1 Thess. 5.20). Interestingly enough, in 2 Cor. 10.10, where it is used to describe Paul's inablility as a speaker, ἐξουθενέω occurs in close proximity with τοῦ σώματος ἀσθενὴς. His opponents charge, 'On the one hand, the epistles are weighty and strong, but on the other hand his presence of body weak and his speech despisable.' Whether τοῦ σώματος ἀσθενὴς in 2 Cor. 10.10 means that Paul was physically ill or not,[91] the meaning of ἐξουθενέω is clear. Its sense in Gal. 4.14 is no doubt quite similar.

The meaning of ἐκπτύω is a bit more difficult to determine. As noted earlier, it is sometimes argued that ἐκπτύω should be taken literally in the sense of 'to spit' and would indicate that the Gala-

---

[85] Cf. esp. Bonnard, *Galates*, p. 92.

[86] Ramsay, *Galatians*, pp. 423 and 426; Ridderbos, *Galatians*, p. 167; Neil, *Galatians*, p. 69; Krentz, *Galatians*, p. 63; and Fung, *Galatians*, p. 198.

[87] Beet, *Galatians*, p. 124.

[88] Guthrie, *Galatians*, p. 126.

[89] Bruce, *Galatians*, p. 209.

[90] Bligh, *Galatians*, p. 386.

[91] A suggestion made but dismissed by R.P. Martin, *2 Corinthians* (Dallas: Word, 1986), p. 312.

tians assumed a demonic origin for Paul's illness.[92] However, it is likely that ἐκπτύω should be taken in its figurative sense, meaning 'to despise'. Several pieces of evidence might be offered in favor of such a rendering. First, the term eventually comes to function as a synonym for ἐξουθενέω. Second, the same two terms that appear together here in Gal. 4.14 also occur together in *Joseph and Aseneth* 2.1, where there is not a hint of its earlier demon-related nuance. Third, that ἐκπτύω was regarded as a synonym for ἐξουθενεώ may explain the omission of ἐκπτύω from Gal. 4.14 by $\mathfrak{P}^{46}$, the earliest extant text of the Pauline materials. Apparently, the scribe regarded ἐκπτύω as redundant and, therefore, unneeded.[93] Consequently, it seems safe, with the majority of scholars, to take ἐκπτύω in a figurative sense.[94]

It would appear, then, that Paul may have feared being despised as one rejected by God, owing to his illness. But on the contrary, the Galatians received him as an angel of God, even as Christ Jesus. Paul's rather startling words serve to emphasize the contrast between his anticipated reception by the Galatians and their actual reception of him.[95]

Verse 15

Having reminded the Galatians of the loving reception they gave him, Paul now (οὖν) queries them as to where their happiness has gone. He follows this question up very quickly with yet another reminder of their (former?) devotion, only on this occasion he uses legal terminology to emphasize the trustworthiness of his statement (μαρτυρῶ γὰρ ὑμῖν). Their love for him was so great that, if possible, the Galatians would have gouged out their eyes and given them to Paul. While such a graphic statement could be taken as evi-

---

[92] Cf. esp. Bonnard, *Galates*, p. 92; H. Schilier, 'ἐκπτύω,' *TDNT*, II, p. 448; Betz, *Galatians*, p. 225; and apparently Krentz, *Galatians*, p. 64.

[93] Cf. Longenecker, *Galatians*, p. 192.

[94] Cf. Lightfoot, *Galatians*, p. 175; Burton, *Galatians*, p. 242; M.-J. LaGrange, *Saint Paul épitre aux Galates* (Paris: Gabalda, 1950), p. 114; Ridderbos, *Galatians*, p. 167; Guthrie, *Galatians*, p. 126; Bruce, *Galatians*, p. 209; Stott, *Galatians*, p. 114; Fung, *Galatians*, p. 198; Cole, *Galatians*, p. 123; and H. Balz, 'ἐκπτύω', *EDNT*, I, p. 421.

[95] Cf. Guthrie, *Galatians*, p. 126 and Longenecker, *Galatians*, p. 192. There is no justification in thinking that Paul considered himself to be an angel or Christ Jesus, as the ὡς makes clear in both instances. Cf. Betz, *Galatians*, p. 226.

dence that Paul suffered from some sort of eye ailment,[96] it in all likelihood illustrates the Galatians' devotion to Paul generally, in that the eye was commonly regarded as one's most precious possession (cf. Deut. 32.10, Ps. 17.8; Zech. 2.8).[97]

Perhaps the nearest parallel to the kind of sacrifice the Galatians were willing to make for Paul is found in Lucian's (*Toxaris* 39-41) account of two Scythian friends, Dandamis and Amizoces. Lucian narrates through a fictional character named Toxaris that when attacked by tens of thousands of Sauromatae troops all the Scythians sought to escape by swimming across the river. Amizoces, who was captured, called out to Dandamis for help. Swimming back to Amizoces' aid Dandamis himself was captured, but still sought to bargain for his friend's release. Having no possessions with which to bargain, Dandamis agreed to his adversary's proposal of Amizoces' release in exchange for Dandamis' eyes. Having gained the release of his friend through the sacrifice of his own eyes, they swam back to safety together. Although this gesture of friendship renewed the Scythian resolve to fight, Amizoces could not bear to have his vision while Dandamis was blind, so Amizoces put out his eyes with his own hands.

While it would be presumptuous to assume that Paul and the Galatians would have been familiar with such a story (since Lucian writes ca. 163 CE, though the story itself appears to be much older), it does suggest the proverbial nature that 'giving one's eyes' may have attained by the first century. If this interpretation is anywhere near the mark, Paul is saying that the Galatians would have made any sacrifice necessary for his benefit.

Paul closes this section (vv. 16-20) by noting that despite their past actions and affections, the Galatians now consider Paul an enemy. They have succumbed to the influence of his opponents.

What are the implications of Gal. 4.13-15 for this study on the Devil, disease, and deliverance? 1) It is, quite obviously, important to note that in this passage Paul himself says that he suffered from some physical infirmity. That one who was regarded as an apostle

---

[96] So Guthrie, *Galatians*, p. 126 and less certain Bonnard, *Galates*, p. 93.

[97] Beet, *Galatians*, p. 125; Loisy, *Galates*, p. 170; Burton, *Galatians*, p. 244; LaGrange, *Galates*, p. 114; Neil, *Galatians*, p. 69; Betz, *Galatians*, p. 228; Krentz, *Galatians*, p. 64; Fung, *Galatians*, p. 199; Cole, *Galatians*, p. 172; Longenecker, *Galatians*, p. 193; and Hansen, *Galatians*, p. 134.

could suffer from an illness implies that sickness was known at every 'level' in the early church. 2) Although he feared that the Galatians would reject him as under divine judgment owing to his illness, Paul gives no indication that his illness was the result of sin or, for that matter, a demonic attack. Simply because he feared the Galatians would make such associations in no way indicates the source to which Paul himself attributed this infirmity. He could very well have considered this illness simply to be part of the human experience. 3) Perhaps most significant for this enquiry is the way in which Paul regards the illness as the reason for his ministry to the Galatians in the first place. Is this acknowledgement tantamount to saying that Paul regarded his illness as a providential one? If so, then Paul not only believed that God could use illness as discipline for believers who had sinned (as in 1 Cor. 11.30), but he could also use it as a means to accomplish his will through the preaching of the gospel.

Gal. 4.13-15 thus reveals another dimension of Paul's thought regarding the Devil, disease, and deliverance. But does Paul ever attribute illness directly to Satan? This question is the concern of the next section of this chapter.

2 Corinthians 12.7-10 – Paul's Thorn in the Flesh

In only one place (2 Cor. 12.7-10) does Paul appear to attribute the origin of an illness to the Devil: a text which is located in a section of 2 Corinthians that has been the subject of intense debates. The primary issue concerns the epistle's literary integrity, with several scholars questioning whether it is proper to regard chapters 10-13, in particular, as originally part of the letter as a whole. Whether one agrees with such a judgment or not, when reading these chapters it is not difficult to understand why questions are raised concerning its integrity. For in these chapters one encounters a perceptible change of tone from that in chapters 1-9.

Paul's primary purpose in 2 Corinthians 10-13 is to defend his apostolic ministry against what appear to be vicious attacks on the part of his opponents who themselves pose as apostles. As a means of response, Paul agrees to 'play the fool' and boast about his 'qualifications', which include numerous trials, persecutions, and periods of suffering.

In 12.1-7a, Paul reveals that he had an extraordinary spiritual experience that defied explanation. Not only did it include a journey to the third heaven, but also the hearing of sacred words which 'are not proper for anyone to tell' (v. 4). After affirming the trustworthiness of his words, Paul refuses to reveal anything else so that no one would think too highly of him (v. 6). At this point he writes:

> And concerning the extraordinary nature of the revelations; therefore, in order that I might not be puffed up, there was given to me a thorn in the flesh, an angel of Satan, in order that it (he) might beat me, in order that I might not be puffed up. Concerning this I called unto the Lord three times in order that he might take it from me. And he said to me, 'My grace is enough for you. For the power is completed in weakness'. Therefore all the more gladly will I boast in my weakness, in order that the power of Christ might rest upon me. Therefore, I delight in weaknesses, in insults, in hardships, in persecutions and difficulties for the sake of Christ. For when I am weak, then I am strong.

Verse 7

The first issue facing the interpreter of 2 Cor. 12.7-10 is to determine what to do with the phrase translated, 'And concerning the extraordinary nature (τῇ ὑπερβολῇ) of the revelations'. Grammatically this phrase concludes the thought of v. 6b, with 'therefore' (διό) beginning the next sentence.[98] However, since διό is omitted by some leading manuscipts, it is also grammatically possible to take this phrase as beginning the thought of v. 7.[99] Yet, even when διό is retained, it still appears that the phrase, while concluding the thought of v. 6, serves to introduce the reader to what follows, despite the grammatical problems.[100] Therefore, the context of what

---

[98] B.M. Metzger, *A Textual Commentary on the Greek New Testament* (London: UBS, 1971), p. 585; V.P. Furnish, *II Corinthians* (Garden City: Doubleday, 1984), p. 528; and R.P. Martin, *2 Corinthians* (Waco: Word, 1986), p. 410.

[99] R.V.G. Tasker, *II Corinthians* (London: Tyndale Press, 1958), p. 173; J. Héring, *The Second Epistle of Saint Paul to the Corinthians* (trans. A.W. Heathcote and P.J. Allcock; London: Epworth, 1967), p. 92; Bruce, *1 and 2 Corinthians*, p. 248; and R. Bultmann, *The Second Letter to the Corinthians* (trans. R.A. Harrisville; Minneapolis: Augsburg, 1985), p. 224.

[100] Beet, *Corinthians*, p. 458 and A. Plummer, *The Second Epistle of Saint Paul to the Corinthians* (Edinburgh: T & T Clark, 1915), p. 347. Cf. esp. F.W. Danker, *II Corinthians* (Minneapolis: Augsburg, 1989), pp. 192-93, who notes, '(1) The phrase

follows is the extraordinary nature of the revelations[101] which Paul received.

The nature of such spiritual experiences could have led Paul to a position of pride. Therefore, in order that he not become full of pride 'a thorn in the flesh, an angel of Satan was given' to him. The identical language of the first and third of the three purpose (ἵνα) clauses in v. 7 (ἵνα μὴ ὑπεραίρωμαι) makes clear Paul's understanding of the goal behind the thorn in the flesh.[102] Such duplication led more than one scribe to omit the second of these identical phrases. However, the phrase is well supported, 'and the repetition has special emphasis in the context'.[103] The danger of such pride for Paul is reflected by the fact that the only other place where ὑπεραίρομαι occurs in the Pauline corpus (or the New Testament as a whole) is in a description of the man of Lawlessness (2 Thess. 2.4), who exalts himself above everything that is called God or is worshipped.

In order that Paul might fight any possible inclination toward such pride there was given to him a thorn in the flesh. Although the giver of the thorn is left unnamed, there can be little doubt as to his identity. To understate the case, the vast majority of scholars identify the giver as God.[104] Primarily this identification is made because

---

is to be taken with v. 6 ... (2) The connection between this phrase and the succeeding clauses is expressed colloquially. The apostle's thought leaps ahead of his grammar'.

[101] With Beet, *Corinthians*, p. 458; Héring, *2 Corinthians*, p. 92; and apparently Martin, *2 Corinthians*, p. 410 rather than taking τῇ ὑπερβολῇ τῶν ἀποκαλύψεων as 'excess of revelations' as does C. Hodge, *An Exposition of the Second Epistle to the Corinthians* (Grand Rapids: Eerdmans, 1953), p. 285.

[102] J. Denny, *The Second Epistle to the Corinthians* (London: Hodder and Stoughton, 1894), p. 352; Plummer, *II Corinthians*, p. 347; E.B. Allo, *Saint Paul: seconde épitre aux Corinthiens* (Paris: Gabalda, 1956), p. 310; and Martin, *2 Corinthians*, p. 411.

[103] Metzger, *Textual Commentary*, p. 585. For an opposing view cf. Héring, *Second Corinthians*, p. 92.

[104] Wesley, *Explanatory Notes*, p. 469; Beet, *Corinthians*, p. 458; Denny, *Second Corinthians*, p. 353; Plummer, *II Corinthians*, p. 348; Deissmann, *Light*, p. 158; R.H. Strachan, *The Second Epistle of Paul to the Corinthians* (London: Hodder and Stroughton, 1935), p. 32; Hodge, *Second Corinthians*, p. 285; Allo, *Saint Paul: seconde épitre aux Corinthiens* , p. 310; Tasker, *II Corinthians*, p. 173; J. Heading, *Second Epistle to the Corinthians* (London: A. & C. Black, 1973), p. 316; Bultmann, *Second Corinthains*, p. 225; M.L. Barré, 'Qumran and the Weakness of Paul', *CBQ* 42 (1980), p. 223; Furnish, *II Corinthians*, p. 528; D.A. Carson, *From Triumphalism to Maturity*

the verb, δίδωμι, occurs in the passive voice. This form, commonly known as the divine passive, is frequently used in the New Testament to make reference to the activity of God without naming him as subject. Even though that which was given to Paul was something he wanted to be removed and despite the fact that the thorn was related in some way to Satan, it should be remembered that the thorn was given to assist Paul in his struggle against pride, a fight for which Satan would have offered Paul no aid. Therefore, it is best to understand the thorn as something which came from God for Paul's own good.[105]

Before attempting to identify this thorn in the flesh, the phrase σκόλοψ τῇ σαρκί itself merits some attention. Two issues, in particular, are unclear. First, does σκόλοψ mean thorn or stake? Second, should τῇ σαρκί be translated 'in the flesh' or 'for the flesh'? Although σκόλοψ may be translated as stake[106] owing to that meaning in a number of Greek texts set within military contexts,[107] the preferred meaning here is thorn.[108] For not only does σκόλοψ mean thorn in the LXX (Num. 33.55; Ezek. 28.24; Hos. 2.6; and Sir. 43.19), but it also aligns better with how Paul describes the thorn in this passage. It was an affliction which was extremely aggravating and caused a great deal of pain, but it does not seem to have been

(Grand Rapids: Baker, 1984), p. 145; Martin, *2 Corinthians*, pp. 412 and 416; P. Barnett, *The Message of 2 Corinthians* (Leicester: IVP, 1988), p. 178; G. Voigt, *Die Kraft des Schwacher* (Göttingen: Vandenhoeck & Ruprecht, 1990), p. 91; and J. Murphy-O'Conner, *The Theology of the Second Letter to the Corinthians* (Cambridge: Cambridge University Press, 1991), p. 118.

[105] N.G. Smith ('The Thorn that Stayed: An Exposition of II Corinthians 12.7-9', *Int* 13 [1959], pp. 411-13) goes to extraordinary lengths to insist that God used the thorn but did not send it. However, such denials appear to be more the result of a theological conviction than a reading of the text.

[106] Carpus, 'The Strength of Weakness', *Exp* (First series) 3 (1876), p. 174; Beet, *Corinthians*, p. 458; W.M. Alexander, 'St. Paul's Infirmity', *ExpT* 15 (1903-1904), p. 470; Strachan, *Second Corinthians*, p. 32; R.P.C. Hanson, *The Second Epistle to the Corinthians* (London: SCM, 1935), p. 87; and P.E. Hughes, *Paul's Second Epistle to the Corinthians* (London: Marshall, Morgan, & Scott, 1962), p. 447.

[107] Cf. esp. D.M. Park, 'Paul's σκόλοψ τῇ σαρκί: Thorn or Stake? (2 Cor. XII 7)', *NovT* 32 (1980), pp. 179-83.

[108] Plummer, *Corinthians*, p. 349; Tasker, *II Corinthians*, p. 173; H.R. Minn, *The Thorn that Remained or St. Paul's Thorn in the Flesh* (Auckland: G.W. Moore, 1972), p. 10; Barrett, *II Corinthians*, p. 315; Martin, *2 Corinthians*, p. 412; and C. Kruse, *2 Corinthians* (Grand Rapids: Eerdmans, 1987), p. 205.

life threatening.[109] The translation 'in the flesh' is to be preferred[110] to 'for the flesh'[111] owing to Paul's subsequent mention of being struck or abused[112] and the phrase's close tie to the substantive 'by analogy'.[113]

The thorn in the flesh is closely associated with an angel of Satan. In fact, ἄγγελος Σατανᾶ stands in apposition to the thorn. Earlier in 2 Corinthians Paul mentioned Satan, warning his readers not to be outwitted by him (2.11) and warning that Satan can transform himself into an angel of light (11.14). The same is true of Satan's servants (11.15). Although Paul does not use the term 'angel of Satan' anywhere else, Matthew (25.4) knows of angels of the Devil, and Revelation (12.7, 9) refers to angels of the Great Red Dragon. Two other passages in the Pauline literature might possibly suggest that Satan has angels. In Rom. 8.34 Paul refers to angels as being in opposition to the believer, while in 1 Cor. 6.3 he states that believers will one day judge the angels. Whether Paul is speaking of angels of Satan in either case is far from certain. However, one must wonder whether Paul would not at the very least have made some connection between Satan and the demons of which he speaks in other contexts (cf. 1 Cor. 10.20, 21 and 1 Tim. 4.1).

Although Paul implies, through the divine passive, that God gave the thorn to him, at the same time he ties this thorn to the work of Satan. It would appear, then, that whatever the exact nature of the thorn, it was inflicted by Satan (or his angel) upon Paul.[114] Such a

---

[109] Cf. Furnish, *II Corinthians*, p. 529.

[110] With Calvin, *II Corinthians*, p. 373; Hodge, *Second Corinthians*, p. 285; *BDF* §190 (3); Furnish, *II Corinthains*, p. 529; and Martin, *2 Corinthians*, p. 413.

[111] Advocates of this translation include: E. Beecher, 'Dispensations of Divine Providence toward the Apostle Paul', *BibSac* 47 (1855), p. 515; Beet, *Corinthians*, p. 458; Plummer, *II Corinthians*, p. 348; Hughes, *Second Corinthians*, p. 447; and J.W. McCant, 'Paul's Thorn of Rejected Apostleship', *NTS* 34 (1988), p. 567.

[112] Furnish, *II Corinthians*, p. 529.

[113] Cf. *BDF*, §190 (3) and Martin, *2 Corinthians*, p. 413.

[114] Wesley, *Explanatory Notes*, p. 469; Beecher, 'Dispensations', p. 515; Beet, *Corinthians*, p. 459; Allo, *Saint Paul: seconde épitre aux Corinthiens* 310; Hughes, *Second Corinthians*, p. 447; Heading, *Second Corinthians*, p. 225; R.M. Price, 'Punished in Paradise (An Exegetical Theory on II Corinthians 12.1-10)', *JSNT* 7 (1980), pp. 33-40; Furnish, *II Corinthians*, pp. 529 and 547; Carson, *From Triumphalism to Maturity*, pp. 144 and 147; and J. Kremer, *2. Korintherbrief* (Stuttgart: Katholisches Bibelwerk, 1990), p. 106. Cf. esp. R.P. Spittler ('The Limits of Ecstasy: An Exege-

statement implies some sort of cooperation on the part of God and Satan, whether one takes the position that God allows Satan to take such action[115] or that Satan unknowingly accomplishes God's will in this work.[116] Other views notwithstanding,[117] it appears that Paul believed his thorn was tied to Satan himself.

While a plethora of proposals have been made in the attempt to identify the precise nature of the thorn itself,[118] only two categories of suggestions are of primary concern for the interests of this study. Namely, is the thorn to be understood as some sort of physical ailment, or does it have reference to something else altogether? If the former, then the implications for this enquiry on the Devil, disease, and deliverance are similar whatever the exact identity of the malady. If the latter, then Paul nowhere attributes illness to Satan.

The idea that Paul's thorn is to be identified as having reference to his opponents is the only major option besides the view that the thorn is a physical ailment.[119] Several reasons may be offered in

sis of 2 Corinthians 12.1-10', in *Current Issues in Biblical and Patristic Interpretation* [Grand Rapids: Eerdmans, 1975], p. 265 n. 39) who asks, 'is it at all conceivable that the phrase *angelos satana* as an appropriate designation of the *skolops* arose in Paul's mind as an alternate to the *angelos tou kyriou*, who may have been the angelic guide during the Himmelsreise? If an angel of the Lord was instrumental in exaltation, would it not be appropriate for an angel of Satan to be the instrument of humiliation?'

[115] Thrall, *Corinthians*, p. 178; Bruce, *1 and 2 Corinthians*, p. 248; Kruse, *2 Corinthians*, p. 87; Talbert, *Reading Corinthians*, pp. 124-25; Barnett, *2 Corinthians*, p. 88; and Voigt, *Die Kraft*, p. 92.

[116] This position is well represented by Danker (*II Corinthians*, p. 193) who writes, 'The humor in Paul's reference to Satan lies in the fact that Satan, who is known in Jewish tradition as God's arch-rival, with a colossal ego, would cross the rhetorical stage as a competitor who sends Paul an antidote to possible pride and arrogance. Since God is ultimately responsible, the humor is doubly sharp.'

[117] For other views concerning the meaning of the angel of Satan cf. Carpus ('Strength', p. 177) who says it is an angel of God and J.J. Thierry ('Der Dorn im Fleische [2 Kor. xii 7-9]', *NovT* 5 [1962], pp. 301-10) who suggests that Paul himself was called an angel of Satan by his opponents.

[118] For surveys of the various proposals cf. Allo, *Saint Paul: seconde épitre aux Corinthiens*, pp. 313-23 and Martin, *2 Corinthians*, pp. 413-16.

[119] Other views include the idea that the thorn was: a) sexual temptation [a view popular in the Middle Ages], b) the temptation to become excessively angry [cf. V.A. Holmes-Gore, 'St. Paul's Thorn in the Flesh', *Theology* 33 (1936), pp. 111-12], and c) Paul's agony over the Jewish rejection of the gospel (cf. P.H. Menoud, 'L'echarde et l'ange satanique [2 Cor. 12.7]' in *Studia Paulina* [ed. J.N. Sevenster and W.C. van Unnik; Haarlem: Bohn, 1953], pp. 163-71).

support of this view. First, the appostitional relationship between angel of Satan and thorn in the flesh is said to suggest a personal source of affliction.[120] Second, the precedent for using 'thorn' to represent an enemy is found in the LXX (Num. 33.55 and Ezek. 28.24).[121] Third, the mention of the angel of Satan in 12.7 is preceded by a reference to the servants of Satan (i.e. Paul's opponents) in 2 Cor. 11.15.[122] Fourth, the term κολαφίζη ('to abuse or beat with a fist') makes much more sense when the thorn is understood as a person or persons.[123] The only other place where this term occurs in the Pauline literature (1 Cor. 4.11) seems to convey the idea of the abuse Paul suffered at the hands of his opponents.[124] Fifth, in the trial lists that surround 2 Cor. 12.7-10 (2 Cor. 11.21b-29 and 12.10a), Paul mentions persecution.[125] Sixth, contrary to most opinions, it is argued that the weakness of Gal. 4.13 and the thorn in the flesh of 2 Cor. 12.7 cannot be equated.[126]

The arguments in favor of understanding the thorn as having reference to a physical infirmity may be set forth as follows. First, it should be noted that thorn-in-the-flesh imagery conveys the idea of physical pain. That the thorn refers to a physical ailment would fit neatly with this imagery. Second, Paul claims to have been given this thorn in close temporal proximity to the heavenly revelation he received. From the primary and secondary sources from which one might deduce information about Paul's life and ministry, it appears

---

[120] Cf. T.Y. Mullins, 'Paul's Thorn in the Flesh', *JBL* 74 (1957), p. 301; Barré, 'Qumran', p. 225; McCant, 'Paul's Thorn', p. 565; L. Woods, 'Opposition to a Man and His Message: Paul's "Thorn in the Flesh" (2 Cor 12.7)', *AusBibRev* 39 (1991), pp. 50-51; and Murphy-O'Conner, *Theology*, p. 119.

[121] Mullins, 'Paul's Thorn', p. 302; Woods, 'Opposition', p. 51; and Murphy-O'Conner, *Theology*, p. 119.

[122] Mullins, 'Paul's Thorn', pp. 301-302; Woods, 'Opposition', pp. 44, 47, and 49; and Murphy-O'Conner, *Theology*, p. 119.

[123] Mullins, 'Paul's Thorn', p. 301 and McCant, 'Paul's Thorn', pp. 566-67.

[124] Barré, 'Qumran', p. 226.

[125] Barré, 'Qumran', p. 225.

[126] McCant ('Paul's Thorn', p. 564) observes, 'A comparison of the texts reveals that (1) in Galatians the construction has ἐν, and the personal pronoun μοῦ; 2 Cor has neither; (2) in Galatians Paul's "condition" is temporary while the present subjunctives in 2 Corinthians indicate a chronic condition; (3) in Galatians it opens the way for preaching (διά with a genitive construction), but in 2 Corinthians the metaphor is related to his rapture to heaven while no such association is made in Galatians; (5) in both passages σάρξ is used but with different cases'. Cf. also Woods, 'Opposition', pp. 49-51.

that Paul was faced with opponents from the very beginning of his ministry. Does this mean that the revelation of 2 Corinthians 12 is to be equated with Saul's conversion experience as depicted in Acts? For, if Acts is to be believed, Paul encountered opponents for the first time as a Christian shortly after his conversion. Third, in 2 Cor. 11.14-15, Satan is referred to as an angel while Paul calls his opponents 'ministers' of Satan. Is it not perhaps reading too much out of the phrase 'angel of Satan' to conclude that it has reference to the ministers of Satan mentioned in 11.15?[127] Fourth, whatever one does with this phrase, it is less likely to have reference to personal opponents as to Satan and/or his angels.[128] Fifth, perhaps the most difficult aspect of the opponent theory to defend is the idea that Paul would have prayed for their removal. Such a conclusion appears to be in diametric opposition to Paul's general attitude concerning the necessity of persecution.[129] Finally, it must be remembered that parts of the biblical tradition do associate the activity of Satan with illness (cf. esp. Job 2.5; Lk. 13.16; and the synoptic texts which link demons and illness). That illness is attributed to an angel of Satan in 2 Corinthains 12 should surprise no one.

Consequently, while the arguments in favor of understanding the thorn as Paul's opponents are impressive, they neither rule out the idea that the thorn was a physical infirmity, nor do they prove to be wholly convincing. In point of fact, the arguments set forth in support of the opponent theory have failed to take certain bits of information into account and may have misinterpreted other pieces. Therefore, it is best to conclude, with the majority of scholars, that Paul's thorn in the flesh was some type of physical infirmity.[130]

---

[127] Cf. Furnish, *II Corinthians*, p. 549.

[128] Furnish, *II Corinthians*, p. 549.

[129] Martin, *2 Corinthians*, p. 415.

[130] The following scholars conclude that the thorn has reference to illness, but they decline to make a specific identification: Beet, *Corinthians*, p. 459; Denny, *Second Corinthians*, p. 352; Deissmann, *Light*, pp. 158 and 307; Strachan, *Second Corinthians*, p. 31; N.G. Smith, 'The Thorn that Stayed', pp. 409-16; Hughes, *Second Corinthians*, p. 448; Bruce, *1 and 2 Corinthians*, p. 248; Minn, *The Thorn that Remained*, pp. 23-31; Spittler, 'Limits of Ecstasy', p. 265; Furnish, *II Corinthians*, pp. 549-50; Martin, *2 Corinthians*, pp. 415-16; Kruse, *2 Corinthians*, p. 206; Talbert, *Reading Corinthians*, p. 124; Danker, *Second Corinthians*, p. 193; Kremer, *2. Korintherbrief*, p. 107; and Voigt, *Die Kraft*, p. 92. Specific suggestions about the identity of Paul's malady include: a) severe head pain (Tertullian, *de Pudicitia* 13.17 and E.A.

The thorn then was given to Paul to abuse him physically so that the heavenly revelations he received would not lead him into arrogance.

Verse 8

The affliction inflicted by the angel of Satan proved to be so painful that Paul sought to have the Lord remove it. Several aspects of this verse, in which Paul describes his petition, merit comment. The term Paul uses to describe his action (παρακαλέω) was not unknown in first-century petitions for healing.[131] It might be significant that the verb appears in the aorist tense in this verse, perhaps suggesting that at the time of the writing of 2 Corinthians Paul's petitions concerning the removal of the thorn were understood to be confined to the past.[132]

Paul states that he earnestly requested the removal of the thorn/angel three times. Whether Paul meant that he prayed three times after his first attack,[133] or that each of these prayers was offered after three separate attacks respectively[134] is difficult to determine. What may be safely assumed is that Paul's mention of his three times of intercession is intended to emphasize his own desire to have this infirmity removed.[135] Clearly, Paul saw nothing wrong with such prayers. In fact, his three prayers regarding the removal

---

Johnson, 'St. Paul's Infirmity', *ExpT* 39 [1927-28], pp. 428-29); b) epilepsy (D. Donley, 'The Epilepsy of Saint Paul', *CBQ* 6 [1944], pp. 358-60); c) malaria (Allo, *Saint Paul: seconde épitre aux Corinthiens*, p. 311); d) a nervous disorder (Carpus, 'Strength', pp. 176-77); e) Malta fever (Alexander, 'St. Paul's Infirmity', pp. 547-48); f) a form of eye trouble (E.M. Merrins, 'St. Paul's Thorn in the Flesh', *BibSac* 64 [1907], pp. 661-92; P. Nisbet, 'The Thorn in the Flesh', *ExpT* 80 [1969], p. 126; and apparently Hanson, *Second Corinthians*, p. 87); and g) defective speech (E.A. Mangan, 'Was Paul an Invalid?' *CBQ* 5 [1943], pp. 68-72; F.L. Arrington, *The Ministry of Reconciliation* [Grand Rapids: Baker, 1980], p. 166 n. 3; P. Marshall, 'A Metaphor of Social Shame: ΘΡΙΑΜΒΕΥΕΙΝ in 2 Cor. 2.14', *NovT* 25 [1983], pp. 315-16; and apparently Barrett, *II Corinthians*, p. 315.)

[131] Cf. the parallel that Deissmann (*Light from the Ancient East*, p. 153 n. 4 and p. 308) produces.

[132] Cf. the comments of Denny, *Second Corinthians*, p.355; Martin, *2 Corinthians*, p. 417; and Barnett, *Message of Second Corinthians*, p. 178.

[133] So Bruce, *1 and 2 Corinthians*, p. 249.

[134] Cf. Beet, *Corinthians*, p. 460; Hughes, *Second Corinthians*, pp. 449-50; Carson, *From Triumphalism to Maturity*, p. 147; and apparently Martin, *2 Corinthians*, p. 418.

[135] Cf. Allo, *Saint Paul: seconde épitre aux Corinthiens*, p. 312 and Barrett, *II Corinthians*, p. 316.

of the thorn call to mind Jesus' three requests in Gethsemane that his cup be removed if possible.[136] The similarity between Jesus' action and Paul's is even closer when one considers that neither of them witnessed the removal of the thing requested.[137] In both cases the power of God was manifest in their suffering. Whether there is a connection with Jesus' action or not, in all likelihood the Corinthians would have found the mention of three prayers natural, since such seems to have been part of some petitions for assistance in the Graeco-Roman world.[138]

The purpose of such prayers is made clear by the use of a ἵνα clause: ἵνα ἀποστῇ ἀπ᾽ἐμοῦ. Paul was obviously seeking the removal of the infirmity when he prayed. That was the sole purpose of the petitions.

Verse 9

Paul's requests do not go unheard. In point of fact, the risen and exalted Christ, to whom Paul had prayed, speaks to him in a revelatory fashion.[139] This pronouncement of the Lord seems to have made a lasting impression upon Paul. While the content of the message is important, the formula of the quote's introduction (καὶ εἴρηκέν μοι) reveals part of the significance for Paul. In this formula Paul uses the perfect tense form of the verb λέγω. Clearly, one aspect of the perfect conveys the idea that this speech was heard in the past, but here it appears that in true perfect fashion the tense carries with it the idea that the words continue to be heard by

---

[136] Wesley, *Explanatory Notes*, p. 469; Denny, *Second Corinthians*, p. 354; Plummer, *II Corinthians*, p. 353; Allo, *Saint Paul: second épitre aux Corinthiens*, p. 312; Hughes, *Second Corinthians*, p. 449; Héring, *Second Corinthians*, p. 93; Furnish, *II Corinthians*, p. 529; Martin, *2 Corinthians*, p. 417; Kruse, *2 Corinthians*, p. 206; Talbert, *Reading Corinthians*, p.125; Barnett, *Second Corinthians*, p. 178; Kremer, *2. Korintherbrief,* p. 107; and Voigt, *Die Kraft,* p. 92.

[137] Cf. Kruse, *2 Corinthians*, p. 206 and the list of similarities between Jesus and Paul provided by McCant ('Paul's Thorn', p. 571). It is sometimes suggested that Paul was consciously following Jesus' pattern, but such a claim is nearly impossible to demonstrate.

[138] Cf. Furnish, *II Corinthians*, p. 529 and Danker, *Second Corinthians*, p. 194. However, Heading (*Second Corinthians*, p. 225) argues that three times would be sufficient for Paul to know the mind of the Lord.

[139] Furnish, *II Corinthians*, p. 550.

Paul, even while he was writing this epistle.[140] Plummer captures the
meaning when he observes, 'he said it then and the answer still
stands, it holds good'.[141]

The content of the proclamation reveals why it made such a lasting impression on Paul. As the Father did not remove the cup from
Jesus, so the Lord does not remove the thorn from Paul. Rather, he
is told, 'My grace is enough. For the power is made complete in
weakness.' The word order of the Greek text reveals that an emphasis is placed upon the continual sufficiency of God's grace. The
present tense use of the verb, ἀρκεῖν, suggests that the Lord's grace
is continually available for Paul[142] so that nothing, not even the
thorn, will cause him to cease from his ministry.[143]

As found in 2 Corinthians, grace is that which the Lord gives to
believers in order that they might a) make application of Jesus' redemptive sacrifice for their sin (5.21-6.1) even as it reaches more
and more people (4.15), b) minister to others financially (8.1-7 and
9.14), and c) be provided with those things which they need (9.8). It
is the grace of the Lord Jesus Christ that enabled him who was rich
to become poor so that believers might through his poverty become
rich (8.9). This same grace now is to enable Paul to withstand his
thorn in the flesh, for just as believers' wealth comes through
Christ's poverty, so the Lord's power is made complete through
Paul's weakness.[144] If power serves as a synonym of grace in this
verse,[145] then the idea conveyed is that God is giving Paul the
strength to cope with his thorn.[146]

---

[140] Strachan, *Second Corinthians*, p. 32; Hodge, *Second Corinthians*, pp. 286-87;
Tasker, *II Corinthians*, p. 178; Hughes, *Second Corinthians*, p. 451; Bruce, *1 and 2
Corinthians*, p. 249; Furnish, *II Corinthians*, p. 530; and Martin, *2 Corinthians*, p. 418.
Kremer (*2. Korintherbrief*, p. 107) notes, 'Der doppelgliedrige Spruch ist das einzige
direkt an Paulus gerichtete gilt mit Recht als Spitzenaussage der Narrenrede'.

[141] Plummer, *II Corinthians*, p. 354.

[142] Kruse, *2 Corinthians*, p. 206.

[143] Martin, *2 Corinthians*, p. 419.

[144] For a more exhaustive treatment of this theme cf. P.J. Gräbe, *The Power of
God in Paul's Letters* (WUNT 123; Tübingen: Mohr Siebeck, 2000), pp. 132-49.

[145] Denny, *Second Corinthians*, p. 356; Hanson, *Second Corinthians*, p. 87; G.G.
O'Collins, 'Power Made Perfect in Weakness: 2 Cor 12.9-10', *CBQ* 33 (1971), p.
532; Bultmann, *Second Corinthians*, p. 226; Furnish, *Corinthians*, p. 551; Martin, *2
Corinthians*, p. 419; and Voigt, *Die Kraft*, p. 93.

[146] Cf. the comments of Calvin, *Second Corinthains*, p. 377; Hodge, *Second Corinthains*, p. 287; and Carson, *From Triumphalism to Maturity*, p. 148.

This word of the risen Lord produces in Paul a complete change in his thinking. Despite his earlier earnest desire and requests that the thorn be removed, he now sees that this angel of Satan is actually being used to bring about a greater manifestation of God's power in his life and a higher degree of communion with God.[147] As a result of this recognition (οὖν), Paul no longer seeks the thorn's removal, but rather rejoices greatly[148] in his infirmities/weaknesses. Such rejoicing in infirmities is possible because Paul understands that it will result in the power of Christ resting upon him in a way similar to the resting of the shekinah (ἐπισκηνώσῃ) upon the tabernacle.[149]

Verse 10

The grandiose paradox[150] of the apostle delighting in adversities can best be appreciated when the relationship between his weakness and Christ's power is understood. Rather than concluding that their relationship is simply coincidental[151] or that it is by the instrument of weakness that the power of God is manifest,[152] it is more likely that he is saying '… the weaknesses which continue to characterize his life as an apostle … represent the effective working of the power of the crucified Christ in his ministry'.[153] This working is similar to the way in which God chose to establish the church at Corinth in the first place, by use of weak, foolish, and ignoble elements (1 Cor. 1.26-31).[154]

There are at least eight implications of the examination of 2 Cor. 12.7-10 for the primary purpose of this study. 1) There is a clear connection between the heavenly revelation that Paul experienced and the thorn which he was given. Rather than making him immune to infirmities, in this case Paul's visit to the third heaven

---

[147] Martin, *2 Corinthians*, p. 422.

[148] On the superlative ἥδιστα cf. *BDF,* §60 (2).

[149] For this identification, based primarily upon the term ἐπισκηνώσῃ, cf. Plummer, *II Corinthians*, p. 355; Strachan, *Second Corinthians*, p. 33; Hughes, *Second Corinthians*, p. 452; Kremer, *2. Korinterbrief,* p. 108; and cautiously Furnish, *II Corinthians,* p. 531.

[150] Héring, *Second Corinthians*, p. 94.

[151] As O'Collins ('Power Made Perfect', p. 536) argues.

[152] So Wesley, *Explanatory Notes*, p. 469.

[153] Furnish, *II Corinthians*, p. 552.

[154] Cf. Kruse, *2 Corinthians*, p.207.

led to an infirmity. 2) The specific purpose for the giving of the thorn is also very clear: it served to keep Paul from becoming spiritually arrogant or conceited. 3) Paul attributes the ultimate origin of this illness to God. This means that Paul believed that not only could God use illness as discipline for believers who had sinned (as in 1 Cor. 11.30-31) and as a means of accomplishing his will through the preaching of the gospel (Gal. 4.13), but he could also use it as an antidote to spiritual pride. 4) In this one passage, out of the whole Pauline corpus, does Paul go on to assign illness to Satan (or his angel). That he says it was, at one and the same time, given by God and called an angel of Satan implies that there was some kind of multiple agency involving both God and Satan on this occasion. 5) Paul's three prayers for the removal of the thorn suggest that his normal response to sickness was to petition God for healing. The impression left is that Paul would have continued to pray for such if he had not heard from the Lord. 6) Paul's understanding of the words of the risen Christ was that it was not God's will for him to be healed on this occasion. But such an understanding seems to have resulted only from the words of Christ himself. 7) Since it was God's will for Paul to suffer, he was promised a continual supply of grace. 8) It is made extremely clear that the power of God is made manifest not only in the healing of the sick, but also in the faithfulness of those who suffer in obedience to Christ.

Philippians 2.25-30 – Epaphroditus' Illness

Another text which reveals something of Paul's attitude toward illness is found in his letter to the Philippians. Near the end of chapter two, Paul includes information about two fellow workers, Timothy and Epaphroditus. Owing to the fact that it follows a powerful christological confession (2.5-11), with its resulting admonitions (2.12-18), and precedes a rather awkward transition (3.1-2), there has resulted some question concerning the literary integrity of the epistle.[155] Despite such questions, it has recently been demonstrated that not only does the structure of the letter make sense in the light of hellenistic parallels,[156] but also that the theological sig-

---

[155] For example, cf. B.J. Rahtjen, 'The Three Letters of Paul to the Philippians', *NTS* 6 (1960), pp. 167-73.
[156] Cf. L. Alexander, 'Hellenistic Letter-Forms and the Structure of Philippians', *JSNT* 37 (1988), pp. 87-101.

nificance of 2.19-30 is to reinforce, by way of the example of Timothy and Epaphroditus, Paul's earlier words about imitating Christ in servanthood.[157] In 2.25-30 Paul writes:

> But I think it necessary to send back to you Epaphroditus, my brother, fellow worker and fellow soldier, who is also your messenger, whom you sent to take care of my needs. For he longs for all of you and is distressed because you heard he was ill. Indeed he was ill, and almost died. But God had mercy on him, and not on him only but also on me, to spare me sorrow upon sorrow. Therefore I am all the more eager to send him, so that when you see him again you may be glad and I may have less anxiety. Welcome him in the Lord with great joy, and honor men like him, because he almost died for the work of Christ, risking his life to make up for the help you could not give me.

Verse 25

In this verse the reader is introduced for the first time to an individual named Epaphroditus. It is clear that despite bearing a pagan name (which embodies that of the goddess Aphrodite),[158] this man was a Christian and a leading one at that.[159] While it is not impossible that this Epaphroditus be identified with the Epaphras mentioned in Colossians (1.7; 4.12) and Philemon (23),[160] the frequency of the name in antiquity[161] as well as the fact that Epaphroditus and Epaphras appear to have been natives of Philippi and Colossae re-

---

[157] Cf. esp. R.A. Culpepper, 'Co-Workers in Suffering: Philippians 2.19-30', *RevExp* 77 (1980), pp. 349-58. A similar point was made regarding Epaphroditus by F.F. Bruce, *The Pauline Circle* (Grand Rapids: Eerdmans, 1985), p. 85.

[158] H.C.G. Moule, *Studies in Philippians* (Grand Rapids: Kregel, 1977), p. 79.

[159] It was not until the third century CE that Christians began to give their children names drawn from the Hebrew Bible. Origen, for example, bore a pagan name though reared in a Christian home.

[160] A possibility held out by A. Wiesinger, *St Paul's Epistles to the Philippians, to Titus, and the First to Timothy* (trans. J. Fulton; Edinburgh: T. & T. Clark, 1851), p. 87 and M.A. Getty, *Philippians and Philemon* (Wilmington: Michael Glazier, 1980), p. 43.

[161] For example, Josephus' patron was named Epaphroditus (cf. *Ant.* 1.8; *Life* 430; *Against Apion* 1.1; 2.1, 296) as well as the Epaphroditus in Suetonius, *Nero* 49 and *Domitian* 14.

spectively, suggest that these names do not refer to the same individual, as most scholars agree.[162]

Although a shadowy figure to modern readers, Epaphroditus was well known to the Philippians. In 4.18 it is revealed that he had brought a gift from the Philippian church to Paul. For this and perhaps other services, Paul describes Epaphroditus in stellar terms. In fact, Paul uses five terms of compliment in making reference to him. In one phrase Epaphroditus is described as 'my brother, co-worker, and fellow soldier'. These three terms also occur in Philemon 1, 2, but there each term is used to describe different individuals.[163] In Phil. 2.25, all three words have reference to Epaphroditus, evidenced by the fact that the three nouns are governed by a single definite article (τόν)[164] and are qualified by one personal pronoun (μου).[165] Not only does the sheer force of their cumulative weight convey Paul's desire to praise Epaphroditus, but also each of the specific terms individually serve to communicate Paul's affection and esteem for this individual.

In every other occurrence of ἀδελφός in this epistle (1.12, 14; 3.1, 13, 17; 4.1, 8, 21), the term appears in the plural when Paul seeks to address the Philippians directly. As one of Paul's favorite expressions (he uses it some 133 times) it perhaps comes close to serving as a synonym for Christian.[166] In this epistle it is used as a tender and affectionate term to convey the close bond that exists

---

[162] R. Johnstone, *Lectures on the Book of Philippians* (Minneapolis: Klock & Klock, 1977), p. 215; Moule, *The Epistle to the Philippians*, p. 79; M.R. Vincent, *Critical and Exegetical Commentary on the Epistles to the Philippians and to Philemon* (Edinburgh: T. & T. Clark, 1897), p. 75; J.B. Lightfoot, *St. Paul's Epistle to the Philippians* (Grand Rapids: Zondervan, 1953), pp. 122-23; A.T. Robertson, *Paul's Joy in Christ* (Grand Rapids: Baker, 1970), p. 166; A. Plummer, *A Commentary on St. Paul's Epistle to the Philippians* (London: R. S. Roxburghe House, 1919), p. 60; J.H. Michael, *The Epistle of Paul to the Philippians* (London: Hodder and Stoughton, 1928), p. 120; J.H. Müller, *The Epistles of Paul to the Philippians and to Philemon* (Grand Rapids: Eerdmans, 1955), p. 100 n. 1; J.-F. Collange, *The Epistle of Saint Paul to the Philippians* (trans. A. W. Heathcote; London: Epworth, 1979), p. 118; Culpepper, 'Co-Workers in Suffering: Philippians 2.19-30', p. 355; F.F. Bruce, *Philippians* (New York: Harper & Row, 1983), p. 74; G.F. Hawthrone, *Philippians* (Waco: Word, 1983), p. 115; and P.T. O'Brien, *Philippians* (Grand Rapids: Eerdmans, 1991), p. 330.

[163] Michael, *Philippians*, p. 120.

[164] Plummer, *Philippians*, p. 61.

[165] O'Brien, *Philippians*, p. 330.

[166] Cf H.F. von Soden, 'ἀδελφός', *TDNT*, I, p. 145.

between Paul, his readers, and other believers. Paul's use of ἀδελ-φός to describe Epaphroditus demonstrates at the very least that this individual was a valued brother, on par with all those in the Philippian church.

But Paul is not content simply to identify Epaphroditus as a brother; he very quickly describes him as his συνεργός. In the Pauline literature, this term is used almost exclusively to describe those who have labored with Paul in the preaching of the gospel. Timothy (Rom. 16.21 and 1 Thess. 3.2), Urbanus (Rom. 16.9), Apollos (1 Cor. 3.9), Titus (2 Cor. 8.23), Clement (Phil. 4.3), Jesus called Justus (Col. 4.11), Philemon (1), Mark, Aristarchus, Demas, and Luke (Philemon 24) are all singled out for mention by Paul as co-workers. But perhaps the most striking parallel is found in Rom. 16.3, where both Priscilla and Aquilla are called co-workers in Christ, and are described as those 'who risked their lives for me'. Whether the Philippians would have been able to pick up on this association or not, that Paul would describe Epaphroditus in terms similar to those used for Priscilla and Aquilla is noteworthy. The classification as co-worker suggests that Epaphroditus is regarded as an early Christian leader by Paul and perhaps implies that 'he was not previously unknown to Paul'.[167]

Paul goes on to call Epaphroditus his συστρατιώτης. Earlier in the letter, Paul has encouraged his readers to 'stand firm in one spirit, contending as one man for the faith of the gospel' (1.27). Although military imagery is not unknown to Paul (cf. 1 Cor. 9.7; 2 Cor. 10.3, 4), he refers to only one other individual as his fellow-soldier, Archippus (Philm. 2). Perhaps Collange captures Paul's intent in using συστρατιώτης when he notes, 'the Gospel is represented here as a combat which Epaphroditus has not shirked'.[168] Such combat is, no doubt, similar to that which Paul describes in 2 Cor. 10.3, 4, where Paul, *et. al.* (notice the 'we'), tears down the strongholds with divine power. To call Epaphroditus a fellow-soldier underscores Paul's confidence in this individual.

If Epaphroditus was Paul's brother, co-worker, and fellow-soldier, he was also valuable to the Philippians as their ἀπόστολος

---

[167] Cf. Hawthorne (*Philippians*, p. 116) who goes on to suggest that Epaphroditus may even have been involved in the founding of the church in Philippi itself.
[168] Collange, *Philippians*, p. 120.

and λειτουργός. In the Greek text 'my' (μου) and 'your' (ὑμῶν) stand side by side to emphasize the value of Epaphroditus to both Paul and the Philippians. Although Paul often uses ἀπόστολος as a technical term for one commissioned by the resurrected Lord (Rom. 1.1; 1 Cor. 1.1; 9.1, 2; 2 Cor. 1.1; and the extraordinarily terse Gal. 1.15-17), he also can extend its use to those who are messengers or representatives of the churches (ἀπόστολοι ἐκκλησιῶν), that is, those especially commissioned for specific purposes by the individual congregations (2 Cor. 8.23).[169] To translate ἀπόστολος in this context loosely as messenger,[170] or to take it as a sign that Epaphroditus' authority was equal to that of Paul,[171] seems equally to miss the mark. Rather, the term conveys some 'official' sense of commissioning by the Philippian church.

Epaphroditus is not only the Philippians' commissioned messenger, but he is also their minister to Paul's need. Although used almost exclusively in the LXX in contexts dealing with the priests and Levites in the Temple, in the New Testament, where Jesus himself is regarded as Priest (Heb. 8.2), λειτουργός has reference to secular rulers (Rom. 13.6), angelic servants (Heb. 1.7), and Paul, whose priestly duty is to proclaim the gospel to the Gentiles. Without invoking the priestly imagery of the Old Testament, it appears that Paul does think of Epaphroditus in some sort of priestly terms as he later describes the gift which he brought as a θυσία (4.18).[172] Regardless of the precise understanding of λειτουργός, it is clear that Epaphroditus was sent to minister to Paul's need. In all likelihood, χρείας has reference to some material or financial need, as Phil. 4.18 seems to make clear (cf. also Rom. 12.13; Eph. 4.28; 1 Thess. 4.12; and Phil. 4.19).[173]

It is this valuable helper that Paul has decided to send to the Philippians. While it is possible that Epaphroditus had already left Paul for home, it could very well be that πέμψαι serves as an epistolary

---

[169] Cf. O'Brien, *Philippians*, p. 332.

[170] As Collange (*Philippians*, p. 120) suggests.

[171] So Hawthorne (*Philippians*, pp. 116-17).

[172] It is possible to take ἀπόστολον καὶ λειτουργὸν as a hendiadys with the resulting meaning of 'Your apostle sent to minister to my need'. Cf. Bruce, *Philippians*, 74 and O'Brien, *Philippians*, pp. 331-32.

[173] Cf. Bonnard, *L'Épître de Saint Paul aux Philippiens*, p. 57.

aorist,[174] by which Paul seeks to describe his action i
identifies with the readers' context when they receive tl
interpretation is strengthened by the fact that in a
Epaphroditus carried this letter with him on his return to
Philippi.[175] It is perhaps significant that Paul says he has decided to
send Epaphroditus, rather than to send him *back*. This statement
may imply that the Philippians had sent Epaphroditus to stay with
Paul indefinitely[176] and may explain in part the level of Paul's praise
for Epaphroditus.

Verse 26

Paul's rationale for sending Epaphroditus to Philippi is offered in v.
26 and is connected to the preceding sentence by the causal conjunction ἐπευδή. In words very similar to those which Paul uses to
describe his own desire to see the Philippians in 1.8 (ὡς ἐπιποθῶ
πάντας ὑμᾶς), Epaphroditus is described as having an intense
longing for the Philippians (ἐπιποθῶν ἦν πάντας ὑμᾶς). By using
such similar language Paul not only avoids any hint that Epaphroditus' desires were less than noble, but he also continues in his praise
of his companion, although this time in a much more subtle manner. This connection would seem to rule out the idea that ἐπιποθῶν
is to be understood as homesickness, as is sometimes argued.[177] Paul
is intentionally inclusive in noting that Epaphroditus, as Paul himself, longed for all the Philippians, not simply certain groups in the
church.[178]

Epaphroditus' intense longing was in part related to the fact that
word had come to him that the Philippians had learned of his illness. This news had caused Epaphroditus to become extremely distressed. The intensity of his emotional turmoil is revealed by the
fact that the only other New Testament occurrences of the term
ἀδημονέω are found in the gospels (Mt. 26.37 and Mk 14.33) where
it describes the emotional anguish of Jesus in the Garden of Gethsemane shortly before his death. That such longing and distress

---

[174] Martin, *Philippians*, p. 119 and Culpepper, 'Co-Workers in Suffering', p.
353.

[175] O'Brien, *Philippians*, p. 329.

[176] Cf. Michael, *Philippians*, p. 122 and Hawthorne, *Philippians,* p. 117.

[177] Cf., for example, the remarks of Plummer, *Philippians*, p. 61.

[178] O'Brien, *Philippians*, p. 334.

characterized a continual emotional state for Epaphroditus may be indicated by the fact that both ἐπιποθέω and ἀδημονέω are periphrastics.[179] While it might seem odd to modern western readers that Epaphroditus could be caused such anxiety merely by the Philippians' knowledge of his illness, it is certainly in keeping with similar concerns expressed in a letter from a soldier to his mother written early in the second century. Moffatt describes the letter's context:

> A rumor had reached her that he was ill, and he is annoyed to think her mind has been disturbed. The rumour seems to have been caused or at any rate made more credible by the fact that she had not heard from him for some time.[180]

The soldier responds to this situation by saying, 'Do not grieve for me. Nevertheless I was exceedingly grieved when I heard that you had heard of my illness.'[181] The fact that a soldier would be anxious over a rumor of his illness suggests that Epaphroditus' anxiety regarding reports of his actual illness is in keeping with contemporary attitudes. At any rate, in this verse Paul clearly wishes to emphasize the extent of Epaphroditus' love and concern for the Philippians.

Exactly when Epaphroditus began to feel ill and how the Philippians heard about their envoy's troubles is not clear. It is possible that he took ill while en route to Paul,[182] as a result of a sea voyage or land journey. If this is the case, then perhaps Epaphroditus sent word via someone headed for Philippi. However, the evidence is simply too flimsy to know with any degree of certainty[183] and there are arguments in favor of his illness being the result of his time

---

[179] As Vincent (*Philippians*, p. 76), Lightfoot (*Philippians*, p. 123), Plummer (*Philippians*, p. 61), Robertson (*Paul's Joy in Christ*, p. 167 n. 7) and Hawthorne (*Philippians*, p. 117) observe. However, O'Brien (*Philippians*, p. 335) argues that given the relative rarity of the periphrastic construction in the Pauline literature, it is better to take ἐπιποθέω and ἀδημονέω as adjectival.

[180] J. Moffatt, 'Philippians II 26 and 2 Tim. IV 13', *JTS* 18 (1917), p. 312.

[181] O'Brien, *Philippians*, p. 335 n. 42.

[182] Cf. B.S. Mackay, 'Further Thoughts on Philippians', *NTS* 7 (1961), p. 169; C.O. Buchanan, 'Epaphroditus' Sickness and the Letter to the Philippians', *EvQ* 36 (1964), p. 162; Bruce, *Philippians*, p. 71; and Culpepper, 'Co-Workers in Suffering', p. 356.

[183] Cf. K. Grayston, *The Letters of Paul to the Philippians and the Thessalonians* (Cambridge: Cambridge University Press, 1967), p. 31 and Hawthorne, *Philippians*, p. 118.

spent in ministry with Paul.[184] On this view, Paul and/or Epaphroditus would have relied on the normal lines of communication (friends or relatives traveling in that direction). All that can be known for certain is that word somehow reached the church at Philippi that Epaphroditus had been sick.

Verse 27

While the precise nature of the illness is impossible to determine,[185] it is clearly the result of Epaphroditus' sacrificial service to Paul on behalf of the community.[186] The statement of the preceding verse is intensified by the use of καὶ γάρ (indeed).[187] Paul makes explicit that the malady was a very serious illness; in fact Epaphroditus had nearly died (παραπλήσιον θανάτῳ – he was a near neighbor to death). That Paul would go to such lengths to emphasize Epaphroditus' illness, while not revealing its nature, perhaps suggests that Paul anticipated a critical attitude on the part of the Philippians toward Epaphroditus on his (early?) return.[188] However, it should not be overlooked that this emphasis upon Epaphroditus' willingness to serve, even at risk to his own life, once again places him in the same category as Paul, who faced death, and Jesus, who was actually put to death.[189]

Despite Epaphroditus' dire condition, God mercifully intervened! This contrast is brought out in part by the use of ἀλλά. Unfortunately, Paul is as ambiguous in describing Epaphroditus' recovery as he was in discussing his illness, choosing simply to observe that 'God had mercy on him'. Some scholars have interpreted this

---

[184] Cf. Martin, *Philippians*, pp. 120-21.

[185] As Getty (*Philippians and Philemon*, p. 45) notes, although Martin (*Philippians*, p. 121) reasons that '… it was evidently the cause or accompaniment of a nervous disorder and was partly occasioned by his anxious solicitude for the Philippians'.

[186] So A. Wiesinger, *Biblical Commentary on St. Paul's Epistles to the Philippians, to Titus, and the First to Timothy* (trans. J. Fulton and A. M. Garvald; Edinburgh: T. & T. Clark, 1851), p. 89 and Getty, *Philippians and Philemon*, p. 45.

[187] O'Brien, *Philippians*, p. 336.

[188] Cf. O'Brien, *Philippians*, p. 336 and Hawthorne, *Philippians*, p. 118. In contrast, Michael (*Philippians*, p. 124) takes this emphasis of Paul's to suggest 'he suspected that when Epaphroditus reached Philippi he would do his utmost to minimize its gravity'.

[189] A point made by Culpepper ('Co-Workers in Suffering', p. 356) and O'Brien (*Philippians*, p. 336).

somewhat ambiguous phrase to mean that Paul did not or could not use the gift of healing to facilitate Epaphroditus' recovery.[190] But such a conclusion is too simplistic at worst or too premature at best. For one thing, it fails to pay careful enough attention to the way mercy is used in connection with the recovery of health in the New Testament. While it is true that Paul does not normally use ἐλεέω to describe physical healings, preferring to reserve the term to describe salvation either for Israel and the Gentiles (Rom. 9.15-16, 18; 11.30-32) or Paul himself (1 Cor. 7.25; 2 Cor. 4.1), the term does occur in the Synoptics in contexts where individuals cry out to Jesus for healing (Lk. 17.13; 18.38-39 and parallels).[191] Paul's point, of course, *is* that Epaphroditus recovered physically. That he had been at the point of death and now was well enough to travel suggests a supernatural restoration to health. To argue that such language excludes the healing of Epaphroditus at the hands of Paul or others appears to outdistance the text. For there can really be little doubt that Paul and any other Christians with him would have offered earnest prayer on Epaphroditus' behalf. Such a scenario is 'quite possible, and not unlikely'.[192] In point of fact, such actions can be taken more or less for granted.[193] However, the primary point for Paul is that Epaphroditus recovered, not how he recovered.

In the very act whereby God showed mercy to Epaphroditus through his recovery, he also showed mercy to Paul. According to O'Brien the grammatical construction, οὐκ αὐτὸν δὲ μόνον ἀλλὰ καὶ ἐμέ, makes this point explicitly:

> The δέ indicates that not all has been said in the previous clause about the divine mercy, while the οὐκ ... μόνον ἀλλὰ καὶ ('not

---

[190] For example, Moule (*Studies in Philippians*, p. 81) asserts, 'This passage among others (e.g. 2 Tim. iv 20) shews that the mysterious "gift of healing", used by St Paul at Melita (Acts xxviii. 8), was not at the *absolute* disposal of even the faith of its recipient'. Cf. also Plummer, *Philippians*, p. 62 and Hawthorne (*Philippians*, p. 118) who seems to quote Moule with approval.

[191] It is not without significance that in these Synoptic texts the term σώζω occurs in Jesus' pronouncement of healing.

[192] J.A. Beet, 'Epaphroditus and the Gift from Philippi', *Expositor* 9 (1889) Third Series, p. 72.

[193] Collange, *Philippians*, p. 121.

only … but also') introduces, in an emphatic way, the additional point that Paul, too, had been the recipient of divine mercy.[194]

This act of divine mercy had as its purpose the sparing of Paul from receiving sorrow upon sorrow or wave upon wave of misfortune (ἵνα μὴ λύπην ἐπὶ λύπην σχῶ). While it is possible that Paul means Epaphroditus' death would have been a sorrow added to the sorrow of his illness,[195] given Paul's current circumstance, it is more likely that the sorrow of Epaphroditus' death would have been in addition to the pain of his imprisonment.[196]

Verse 28

Because of the illness (and subsequent recovery) Paul conveys his intention to send Epaphroditus to Philippi. The connection between Epaphroditus' illness and Paul's decision to send him to the Philippians is brought out by the use of οὖν, 'therefore'. In fact, Paul reveals that he is sending Epaphroditus to the Philippians much earlier than expected by the use of σπουδαιοτέρως, a comparative[197] here meaning 'most hastily'. It is difficult to avoid the conclusion that both Paul and the Philippians had expected Epaphroditus to remain with Paul for some time, if not permanently, and that Paul's wording reveals his fear that the Philippian church might be upset with Epaphroditus for his premature departure.[198] The purpose (expressed by a ἵνα clause) of Epaphroditus' return is twofold: 1) that seeing him you might rejoice again and 2) that Paul's sorrow might be lessened. Presumably, Paul has reference to the Philippians earlier distress at the news of Epaphroditus' illness. Such anxiety will end, and Paul presumes (perhaps by way of instruction?) the Philippians will rejoice at the sight of their friend. Paul does not say that Epaphroditus' return will make him anxiety-

---

[194] O'Brien, *Philippians*, p. 337.

[195] A possibility suggested by F.W. Beare, *The Epistle to the Philippians* (San Francisco: Harper & Row, 1959), p. 98.

[196] So Wiesinger, *Philippians*, p. 89; Vincent, *Philippians and Philemon*, p. 76; Michael, *Philippians*, p. 125; Martin, *Philippians*, p. 122; and O'Brien, *Philippians*, p. 338.

[197] O'Brien (*Philippians*, p. 339) observes that the comparative σπουδαιοτέρως is being used in this context as a superlative emphasizing utmost urgency.

[198] Michael, *Philippians*, p. 126; Beare, *Philippians*, p. 99; Martin, *Philippians*, p. 122; Hawthorne, *Philippians*, p. 118; and M. Silva, *Philippians* (Chicago: Moody Press, 1988), p. 162.

free (ἄλυπος), but rather his return will make Paul less sorrowful (ἀλυπότερος).

Verse 29

In the light of Epaphroditus' imminent (and sooner than expected) return, therefore (οὖν) the Philippians are instructed to give him a very warm and honorable reception. At first sight this verse would appear to be in accord with Paul's words to a different church (Rome) about another colleague in ministry, Phoebe (cf. Rom. 16.1-2). For her part, Phoebe is called a sister and deacon. She is to be received in the Lord, worthy of the saints. By way of comparsion, Epaphroditus is to be received 'wholeheartedly'[199] or 'with hearts full of joy'[200] (μετὰ πάσης χαρᾶς), in the Lord. The Philippians are further instructed to consider Epaphroditus in the class of those worthy of continued esteem (καὶ τοὺς τοιούτους ἐντίμους ἔχετε).[201] Clearly, Paul is speaking of Epaphroditus in superlative language here.

On balance, Epaphroditus is given a slightly stronger recommendation than Phoebe. Of course, the odd thing about such a situation is that whereas Phoebe is being recommended to a church that presumably does not know her or her ministry, Epaphroditus is being recommended to a congregation to whom he is well known. Such a state of affairs suggests that Paul anticipated that there might be a problem with Epaphroditus' early return.[202]

Verse 30

Paul's praise of Epaphroditus continues in v. 30, as the apostle repeats some of what he has earlier said about his fellow-laborer. He prefaces his further comments with διὰ τὸ ἔργον Χριστοῦ, by which he emphasizes that all the hardships which Epaphroditus faced were on account of the work of Christ, a phrase that, no doubt, encompasses a variety of activities ranging from the proclamation of the gospel to ministering to the needs of Paul. Paul now

---

[199] Hawthorne, *Philippians*, p. 119.

[200] O'Brien, *Philippians*, p. 341.

[201] O'Brien (*Philippians*, p. 341) notes that the present imperative verb should be taken to mean, 'continue to hold [such people] in esteem'.

[202] Cf. H.C.G. Moule, *The Epistle to the Philippians* (Cambridge: Cambridge University Press, 1897), p. 82; Michael, *Philippians*, p. 126; Culpepper, 'Co-Workers in Suffering', p. 356; and Hawthorne, *Philippians*, p. 119.

not only repeats the statement that Epaphroditus came very near to death, owing to his ministerial work, but he also goes on to emphasize this hazard by observing that Epaphroditus had gambled with his life (παραβολευσάμενος τῇ ψυχῇ). The term παραβολευσάμενος was a gambling term meaning 'to wager in a game of chance',[203] which could be used to describe the risk one would undertake in order to see a difficult task accomplished.[204] The purpose (ἵνα) of such a gamble was so that he could render the service (λειτουργίας) which the Philippians were unable to provide. This phrase is in no way meant to shame the Philippians for a lack of support, but rather to praise Epaphroditus and make clear that he had been a very successful representative of the Philippian church in serving the needs of Paul.[205]

What are the primary implications of Phil. 2.25-30 for this enquiry about the Devil, disease, and deliverance? 1) This passage provides additional evidence that leaders in the early church sometimes fell ill, even deathly sick. 2) Although Paul indicates some degree of apprehension regarding Epaphroditus' reception by the Philippians upon his return, he does not give the slightest hint that the illness reflected negatively upon his spirituality. On the contrary, Paul heaps extravagant praise upon Epaphroditus as a Christian leader. 3) Paul does not attribute this illness to God or the Devil, et. al. 4) The remark that God spared Epaphroditus' life may be a very subtle hint that Epaphroditus had been healed, although it could be no more than a hint.

Two passages in the Pastoral Epistles are worthy of mention before concluding this examination of the Pauline literature. Although a host of critical problems surround the authorship of these letters, they are, at the very least, representative of later Pauline thought, whether that of Paul shortly before his death or one of his students.[206] The passages to be examined are Paul's instruction to

---

[203] Moule, *The Epistle to the Philippians*, p. 82.

[204] Cf. esp. Deissmann, *Light from the Ancient East*, p. 88 n. 3.

[205] Cf. 1 Cor. 16.15-18, which parallels this verse to a certain extent.

[206] Most scholars date the Pastorals to the latter part of the first century CE. Cf. P.N. Harrison, *The Problem of the Pastoral Epistles* (London: Oxford University Press, 1921); G. Herdan, 'The Authorship of the Pastorals in the Light of Statistical Linguistics', *NTS* 6 (1959-60), pp. 1-15; M. Dibelius and H. Conzelmann, *The*

Timothy, in 1 Tim. 5.23, to 'Stop drinking only water, and use a little wine because of your stomach and your frequent illnesses', and the revelation in 2 Tim. 4.20 that Trophimus was left sick in Miletus by Paul.

1 Timothy 5.23 – Timothy's Stomach Trouble

Near the end of 1 Timothy 5, in a series of instructions concerning sin, one finds a directive, which at first sight appears to be so hopelessly out of place that it has sometimes been treated as an interpolation.[207] However, this view has not found favor with the majority of scholars.[208] The command for Timothy to stop drinking water only, suggests that he had made a decision to abstain from drinking any wine.[209] It could be that this decision tells of Timothy's own ascetic lifestyle[210] or that he made this decision in reaction to a problem in his circle of influence that some had with drinking too much (of which 1 Tim. 5.3, 8 may be evidence).[211] Another possibility is that such abstinence was a concession to the asceticism of the

---

Pastoral Epistles (Philadelphia: Fortress Press, 1972). However, several scholars argue for a date near the end of Paul's life. Cf. B.M. Metzger, 'A Reconsideration of Certain Arguments Against the Pauline Authorship of the Pastoral Epistles', *ExpT* 70 (1958), pp. 91-101; E.E. Ellis, *Paul and His Recent Interpreters* (Grand Rapids: Eerdmans, 1961), pp. 49-57; J.N.D. Kelly, *A Commentary on the Pastoral Epistles* (Grand Rapids: Baker, 1981), pp. 30-36; G.D. Fee, *1 and 2 Timothy, Titus* (Peabody, MA: Hendrickson, 1988), pp. 23-26; E.E. Ellis, *Pauline Theology* (Grand Rapids: Eerdmans, 1989), pp. 104-11; D. Guthrie, *New Testament Introduction* (Downers Grove: InterVarsity Press, 1990), pp. 607-49; and G.W. Knight, *The Pastoral Epistles* (Grand Rapids: Eerdmans, 1992), pp. 21-52.

[207] Cf. for example, R. Falconer, *The Pastoral Epistles* (Oxford: Clarendon Press, 1937), p. 151.

[208] Cf. the comments of J.H. Bernard, *The Pastoral Epistles* (Cambridge: Cambridge University Press, 1899), p. 89; C. Spicq, *Les Épîtres Pastorales* (Paris: Gabalda, 1947), p. 180; P. Dornier, *Les Épîtres Pastorales* (Paris: Gabalda, 1969), p. 97; and Kelly, *The Pastoral Epistles*, p. 128.

[209] Fee (*1 and 2 Timothy, Titus*, p. 132) notes that '… every other known use of this verb in antiquity means *to drink only water* in the sense of abstaining from wine'.

[210] A possibility mentioned by W. Lock, *The Pastoral Epistles* (Edinburgh: T. & T. Clark, 1936), p. 64. G. Holtz (*Die Pastoralbriefe* [Berlin: Evangelische Verlagsanstalt, 1965], p. 130) and H. Bürki (*Der ertse Brief des Paulus an Timotheus* [Wuppertal: R. Brockhaus, 1974], p. 183) observe that both Jews and Greeks held the drinking of water instead of wine to be a sign of asceticism.

[211] So Bernard, *The Pastoral Epistles*, p. 88 and perhaps Lock, *The Pastoral Epistles*, p. 64

false teachers.[212] If this latter suggestion is correct, then the writer's words about water would clarify his earlier statement about purity, that is, purity is not asceticism.[213] On this view, the writer is either chiding Timothy for adopting a practice of the false teachers or seeking to keep him from inadvertently giving the false teachers support for their ascetic views.[214]

While it is difficult to be certain about the specific background of this statement, what *is* sufficiently clear from the text is that the command not to drink water only is tied very closely to Timothy's health.[215] The instuction to drink a little wine on account of your stomach and frequent illnesses would not have been wholly unexpected in antiquity.[216] Hippocrates († ca. 400 BCE) advocates the use of wine as part of a change of diet for a (hypothetical) man who had drunk only water (*Ancient Medicine*, XIII).[217] In *Advice about Keeping Well* (132), Plutarch († ca. 120 CE) describes wine in this way:

> For wine is the most beneficial of beverages, the pleasantest of medicines, and the least cloying of appetizing things, provided that there is a happy combination of it with the occasion as well as with water.[218]

---

[212] Kelly, *The Pastoral Epistles*, pp. 128-29 and T.D. Lea, *1, 2, Timothy* (Nashville: Broadman Press, 1992), p. 158

[213] E.F. Scott, *The Pastoral Epistles* (London: Hodder and Stoughton, 1936), p. 69; U. Borse, *1. und 2. Timotheosbrief Titusbrief* (Stuttgart: Katholisches Biblewerk, 1985), p. 64; Guthrie, *New Testament Introduction*, p. 120; and H. Merkel, *Die Pastoralbriefe* (Göttingen und Zürich, 1991), p. 46.

[214] Dornier (*Les Épîtres Pastorales*, p. 97) notes, 'L'intention de Timothée était louable … mais elle court le risque de passer pour une approbation implicite de cette ascèse légatiste qui distingue entre le pur et l'impur'. Cf. also Dibelius and Conzelmann, *The Pastoral Epistles*, pp. 80-81; N. Brox, *Die Pastoralbriefe* (Regensburg: Friedrich Pustet, 1969), p. 203; and J. Roloff, *Der erste Brief an Timotheus* (Zürich: Benziger, 1988), p. 23.

[215] A.T. Hanson (*The Pastoral Epistles* [Grand Rapids: Eerdmans, 1982], p. 22) concludes that Paul could not have been reacting against the ascetics because even they were not opposed to taking wine as a medicine.

[216] Dornier (*Les Épîtres Pastorales*, p. 98) points out that Paul advocates the use of wine as medicine without hesitation.

[217] This recommendation is an example of a general rule of thumb that if one is ill, a radical change of diet is needed, not just the substitution of wine for water.

[218] Cited according to the translation of F.C. Babbitt, *Plutach's Moralia*, II (London: Heinemann, 1971), p. 265.

However, Plutarch goes on to offer strong words of advice regarding the misuse of wine and the necessity of diluting it with water, both by adding it to the wine itself and by drinking lots of water as well. Perhaps the most revealing contemporary parallel comes from Pliny († ca. 112 CE) in his *Natural History* (23.22.38).

> Wine is a tonic to the stomach and a sharpener of the appetite; it dulls sorrow and anxiety, expels urine and chills, and induces sleep. In addition it checks vomiting, and pieces of wool, soaked in wine and applied externally, soften abcesses. Asclepiades asserted that the usefulness of wine is hardly exceeded by the power of the gods.[219]

After discussing a variety of additional ailments for which wine might help in effecting a cure, the last of which is cardiac disease, Pliny cautions that one must use discernment in dispensing it.

> It ought at any rate to be given with food, not after sleep nor another kind of drink – that is, there must at any rate be thirst – only in the last resort and to a man rather than a woman, to an old man rather than to a young one, to a young man rather than to a boy, in winter rather than in summer, to those used to wine rather than to teetotalers. The dose to be taken depends upon the potency of the wine and also the amount of water added. The general opinion is that a satisfactory mixture is one cyathus of wine to two of water. If the stomach be disordered, should the food not pass down, the wine must be given once more.[220]

If Pliny's attitude is any indication of how Paul (or one of his followers) may have thought about the use of wine, then it is likely that when he advocates a little wine for the stomach (ἀλλὰ οἴνῳ ὀλίγῳ χρῶ διὰ τὸν στόμαχον) he is thinking medicinally and not necessarily encouraging the use of wine generally (for example, cf.

---

[219] Cited according to the translation of W.H.S. Jones, *Pliny: Natural History*, VI (London: Heinemann, 1961), p. 439.

[220] Cited according to the translation of Jones, *Pliny: Natural History*, VI, p. 449.

Rom. 14.21). As for Timothy's frequent illnesses, the text does not reveal their nature, only their existence.[221]

The primary significance of 1 Tim. 5.23 for this study is that the text acknowledges that Timothy has ongoing bouts with a stomach illness of some sort. The writer both refuses to suggest that this illness was a sign of some flaw in Timothy's spirituality and refrains from attributing its origin to any specific cause. It is also significant that the verse advocates the use of medicine on this occasion.

2 Timothy 4.20 – 'Trophimus I Left Ill'

Very near the end of 2 Timothy, in the final greetings, reference is made to several individuals, one of whom is Trophimus. Although this is the first mention of Trophimus in the Pauline corpus, Luke makes two references to a certain Trophimus in connection with Paul (Acts 20.4 and 21.29). From these passages it is learned that this Trophimus was a Gentile from Ephesus who was one of those who was with Paul in Jerusalem. The Jews charged (wrongly) that Paul had brought Trophimus into the Temple. While it is difficult to discern whether or not the readers of the Pastorals were familiar with the Acts account, it would seem safe to identify the Trophimus of 2 Timothy with the Trophimus of Acts.

Why Trophimus is mentioned at this point is a little hard to determine. It is possible to take this statement as intended to inform Timothy about a friend's illness of which he was unaware[222] or as an explanation of why Trophimus was not with Paul.[223] Literarily, it functions as part of the explanation of why Paul was alone at this point. In any event, this verse states that Trophimus was left ill in Miletus. While the precise nature of the illness is not specified, apparently Trophimus was too sick to travel.[224] More than one scholar

---

[221] Lack of knowledge concerning the nature of the illness has not prevented speculation regarding what troubled Timothy. Cf. the innovative comment of R.A. Ward (*1 & 2 Timothy & Titus* [Waco: Word, 1974], p. 90), 'As Timothy had weighty responsibilities on his hands he would have to guard against dyspeptic choler and the possibility of losing his temper and starting a quarrel.'

[222] Bernard, *The Pastoral Epistles*, p. 151; Guthrie, *New Testament Introduction*, p. 119; and Lea, *1, 2 Timothy*, p. 260.

[223] Falconer, *The Pastoral Epistles*, p. 100.

[224] E.F. Brown, *The Pastoral Epistles* (London: Methun & Co, 1917), p. 90.

has noted than Paul did not heal Trophimus on this occasion.[225] Unfortunately, the reason is not known. However, the significance of the verse for this enquiry is that, like Timothy, Trophimus' experience is evidence that not everyone in the early church was always healthy, even leaders (!), and that again the writer does not insinuate that the illness reflected badly on Trophimus, nor does he speculate about its origin.

Whether the Pastorals are from Paul's hand or not, these verses continue the thematic trajectory, which began with Epaphroditus, that illness is not necessarily a reflection on one's spiritual condition. The major difference between Epaphroditus' situation and that of Timothy and Trophimus is that the former recovered (perhaps by means of healing?) while the latter had not.

Conclusions and Implications

Having examined several texts relating to the issue of the Devil, disease, and deliverance in the Pauline literature, it is time to identify the conclusions which may be drawn in the attempt to summarize Paul's thought on the subject. Each set of conclusions are grouped under a question which should facilitate the process. The conclusions are numbered sequentially throughout this section.

To whom or what may the origin of illness be attributable?

1) In ways somewhat similar to James, Paul is not hesitant to assign the origin of certain illnesses to God.

2) Although not always the case, Paul sometimes sees a clear connection between sinful behavior and sickness or death.

3) In only one text does Paul identify the Devil as having a hand in illness, but even there, Paul suggests that Satan does not work apart from the ultimate agency of God himself. The precise nature of that co-agency is not altogether clear.

4) Paul and the 'Paul of the Pastorals' (if such a distinction needs to be made) can also treat illness as a 'normal' part of Christian existence.

What are the purposes of divinely approved or inflicted illness?

---

[225] Cf. esp. Spicq, *Les Épîtres Pastorales*, p. 397; Ward, *1 & 2 Timothy & Titus*, p. 223; Knight, *The Pastoral Epistles*, p. 477; and Lea, *1, 2 Timothy*, p. 261.

5) Some illnesses function as pedagogical chastisement of those believers who are guilty of specific sinful behavior. This conclusion, while not a universally applicable principle, dovetails neatly with the idea in James 5 that God sometimes chastizes some believers through illness.

6) Providential intervention in the form of illness sometimes occurs in order that the gospel might be proclaimed.

7) The purpose of the thorn in the flesh was to aid Paul in his struggle against becoming arrogant on the basis of the extraordinary heavenly revelations which he received. Here too a redemptive purpose is discernible.

What was Paul's response to illness?

8) It appears that Paul's normal response was to pray, both privately and corporately, for healing. This assessment is based in part upon Paul's actions when he was inflicted with the thorn in the flesh. It also draws upon Paul's mention of those with gifts of healings in the church at Corinth and the ways in which signs and wonders accompanied his preaching, both of which imply that healings were somewhat regular in the Pauline communities.

9) In cases where healing did not occur, one might assume that Paul's practice was to keep praying until he heard from the Lord.

10) If the observations drawn from the Pastorals can be trusted, it seems that Paul is not opposed to advocating the use of certain 'medical' remedies in the case of recurring sickness.

3

THE JOHANNINE LITERATURE

Although not an overriding concern, the relationship between sin and sickness is given some attention in the literature examined to this point. Generally speaking, while James and Paul both believe illness is sometimes the direct result of sin, neither of them imply that such a causal relationship always exists. Somewhat surprisingly, in cases where these writers make an identification between sin and sickness, neither James nor Paul is reluctant to attribute illness to God. In point of fact, neither of them implies that the Devil is ever the cause of illness which results from sin, though Paul seems to allow a role for Satan in inflicting what might be called pedagogical afflictions. In such cases, it would appear that Satan unwittingly aids the believer.

While acknowledging the role God plays in affliction, both James and Paul also indicate that sin is not always the cause of an illness. Although James does not reveal his thinking about such cases, Paul seems to suggest that some 'unattributed' illnesses may be used by God for the preaching of the gospel, while others are described without judgment as to origin. Most of the evidence suggests that the general course of action was to respond to any affliction with prayer.

This investigation now takes up the Johannine literature, which is one of the major strands of the New Testament writings. Distinct grammatically and theologically from other New Testament documents, the Johannine literature includes three different literary genres (narrative, epistle, and apocalypse), each of which requires specific hermeneutical approaches. This chapter focuses upon the relevant materials in the gospel and the epistles.

The Fourth Gospel describes several miraculous events performed by Jesus known as signs. These signs play a prominent role in the overall purpose of the gospel (cf. 20.30, 31) and are often intricately related to long discourses by Jesus which follow, where the theological significance of the individual sign is the subject of a good deal of theological reflection. Despite its similarity to the Synoptic Gospels in the recounting of miracle stories, the Fourth Gospel is distinct from them in that there is no attention given to exorcism. In point of fact, while the Devil is the topic of some discussion, the only references to demon possession come in 7.20 and 8.48, 49, where it is Jesus that is charged with being demon possessed.

The Fourth Gospel, which appears to have come into final form sometime near the end of the first century CE, contains two stories that directly relate to the major topic of this enquiry: 5.1-16 and 9.1-12. Most scholars divide the Gospel of John into two major sections, the Book of Signs (1-12), which is devoted primarily to the public ministry of Jesus, and the Book of Glory (13-21), which describes Jesus' farewell actions and his passion and resurrection.[1]

John 5.1-16 – 'Stop Sinning Lest Something Worse Come upon You'

Chapter five marks a new section of the story of Jesus in the Fourth Gospel. Following the prologue, the first section of the gospel (1.19-4.54) chronicles the near universally positive response to Jesus by various individuals. This begins with the response of the initial disciples (1.35-51, 2.11, 22), the belief of the Samaritans (4.27-30, 39-42), and the faith of the official (and his family) whose son was healed by Jesus (4.50-53). The most negative responses to Jesus are the conflict over the cleansing of the temple (2.13-20), the (inadequate) belief of the crowds generated by the signs which Jesus performed (2.23-25), and the somewhat enigmatic response on the part of Nicodemus (3.1-15), who seems to vanish from the story after v. 9.

---

[1] For an extensive survey of the scholarly views on the literary structure of the Fourth Gospel, cf. G. Mlakuzhyil, *The Christocentric Literary Structure of the Fourth Gospel* (Rome: Pontifical Biblical Institute, 1987), pp. 137-68.

The (sometimes eager) responsiveness found in the first four chapters all but disappears with the onset of chapter five, which is the beginning of a series of confrontations between Jesus and the Jews.[2] The first of these stories recounts the healing at the pool of Bethesda of a man afflicted for thirty-eight years. His encounter with Jesus not only results in his own healing, but also in opposition to Jesus on the part of the Jewish leaders who are upset that these actions take place on the Sabbath.

> After these things there was a feast of the Jews, and Jesus went up into Jerusalem. And there is in Jerusalem by the Sheep Gate a pool called in Hebrew Bethesda, having five porches. In these porches lay many sick people, blind, lame, and paralyzed. And there was a certain man there who had been ill for thirty-eight years. Jesus, seeing this one lying and knowing that he had already been there a long time, said to him, 'Do you wish to be whole?' The sick man answered him, 'Sir, I have no man in order that when the waters are troubled he might put me in the pool. And while I come another goes down before me.' Jesus said to him 'Raise up, take your mat and walk'. And immediately the man became whole and he took his mat and walked.

> And that day was a Sabbath. Therefore the Jews were saying to the one who had been healed, 'It is the Sabbath, and it is not lawful for you to carry your mat.' And he answered them, 'The one who made me whole, that one said to me, "Take up your mat and walk".' They questioned him, 'Who is the man who said to you, "Take up your mat and walk"?' And the healed one did not know who he was, for Jesus had disappeared in the crowd of the place. After these things Jesus found him in the temple and said to him, 'See you have become whole! Stop sinning, in order that something worse does not come to you.' The man departed and proclaimed to the Jews that Jesus was the one who made him whole. And on account of this the Jews were persecuting Jesus, because he did these things on the Sabbath.

The passage follows a somewhat typical Johannine structure in that it begins with a narrative introduction (vv. 1-5), is followed by

---

[2] This statement should not be taken to imply that there are no responses of faith in chapters 5-11, but to note that such responses are rarer.

dialogue, in this case a series of dialogues (vv. 6-18), and gives way to an extended discourse on the part of Jesus (vv. 19-47). Verses 1-18 may also be broken down into the following outline:

(a) Introduction (vv. 1-3)
(b) Jesus and the man at the pool (vv. 5-9a)
(c) The Jews and the man who had been healed (vv. 9b-13)
(d) Jesus and the man (v. 14)
(e) The man and the Jews (v. 15)
(f) Jesus and the Jews (vv. 16-18).[3]

This outline will be utilized in the study which follows.

The Narrative Introduction (vv. 1-4)

Verse 1

This passage begins with μετὰ ταῦτα, which can sometimes be used merely as a designation for an uncertain period of time in the Johannine literature,[4] but here its appearance is rather clearly intended to mark a new beginning.[5] Not only does μετὰ ταῦτα introduce the next section of the gospel (chaps. 5-12), but it also introduces the story of the healing at Bethesda. The story opens with the statement that there was a feast in Jerusalem and as was his custom Jesus went up to Jerusalem.[6] While the identity of the feast is surprisingly unclear, given the Fourth Gospel's apparent interest in

---

[3] This basic outline is found in R.A. Culpepper, 'Un Exemple de Commentaire Fondé sur la critique narrative: Jean 5,1-18', in *La Communiuté Johannique et son historie: La trajectorie dé l'évangile de Jean aux deux premiers siècles* (Genéve: Labor et Fides, 1990), p. 143.

[4] J.R. Michaels (*John* [Peabody: Hendrickson, 1984], p. 84) can refer to it as a 'vague connective'.

[5] J.H. Bernard, *The Gospel according to St. John*, I (Edinburgh: T. & T. Clark, 1928), p. 225 and Culpepper, 'Un example', p. 138.

[6] Cf. the remarkably similar statement describing Jesus' journey to Jerusalem for the feast of Passover in John 2.13.

Jewish feasts[7] (Passover,[8] Pentecost,[9] and New Years[10] all have their advocates), mention of the unnamed feast in the narrative serves to explain Jesus' presence in Jerusalem.[11]

Verse 2

From the description of Jesus' previous visit to Jerusalem in John 2.13, the reader expects next to find Jesus in the temple. However, the Evangelist focuses attention upon an unexpected site, a pool where the infirm gather.[12] This pool, which was located near the Sheep Gate[13] and had five porches or archways under which the sick

---

[7] Cf. the comments of R. Schnackenburg, *The Gospel according to St. John*, II (trans. C. Hastings; New York: Crossroads, 198 7), p. 93 and Michaels, *John*, p. 84.

[8] E.W. Hengstenberg, *Commentary on the Gospel of John*, I (Edinburgh: T. & T. Clark, 1865), pp. 253-56; Bernard, *John*, I, p. 225; P. Beeckman, *L'Evangile selon Saint Jean* (Paris: Beyaert-Bruges, 1951), p. 109; R. Bultmann, *The Gospel of John* (trans. G. Beasley-Murray; Philadelphia: Westminster, 1971), p. 240; W. Nicol, *The Semeia in the Fourth Gospel* (Leiden: E.J. Brill, 1972), p. 32; and apparently J.N. Sanders, *A Commentary on the Gospel according to St. John* (ed. B.A. Mastin; London: A. & C. Black, 1968), p. 158.

[9] J. Calvin, *The Gospel according to St. John* (Grand Rapids: Eerdmans, 1959), p. 116; G.H.C. MacGregor, *The Gospel of John* (London: Hodder & Stoughton, 1928), p. 166; M.E. Boismard and A. Lamouille, *L'évangile de Jean* (Paris: Cerf, 1977), pp. 160-61; and P. Ellis, *The Genius of John: A Composition-Critical Commentary on the Fourth Gospel* (Collegeville, MN: Liturgical Press, 1984), p. 88.

[10] A. Guilding, *The Fourth Gospel and Jewish Worship* (Oxford: Clarendon, 1960), pp. 69-91.

[11] C.K. Barrett, *The Gospel according to St. John* (Philadelphia: Westminster Press, 1978), p. 251 and D.A. Carson, *The Gospel according to John* (Grand Rapids: Eerdmans, 1990), p. 241.

[12] See the perceptive comments on this point by E.C. Hoskyns, *The Fourth Gospel* (ed. F.M. Davey; London: Faber & Faber, 1956), p. 278.

[13] There is some degree of uncertainty as to the original reading in the Greek text at this point. This problem is compounded by the fact that in either major reading a word must be supplied in order for the sentence to make sense. Should one read, 'There is in Jerusalem, near the Sheep Gate a pool', in this case supplying the word Gate, or 'There is in Jerusalem a Sheep Pool near the place', in which case the word place must be supplied. The former is favored by Hengstenberg, *John*, p. 257; B.F. Westcott, *The Gospel according to St. John* (London: Murray, 1881), p. 81; Bernard, *John*, I, p. 227; M.J. LaGrange, *Evangile selon Saint Jean* (Paris: Gabalda, 1936), p. 132; M. Dods, *The Gospel of St. John* (New York: Armstrong and Son, 1903), p. 177; Beeckman, *Jean*, p. 110; D.J. Wieand, 'John 5.2 and the Pool of Bethseda', *NTS* 12 (1966), p. 394; Bultmann, *John*, p. 240; B. Lindars, *The Gospel of John* (London: Oliphants, 1972), p. 212; F.F. Bruce, *The Gospel of John* (Grand Rapids: Eerdmans, 1983), pp. 121-22; Michaels, *John*, p. 88; G.R. Beasley-Murray, *John* (Waco: Word, 1987), p. 70; and Carson, *John*, p. 241. The latter is

could take shelter, was called Bethesda.[14] If the pools discovered at St. Anne's church reveal the authentic site,[15] the place actually consisted of two pools with one porch in between the bodies of water and two porches on either side of each pool.[16]

Verse 3

The description of the scene, which began with the physical identification of the pool and its porches, continues in this verse as the Evangelist now discloses that the place was full of people. Such an observation is not unexpected, given that a feast was being celebrated in Jerusalem. However, rather than learning of religious pilgrims, the reader discovers that this crowd is composed of society's abandoned, the physically ill: the blind, lame, and paralyzed.

For a couple of reasons, the reader's expectancy level is rather high at this point in the narrative. First, the mention of the pool of water serves to remind the reader that the appearance of water thus far in the Fourth Gospel has been in rather remarkable contexts. These include the significance and origin of John's baptism (1.25-28, 33; 3.23), Jesus' turning water into wine (2.1-11), the fact that one must be born of water and spirit in order to see the Kingdom of God (3.5), that Jesus (3.23) and/or his disciples (4.2) baptized others in water, and Jesus' discussion of living water with the Samaritan woman (4.9-15). The significant use of water continues in the Fourth Gospel after chapter five. Jesus makes a proclamation regarding rivers of living water (7.37-39), a blind man receives his

---

favored by: R.V.G. Tasker, *The Gospel according to St. John* (Grand Rapids: Eerdmans, 1965), p. 90; R.E. Brown, *The Gospel according to John*, I (Garden City, NY: Doubleday, 1966), p. 206; A.M. Hunter, *According to John* (London: SCM Press, 1968), p. 56; L. Morris, *The Gospel according to John* (Grand Rapids: Eerdmans, 1971), p. 300; Barrett, *John*, p. 251; Schnackenburg, *John*, II, p. 94; E. Haenchen, *John*, I (trans. R.W. Funk; ed., R.W. Funk and U. Busse; Philadelphia: Fortress Press, 1984), p. 244; J.A.T. Robinson, *The Priority of John* (London: SCM Press, 1985), p. 56.

[14] There is also a question as to the original name of this pool.

[15] A preponderance of modern scholars make this identification. Cf. esp. J. Jeremias, *The Rediscovery of Bethesda* (Louisville: Southern Baptist Theological Seminary, 1966). Cf. also Brown, *John*, I, p. 207; Sanders, *John*, p. 160; Morris, *John*, p. 301; Lindars, *John*, p. 213; Barrett, *John*, p. 253; Schnackenburg, *John*, II, p. 94; Bruce, *John*, p. 122; Haenchen, *John*, I, p. 244; R. Kysar, *John* (Minneapolis: Augsburg, 1986), p. 76; and Carson, *John*, p. 242.

[16] However, cf. the vigorous challenge of this identification by Robinson, *John*, pp. 54-59.

sight by washing in water (9.7), Jesus washes the disciples' feet (13.1-20), at the crucifixion blood and water come forth from a wound in Jesus' side (19.34), and a miraculous catch of fish takes place in the water (21.1-14). The second reason for this high level of expectancy is the action of Jesus in the gospel to this point. Not only has he performed so many signs (most of which are not de-scribed in the text but alluded to) that numbers of people 'believe' in him, but also his most recent act, which immediately precedes chapter five, the healing of an official's son, results in the official (and his whole house) believing in Jesus. Therefore, although the reader is not immediately informed as to the reason for this collec-tion of infirm individuals, he/she is prepared for some significant event to take place.[17]

Verse 5

As the Evangelist continues his description, he focuses the reader's attention on one particular man in this mass of people. This tech-nique, not dissimilar to the effect of a zoom lens on a camera,[18] so effectively concentrates the focus of the reader upon this specific person that the rest of the crowd fades from view.

In this verse the Evangelist reveals that the man had been ill for 38 years. Although it is possible that the number is meant to be taken as a symbol of Israel's wilderness wanderings,[19] if the number has any symbolic meaning perhaps it is that thirty-eight years 'is the time of a whole generation, as in Deut. 2.14'.[20] While such secon-dary significance of the number is possible, its presence clearly in-

---

[17] An early (Tertullian) interpolation inserted into the text appears in a num-ber of manuscripts at this point (v. 4), in order to explain why so many sick peo-ple had gathered around this particular pool. Given the drama of the narrative, this addition seems particularly misplaced. In fact, if a statement of clarification were needed at all, one would expect the insertion in v. 7, not here. Major advo-cates for the authenticity of v. 4 include A. Duprez, *Jésus et les dieux guérisseurs* (Paris: Gabalda, 1970), pp. 135-36 and Z.C. Hodges, 'The Angel at Bethseda – John 5.4', *BibSac* 136 (1979), pp. 25-39. The secondary nature of v. 4 has been convincingly demonstrated by G.D. Fee, 'On the Inauthenticity of John 5.3b-4', *EvQ* 54 (1982), pp. 207-18.

[18] Culpepper, 'Un Example', p. 144.

[19] Cf. Hengstenberg, *John*, I, p. 264; A Loisy, *Le quatrième évangile* (Paris: Emile Nourry, 1921), p. 202; Ellis, *John*, p. 88; and apparently MacGregor, *John*, p. 169.

[20] K. Grayston, *The Gospel of John* (London: Epworth, 1990), p. 48.

dicates that the illness was not a temporary one[21] and that the subsequent healing was miraculous.[22]

What is a bit surprising is that although the Evangelist provides information regarding the length of the illness, he does not disclose its identity.[23] However, it may reasonably be deduced from the fact that the man is described as lying and is later commanded to walk that he suffered from some sort of paralysis,[24] and if not that, some infirmity that left him extraordinarily weak.[25]

Jesus and the Man (vv. 6-9a)

Verse 6

The single focus upon this man who had been ill for thirty-eight years expands to include Jesus who now shares the stage with him, albeit gradually (notice that as v. 6 begins it is the man, τοῦτον, who is mentioned first in the Greek text). The reader next learns that the infirm man is lying down, perhaps suggesting that he is one of the lame or paralyzed mentioned in v. 3.

It comes as no surprise to the reader that even as he sees the man, Jesus knows that he has already been there a long time. Although it is theoretically possible that Jesus knew this naturally,[26] either by deduction or enquiry, it would seem to ignore too many indicators in the text not to take his knowledge as a supernatural one.[27] For not only has the Fourth Gospel given various examples

---

[21] Westcott, *John*, p. 82; Bernard, *John*, I, p. 229; M.C. Tenny, *John: The Gospel of Belief* (London: Marshall, Morgan & Scott, 1948), p. 125; Brown, *John*, I, p. 207; and Morris, *John*, p. 302 n. 17.

[22] MacGregor, *John*, p. 169; Lindars, *John*, p. 214; Schnackenburg, *John*, II, p. 95; and R. Kysar, *John*, p. 76.

[23] As Boismard (*Jean*, p. 161) remarks, 'Il est étrange que le recit johannique indique depuis cobien de temps l'homme était malade temdis qúil néglige de nous dire quelle étaide sa maladie!'

[24] Hengstenberg, *John*, I, p. 264; LaGrange, *Jean*, p. 136; Beeckman, *Jean*, p. 112; Bultmann, *John*, p. 240; Morris, *John*, p. 302; and Kysar, *John*, p. 76.

[25] An idea suggested by Carson, *John*, p. 242.

[26] An interpretation set forth by: B.E. Weiss, *Das Johannes-Evangelium* (Göttingen: Vandenhoeck & Ruprecht, 1902), p. 164; Bernard, *John*, I, p. 230; LaGrange, *Jean*, p. 136; Beeckman, *Jean*, p. 113; Morris, *John*, p. 303; Lindars, *John*, p. 215; and Michaels, *John*, p. 88.

[27] Hengstenberg, *John*, I, p. 265; Westcott, *John*, p. 82; H. Strathmann, *Das Evangelium nach Johannes* (Göttingen: Vandenhoeck & Ruprecht, 1955), p. 101;

of Jesus' extraordinary knowledge to this point in the narrative, but there is also a clear statement regarding his knowledge of the hearts of men (cf. 1.47-50; 2.25; 3.1-10; 4.16-19).

The question which Jesus now asks comes from his knowledge regarding the man and his condition, 'Do you wish to be whole?' The rationale behind this question is not immediately evident to the reader, with diametrically opposed explanations having been offered by a variety of interpreters. Some have seen in this question a rebuke of a man, who does not really want to get well,[28] or at least a test of the man's will to regain his health.[29] But such a negative assessment seems to be based in part upon the secondary reading in v. 4. That is to say, even though most interpreters regard the explanatory note found in v. 4 as a later insertion into the text, they often still allow it to color their interpretation of the dialogue between Jesus and the infirm man. It should be remembered that the Evangelist is fully capable of making clear when Jesus desires to test someone through a question (cf. 6.5, 6). More sympathy can be given to those explanations which see in Jesus' question an attempt to elicit hope from the man[30] or awaken a receptive spirit within him.[31] But even these attempts do not completely satisfy.

Given the sense of drama in the narrative at this point, Jesus' question in v. 6 most likely should be interpreted as continuing the dramatic buildup in the narrative and preparing the reader for that which follows. The reader, who knows of Jesus' previous actions, especially the healing of the official's son, appreciates the fact that Jesus has the authority to heal this man. His question focuses attention upon his intended action and allows the reader to anticipate

---

Brown, *John*, I, p. 207; Boismard, *Jean*, p. 162; Barrett, *John*, p. 254; Haenchen, *John*, p. 245; L.T. Witkamp, 'The Use of Traditions in John 5.1-18', *JSNT* 25 (1985), p. 22; Kysar, *John*, p. 76; and Carson, *John*, p. 243.

[28] M. Dods, *The Gospel of St. John*, p. 178; J.R. Morton, 'Christ's Diagnosis of Disease at Bethseda', *ExpT* 33 (1921-22), pp. 424-25; W. Barclay, *The Gospel of John*, I (St. Andrews: St. Andrews Press, 1955), p. 179; and W.O. Fitch, 'The Interpretation of St. John 5,6', in *Studia Evangelica*, IV (ed. F.L. Cross; Berlin: Akademie-Verlag, 1968), p. 195; and Culpepper, 'Un example', p. 148.

[29] Beasley-Murray, *John*, p. 74.

[30] Westcott, *John*, p. 82.

[31] MacGregor, *John*, p. 169. Lindars' (*John*, p. 215) conjecture that, 'It is possible to imagine that Jesus' question has been prompted by the fact that this man has made no attempt to reach the water when it last bubbled up' still seems to be dependent upon the reader's knowledge of v. 4 to make sense.

what happens next.[32] The reader also knows that Jesus' words are often misunderstood by his dialogue partners.

In this regard, it is perhaps significant that Jesus does not ask the man whether he desires to be healed,[33] but rather, does he desire to be whole. While it is obviously the case that the man is healed in v. 9, and is described as such in v. 10 and v. 13, the reference to this man in 7.23 suggests that ὑγιής is not to be understood simply as a synonym for healing. It is possible that ὑγιής is being used in a fashion here not unlike the use of ἄνωθεν and ὕδωρ ζῶν in 3.3 and 4.10 respectively. These possible parallels may suggest that double meaning will come into play in this dialogue as well.

Verse 7

The dialogue begun by Jesus in v. 6 continues in this verse with the answer of the sick one. Rather than taking the man's response as mere complaint[34] or as a sign that he does not truly desire healing,[35] his words appear to function, in typically Johannine style, as a misunderstanding,[36] for they quite miss the intent of Jesus' question. Although the official in 4.47 heard that Jesus was in Galilee and, consequently, came for him to heal his son, there is no indication that this infirm man had ever heard of Jesus. So it is unlikely that he should be expected to respond with unbridled faith in Jesus' ability to heal. Rather, just as the Samaritan woman mistook Jesus to be a weary traveler, so this sick man mistakes Jesus to be only a possible

---

[32] Loisy, *Jean*, p. 202; Haenchen, *John*, I, p. 245; and J.F. Staley, 'Stumbling in the Dark, Reaching for the Light: Reading Character in John 5 and 9', *Semeia* 52 (1990), p. 59.

[33] Jesus uses the adjective ὑγιής in this question, not ἰάομαι or θεραπεύω.

[34] Beasley-Murray, *John*, p. 74.

[35] Cf. Tenny, *John*, p. 105; C.H. Dodd, *The Interpretation of the Fourth Gospel* (Cambridge: Cambridge University Press, 1953), pp. 319-20; and Brown, *John*, I, p. 209. Carson (*John*, p. 243) describes the man's response as, 'the crotchety grumblings of an old and not very perceptive man who thinks he is answering a stupid question'.

[36] For this interpretation cf. Witkamp, 'Use of Traditions', pp. 24-25 and S. van Tilborg, *Imaginative Love in John* (Leiden: Brill, 1993), p. 216. For example, this passage receives no attention in the works devoted to misunderstanding in the Fourth Gospel; cf. H. Leroy, *Rätsel und Missverständnis: Ein Beitrag zur Formgeschichte des Johannesevangeliums* (Bonn: Hanstein, 1966) and D.A. Carson, 'Understanding Misunderstanding in the Fourth Gospel', *TynB* 33 (1982), pp. 59-91. Cf. esp. the chart in Carson p. 90, which documents the lack of scholarly consideration of this passage as an example of misunderstanding.

helper in his quest to get into the pool quickly when the water is troubled. Therefore, despite the rhetoric to the contrary, the man's words are best taken as an honest, if misguided, response.[37] Nothing to this point suggests otherwise.

The man's response reveals several things. First, he has no man to help him. The irony, of which the reader is aware, is that one stands before this infirm one who is more than a man who can help him into the pool, he is the Son of God! Second, the man reveals that apparently the water is (periodically) troubled. When this happens, there was a mad dash to get into the water. The word βάλλω here implies the necessity of haste[38] or rapidity of motion.[39] It is impossible to determine why there was such a mad rush to get into the water (first?). If there is any truth in the information offered in the explanatory gloss of v. 4, then only the first person into the pool at the troubling of the water would be healed. But if that information is wholly spurious, one cannot even be certain that the water was considered to have miraculous qualities. From the text itself, the pool may have simply been considered a therapeutic bath when the waters were troubled. In that case the man finds no place in the pool owing to the massive crowd (ἐν ᾧ δὲ ἔρχομαι ἐγὼ ἄλλος πρὸ ἐμοῦ καταβαίνει).

Verse 8

Instead of responding to the man's statement, Jesus speaks directly to the situation with a synoptic-like command, 'Rise, take up your mat and walk!' The mention of the mat and the command to walk may be additional reasons to believe that the man was lame.[40] It is likely that the commands are intended, in part, to demonstrate that the cure was complete and visible.[41]

Verse 9a

No sooner had Jesus spoken these commands than they took place. The man was immediately made whole and did just as Jesus com-

---

[37] Bruce, *John*, p. 124 and Haenchen, *John*, I, pp. 245-46.

[38] Westcott, *John*, p. 82.

[39] Bernard, *John*, I, p. 231.

[40] R.T. Fortna, *The Gospel of Signs* (Cambridge: Cambridge University Press, 1970), p. 51.

[41] For this opinion cf. Hengstenberg, *John*, I, p. 265; Barrett, *John*, p. 254; Haenchen, *John*, I, p. 246; and Carson, *John*, p. 244.

manded, obedience in the tradition of Mary's instructions in 2.5, 'Whatever he says to you do it!' Clearly, the Evangelist intends this healing to be understood to have been at the word of Jesus.[42]

The Man and the Jews (vv. 9b-13)

Verse 9b

In v. 9b, John mentions that the day on which this healing occurred was a Sabbath. By means of this observation, the reader discovers that this story is not at an end but is to take a distinct turn. For just as the reader is expected to pick up on the subtle detail about the bronze serpent in 3.14, so here, mention of the Sabbath could very well be expected to call to mind biblical stipulations such as Exod. 20.8-11, Jer. 17.2-22, and Neh. 13.19, as well as some first-century prohibitions.

Verse 10

At this point the Jews are introduced into the pericope. Thus far in the Fourth Gospel, the term οἱ Ἰουδαῖοι has been used in a neutral sense (2.6, 13; 4.9; 5.1), but also has been and increasingly will be used to identify the Jewish religious leaders (cf. 1.19; 2.18, 20; 3.1). Their appearance in v. 10 marks the beginning of a period of open hostility to Jesus.[43] Their first words, directed to the formerly infirm man, now referred to as 'the one who had been healed' (τῷ τεθεραπευμένῳ), charge him with breaking the Sabbath by carrying his mat. The use of ἔλεγον suggests that their accusation was ongoing. In particular, it appears that the man violated the (emerging rabbinic) regulation that deals with transporting an object from one domain to another (m. Šab. 11.1-11).[44] It should be noted that the charge, in this case, is made against the formerly ill man and not Jesus directly.[45]

---

[42] Bernard's (*John*, I, p. 230) observation that the healing may have not been supernatural is particularly difficult to understand.

[43] Cf. esp. U.C. von Wahlde, 'The Johannine "Jews": A Critical Survey', *NTS* 28 (1982), pp. 33-60 and R.A. Culpepper, 'The Gospel of John and the Jews', *RevExp* 84 (1987), pp. 273-88.

[44] For a more comprehensive discussion cf. J.C. Thomas, 'The Fourth Gospel and Rabbinic Judaism', *ZNW* 82 (1991), pp. 169-72.

[45] Bultmann, *John*, p. 242 and Barrett, *John*, p. 255.

Verse 11

In response to this accusation of Sabbath violation, the man appeals to the command of Jesus. It is, of course, possible to see in the man's words a shifting of blame from himself to his healer.[46] But in truth, what else could the man say? Would he have been carrying the mat if he had not been healed? Three things militate against a negative assessment of his answer. 1) The emphasis of the sentence is upon the reality of his healing, if word order means anything in Greek. 2) Nothing in the text to this point suggests that he is antagonistic toward Jesus or desires to act in a malevolent way toward him. 3) In all honesty, the man makes in a general way, the very point that Jesus himself will make in the discourse that follows: the Son has authority to act and judge as he does! In other words, for the healed man it is an issue of authority.[47] Perhaps Lindars is not too far from the truth when he remarks:

> Rather in the style of a rabbinic disputation, the healed man sets against the halakic ruling of verse 10 the ruling of another authority – Jesus himself.[48]

It could be concluded then that this verse provides the key to understanding the passage – the one who has authority to heal, has power over the Law.[49]

Verse 12

Not satisfied with his answer, and not remotely interested in the man's healing (it is never mentioned by them once in this pericope), the Jews demand to know the name of the man who said, 'Take up and Walk'![50] The word used to describe their enquiry (ἐρωτάω) can be used in the Fourth Gospel to mean interrogation (cf. 1.19, 21, 25; 9.15, 19; 18.19) and may likely have that meaning here.

---

[46] For this interpretation cf. Sanders, *John*, p. 162; Morris, *John*, p. 306; Barrett, *John*, p. 255; Michaels, *John*, p. 86; Kysar, *John*, p. 77; and Carson, *John*, p. 245.

[47] Cf. Westcott, *John*, p. 83; Bernard, *John*, I, p. 233; and Bruce, *John*, p. 125.

[48] Lindars, *John*, p. 216.

[49] MacGregor, *John*, p. 170.

[50] It is possible that the phrase, Τίς ἐστιν ὁ ἄνθρωπος, is meant to be pejorative. So LaGrange, *Jean*, p. 139; Beeckman, *Jean*, p. 115; and Morris, *John*, p. 306. For a contrasting assessment cf. Bultmann, *John*, p. 243 and Lindars, *John*, p. 216.

Verse 13

But the man (who is now referred to as ὁ ἰαθείς) does not himself know who healed him, as Jesus vanished owing to the enormous crowd in the place. Such a lack of knowledge concerning Jesus' identity may prepare the reader for a lack of knowledge on the part of another healed person later in the gospel (cf. 9.25, 36). And with this observation, the section draws to a close.

Jesus and the Man (v. 14)

The short pause created by the mention of Jesus' departure in the previous verse[51] gives way with the appearance of μετὰ ταῦτα, here used to convey a short passage of time. Sometime later, Jesus finds the man in the temple. The expectation created in v. 1 by the mention of a feast of the Jews and Jesus' trip to Jerusalem is now satisfied in that Jesus finally reaches the temple. If his presence within the temple precincts is understandable on the basis of the feast, the healed man's presence is even easier to explain. He has, no doubt, gone to celebrate the feast with a special thanksgiving and praise upon his heart.[52] Perhaps the fact that Jesus found this man in the temple at a feast time should not be passed over quickly. Given the sheer number of people in attendance at the feast, this observation may be a somewhat subtle hint about Jesus' (supernatural) abilities.

For the primary purpose of this enquiry v. 14 is crucial. Upon finding the healed man Jesus gives him a final admonition, which can be divided into three parts for the sake of investigation: 1) 'Behold, you have been made whole', 2) 'Stop sinning', 3) 'in order that something worse might not come upon you'. Each of these clauses requires specific attention.

'Behold you have been made whole.'

Two things about this phrase are noteworthy. a) It is very difficult to avoid the conclusion that there is something significant about the term ὑγιής as used by John, since all six of its occurrences in the Fourth Gospel have reference to this one individual and five of the uses occur in Jn 5.6-15.[53] Jesus begins this emphasis in v. 6 by asking

---

[51] Schnackenburg, *John*, II, p. 97.

[52] Hengstenberg, *John*, I, p. 267 and Beeckman, *Jean*, p.115.

[53] J. Painter, 'Text and Context in John 5', *AusBR* 35 (1987), p. 30.

if the infirm man desires to be whole. The narrator reports in v. 9 that he had been made whole. The man himself claims that Jesus has made him whole in v. 11, and now Jesus reminds the man through a pronouncement that he has been made whole. Is it possible that in such emphasis the Evangelist is suggesting that the man has not only been healed, but forgiven of his sins as well?[54] If so, Jesus' words in 7.23 might be relevant to this issue. In that passage Jesus points out that the Jewish practice of circumcision on the eighth day sometimes violates the Sabbath. He contrasts this practice with his own and asks, 'ἐμοὶ χολᾶτε ὅτι ὅλον ἄνθρωπον ὑγιῆ ἐποίησα ἐν σαββάτῳ'? It is, of course, possible that Jesus is contrasting the Jewish action of circumcision, which effects one part of the body with his healing that affected the entire body. But is it not also possible that the use of ὅλον ἄνθρωπον ὑγιῆ signifies more (cf. also the use of ὅλος in 13.10)? b) This line of interpretation may be strengthened by the formula Jesus uses in declaring the man whole. In four other passages in the Fourth Gospel an individual sent by God sees a person, says '"Ἴδε', and then describes the person in such a way so as to reveal something about his or her situation, mission, or destiny (cf. 1.19-34; 1.35-39; 1.47-51; and 19.24b-27).[55] In this case Jesus finds the person, says '"Ἴδε', and pronounces that he has been made whole. Perhaps this formula is used intentionally to draw attention to the nature of his wholeness.

Although the second and third phrases go together grammatically, they will be considered separately.

'Stop sinning'
This phrase is a surprise to the reader at this point for he/she has not seen sin terminology in the narrative since Jn 1.29, where the Baptist declared, 'Behold the Lamb of God who takes away the sin of the world!' This previous statement by John has already prepared the reader to expect that Jesus would at some point in the narrative remove (forgive?) sin. Is this the time? Grammatically, μηκέτι ἁμάρτανε is a present imperative prohibition, a construction ordi-

---

[54] Cf. Boismard, *Jean*, p. 162.
[55] Cf. the discussion of M. de Goedt, 'Un schème de Révélation dans le quatrième évangile', *NTS* 8 (1961-62), pp. 142-50.

narily used to forbid what one is already doing.[56] The command may very well imply that when the man was made whole, his previous sins were forgiven,[57] an idea which would make sense to the reader on the basis of 1.29.[58]

'In order that something worse might not come upon you'
More importantly for the purpose of this study, Jesus appears to see a connection between the man's infirmity and sin. Specifically, Jesus implies that the man had been ill because he had personally sinned, the prohibition suggests that the man would understand the sin Jesus was talking about. While not all admit a connection between sin and illness here,[59] several reasons may be offered in support of this interpretation. a) Following fast on the heels of the healing of the official's son in 4.46-53, where there is no hint that sin is the cause of the disease, a specific mention of sin in 5.14 nearly leaps off the page at the reader. b) If a view was held in certain early Christian circles that there was some connection between sin and illness, as the evidence from James 5 and 1 Corinthians 11 indicates, then to mention sin in the context of Jn 5.14, without further explanation,

---

[56] A.T. Robertson, *A Grammar of the Greek New Testament* (New York: Hodder & Stoughton, 1919), p. 890.

[57] For this interpretation cf. Loisy, *Jean*, p. 206; Sanders, *John*, p. 162; Boismard, *Jean*, p. 162; Barrett, *John*, p. 255; Schnackenburg, *John*, II, p. 97; and Ellis, *John*, p. 89. Cf. esp. the conclusion of J. Wilkinson ('Healing in the Fourth Gospel', *SJT* 20 [1967], p. 455), 'It may imply his forgiveness which in turn suggests that the man had come to faith in Jesus as the Son of God on which that forgiveness is based'. As additional support Wilkinson argues that since each of the other healings in the Fourth Gospel (4.46-53; 9.1-41; and 11.1-45) result in belief in Jesus, it is likely that this one does too.

[58] Grayston (*John*, p. 48) interprets the command to mean, 'Give up your appalling doctrine of God' which requires you to wait at this pool so long for your healing. Staley ('Stumbling in the Dark', p. 63) suggests that the sin had something to do with the man's previous conversation with the Jews.

[59] Most notably Barrett, *John*, p. 255; Kysar, *John*, p. 78; Culpepper, 'Un example', p. 147; and apparently Michaels, *John*, p. 86. Cf. Tilborg's (*Imaginative Love*, p. 217-18) somewhat idiosyncratic interpretation; 'The sentence connects sin and sickness, a connection which in other places (Jn 9,3) is rejected by Jesus. I suppose, then, that the connection is not made here either. One can think of all manner of sin, but in the story the only one mentioned is the description of the sabbath, because he carries his bed. Can we not suppose that Jesus says to the man that he should not continue to sin (μήκετι), because otherwise something worse might happen to him; that the man should not carry his bed any longer, because otherwise he might be condemned to death as punishment for this offence against the law?'

almost certainly ensures that the readers would have made a connection between sin and illness.[60] c) It is very clear that 'the two
clauses, 'Stop sinning' and 'something worse may happen to you'
cannot be interpreted independently.'[61] Therefore, it would appear
safe to assume some connection between sin and sickness in this
verse.[62]

But what was the precise relationship between the man's sin and
his illness? Judging from the purpose clause that follows the prohibition, the relationship seems to be a one to one correspondence.
For if the man continued in sin, after having been made whole, he
is certain to meet with a worse fate. Before moving to an attempt to
determine the identity of the worse thing that possibly awaits this
man, it should be reiterated that Jesus seems deadly serious that not
only has this illness been the consequence of sin, but that even
more dire consequences await the man if he does not heed the caution of Jesus.

In reflecting upon the 'worse thing', it is important to remember
that the man had been ill for thirty-eight years and, apparently, had
limited mobility, perhaps being confined to his mat for the most
part. Such a desperate illness has made it difficult for most interpreters to believe that the something worse could be some other,
more devastating physical ailment.[63] Most settle on the idea that the
worse thing is either physical death[64] or some sort of eternal consequence.[65] The idea that the worse thing is physical death might find
support in 1 Jn 5.16, which mentions a 'sin unto death',[66] and 1
Corinthians 11, which states that many had fallen asleep (κοιμῶν-

---

[60] Hengstenberg, *John*, I, p. 267.

[61] Carson, *John*, p. 245.

[62] Cf. Hengstenberg, *John*, I, pp. 267-68; Westcott, *John*, p. 83; Dods, *John*, p. 186; MacGregor, *John*, pp. 170-71; Tenny, *John*, p. 105; Beeckman, *Jean*, p. 116; Sanders, *John*, p. 162; Morris, *John*, p. 307; Boismard, *Jean*, p. 162; Bruce, *John*, p. 126; Beasley-Murray, *John*, p. 74; Carson, *John*, pp. 245-46; and Bernard, *John*, I, p. 234.

[63] MacGregor (*John*, p. 171) is one of the few scholars who considers this a possibility.

[64] Dods, *John*, p. 137 and Schnackenburg, *John*, II, p. 98.

[65] Loisy, *Jean*, p. 206; MacGregor, *John*, p. 171; LaGrange, *Jean*, 140; Beeckman, *Jean*, 116; Morris, *John*, p. 307; Lindars, *John*, p. 217; Barrett, *John*, p. 255; Bruce, *John*, p. 126; Beasley-Murray, *John*, p. 74; and Carson, *John*, p. 246.

[66] W. Grundmann, 'ἁμαρτάνω', *TDNT*, I, pp. 307-308 n. 151.

ται) because they abused the Lord's Table. However, given the rather tight interplay between present and future realities in the Fourth Gospel, it might be unwise to be dogmatic about any one of these options.

The Man and the Jews (v. 15)

The man's action, after this admonition by Jesus, is at first a bit puzzling, for it appears that after his miraculous cure he turns traitor and in a cowardly fashion reports Jesus to the authorities to get himself off the hook regarding the Sabbath violation.[67] At best, it is suggested, the man is dull[68] or persistently naive.[69] It has even been suggested that the man commits the very sin about which Jesus has just warned him.[70] But such interpretations falter at three points.[71] First, they build, to a certain extent, upon a rather negative view of this man previously in the narrative, which is perhaps not the best reading of the text. Second, they overlook entirely the fact that the word used to describe the man's report to the Jews is ἀναγγέλλειν. In every other occurrence in the Johannine literature, this term is used in an extraordinarily positive fashion: to describe the activity of the Messiah (4.25), the Paraclete (16.13, 14, 15), and the authoritative proclamation of the Johannine church (1 Jn 1.5). The Evangelist had at his disposal another way to describe reports of Jesus' activities to the Jews if he had desired to put things in a less positive light (cf. 11.46). Such philological evidence suggests that the man is intended to be viewed more positively.[72] Third, if, as John Chrysostom has observed, the man had wished to disparage Jesus, he could have emphasized the offense, which was the main interest

---

[67] Morris, *John*, p. 307 n. 37.

[68] Carson, *John*, p. 246.

[69] Brown, *John*, I, p. 209.

[70] Kysar, *John*, p. 78. He goes on to observe, 'Those who benefit from Jesus' wondrous works are not necessarily brought to faith.'

[71] Numerous interpreters have not felt comfortable with an overly suspicious interpretation of the man's action. Cf. Hengstenberg, *John*, I, p. 269; Westcott, *John*, p. 83; Bernard, *John*, I, p. 235; Beeckman, *Jean*, p. 116; Schnackenburg, *John*, II, p. 98; and Ellis, *John*, p. 89.

[72] Cf. the perceptive comments of Tilborg, *Imaginative Love*, pp. 218-19. Staley ('Stumbling in the Dark', pp. 63-64) also argues for a more positive view of the man.

of the Jews. But he does not mention Jesus' command to take up his mat, rather he says that it was Jesus who made him whole.[73]

The Man and the Jews (v. 16)

Just as testimony regarding Jesus brought belief in him in the first portion of the gospel (John 1-4), so in the next portion (John 5-12) word of Jesus' activity brings persecution (cf. 9.13-34 and 11.46).

Implications

There are several implications of the examination of Jn 5.1-16 for the primary purpose of this study. 1) It is clear that at least in this context the Johannine Jesus sees a connection between illness and sinful behavior. 2) In this case, the connection between sin and illness is so strong that future suffering is viewed as a real possibility if the sinful activity continues. 3) It seems that Jesus assumed the man would know the nature of the sinful action which he prohibits. 4) There appears to be little doubt that knowledge of the connection between sin and illness, in this case, is attributable to Jesus' discernment and/or supernatural knowledge. 5) Owing to the fact that Jesus does not hint at a satanic or demonic origin for this illness nor does he rule out the possibility of a future one, it is highly probable that he regarded this infirmity as coming from God. 6) While thus far in the Fourth Gospel not all suffering is directly tied to sinful behavior (i.e. 4.46-53), this story must have been a powerful reminder for the Johannine community of the seriousness of sin and the power of God.

John 6.1-8.59: An Overview

The next Johannine text of particular relevance for this enquiry is found several chapters later in John 9. In order to appreciate more fully the narrative context of the story about the healing of the blind man, a brief overview of several significant features of the story-line should prove helpful.

Following the healing of the infirm man in John 5 and its resulting discourse which emphasizes the works of God, is the miracu-

---

[73] John Chrysostom, *Homilies on John* 38.2. For the thoughts of the Fathers on this pericope cf. Thomas Aquinas, *Commentary on the Four Gospels Collected out of the Works of the Fathers: St. John* (Oxford, 1844) and M. Mees, 'Die Heilung des Kranken vom Bethesdateich aus Joh 15.1-18', *NTS* 32 (1986), pp. 596-608.

lous feeding of the 5,000. The initial portion of the Bread of Life discourse (6.29) defines the works of God, mentioned earlier in 5.17, as 'belief in the one who sent Jesus'. This mention sets up a later contrast with the evil works of the world (7.7). Two other not insignificant points in chapter 6 are Jesus' statement that 'the one who comes to me I will never cast out' (6.37) and the note that Jesus' Bread of Life discourse was given in a synogogue in Capernaum (6.59).

Chapter 7 reveals that the hostility to Jesus continues to be quite intense as the Jews continue in their attempt to kill him (7.1). Their searching for him at the Feast of Tabernacles in Jerusalem (7.11) resulted in people not speaking openly of him 'on account of the fear of the Jews' (7.13), the first mention of this theme in the Fourth Gospel (cf. 9.22; 19.38; 20.19; cf. also 12.42 and 19.8). But despite the opposition, Jesus shows up teaching in the temple (7.14). Later in the chapter, the Jews accuse Jesus of having a demon because he says someone is trying to kill him (7.20) – a threat of which the crowd knows (7.25). The attempt to arrest Jesus is put into motion (7.32) but to no avail (7.44). As the chapter draws to a close (7.45-52), there can be no doubt that the Jews have made their decision regarding Jesus.

In chapter 8, Jesus is once again found teaching in the temple (8.20) and confronts the Jews about their desire to kill him (7.37-40). This includes a discussion about parentage: the Jews' claim that they are Abraham's seed (8.33) and not born of fornication (8.41); Jesus charges that they do not do the works of Abraham (8.39) but are indeed children of the Devil, who was a murderer from the beginning (8.44); the Jews' counter charge is that Jesus is a Samaritan and has a demon (8.48, 52). Finally, Jesus appeals to his existence before Abraham and the fact that Abraham 'saw' Jesus' day and rejoiced (8.56-58). Such a claim prompts the Jews to pick up stones in order that they might cast them at Jesus (8.59).

John 9.1-41 – 'Who Sinned This Man or his Parents?'

Verse 1

With regard to the passage itself, although the story has many intriguing aspects which are deserving of study, for the purpose of this investigation only portions of this text are examined: the account of the miracle itself (vv. 1-7) and those verses that continue the theme of sin/sinner in one way or another (vv. 24, 25, 31, and 34).

> And going along he saw a man blind from birth. And his disciples asked him, 'Rabbi, who sinned, this man or his parents, that he was born blind?' Jesus answered, 'Neither this man nor his parents sinned, but (this man was born blind) in order that the works of God might be manifested. It is necessary for us to work the works of the one who sent me while it is day. Night comes when no one is able to work. As long as I am in the world, I am the light of the world.' Having said these things he spit on the ground and made mud out of the spittle, and placed the mud upon the eyes and said to him, 'Go, wash in the pool of Siloam' (which means Sent). Therefore, he went and washed, and he came seeing.... Therefore they (the Jews) called the man who was blind a second time and said to him, 'Give glory to God: We know that this man is a sinner.' Therefore that one answered, 'If he is a sinner I do not know; one thing I know, that I was blind, now I see'.... 'We know that God does not hear sinners, but he hears those who fear him and do his will'.... They answered and said to him, 'In sin you were wholly conceived, and you would teach us?' And they cast him out.

Clearly, the sense of drama is at its height as chapter 9 opens. The Jews' hostility and intent are obvious and the reader might be tempted to think that, despite the fact that no one can arrest him until his hour comes (8.20), Jesus might at this point withdraw from Jerusalem, as he had done earlier (4.1) and would later (11.55–12.1). Therefore, it is quite surprising to find as v. 1 opens that Jesus has simply left the temple, not Jerusalem. In fact, the text states that 'as he was going along, he saw a man blind from birth'. It would appear, then, that in terms of the narrative one envisions Jesus having just left the temple.[74] But given the fact that the Fourth Gospel does

---

[74] So Westcott, *John*, p. 143; Loisy, *Jean*, p. 307; T. Torrance, 'The Giving of Sight to the Man Born Blind', *EvQ* 9 (1937), p. 75; Hoskyns and Davey, *Fourth Gospel*, p. 405; Hunter, *John*, p. 95; and Tilborg (*Imaginative Love*, p. 220) who argues that while the events of Jn 9.1-12 occurred on the day Jesus departed from the temple, the events described in Jn 9.13 and following occur some time afterwards.

not adhere to anything like a strict chronology,[75] as well as the fact that there is a lack of continuity between the hostility of the Jews in chapter 8 and their less intense attitude in chapter 9, it is possible to take this verse as a fresh beginning with no true tie to the previous passage[76] and/or to assume that some amount of time had passed since 8.59.[77] It might, however, be better to recognize that there is no break in the narration while at the same time acknowledging the problems of continuity that exist.[78] At any rate, the reader would hardly have caught his or her breath from the previous exchange and would not likely have discerned that Jesus was far removed from the temple.

Significantly, v. 1 notes that the man was blind from birth. This description may signify that the man was a well-known figure, as the disciples' question in v. 2 and the neighbors' response in vv. 8-12 would seem to indicate.[79] It could also indicate that the man's situation was very grave,[80] since the healings of no other people blind from birth are described in the gospels (however, cf. Acts 3.2 and 14.8), and this would, consequently, emphasize the greatness of the cure. In point of fact, the text itself supports this very idea when the former blind man asks (v. 32), 'From the age it has not been heard that anyone opened the eyes of the blind'.[81] In addition to these other dimensions, the phrase could also function symbolically so that the one born blind physically would be a symbol of those who are born blind spiritually.[82]

Verse 2

In this verse the disciples reappear after a lengthy absence from the narrative, their last clear presence coming in 6.60-71 (although they

---

[75] Haenchen (*John*, II, p. 37) argues, 'One cannot draw conclusions regarding the sequence of individual events from the sequence given in the text'.

[76] Bernard, *John*, I, p. 323; MacGregor, *John*, p. 224; Brown, *John*, I, p. 371; Bultmann, *John*, p. 330; Lindars, *John*, p. 341; and Beasley-Murray, *John*, p. 148.

[77] Beeckman, *Jean*, p. 209; Guilding, *John*, p. 121; and Morris, *John*, p. 477.

[78] Lightfoot, *John*, p. 199; Sanders, *John*, p. 236; Schnackenburg, *John*, II, p. 240; and Michaels, *John*, p. 159.

[79] Bernard, *John*, II, p. 323 and Morris, *John*, p. 477.

[80] LaGrange, *Jean*, p. 258.

[81] For a similar assessment cf. J. Painter, 'John 9 and the Interpretation of the Fourth Gospel', *JSNT* 28 (1986), p. 35.

[82] Cf. Michaels, *John*, p. 160.

are perhaps mentioned in 7.3). Aside from the question they raise, it is a bit difficult to determine the purpose of their presence in this verse, for they will not be heard from again until 11.7.[83] Despite their brief mention, the question they raise not only introduces a major theme of this pericope, but also is central to the concerns of this investigation.

Their first word to Jesus, 'Ραββί', is one of the disciples' standard forms of address to Jesus (cf. 1.39, 50; 4.31; and 11.8)[84] and perhaps is used here to indicate their desire to learn from him. Their question, 'Who sinned, this man or his parents, in order that he was born blind?' reveals that as far as they are concerned there must be a connection between sin and this blind man's condition.[85] But what prompted such an inquiry in the first place? Was it the widespread nature of a belief in the relationship between sin and sickness[86] or may some other rationale be offered as the reason for their question?

It is a bit surprising that most interpreters do not explore the hints in the text which relate to this topic. For the reader, the most obvious reason why the disciples make a connection between sin and illness in this chapter is owing to the fact that Jesus himself affirmed such a connection in chapter 5. Although the disciples are not present in John 5, the readers, having heard Jesus speak on the subject, are likely to assume that the disciples will have taken their cue from their teacher.[87]

It is perhaps understandable why the disciples wonder whether the parents might be at fault. After all, the Old Testament contains some texts that could be understood to imply such a connection. For example, Exod. 20.5 states:

---

[83] LaGrange (*Jean*, p. 258) also expresses surprise at their appearance here.

[84] The title is also used by 'would-be disciples' to address Jesus (3.2 and 6.25) and as a form of address to John the Baptist (3.26).

[85] Cf. Westcott, *John*, p. 144; Loisy, *Jean*, 308; LaGrange, *Jean*, p. 258; Tenny, *John*, p. 155; Beeckman, *Jean*, 209; and Carson, *John*, p. 361.

[86] M. Gourgues' ('L'aveugle-né (Jn 9). Du miracle au signe: typologie des réactions à l'égard du Fils de l'homme', *NRT* 104 [1982], p. 386) words are representative of this opinion, 'Cette question reflècte la croyance ancienne, bien attestée dans l'Ancien Testament, selon laquelle la maladie est une conséquence du péche'.

[87] Beeckman (*Jean*, 209) is one of the few scholars to make this connection.

You shall not bow down to them (idols) or worship them; for I, the Lord your God, am a jealous God, punishing the children for the sin of the fathers to the third and fourth generation of those who hate me.

A near identical statement is found later in Exodus (34.7) as well as in Numbers (14.18). Psalm 79.8 contains a prayer in which the Psalmist asks God not to hold the sin of the fathers against the children, implying that he normally does. But in Psalm 109.14, the Psalmist prays that God *would* hold his enemy accountable for the sins of his father and mother. According to Isa. 65.14, God himself seems to make a connection between the sins of the fathers and their children's sins. That the disciples in the Fourth Gospel would think of such a possibility would surely not surprise many first-century Christian readers.[88]

If the suggestion that the parents might be to blame is rather easy to understand, the other option which the disciples suggest is much more difficult to comprehend. How exactly, could the disciples have conceived of a man having sinned before his birth? What could they possibly mean by such a question? As one might expect, numerous suggestions have been made as to what the disciples were thinking.

It is possible that the disciples' question reveals a belief on their part in the pre-existence of the soul.[89] Evidence for such a view comes from Wis. 8.19-20, which reads, 'I had received a good soul as my lot, or rather, being good, I had entered an undefiled body'. A similar view is found in the writings of Philo. In one discussion on the nature of the soul (*On Dreams*, 1.138) Philo observes:

Of these souls some, such as have earthward tendencies and material tastes, descend to be fast bound in mortal bodies, while

[88] A. Jaubert (*Approches de l'Evangile de Jean* [Paris: Editions du Seuil, 1976], p. 90) relying on Strack-Billerbeck, notes, 'la plupart (rabbins) pensaient qu'il (péche) avait hérité de la faute de ses parents'.

[89] For this view cf. Loisy, *Jean*, 308; MacGregor, *John*, p. 225; LaGrange, *Jean*, p. 258; and apparently Westcott, *John*, p. 144. Lightfoot (*John*, p. 202) and Hunter, (*John*, p. 95) also mention this as a possibility.

others ascend, being selected for return according to the numbers and periods determined by nature.[90]

Additional support is sometimes claimed from Josephus' (*Jewish Wars* 2.154-55) description of the Essenes' view of the soul.

> For it is a fixed belief of theirs that the body is corruptible and its constituent matter impermanent, but that the soul is immortal and imperishable. Emanating from the finest ether, these souls become entangled, as it were, in the prison-house of the body, to which they are dragged down by some sort of natural spell; but when once they are released from the bonds of the flesh, then, as though liberated from a long servitude, they rejoice and are borne aloft.[91]

However, this view of the soul has not been confirmed by the scrolls from Qumran, which may raise some questions regarding the accuracy of Josephus' description.

Another possible explanation regarding the sin of the man born blind is the idea that somehow he was guilty of a pre-natal sin.[92] In addition to various rabbinic discussions about possible sinful inclinations of a fetus in the womb, it was apparently thought that if a pregnant woman were to commit idolatry, the child would be involved in the act of bending in worship.[93] The primary problem with this suggestion, widespread though it be in the secondary literature, is that all the rabbinic evidence appealed to is a good bit later than the Fourth Gospel. A still more radical explanation concerning the man's sin is that the disciples are making reference to a belief in reincarnation.[94] The only evidence offered in support of

---

[90] Cited according to the translation of F.H. Colson and G.H. Whitaker, *Philo*, V (London: Heinemann, 1988), p. 371. Cf. also Philo's discussion in *On the Giants*, 7.31.

[91] Cited according to the translation of H.S.J. Thackeray, *Josephus* II (Cambridge, MA: Harvard University Press, 1939), pp. 381-83.

[92] For this view cf. Bernard, *John*, II, p. 325; Brown, *John*, II, p. 371; Boismard, *Jean*, 255; Bruce, *John*, p. 208; Michaels, *John*, p. 163; Beasley-Murray, *John*, p. 155; and Carson, *John*, p. 362. Lightfoot (*John*, p. 202) and Hunter, (*John*, p. 95) also mention this as a possibility.

[93] Cf. Lindars, *John*, p. 342.

[94] S. Band, 'Re-incarnation (Matthew xi. 14 and John ix. 2)', *ExpT* 25 (1913-14), p. 474.

this view is its antiquity generally and its alleged prominence in the far east.

While such explanations have left some interpreters shaking their heads,[95] there is another option which can claim the support of both Old Testament and first-century evidence, that, strangely has received very little consideration. John Bligh has suggested that perhaps the disciples had in mind sin which God knew the person would commit in his life after birth.[96] In other words, the answer to this dilemma is God's foreknowledge. Such an idea was not unknown in ancient Judaism. According to Jer. 1.5 God said:

> Before I formed you in the womb I knew/chose you, before you were born I set you apart; I appointed you as a prophet to the nations.

In a similar vein Ps. 139.15-16 reads:

> My frame was not hidden from you when I was made in the secret place. When I was woven together in the depths of the earth, your eyes saw my unformed body. All the days ordained for me were written in your book before one of them came to be.

To this evidence might be added the strongly predestinarian outlook of the Qumran community. One citation from the Community Document (1QS 3.13-14) is given here:

> The Master shall instruct all the sons of light and shall teach them the nature of all the children of men according to the kind of spirit which they possess, the signs identifying their works during their lifetime, their visitation for chastisement, and the time of their reward.
>
> From the God of Knowledge comes all that is and shall be. Before ever they existed He established their whole design, and when, as ordained for them, they come into being, it is in accord with his glorious design that they accomplish their task without

---

[95] Cf. esp. the comments of Morris, *John*, p. 478; Bultmann, *John*, p. 331; and Schnackenburg, *John*, II, pp. 240-41.

[96] Cf. J. Bligh, 'The Man Born Blind', *HeyJ* 7 (1966), p. 131.

change. The laws of all things are in his hand and He provides them with all their needs.[97]

Although other possibilities cannot be ruled out completely, this interpretation may have more to commend it than the others and would certainly prepare the way for Jesus' response in the next verse.

However one comes out on these many interpretive challenges, it is clear that the disciples assume a connection between sin and the man's blind condition and in all likelihood, the reader understands this to be Jesus' position, based on 5.14.

Verse 3

Jesus, who is named here for the first time in this pericope, no doubt surprises both the disciples and the readers with his answer. Although he had earlier spoken of a connection between sin and illness in 5.14, here he denies that any such link exists. In other words, Jesus' earlier statement, which might have mistakenly been taken to imply that there was always (or usually) a causal relationship between sin and illness, is qualified by his answer here in 9.3. To put it the other way around, in this verse he does not deny that there is ever a relationship between the two, but as for this particular blind man, sin is not the cause.[98] Clearly, his words are not meant to imply that neither the man nor his parents had ever sinned, nor should this verse be taken as a statement regarding original sin.[99] Jesus simply notes that in this case neither of the alternatives which the disciples present are acceptable.[100]

Rather than attributing the man's condition to sin, Jesus appears to attribute it to God. The first hint that this is the case is the use of the strong adversative ἀλλ᾽,[101] which forcefully sets the first part of the sentence, the disciples' question, off against the latter part, Jesus' answer. This conclusion is also supported by the ἵνα clause,

---

[97] Cited according to the translation of G. Vermes, *The Dead Sea Scrolls in English* (London: Penguin, 1987), p. 65

[98] For this position cf. Dods, *John*, p. 306; Loisy, *John*, p. 308; Bligh, 'Man Born Blind', p. 131; Bultmann, *John*, p. 331; Lindars, *John*, p. 342; Haenchen, *John*, II, p. 37; and Carson, *John*, p. 362.

[99] As Beeckman (*Jean*, p. 210) correctly observes.

[100] Bernard, *John*, II, p. 325.

[101] Morris, *John*, p. 478.

which follows the ἀλλ᾽, indicating purpose. Simply put, the purpose of the man's being born blind was in order that the works of God might be manifest.

However, some scholars find such a view of God too difficult to reconcile with his goodness[102] and seek to soften the impact of the statement in some manner. These attempts include the suggestions that 1) the ἵνα clause be taken as showing result rather than purpose[103] and 2) the sentence be repunctuated to read 'Neither this man nor his parents sinned. But in order that the works of God might be manifested, it is necessary for us to work the works of God'.[104] F.F. Bruce, who takes the construction to be a purpose clause, thinks there is another way around the dilemma. He interprets the verse to mean:

> This does not mean that God deliberately caused the child to be born blind in order that, after many years, his glory should be displayed in the removal of the blindness; to think so would again be an aspersion on the character of God. It does mean that God overruled the disaster of the child's blindness so that, when the child grew to manhood, he might, by recovering his sight, see the glory of God in the face of Christ, and others, seeing this work of God, might turn to the true Light of the World.[105]

Yet, despite these arguments to the contrary it is difficult not to take this verse to mean exactly what it says. This man was born blind in order that the works of God might be done in him.[106] As noted in 6.29, the work of God is belief in the one who sent Jesus, therefore, that which is about to happen to the blind man is done to lead the blind man (and others?) to faith in the Father, the one who sent Jesus.

---

[102] Tenny (*John*, p. 154) calls it repugnant.

[103] Tenny, *John*, p. 154.

[104] This suggestion by W.H. Spencer ('John ix. 3', *ExpT* 55 [1943-44], p. 110) is strongly criticized by Tenny (*John*, p. 154-55).

[105] Bruce, *John*, p. 209.

[106] Barrett (*John*, p. 356) notes, 'In any case John would not suppose that the man's birth and blindness were outside the control and purpose of God'. Others who assign the man's condition to the providence of God include: Bernard, *John*, II, p. 325; Beeckman, *Jean*, p. 210; Tasker, *John*, p. 123; Kysar, *John*, p. 149; and Carson, *John*, p. 362.

Verses 4-5

Verse 4 continues the thought of v. 3 by bringing further definition to the theme of the works of God by use of other familiar themes in the Fourth Gospel. Emphasis is placed not only upon the necessity (δεῖ) of such work, but also upon those who are to do it. There is a textual corruption at this point in the Greek text with some manuscripts reading, 'It is necessary for me (ἐμὲ) to work ...', and others reading, 'It is necessary for us (ἡμᾶς) to work ...' Although the manuscript evidence is split, the vast majority of scholars opt for the plural 'us'. But what does this statement mean, 'It is necessary for us to work the works of the one who sent me'? For the reader such a statement would mean that the disciples are to be involved in the work of Jesus (cf. 4.31-38),[107] but on another level would be understood to include the reader and/or the Johannine community.[108]

The works are identified as belonging to 'the one who sent me', an idea that has appeared frequently throughout the Fourth Gospel to this point (4.34; 5.23, 24, 30, 37; 6.38-40, 44; 7.16, 18, 28, 33; 8.16, 18, 26, 29) and will continue to be a prominent theme (12.44, 45, 49; 13.16, 20; 14.24, 26; 15.21; 16.5, 7; cf. also 20.21). Its appearance here underscores the fact that what follows is at the behest of the one who sent Jesus and in accordance with the Father's will.

To highlight the urgency of his mission,[109] Jesus challenges the disciples to work while it is still day. The context for such imagery is clearly based in a civilization where one's work is dependent upon the sun's illumination.[110] When darkness comes work ceases, owing to the lack of light. The primary point is captured quite well by Michaels who notes:

---

[107] LaGrange, *Jean*, p. 259; Beeckman, *Jean*, p. 210; Hoskyns and Davey, *The Fourth Gospel*, p. 406; Lightfoot, *John*, p. 202; Brown, *John*, I, p. 372; Hunter, *John*, p. 95; Schnackenburg, *John*, II, p. 241; Kysar, *John*, p. 149; Heanchen, *John*, II, p. 38; and Carson, *John*, p. 362.

[108] J.L. Martyn, *History and Theology in the Fourth Gospel* (New York: Harper & Row, 1968), p. 8-10; Nicol, *Semeia*, p. 119; Boismard, *Jean*, p. 258; Barrett, *John*, p. 357; and Kysar, *John*, p. 149.

[109] Ellis, *John*, p. 161.

[110] LaGrange, *Jean*, p. 260.

Like a laborer determined to finish his work before nightfall, Jesus summons his disciples to join him in taking full advantage of the remaining daylight hours.[111]

The rest of v. 4 contains the remainder of this somewhat proverbial saying. Although many interpreters take the mention of night as a reference to the end of Jesus' public ministry,[112] or to his death and/or departure,[113] this brief parable about the ministry of Jesus should not be pressed to mean that when Jesus has gone there is no more light. Again, Michaels' observations are most helpful:

> It should be remembered that the references to day and night constitute a brief parable about the ministry of Jesus. They do not look beyond it. Elsewhere the Gospel writer can look back on Jesus' ministry with the comment that still 'the light shines in the darkness, and the darkness has not overcome it' ... From the writer's viewpoint, the time since Jesus' departure from the world is a time for doing 'greater things' than Jesus did (14.12), not a time of darkness in which 'no one can work.' The focus in chapter 9 is on Jesus' impending Passion. The point of verses 4-5 is not that the work of God stops when Jesus' life on earth ends but that Jesus has a certain task assigned to him and a limited time in which to complete it.[114]

Verse 5, which provides a bit of commentary on this proverb, reemphasizes the urgency of Jesus' mission by use of the now familiar 'I am (the) Light of the world'. From the outset the reader has known that Jesus is the Light (cf. 1.4-5, 7-9; 3.19-21; 8.12). Interestingly, this theme is confined to the Book of Signs (cf. 11.9-10; 12.35-36, 46).

Of course, talk about working the works of God and being the Light of the world would not have been lost on this blind man, who is, no doubt, curious that he is described by Jesus to have been born

---

[111] Michaels, *John*, p. 160.

[112] Cf. Bernard, *John*, II, p. 327 and Beeckman, *Jean*, p. 210.

[113] Loisy, *Jean*, p. 307; MacGregor, *John*, p. 226; Lindars, *John*, p. 343; Nicol, *Semeia*, p. 119; Barrett, *John*, p. 357; Bruce, *John*, p. 209; and Carson (*John*, p. 363) who argues that night has reference to the first period after Jesus was taken away.

[114] Michaels, *John*, pp. 160-61. Cf. also Schnackenburg, *John*, II, p. 242.

blind so that the works of God might be manifest in him and to have been desirous to see the Light.

Verse 6

The sense of narrative drama is heightened when the reader learns that Jesus has finished speaking (ταῦτα εἰπών) and begins to learn of his actions. However, nothing to this point in the gospel will have prepared the reader for what Jesus now does. First, he spits upon the ground. Although spittle may have been considered to have healing properties in antiquity,[115] the evidence seems to suggest that the emphasis was more upon the person from whom the spittle came than the spittle itself.[116] In this case, it appears that the emphasis is upon the spittle as a symbol of healing power.[117] Next, he made mud and pasted it upon the man's eyes, prompting more than one commentator to see here a reference to creation (Gen. 2.7); Jesus created eyes in this blind man.[118]

Verse 7

Now for the first time, the blind man is addressed directly. He receives two commands from Jesus: Go and Wash.[119] While it is possible that there is a subtle reference to baptism in the command to wash,[120] owing in part to the close tie developed later in the discourse between physical and spiritual blindness, such an interpretation is not likely[121] especially in the light of the use of the term νίπτω, which is used for partial washings, as opposed to λούω, a

---

[115] Cf. Bernard, *John*, II, p. 327.

[116] Cf. Tacitus, *Histories*, 4.81 who tells of a blind man who, at the direction of the god Serapis, threw himself before Emperor Vespasian, begging him to wet his cheeks and eyes with his spittle. Tacitus says that the man was subsequently healed. For a similar assessment cf. Wilkinson, 'Healing', p. 450.

[117] Hengstenberg, *John*, I, p. 484 and Torrence, 'Giving Sight', p. 75.

[118] Bernard, *John*, II, p. 328; Hoskyns and Davey, *Fourth Gospel*, p. 407; Sanders, *John*, p. 239; Lindars, *John*, p. 343; Kysar, *John*, p. 150; and, though tentatively, Michaels, *John*, p. 162.

[119] Cf. T.L. Brodie ('Jesus as the New Elisha: Cracking the Code', *ExpT* 93 [1981-82], p. 40) who sees a number of parallels between these instructions and those given to Naaman in 2 Kgs 5.10-14.

[120] Cf. Loisy, *Jean*, p. 310; Sanders, *John*, p. 239; Lindars, *John*, p. 344; and B. Grigsby, 'Washing in the Pool of Siloam – A Thematic Anticipation of the Johannine Cross', *NovT* 27 (1985), pp. 227-35.

[121] Cf, esp. Kysar, *John*, p. 150; Grayston, *John*, p. 81; and Carson, *John*, p. 366.

term which designates a complete bath.[122] Even the name of the pool in which the man is to wash is not without significance for the story, in that the Evangelist not only gives the name of the pool, Siloam, but provides the word's translation, 'which means Sent'. In all likelihood the name originated from the fact that the water was sent via subterranean channels.[123] Although other options are sometimes suggested concerning the symbolism of the name,[124] considering the numerous references to Jesus being sent by the Father, it is next to impossible not to see in the pool's name a reference to Jesus and his mission.[125]

Without a question, the man does exactly what Jesus told him to do.[126] His obedience is not dissimilar to that of the infirm man in chapter 5 and also conforms to the instructions of the mother of Jesus in 2.5. The end result is that the man born blind now sees. So ends this part of the pericope.

In the ensuing verses, several groups of characters enter the picture. First, the man dialogues with his neighbors who can hardly believe such a thing has happened (vv. 8-12). Next, the Jews interrogate the man (vv. 13-17) and his parents (vv. 18-23), who are reluctant to speak because they were afraid of the Jews who had already decided to throw out of the synagogue anyone who confessed Christ. The primary concern seems to be that these actions took place on the Sabbath.

---

[122] For a more exhaustive treatment of the Johannine usage of these two terms cf. Thomas, *Footwashing in John 13 and the Johannine Community*, pp. 97-104.

[123] Westcott, *John*, p. 145 and Bernard, *John*, II, p. 329.

[124] Cf. for example the comments of Bernard (*John*, II, p. 329) who says that to seek symbolism here is perverse, Michaels (*John*, p. 164) who argues that the name has reference to the Spirit who will be sent, and Grayston (*John*, p. 81) who identifies the blindness as being sent away!

[125] For this identification cf. Hengstenberg, *John*, II, pp. 487; Dods, *John*, p. 310; MacGregor, *John*, p. 207; Dodd, *Interpretation*, p. 357; Hoskyns and Davey, *Fourth Gospel*, p. 408; Lightfoot, *John*, p. 203; Bligh, 'Man Born Blind', p. 132; Hunter, *John*, p. 96; Sanders, *John*, p. 239; Morris, *John*, p. 481; Bultmann, *John*, p. 333; Lindars, *John*, p. 344; Nicol, *Semeia*, p. 35; Barrett, *John*, p. 359; Schnackenburg, *John*, II, p. 243; Bruce, *John*, p. 210; Ellis, *John*, p. 162; Beasley-Murray, *John*, p. 156; J.L. Resseguie, 'John 9: A Literary-Critical Analysis', in *Literary Interpretations of Biblical Narratives*, II (ed. K.R.R. Gros Louis; Nashville: Abingdon, 1982), p. 297; Haenchen, *John*, II, p. 38; and Carson, *John*, p. 365.

[126] Loisy (*Jean*, p. 310), Bernard (*John*, II, p. 329), and Bruce (*John*, p. 210) all call attention to the man's obedience.

Verses 24-25

Not satisfied with their interrogation of the man's parents and suspicious that the man is not telling the truth, the Jews seek to intimidate him into a confession. John conveys this by the Jews' demand that the man take an oath on the order of Josh. 7.19 ('Give glory to God!'), and accordingly, admit that he has taken the part of a sinner. Additionally, their role as the authoritative teachers of the Law is conveyed by the emphatic use of the personal pronoun ἡμεῖς with the verb οἴδαμεν,[127] which pits their role and conclusion ('This man is a sinner') over against the testimony of the formerly blind man. But the man will not be intimidated,[128] refusing to be drawn into a debate as to whether or not Jesus was a sinner and at the same time continuing to bear witness on Jesus' behalf. The facts speak for themselves as far as the man is concerned, 'I was blind, now I see!' This same line of response is seen again in v. 30, the reality of the healing necessitates a different conclusion than that of the Jews.[129] This reasoning is developed in vv. 31-33.

Verse 34

Completely frustrated by this point, the Jews viciously reproach the man.[130] They angrily conclude that the man was wholly conceived in sin. Their conclusion reveals two things. First, they inadvertently admit that the man had been born blind and that a miracle had taken place. Second, they align themselves with a position regarding the relationship of sin and the man's blind condition[131] that has already been shown to be invalid by Jesus in v. 3.[132]

---

[127] Westcott, *John*, p. 148; Loisy, *Jean*, p. 314; Beeckman, *Jean*, p. 218; Lindars, *John*, p. 362; Barrett, *John*, p. 362; Schnackenburg, *John*, II, p. 251; and Kysar, *John*, p. 152.

[128] Westcott, *John*, p. 148; Loisy, *Jean*, p. 314; and Haenchen, *John*, II, p. 40.

[129] Barrett (*John*, p. 362) concludes, 'It is beyond question that he has received sight at the hands of Jesus. The only possible conclusion that could be drawn from the two given facts … was that the Law itself was now superseded'.

[130] Bernard (*John*, II, p. 357) notes, 'Every word is scornfully emphatic'.

[131] Hengstenberg, *John*, II, p. 496; Westcott, *John*, p. 149; Loisy, *Jean*, p. 316; Bernard, *John*, II, p. 335; MacGregor, *John*, p. 230; Beeckman, *Jean*, p. 221; Hoskyns and Davey, *The Fourth Gospel*, p. 413; Brown, *John*, II, p. 375; Morris, *John*, p. 493; Bultmann, *John*, p. 337; Lindars, *John*, p. 349; Schnackenburg, *John*, II, p. 252; Bruce, *John*, p. 219; Michaels, *John*, p. 170; Kysar, *John*, p. 155; and Carson, *John*, p. 375.

[132] Cf. Tilborg, *Imaginative Love*, p. 228.

Later, Jesus, who will never cast out anyone who comes to him, goes to the one who had been cast out of the synagogue. The man comes to believe in Jesus as the Son of Man and as a result sees Jesus, which reminds the reader that earlier in the narrative it was said that Abraham saw Jesus' day. As for the Jews, it turns out that they are the ones with the sin problem (v. 41), not the blind man.

Implications
Several implications for the major purpose of this enquiry emerge from this study of John 9. 1) While not denying that there is ever a connection between illness and sin, in this text the Johannine Jesus makes very clear that there is not always a causal relationship between the two. Therefore, the statement in 5.14 is not a universal principle for the Johannine community. 2) Rather than viewing physical infirmities as 'neutral', this text indicates that some physical infirmities may be understood to exist in order that the works of God might be manifest in those who are suffering. 3) It is very difficult to avoid the conclusion that in this case, God is responsible for the man's blindness. 4) This passage suggests that when one has been healed so that the works of God might be manifest, testimony is an essential part of that person's response. 5) The possibility that some illnesses could be in accord with the divine will would no doubt have caused those in the Johannine community to ponder this possibility when faced with illness.

3 John 2 – 'That You Prosper and Be in Good Health'

A final Johannine text of relevance for this enquiry is found outside the Fourth Gospel in the little letter known as 3 John. It merits inclusion in this study owing to the possible attitude revealed toward illness in the believer's life generally and the place of this passage in charismatic theology at the popular level.[133]

Following closely the opening of the letter in which the writer reveals something of his identity and that of his addressee, Gaius, the Elder in v. 2 continues his greeting with a wish for his reader's health.

---

[133] Oral Roberts credits this passage with substantially changing his views on suffering in the life of the believer. Cf. D. Harrell, *Oral Roberts: An American Life* (San Francisco: Harper & Row, 1987), pp. 65-66.

Beloved, in all things I desire that you prosper and are in good health, just as your life prospers.

Taken out of its first-century context and in isolation from the rest of the Johannine literature, this verse could appear to advocate a view of the Christian life that had little or no place for any deficiency in health or material means. But, is such an understanding of this text its most natural meaning, or has this reading neglected data crucial to its proper interpretation? Before offering an interpretation of this interesting verse more attention must be given to the nature and purpose of the epistle in which it occurs.

The letter known as 3 John offers a most intriguing glimpse into the Johannine community. It reveals a complex of congregations tied together by a series of messengers/emissaries. This letter also reveals a rift in the community particularly between the Elder and Diotrephes.

This letter has the distinction of being the shortest book in the New Testament, consisting of 219 words in the Greek text. As such, 3 John would have rather easily fit on a single sheet of papyrus, the normal length of Graeco-Roman letters of the day.[134] 3 John not only resembles a number of secular Graeco-Roman letters in its brevity, but it also shares a number of structural and literary features. The broad outline of such letters may be delineated as follows:

I. An A (author) to B (recipient) Greeting
II. A Wish for Health
III. Expressions of Thanks for the Receipt of Good News
IV. Body (Opening) – Occasion
V. Body (Closing) – Recapitulation and Promise of Visit
VI. Closing Formula – Greetings of Mutual Friends.[135]

As this outline indicates, a wish for the reader's health ordinarily follows the greeting. In fact, the health wish appears so regularly '... in Latin letters that it was customarily expressed by the use of ini-

---

[134] M. Hengel (*The Johannine Question* [Philadelphia: Trinity Press International, 1989], p. 29) suggests that the length of 2 and 3 John would be equivalent to the modern day postcard.

[135] J. Lieu, *The Second and Third Epistles of John* (Edinburgh: T. & T. Clark, 1986), pp. 38-39. Cf. also the discussion in R.E. Brown, *The Epistles of John* (Garden City, NY: Doubleday, 1982), pp. 788-95.

tials, S V B E E V (si uales, beve esti ego ualeo, 'if you are well, that is good; I am well')'.[136] Since 3 John 2 is, properly speaking, a health wish, it might be beneficial to compare its use here with the function and purpose of the health wish in letters of the day. Two roughly contemporary examples are cited here. The first is a letter from one brother to another:

> Irenaeus to Apollinarius his dearest brother many greetings. I pray continually for your health, and I myself am well. I wish you to know that I reached land on the sixth of the month Epeiph and we unloaded our cargo on the eighteenth of the same month. I went up to Rome, on the twenty-fifth of the same month and the place welcomed us as the god willed, and we are daily expecting our discharge, it so being that up till to-day nobody in the corn fleet has been released. Many salutations to your wife and to Serenus and to all who love you, each by name. Goodbye. Mesore 9. [Addressed] To Apollinarius from his brother Irenaeus.[137]

Another example comes from an Egyptian soldier in the Roman Navy to his father:

> Apion to Epimachus his father and lord many greetings. Before all things I pray that thou art in health, and that thou dost prosper and fare well continually together with my sister and her daughter and my brother. I thank the lord Serapis that, when I was in peril in the sea, he saved me immediately. When I came to Miseni I received as viaticum (journey-money) from the Caesar three pieces of gold. And it is well with me. I beseech thee therefore, my lord father, write unto me a little letter, firstly of thy health, secondly of that of my brother and sister, thirdly that I may do obeisance to thy hand because thou hast taught me well and I therefore hope to advance quickly, if the gods will. Salute Capito much and my brother and sister and Serenilla and my friends. I sent [*or* 'am sending'] thee by Euctemon a little picture of me. Moreover my name is Antonis Maximus. Fare thee well, I pray. Centura Athenonica. There saluteth thee Serenus the son

---

[136] F.F. Bruce, *The Epistles of John* ((London: Pickering & Inglis, 1970), p. 147.

[137] Cited according to the translation found in C.K. Barrett, *The New Testament Background: Selected Documents* (New York: Harper & Row, 1987), p. 30.

of Agathus Daemon, and ... the son of ... and Turbo the son
of Gallonius and D[...]sen [...] ... [138]

While the general similarities between these two letters and 3 John
are difficult to miss, the similarity of most significance for this particular study is the regularity, role, and function of the health wish.
Simply put, the wish for health seems to have been a literary device
by which the author assured the reader of his or her genuine concern for the welfare of the reader.

In the light of its similarities to other ancient letters, part of the
interpretive task in approaching 3 John 2 is to determine whether
the verse is intended to function simply as a health wish or if it has
been modified in order to convey a deeper, theological meaning.

Verse 2

John begins v. 2 by referring to Gaius a second time as Beloved (cf.
v. 1), using this term at the beginning of his expression of the
health wish for Gaius, as he continues his attempt to identify with
his reader. Such a term of endearment would perhaps make this
health wish sound less formalistic, but it is difficult to believe that
this addition alone would cause Gaius to interpret the health wish in
any other fashion than most readers (both secular and Christian)
would have, as a polite good wish for health and prosperity.[139]

Following this term of endearment, the Elder describes his desire for Gaius. In doing this he uses the term εὔχομαι, which
ranges in meaning from wish to pray. Although it is possible to take
the term as prayer here,[140] normally one would expect to find the
verb followed by some reference to God by name if the specific
idea of prayer were intended.[141] Given this omission and the frequency of εὔχομαι language in other health wishes in antiquity, it is
probably nearer the mark to understand εὔχομαι here as having
reference to the Elder's (genuine) desire for Gaius,[142] while leaving

---

[138] Cited according to the translation in Deissmann, *Light from the Ancient East*, p. 180.
[139] Brown, *The Epistles of John*, p. 703.
[140] As does M.M. Thompson, *1-3 John* (Downers Grove; IVP, 1992), p. 159.
[141] Brown, *The Epistles of John*, p. 703.
[142] For this conclusion cf. J.E. Huther, *Handbuch über die drei Briefe des Apostel Johannes* (Göttingen: Vandenhoeck und Ruprechte, 1880), p. 303; R. Bultmann,

open the possibility that the term might convey a meaning some-
where between the two.[143] It should be clear, however, that to understand the Elder's remark to mean fervent prayer is to outdistance
the evidence.

The Elder's desire is expressed by use of two verbs in the infinitive mood. The first is εὐδοῦσθαι, which literally means to have a
good journey. In the New Testament it never has this meaning but
is only used in a figurative sense.[144] While the idea is broad enough
to cover a wide variety of issues it certainly includes things like material or temporal success and prosperity.[145] The other verb used is
ὑγιαίνειν, which has to do with physical wholeness. Although the
use of this term is sometimes taken to mean that Gaius was not in
the best of health,[146] in the light of the frequent use of this verb in
health wishes of the day such an interpretation seems to be ill-
founded.[147] The extent of the Elder's good wishes for Gaius is
made clear by the fact that the phrase 'in all things' is placed in an
emphatic position in the sentence following Ἀγαπητέ.[148] These

---

The Johannine Epistles (ed. R.W. Funk; trans. R.P. O'Hara, L.C. McGaughty, and
R.W. Funk; Philadelphia: Fortress, 1973), p. 97 n. 1; I.H. Marshall, *The Epistles of
John* (Grand Rapids: Eerdmans, 1978), p. 82; Brown, *Epistles*, p. 703; and Thomas,
'εὐχή', *The Complete Bible Library: The New Testament Greek-English Dictionary –
Delta-Episilon*, pp. 658-59.

[143] Marshall, *Epistles of John*, p. 82 and S. Smalley, *1, 2, 3 John* (Waco: Word,
1984), p. 345.

[144] S. Peterson, 'εὐοδόω', *EDNT*, II, p.84.

[145] Cf. J. Chaine, *Les Épîtres Catholiques* (Paris: Gabalda, 1939), p. 252 and C.H.
Dodd, *The Johannine Epistles* (London: Hodder & Stoughton, 1946), p. 158.

[146] Westcott, *Epistles of John*, p. 236; Marshall, *Epistles of John*, p. 83; and Smalley, *1, 2, 3, John*, p. 346.

[147] For this conclusion cf. J.H.A. Ebrard, *The Epistles of St John* (Edinburgh: T.
& T. Clark, 1860), p. 398; Huther, *Handbuch*, p. 303; D.F. Büchsel, *Die Johannesbriefe*
(Leipzig: Deichert, 1933), p. 98; Chaine, *Les Épîtres Catholiques*, p. 252; A. Nicole,
La marche dans l'obeissance et dans l'amour: commentaire sur les trois epîtres de Jean (Vevey:
Editions des Groupes Missionaires, 1961), p. 289; D.E. Hiebert, 'An Exposition
of 3 John 1-4', *BibSac* 144 (1987), p. 62; Brown, *Epistles of John*, p. 739; and
Schnackenburg, *The Johannine Epistles* (trans. R. and I. Fuller; London: Burns &
Oates, 1992), p. 292.

[148] D.E. Hiebert, 'An Exposition of 3 John 1-4', p. 61; D. Watson, 'A Rhetorical Analysis of 3 John: A Study in Epistolary Rhetoric', *CBQ* 51 (1989), p. 488;
and S. Smalley, *1, 2, 3, John*, p. 345.

words indicate that the Elder's desire for Gaius' health and prosperity extend to every area of his life.[149]

It is possible to take the second phrase in the verse, 'just as your soul prospers', as a reference to spiritual prosperity, balancing the reference to physical prosperity in v. 2a.[150] However, this interpretation is not likely in the light of John's use of ψυχή elsewhere. The majority of occurrences of ψυχή in Johannine literature denotes life which one may lay down, not simply the spiritual side of the human being. On this view, the Elder prays for prosperity and health in the light of Gaius' life generally. This understanding of ψυχή does not exclude what might be called Gaius' spiritual welfare, but certainly does not restrict such well being to his soul. The prayer, then, is not for some docetic spirituality but the sum total of Gaius' life,[151] which no doubt is positively assessed because he is 'walking in the truth'.[152]

Implications

What are the major implications of this study of 3 Jn 2 for an understanding of the Devil, disease, and deliverance in Johannine thought? 1) Owing to the similarities between 3 Jn 2 and the standard wish for health that appears in many secular letters of the day, it is very unlikely that Gaius would have read this verse to be more than a polite (and very genuine) wish for health. Therefore, it would

---

[149] The phrase itself is rare, with πρὸ παντος or πρὸ παντων (meaning 'above all') normally occurring in such wishes. Cf. Lieu, *Second and Third John*, p. 44.

[150] Ebard, *Epistles of John*, p. 398; Huther, *Handbuch*, p. 303; Westcott, *Epistles of John*, p. 236; Loisy, *Jean*, p. 587; Chaine, *Les Épîtres Catholiques*, p. 252; Stott, *Epistles of John*, pp. 218-19; E. Schweizer, 'ψυχή', *TDNT*, IX, pp. 651-52; J.B. Pohill, 'An Analysis of II and III John', *RevExp* 67 (1970), p. 467; Bruce, *Epistles of John*, p. 147; Marshall, *Epistles of John*, p. 83; Hiebert, 'An Exposition of 3 John 1-4', p. 62; G. Harder, 'Soul', *DNTT*, III, p. 684; K. Grayston, *The Johannine Epistles* (Grand Rapids: Eerdmans, 1984), p. 159; Watson, 'A Rhetorical Analysis', p. 488; R. Kysar, *I, II, III John* (Minneapolis: Augsburg, 1986), p. 139; and D. Jackman, *The Message of John's Letters* (Leicester: IVP, 1988), p. 192.

[151] Bultmann, *The Johannine Epistles*, p. 97; J.L. Houlden, *A Commentary on the Johannine Epistles* (London: A. & C. Black, 1973), p. 151; K. Wengst, *Der erste, zweite und dritte Brief des Johannes* (Würzburg: Gütersloher, 1978), p. 246; Brown, *Epistles of John*, p. 704; G. Strecker, *Die Johannesbriefe* (Göttingen: Vandenhoeck & Ruprecht, 1989), p. 361; D.M. Smith, *First, Second, Third John* (Louisville, John Know Press, 1991), p. 151; W. Loader, *The Johannine Epistles* (London: Epworth, 1992), p. 102; Schnackenburg, *The Johannine Epistles*, p. 292; and Thompson, *1-3 John*, p. 139.

[152] P. Bonnard, *Les Épîtres johanniques* (Genève: Labor et Fides, 1983), p. 130.

be unwise to take this verse as encapsulating a Johannine theology of health and prosperity despite the genuineness of the Elder's concern.[153] 2) If, despite its similarities to other health wish formulas, one insists that there are more to the words of the Elder in this case, from the text of 3 John one would have to conclude that the Elder felt a freedom to offer such a 'prayer' for Gaius precisely because he had been such a good steward of his resources in supporting the work of the Johannine emissaries. But even this modest statement may go beyond the Elder's intent.

Conclusions and Implications

What may be concluded about the Devil, disease, and deliverance from this examination of the Johannine literature?

1) It is clear that on at least one occasion, there is a connection between sin and illness. The tie is so strong between the two that a warning of an additional (worse) 'illness' is given if the person continued to sin.

2) Where there is a connection between sin and illness, it is assumed that the person who had been ill would know the identity of the sin which resulted in the illness.

3) However, the Johannine literature does not indicate that there is always a causal relationship between sin and illness. In fact, the attitude which assumes that illness is always the direct result of sin is roundly condemned.

4) In ways not dissimilar to James and Paul, the Johannine literature appears comfortable in assigning the origin of certain illnesses to God.

5) When illness is the direct result of sin, it appears that God has sent the illness as a sort of punishment. There is no real reflection upon the pedagogical purpose of such illnesses, as there is in James and Paul.

---

[153] Nicole (*Obéissance et Amour*, p. 289) offers this balanced assessment, 'Nous pouvons conclure de ce passage qu'il est légitime de souhouter la prospérité et la santé pour soi et pour les autres, et de prier dans ce sens. Cependant, la tournure de la phrase montre que la santé du corps et la prospérité matérielle ne découlent pas automatiquement d'un bon état de l'âme. Il y a des âmes d'élite qui ont glorifié Dieu dans l'infortune et dans la maladie.'

6) In the Fourth Gospel, illness can be used as an occasion for the manifestation of the works of God and apparently can be sent by God for that specific purpose. The implication is that sometimes suffering is in accord with the divine will.

7) The Johannine literature never attributes illness to the Devil or demons and shows no real interest in the topic.

8) Sometimes the origin of an illness is left unattributed, the inference being that some illnesses are the result of 'natural causes'.

9) The basis on which the origin of illness is determined in the Johannine literature is discernment, particularly the supernatural knowledge of Jesus.

10) In the Fourth Gospel when one has been healed in order that the works of God might be manifest, testimony is an essential part of the healed person's response.

11) If the narratives of the Gospel according to John are intended to serve as a paradigm for the praxis of the community, one may deduce that when faced with illness, the church would have prayed for those who were ill, with perhaps a reliance upon the Paraclete for direction in discerning the purpose of the particular illness.

12) In any case, the fact that illness could be either the result of sin or in order that the miraculous work of God be accomplished would have resulted in the community's giving very special attention to illness within its ranks.

13) Despite the claims sometimes made for 3 Jn 2, there is no evidence that the Johannine community advocated a theology of health and prosperity. The texts examined in the Fourth Gospel undermine such a use of this text.

4

THE GOSPEL ACCORDING TO MARK

In the literature examined to this point, there is little evidence that illness was ever attributed to the Devil and/or demons.[1] This picture slowly begins to change as each of the Synoptic Gospels are read, for here Jesus is in conflict with a host of demonic forces and, for the first time in this study, one finds various sorts of infirmities attributed to demons or unclean spirits. It would be a mistake, however, to assume that the Synoptics are filled with such stories for, in truth, illnesses attributed to demonic origins are rare in Mark and Matthew, occurring much more frequently in Luke-Acts. But the appearance of even one such story indicates that for the purposes of this study there is a very important dimension of the Devil, disease, and deliverance that has yet to be explored. So it is to the Synoptics that this investigation turns.

Given the unique nature of the literary relationship amongst the synoptic gospels and the methodological challenges which result, a word of explanation is perhaps in order regarding the treatment of the materials presented in the following three chapters; specifically, the order of examination and the scope of each chapter. The books are examined in the following order: Mark, Matthew, and Luke-Acts. This approach reflects the generally agreed upon sequence of the Synoptics' composition[2] and allows the Acts material to form a conclusion to this section. With regard to the content or scope of each chapter, those passages of relevance to this study are treated in

---

[1] The lone exception being Satan's role, or more properly his angel's role, in inflicting Paul with the thorn in the flesh, but even here the affliction is one in which God himself is involved.

[2] It is, of course, still unclear as to whether or not Matthew was written before Luke.

each gospel. While examination of parallel passages is not duplicated, significant contributions of the specific evangelists are noted. This particular chapter focuses upon the Gospel according to Mark, which is considered by the majority of scholars to be the first of the Synoptics written,[3] with a date of composition sometime around the late 60's of the first century CE. One of the major thematic emphases of Mark's Gospel is the issue of discipleship; its purpose, development, and cost.[4]

For the purposes of this investigation, two specific passages in Mark's Gospel merit detailed examination. First, in Mk 2.1-12 Jesus forgives the sins of a paralytic shortly before healing him. Second, there is recorded in Mk 9.14-29 the healing of a young boy who was mute owing to demon possession. Finally, there are a few places where exorcisms and healings are described in close proximity.

Mark 2.1-12 – 'Which Is Harder to Say?'

As is well known, Mark begins his Gospel with a description of the ministry of John the Baptist, who comes proclaiming a conversion baptism for the forgiveness of sin. His ministry produces phenomenal results as the whole of Judea and all the inhabitants of Jerusalem come out to him for baptism. No sooner has John foretold the coming of a mightier one than Jesus appears for baptism, which results in the anointing by the Holy Spirit and confirmation from the Father for Jesus. Immediately, Jesus is cast out into the wilderness by the same Spirit who has just anointed him, to be tested by Satan. With the imprisonment of John the Baptist, Jesus himself begins to preach a gospel of conversion and shortly thereafter, acquires four fishermen as followers.

Entering Capernaum, his teaching amazes his hearers for *he* taught as one with *authority*, not like the scribes. A man with an unclean spirit makes contact with him in the synagogue and begins to call him the Holy One of God. The exorcism of this spirit by Jesus and his teaching results in the crowd's astonishment at its newness.

---

[3] While there are notable challenges to this position, a great preponderance of scholars hold to some sort of Marcan priority.

[4] For my own thoughts on this topic cf. J.C. Thomas, 'Discipleship in Mark's Gospel', *Faces of Renewal* (ed. P. Elbert; Peabody, MA: Hendrickson, 1988), pp. 64-80.

From the synagogue, Jesus goes to the house of Peter and Andrew where Peter's mother-in-law was in bed with a fever. Her healing at the touch of Jesus' hand produces a throng of sick people and those demon possessed being brought to his door, all of whom Jesus heals, on the one hand, and exorcises, on the other hand.

Seeking refuge from the crowds in a desert place, he prays. Despite the requests of those seeking him, Jesus goes throughout Galilee preaching and casting out demons, at which time a man suffering from leprosy cries out for cleansing. Upon being healed, the former leper himself begins to preach (κηρύσσειν) many things and to spread around the word (τὸν λόγον), despite the fact that Jesus seeks to keep the man silent. The cumulative effect is that Jesus could no longer enter any city openly, having to stay in desert places. And yet, the people still come!

The euphoria of chapter one is tempered in the next section as the author chronicles the growing hostility toward Jesus on the part of the Jewish religious leaders. While this observation should not be taken to imply that Jesus will no longer attract a large following, for he does, it does indicate that Mark consciously leads his readers into the next phase of the story by chronicling the opposition which is ever mounting against Jesus.

Despite the fact that 2.1-12 has certain points of contact with that which precedes it in the narrative,[5] it is also clear that this passage stands at the beginning of a larger section, which consists of five passages, devoted to the increasing hostility and opposition to Jesus on the part of a variety of Jewish religious leaders.[6] Each peri-

---

[5] W. Wink ('Mark 2.1-12', *Int* 36 [1982], p. 62 [63-67]) notes that in 2.1-12 the gospel's progression reaches a crescendo with the announcement of a theme that will continue throughout the book. Cf. also R. Kernaghan, 'History and Redaction in the Controversy Stories in Mark 2.1-3.6', *Studia Biblica et Theologica* 9 (1979), pp. 23-47, esp. 38-41.

[6] For this conclusion cf. M. Albertz, *Die synoptischen Streirgespräche* (Berlin: Trowitzsch & Sohn, 1921), pp. 5-6; P.M. Beernaert, 'Jésus controversé: structure et theologie de Mark 2, 1-3, 6', *NRT* 95 (1973), pp. 129-49; J. Dewey, 'The Literary Structure of the Controversy Stories in Mark 2.1-3.6', *JBL* 92 (1973), pp. 394-401; W. Lane, *The Gospel according to Mark* (Grand Rapids: Eerdmans, 1974), p. 91; H. Anderson, *The Gospel of Mark* (London: Oliphants, 1976), p. 99; B. Standaert, *L'évangile selon Marc: Composition et littéraire* (Brugge: Zevenkerken, 1978), p. 271 n. 1; W. Harrington, *Mark* (Wilmington: Michael Glazier, 1979), p. 24; J. Dewey, *Mark and Public Debate* (SBLDS 48; Chico: Scholars Press, 1980); M. Beernaert, *Saint Marc* (Bruxelles: Lumen Vitae, 1985), pp. 37-39; J.D.G. Dunn, 'Mark 2.1-3.6:

cope reveals that the opposition steadily increases from the first
passage to the last. In the initial text of this section (2.1-12) the opposition of the Jewish leaders is unspoken ('they question in their
hearts' – v. 6). The second story (2.13-17) relates the opposition by
means of a question raised with the disciples about the conduct of
Jesus ('Why does he eat with sinners and tax collectors?' – v. 16). In
the next pericope (2.18-22) the opponents pose a question directly
to Jesus regarding the practice of his disciples ('Why do your disciples not fast?' v. 18). This question is followed by a charge made to
Jesus in the following text (2.23-28) that his disciples are doing that
which is unlawful on the Sabbath (v. 24). The opposition of the
Pharisees, joined by the Herodians, is complete in the last pericope
of the section (3.1-6), where as a result of Jesus healing on the Sabbath, these two groups conspire as to how they might put him to
death.[7] It is the first of these stories that is of specific relevance for
this study.

> And having entered again into Capernaum after a few days it was
> heard that he was at home. And so many people gathered that
> there was no room even at the door, and he spoke to them the
> word. And they came bringing to him a paralytic, being carried
> by four. And not being able to bring (the paralytic) to him on ac-
> count of the crowd, they opened the roof where he was, and
> having dug through it they lowered the cot upon which the para-
> lytic was lying. And Jesus, seeing their faith, says to the paralytic,
> 'Child, your sins are forgiven'. And there were some scribes sit-
> ting there and questioning in their hearts, 'What is this he says?
> Blasphemy! Who is able to forgive sins except One, God?' And
> immediately Jesus, knowing in his spirit that they were question-
> ing in their hearts, says to them, 'Why do you question in your

---

Between Jesus and Paul', *NTS* 30 (1984), pp. 397-98; R. Latourelle, *Miracles de Jésus
et théologie du Miracle* (Paris: Cerf, 1986), p. 120; and R. Gundry, *Mark: A Commentary on His Apology for the Cross* (Grand Rapids: Eerdmans, 1993), p. 109. Several
scholars argue for a concentric or chiastic structure for this section. Cf. esp.
Dewey, 'The Literary Structure of the Controversy Stories in Mark 2.1-3.6', pp.
394-401; Standaert, *L'évangile selon Marc: Composition et littéraire*, pp. 175-80; Harrington, *Mark*, pp. 24-25; Dewey, *Mark and Public Debate*, pp. 131-80; and S.
Kuthirakkattel, *The Beginning of Jesus' Ministry according to Mark's Gospel (1,14-3,6): A
Redaction Critical Study* (Rome: Pontifical Biblical Institute, 1990), pp. 73-77.
[7] Standaert (*L'évangile selon Marc: Composition et littéraire*, p. 217 n. 1) gives a
good description of this process.

hearts? Which is easier, to say to a paralytic – "your sins are forgiven", or to say, "rise, take up your cot and walk?" But in order
that you might know that the Son of Man has authority to forgive sin upon the earth …', – he says to the paralytic, 'I say to
you, rise, take up your cot and go to your (own) house'. And he
arose, and immediately taking up his cot he went out before
them all, so that all were amazed and glorified God saying, 'We
have never seen anything like this!'

The passage can be divided into the following sections:

a)   Narrative Introduction (vv. 1-2)
b)   The Bringing of the Paralytic (vv. 3-4)
c)   Jesus' Words of Forgiveness to the Paralytic (v. 5)
d)   The Reaction of the Scribes (vv. 6-7)
e)   Jesus' Words to the Scribes (vv. 8-10a)
f)   Jesus' Words of Healing to the Paralytic (v. 10b-11)
g)   The Healing of the Paralytic and its Results on the Crowd
     (v. 12).[8]

This outline is utilized in the study of this passage.

Narrative Introduction (vv. 1-2)
As noted in the survey of chapter one, Mk 1.45 indicates that Jesus
could no longer enter a city openly owing to the enormous crowds
that followed him, even into desert places. Yet the opening verse of
chapter two reveals that, surprisingly, Jesus has returned to the city.
But what contributes to an extremely high expectancy level on the
part of the reader is that Jesus has not entered just any city, but has
returned to Capernaum.[9] Specific mention of a return to Capernaum (πάλιν) calls to the reader's mind Jesus' previous visit (1.21-
28), which included his teaching in the synagogue, the casting out
of a demon, and the resulting amazement of the populace and continuing increase of Jesus' reputation. While Mark does not specify

---

[8] R.T. Mead ('The Healing of the Paralytic – A Unit?', *JBL* 80 [1961], p. 352)
suggests that the structure of this pericope follows the tripartite pattern of 'revo-
lutionary action, protest, and silencing of the remonstrants', found in some rabbinic literature, while Kuthirakkattel (*The Beginning of Jesus' Ministry according to
Mark's Gospel*, p. 181) argues for a concentric structure with v. 7 standing in the
middle.
[9] L.W. Hurtado (*Mark* [New York: Harper & Row, 1983], p. 22) suggests that
Capernaum was Jesus' Galilean home base.

the precise amount of time which had passed between the visits (δι᾽ ἡμερῶν),[10] it has not been long in terms of narrative time. Not surprisingly, word gets out that Jesus is 'at home' (ἐν οἴκῳ). Given the fact that Jesus was received in the home of Simon and Andrew previously in Capernaum (1.29-31), the reader suspects this is the house to which Jesus has come.[11]

As the reader very well expects by this time, word of Jesus' presence produces a flood of individuals anxious to see him. In fact, the house was not able to accommodate such a crowd so that a number of them were outside the door, perhaps standing in the street.[12] In accordance with the purpose of his coming (1.38), Jesus speaks to them 'the word'. Such an action is fully consistent with Jesus' previous activity in Mark, as he had preached and taught often (1.14-15, 21, and 38-39). In this preaching there is some continuity with the preaching of John the Baptist and perhaps with the preaching of the former leper in 1.45. While much of the former leper's preaching was, no doubt, devoted to his own miraculous healing, Mark may intimate that the leper said more, for aside from this instance, '"the word' in Mark always refers to Jesus' message'.[13] The content of Jesus' 'word' (λόγος) on this occasion is surely similar to his earlier sermons which included a call for conversion and belief in the

---

[10] For taking διά with the genitive to mean 'after', cf. *BDF*, p. 119 §223 (1).

[11] An idea which many scholars entertain. Cf. Wesley, *Explanatory Notes upon the New Testament*, p. 101; H.B. Swete, *The Gospel according to St Mark* (London: MacMillan, 1909), p. 32; M.-J. LaGrange, *Évangile selon Saint Marc* (Paris: Gabalda, 1947), p. 32; J. Huby, *Évangile selon Saint Marc* (Paris: Beauchesne, 1948), p. 45; V. Taylor, *The Gospel according to St. Mark* (London: MacMillan, 1952), p. 193; C.E.B. Cranfield, *The Gospel according to Saint Mark* (Cambridge: Cambridge University Press, 1972[4]), p. 96; S.E. Johnson, *A Commentary on the Gospel according to Mark* (London: A & C Black, 1960), p. 55; A. Johnes, *The Gospel according to St Mark* (London: Chapman, 1965), p. 77; H. van der Loos, *The Miracles of Jesus* (Leiden: E.J. Brill, 1965), p. 442; Lane, *Mark*, p. 93; Latourelle, *Miracles de Jésus et théologie du Miracle*, p. 120; H.C. Waetjen, *A Reordering of Power: A Socio-Political Reading of Mark's Gospel* (Minneapolis, MN: Fortress, 1989), p. 86; Kuthirakkattel, *The Beginning of Jesus' Ministry*, p. 183; J.A. Brooks, *Mark* (Nashville: Broadman Press, 1991), p. 58; M.D. Hooker, *The Gospel according to St Mark* (London: A & C Black, 1991), p. 85; and Gundry, *Mark*, p. 110.

[12] Perhaps this note indicates that the house envisioned had no courtyard so those on the outside were, in effect, standing in the street. Cf. esp. C.S. Mann, *Mark* (Garden City: Doubleday, 1986), p. 223. Cf. also Taylor, *Mark*, p. 193; Waetjen, *Reordering of Power*, p. 86; and Hooker, *Mark*, p. 85.

[13] R.A. Guelich, *Mark 1-8.26* (Dallas: Word, 1989), p. 84.

gospel as a result of the nearness of the Kingdom of God.[14] But apparently at this point in the narrative, Mark intends his readers to pay more attention to the fact that his teaching possesses a unique authority and that healings and exorcisms regularly accompanied it, all of which the reader would expect when it is learned that Jesus is teaching.

The Bringing of the Paralytic (vv. 3-4)

From 1.32 the reader has learned that when Jesus is in the house a number of infirm people are brought (ἔφερον) to him. So here in v. 3 a similar activity is taking place, only this time the focus is upon a specific sufferer, a paralytic, and the four who were bringing (φέ-ροντες) him.[15] Since on the previous occasion many of those brought to Jesus were healed, the reader rightly anticipates a positive outcome for this poor man.

There is, however, a complication. In 1.33, the crowd, which gathered at the door, was apparently no obstacle for those who desired healing or were brought for exorcism. In 2.4, the crowd is so large that access through the door is impossible. But before the reader is able to reflect on the implications of such a situation for this man, Mark quickly reveals the drastic steps taken by the four bearing the paralytic. In order to allow their friend to have access to Jesus,[16] the men gain access to the roof (of this one story dwelling), perhaps via an outside staircase.[17] Digging through the roof com-

---

[14] For this interpretation cf. E.P. Gould, *A Critical and Exegetical Commentary on the Gospel According to Saint Mark* (New York: Scribners, 1907), p. 36; Huby, *Saint Marc*, pp. 44-45; Cranfield, *Mark*, p. 97; and Lane, *Mark*, p. 93. LaGrange (*Saint Marc*, p. 33) defines 'the word' here as 'la bonne nouvelle du salut', while W. Thissen (*Erzählung der Befreiung: Eine exegetische Untersuchung zu Mk 2,1-3,6* [Würzburg: Echter Verlag, 1976], pp. 300-33) argues that it has reference to the missionary preaching of the early church.

[15] LaGrange (*Saint Marc*, p. 33) believes that the man's parents are among the four who bring him.

[16] Not to hide the house door from a demon thought to have caused the paralysis, as argued by H. Jahnow, 'Das Abdecken des Daches Mc 2.4 Lc 5.19', *ZNW* 24 (1925), p. 156; L. Schenke, *Die Wundererzählungen des Markusevangeliums* (Stuttgart: Katholisches Bibelwerk, 1974), p. 153; J. Gnilka, *Das Evangelium nach Markus*, I (Zürich: Benziger, 1978), pp. 97-98; and D.J. Doughty, 'The Authority of the Son of Man', *ZNW* 74 (1983), p. 163.

[17] For this suggestion cf. Gould, *Mark*, p. 36; Swete, *Mark*, p. 33; Taylor, *Mark*, p. 194; Cranfield, *Mark*, p. 97; Johnson, *Mark*, p. 55; D.E. Nineham, *The*

posed of mud and thatch, the men not only make a passageway for
this poor man's cot (κράβαττον),[18] but perhaps also clear a place
for him in the house itself as, no doubt, individuals would have
sought to move out of the way of the debris falling from the ceil-
ing.

Jesus' Words of Forgiveness to the Paralytic (v. 5)

At this point in the narrative, the reader fully expects Jesus to heal
the paralytic. After all, that is what one has come to anticipate from
the first chapter of Mark's Gospel when the sick are brought to Jesus. This expectancy is further encouraged by the words, 'And Jesus,
seeing their faith …', a phrase that certainly focuses upon the extraordinary actions of the infirm man's companions,[19] but does not
necessarily exclude the faith of the paralytic,[20] (it is hard to imagine
the man being brought against his will!). Although it is possible
formally to describe the actions of these men as a 'nonverbal request for healing',[21] and a confident one at that,[22] perhaps this is to
move too quickly. For as the reader remembers, the concept of belief has appeared only once in Mark to this point, and there it was
not in the context of healing but belief in the Gospel (1.15). This
fact in itself suggests that Jesus' recognition of their faith is intended to be seen, at least in part, as their compliance with his earlier proclamation to believe in the Gospel (1.15). This observation
does not deny the developing relationship between healing and be-

Gospel of St Mark (London: A & C Black, 1963), p. 92; Lane, *Mark*, p. 93; Anderson, *Mark*, p. 100; Guelich, *Mark*, p. 85; Brooks, *Mark*, p. 58; and Hooker, *Mark*,
p. 85.

[18] Swete, *Mark*, p. 34; Johnson, *Mark*, p. 56; Taylor, *Mark*, p. 194; Cranfield,
Mark, p. 97; Nineham, *Mark*, p. 92; Hiebert, *Mark*, p. 63; Gnilka, *Markus*, I, p. 98;
Mann, *Mark*, p. 86; Kuthirakkattel, *The Beginning of Jesus' Ministry according to Mark's
Gospel*, p. 186; Hooker, *Mark*, p. 85; and J.F. Williams, *Other Followers of Jesus: Minor
Characters as Major Figures in Mark's Gospel* (JSNTSup 102; Sheffield: JSOT Press,
1994), p. 99.

[19] Johnson, *Mark*, p. 56; A. Cole, *Mark* (Grand Rapids: Eerdmans, 1989[2]), p.
120; Hurtado, *Mark*, p. 22; and Gundry, *Mark*, p. 112.

[20] So Gould, *Mark*, p. 36; Taylor, *Mark*, p. 194; A. Cabaniss, 'A Fresh Exegesis
of Mark 2.1-12', *Int* 11 (1957), p. 325; Cranfield, *Mark*, p. 97; Nineham, *Mark*, p.
92; van der Loos, *Miracles of Jesus*, p. 443; Kuthirakkattel, *The Beginning of Jesus'
Ministry*, p. 186; Brooks, *Mark*, p. 58; Hooker, *Mark*, p. 85; and Williams, *Other
Followers of Jesus*, pp. 99-100.

[21] As does Guelich (*Mark*, p. 85).

[22] Cf. R. Pesch, *Das Markusevangelium*, I (Freiburg: Herder, 1976), p. 158.

lief in Mark's Gospel which seems to begin here,[23] but simply to note that with respect to this narrative it is a mistake to ignore the connection between the faith of these men and Jesus' earlier words to believe.

Jesus says, 'Child, your sins are forgiven'. Several aspects of this sentence are worthy of comment. First, Jesus' initial word to the paralytic, 'Child' (Τέκνον), is a term of endearment[24] which conveys to the reader Jesus' compassionate reception of this individual. Second, Jesus' statement that the man's sins are forgiven appears in the present tense, which indicates that his sins were forgiven in that instant.[25] Third, grammatically it is possible to take this pharse (ἀφίενταί σου αἱ ἁμαρτίαι) as a divine passive.[26] Taken this way, Jesus was not himself pronouncing the forgiveness of sin, but, in line with the action of certain Old Testament prophets (cf. the words of Nathan to David in 2 Sam. 2.12-13),[27] he was saying that *God* had forgiven the man's sins. Another possible way of understanding Jesus' statement is as a word of assurance to the man that his sins had been forgiven (at some point) by God.[28] Although theoretically Jesus' pronouncement might be ambiguous enough to suggest that he may have been speaking as a prophetic figure,[29] neither the scribes in the narrative nor the Evangelist himself take the statement in that way. In point of fact, the purpose of the story in the narrative is ultimately to emphasize the authority of the Son of

---

[23] Cf. esp. 5.34 and 10.52 where those healed are told, 'Your faith has saved/healed (σέσωκέν) you.'

[24] Cranfield, *Mark*, p. 97 and Mann, *Mark*, p. 224.

[25] Swete, *Mark*, p. 34; LaGrange, *Saint Marc*, p. 35; A. Feuillet, 'L'exousia du fils de l'homme (d'après Mc. II, 10-28 et parr.)', *RSR* 42 (1954), p. 166; Taylor, *Mark*, p. 195; Mann, *Mark*, p. 224; Kuthirakkattel, *The Beginning of Jesus' Ministry*, p. 187; and Gundry, *Mark*, p. 112. As for the aoristic present, Blass, DeBrunner, and Funk (*BDF*, p. 167 §320) note, 'In those few cases where a punctiliar act taking place at the moment of speaking is to be denoted, the present is usually used since the punctiliar aorist stems form no present....'

[26] So Lane, *Mark*, p. 94 n. 9; D.E. Hiebert, *Mark: A Portrait of a Servant* (Chicago: Moody Press, 1974), p. 65; W. Grundmann, *Das Evangelium nach Markus* (Berlin: Evangelische Verlagsanstalt, 1968), p. 56; Pesch, *Das Markusevangelium*, I, p. 156; D.H. Juel, *Mark* (Minneapolis: Augsburg, 1990), p. 47; Brooks, *Mark*, p. 58; and apparently Guelich, *Mark*, pp. 86, 94-95.

[27] So Nineham, *Mark*, p. 93 and J. Murphy-O'Conner, 'Pêchê et Communauté dans le Nouveau Testament', *RB* 74 (1967), p. 182.

[28] Which is apparently Guelich's (*Mark*, p. 94) point.

[29] Cf. Cranfield, *Mark*, p. 99.

Man to forgive sins upon the earth. Therefore, this interpretive option appears to be ruled out.

Fourth, there is some degree of uncertainty with regard to the precise meaning and purpose of Jesus' statement about forgiveness of sin. A large number of scholars interpret this phrase in the light of the belief in antiquity that there was a connection between sin and sickness. These views range from those who see a strong connection between this man's sin and his illness[30] to those who see a general link between sin and sickness.[31] However, others are not so quick to see such a connection here as the text does not make one[32] and one would expect that if sin were the direct cause for the paralysis, immediately upon hearing the words of forgiveness the man would have been healed,[33] as appears to have been the case in John 5.

But if there is no overt connection between sin and sickness on this occasion, why does Jesus pronounce the paralytic's sins as forgiven? The previous discussion about the faith which Jesus saw may provide the route to an answer. If the belief of these individuals (the paralytic and his friends) is connected with belief in the gospel as called for earlier in the preaching of Jesus (1.15), no doubt the content of the 'word' which he was speaking to them in the house, then his words to the paralytic are easier to interpret. The imperative of Jesus' message in 1.15 is two-fold: 'Convert (μετανοεῖτε) and believe in the gospel'. As Mark does not redefine his message in the remainder of chapter one, it seems likely that the readers are to assume that its content is still the same when the 'word' is spoken

---

[30] B.H. Branscomb, *The Gospel of Mark* (London: Hodder and Stoughton, 1937), pp. 42, 45-47; LaGrange, *Saint Marc*, p. 35; Huby, *Saint Marc*, pp. 45-46; Taylor, *Mark*, p. 195; Gnilka, *Markus*, I, p. 99; J. Calloud, 'Toward a Structural Analysis of the Gospel of Mark', *Semeia* 16 (1980), pp. 148-49; Dewey, *Markan Public Debate*, p. 77; D. Lührmann, *Das Markusevangelium* (Tübingen: J.C.B. Mohr, 1987), p. 57; D.E. Garland, '"I Am the Lord Your Healer": Mark 1.21-2.12', *RevExp* 85 (1988), p. 338; Waetjen, *Reordering of Power*, p. 87; Juel, *Mark*, p. 46; and Hooker, *Mark*, p. 85.

[31] Gould, *Mark*, p. 37; Cranfield, *Mark*, p. 99; Lane, *Mark*, p. 94; Anderson, *Mark*, p. 100; and Kuthirakkattel, *The Beginning of Jesus' Ministry*, p. 187.

[32] Heibert (*Mark*, p. 64) concludes, 'That personal sins had caused his affliction is not asserted nor explicitly ruled out'. Cf. also Williams, *Other Followers of Jesus*, p. 100.

[33] Cf. W. Wink ('Mark 2.1-12', p. 60), who observes that after his sins were 'forgiven he was still on the pallet', and Gundry, *Mark*, p. 112.

by Jesus in 2.2. When faith is mentioned in connection with the actions of the paralytic and his friends, the reader is reminded of Jesus' earlier words as this is the first mention of faith since 1.15. Knowing that conversion involves the confessing of sins (cf. 1.4-5) and subsequent forgiveness, the reader is not totally unprepared for Jesus' words of forgiveness in v. 5. That is to say, the forgiveness of sin spoken to the paralytic would appear to indicate that these individuals not only have come believing in the gospel (Jesus sees their faith) but also have hearts of repentance/conversion (Jesus forgives sins). Jesus' words are the natural reward of such faith. Thus, v. 5 develops a theme which goes back to the beginning of the Gospel and which becomes the focus for what follows in the remainder of this pericope. This verse also continues to develop the idea of authority to which much of 2.1-3.6 is devoted.

The Reaction of the Scribes (vv. 6-7)

At this point the presence of certain scribes is revealed. The scribes were those individuals with special training to interpret the Torah as it related to various aspects of religious, social, and domestic life. They were generally revered for their function in Jewish society and devoted themselves to ensuring that the Torah was properly observed.[34]

In Mark's Gospel, the scribes function as Jesus' antagonists. While they do not appear in the Marcan narrative until this verse, reference has earlier been made to them when their teaching was unfavorably compared to that of Jesus (1.22). In that passage, although the scribes are the authoritative teachers, it is Jesus' teaching that is said to have authority. By means of this contrast Mark prepares the reader for Jesus' later conflict with the scribes and the controversy over his authority, both of which appear in 2.1-12. Despite the crowded conditions, here in this their first appearance, the scribes are seated, the position of honor,[35] quietly (on this occasion) assessing (διαλογιζόμενοι) the words and actions of Jesus.

As the reference to the scribes in 1.22 suggested, the content of their internal deliberation in this verse reveals that the scribes are

---

[34] Cf. the discussion of Torah scholars in E. Schürer, *The History of the Jewish People in the Age of Jesus Christ*, II (ed. G. Vermes, F. Millar, and M. Black; Edinburgh: T. & T. Clark, 1979), pp. 321-36.

[35] Swete, *Mark*, p. 35 and Hiebert, *Mark*, pp. 64-65.

Jesus' antagonists indeed. For their ponderings not only disclose their contempt for 'this fellow' (Jesus),[36] perhaps resentment for their earlier unfavorable comparison to one without the proper training in the Torah(?), but they mentally charge Jesus with the most heinous crime, he blasphemes! According to the Torah (Lev. 24.10-16), blasphemy is to curse or slander the name of God. One could then blaspheme by slandering or cursing the name of God, or, extending the idea, by attributing to themselves the powers or dignity reserved for God alone.[37] So serious was the charge of blasphemy that if guilty, the offender was to be put to death by stoning.[38] Needless to say, such a charge is too strong if Jesus is merely taking a prophetic position in pronouncing that the man's sins have been forgiven by God.[39]

For Mark, the introduction of blasphemy language accomplishes several things. First, it clearly marks the scribes off as opponents of Jesus. Second, their charge reveals their own culpability in that it is made in the context of belief in Jesus (2.5).[40] In addition, although it is Jesus who is charged with blasphemy, ultimately those who identify with his crucifiers are the ones who blaspheme (15.29), and in the same context, the obdurate rejection of Jesus by the scribes is made complete in their challenge for Jesus to come down from the cross so that they might 'see and believe' (15.32), again underscoring the relationship between blasphemy and lack of belief. Third, the charge of blasphemy points the reader ahead to the death of Jesus. In the last pericope of this section devoted to the escalating hostility toward Jesus (3.1-6) there is a conspiracy to put Jesus to death (3.6). Ultimately, it is blasphemy of which Jesus is convicted in his trial (14.60-64), although the specific reason for the charge has changed.

The scribes reach their conclusion that Jesus blasphemes on the basis of his words of forgiveness spoken to the paralytic, for 'Who

---

[36] A possible meaning for οὗτος in this context. So Kuthirakkattel, *The Beginning of Jesus' Ministry*, p. 189; Hooker, *Mark*, p. 86; and Gundry, *Mark*, p. 112.

[37] O. Hofius, 'Βλασφημία', *EDNT*, I, p. 220.

[38] According to m. *Sanh.* 7.5 a person is culpable of blasphemy only if the divine name itself has been pronounced by the offender. However, it is unclear whether this stipulation was fixed by the late 60's in the first century CE.

[39] Gundry, *Mark*, pp. 117-18.

[40] Cf. Williams, *Other Followers of Jesus*, p. 100.

is able to forgive sins except one, God?' On the basis of the Hebrew Scriptures, the scribes were justified in their conclusion, for only God is able to forgive sins.[41] Clearly, the scribes understand Jesus to be ascribing for himself God's prerogative to forgive sins.[42] This charge, and the rationale behind it, stand at the heart of the passage, as v. 7 is bounded on either side by the phrase, 'pondering in their/your hearts'.[43]

Jesus' Words to the Scribes (vv. 8-10a)

In sharp contrast to the deliberations in the hearts of the scribes is the knowledge in the spirit of Jesus.[44] His knowledge of the scribes' pondering is immediate and accurate. While it is possible that such knowledge comes intuitively,[45] after his displays of authority and power in chapter one and the pronouncement of forgiveness of the paralytic's sins in this pericope, the reader is not surprised at Jesus' ability to know the hearts of his opponents.[46] In order to emphasize the deliberation of the scribes, for the third time Mark uses a form of διαλογίζομαι, this time in the question which Jesus poses directly to the scribes. Perhaps the purpose of such emphasis is to

---

[41] Cf. Feuillet, 'L'exousia du fils de l'homme (d'après Mc. II, 10-28 et parr.)', p. 166; Nineham, *Mark*, p. 90; W.E. Keller, 'The Authority of Jesus as Reflected in MK 2.1-3.6: A Contribution to the History of Interpretation', (PhD thesis, Cambridge University, 1967-68), p. 299; I. Maisch, *Die Heilung des Gelähmten: Eine exegetisch-traditiongeschichtliche Untersuchung zu Mk 2,1-12* (SBS 52; Stuttgart: KBW Verlag, 1971), pp. 89-90; K. Kertelge, 'Die Vollmacht des Menschensohnes zur Sündenvergebung (Mk 2, 10)', *Orientierung an Jesus* (ed. P. Hoffmann *et al.*; Freiburg: Herder, 1973), p. 208; J. Gnilka, 'Das Elend vor dem Menschensohn (Mk. 1, 1-12)', in *Jesus und der Menschensohn* (ed. R. Pesch *et al.*; Freiburg: Herder, 1975), p. 202; and Harrington, *Mark*, p. 29.

[42] The nearest parallel to Jesus' actions is said to be found in an Aramaic fragment from Qumran (4QPrNab), the Prayer of Nabonidus, where an exorcist pardons the sins of the king. Cf. A. Dupont-Sommer, 'Exorcismes et guérisons dans les écrits de Qoumân', in *Congress Volume, Oxford 1959* (VTSup 7; ed. G.W. Anderson *et al.*; Leiden: E.J. Brill, 1960), pp. 254, 259-60. For a critical examination of the somewhat questionable reconstruction of the text upon which the translation is based cf. B. Blackburn, *Theios Aner and the Markan Miracle Traditions* (Tübingen: J.C.B. Mohr, 1991), pp. 138-40.

[43] For this observation cf. Kuthirakkattel, *The Beginning of Jesus' Ministry*, p. 190.

[44] Gundry, *Mark*, p. 113.

[45] Gould, *Mark*, p. 37.

[46] Closer to the mark are those scholars who attribute this knowledge to some divine or prophetic aid. Cf. LaGrange, *Saint Marc*, p. 36; Huby, *Saint Marc*, p. 46; and Pesch, *Markus*, I, p. 159.

contrast the uncertainty (or unbelief?) of the scribes with regard to Jesus' identity with the certainty on the part of those who believe (the paralytic and his friends) and/or with Jesus' attempt to reveal himself, even to the scribes.[47]

The direct question of v. 8 is followed up by one of a more rhetorical nature in v. 9. Owing to the scribes' charges of blasphemy because of what Jesus said in v. 5, he now asks a question about what is easier to say.[48] In one sense, the question centers upon the issue of verification. While, on the one hand, it may be easy simply to say someone's sins are forgiven, there is no way of verifying the claim; on the other hand, to tell a paralytic to rise and walk is obviously open to verification.[49] But, in point of fact, the purpose of the question is rhetorical,[50] in that Jesus has no intention of providing an answer, and in that both pronouncing forgiveness and speaking words of healing are the work of God,[51] each of which Jesus will do! Interpretations which take this question as an attempt to make a direct connection between sin and the paralysis seem misguided,[52] especially if the reading of vv. 4-5 offered earlier is correct.

Several aspects of v. 10a merit comment. First, following the two previous questions is a purpose clause which governs the rest of the statement.[53] It indicates that the action which Jesus takes in v. 11 (the healing of the paralytic) is for the specific purpose of belief in the authority of the Son of Man to forgive sins on the earth.

Second, the term 'Son of Man' is introduced into Mark's Gospel for the first time at this point. The presence of this controversial term in v. 10 and its extraordinary context, that he has authority to forgive sins, have prompted more than one scholar to take v. 10a as

---

[47] In 12.34 it becomes evident that not all scribes are without hope.

[48] LaGrange, *Saint Marc*, p. 37.

[49] Huby, *Saint Marc*, p. 48 and Guelich, *Mark*, p. 88.

[50] T.L. Budesheim, 'Jesus and the Disciples in Conflict with Judaism', *ZNW* 62 (1971), p. 192.

[51] Cranfield, *Mark*, pp. 99-100 and Brooks, *Mark*, p. 59.

[52] Cf. Taylor, *Mark*, p. 197; Hurtado, *Mark*, p. 23; Doughty, 'The Authority of the Son of Man', p. 166; and Garland, '"I Am the Lord Your Healer": Mark 1.21-2.12', p. 339.

[53] Guelich, *Mark*, p. 88.

a parenthetical statement directed to Mark's Christian audience.[54] However, while such a move may clear up certain 'historical' problems relating to Jesus' use of the 'Son of Man' title this early in his ministry, it disrupts the flow of the text, as the saying is integral to the interpretation of the passage.[55] For the purposes of this study, no attempt is made to follow the enormous debate regarding the meaning of the term Son of Man,[56] rather Mark's own usage is allowed to define the meaning of the term. Three things stand out in this verse about the Son of Man. 1) It is obvious that Jesus uses this title to refer to himself. 2) Although the title emphasizes his existence as part of humankind, it is clear that this Son of Man assumes a divine prerogative – the authority to forgive sins. 3) This is the first of two appearances of 'Son of Man' in the first half of Mark's Gospel, both of which deal with authority. Although the word ἐξουσία does not appear in 2.28, the concept is certainly present in that the Son of Man claims to be Lord of the Sabbath.[57]

The third aspect of v. 10a worthy of mention is the issue of authority (ἐξουσία) to forgive sins. Thus far in Mark's narrative, authority has twice been explicitly attributed to Jesus. In 1.21, his teaching is described as having authority, being unlike the teaching of the scribes. Later in that pericope (1.27) the attribution of a new and authoritative teaching seems to be related to his ability to speak to unclean spirits and have them obey him. Although the word 'authority' will not appear again until 2.10a, the concept of Jesus' authority over infirmity and demon possession is clearly present in his activities. Therefore, for Jesus now to claim authority to forgive sins is not completely unexpected, for from the reader's perspective the revelation of Jesus' authority continues to build in an unhin-

---

[54] G.H. Boobyer, 'Mark 2, 10a and the Interpretation of the Healing of the Paralytic', *HTR* 47 (1954), p. 120; Murphy-O'Conner, 'Pêchê et Communauté dans le Nouveau Testament', p. 182; L.S. Hay, 'The Son of Man in Mark 2.10 and 2.28', *JBL* 89 (1970), p. 71; Lane, *Mark*, p. 98; and Doughty, 'The Authority of the Son of Man', p. 165.

[55] As Dewey (*Markan Public Debate*, p. 77-79) has shown from her rhetorical analysis of this text.

[56] The scholarly contributions on the various aspects of the meaning of 'Son of Man' is nearly becoming too unwieldy to be treated by a single scholar. Fortunately, the results of this study do not depend upon mastery of this voluminous literature.

[57] For one of the better discussions of Mark's use of the 'Son of Man' title at this point in the narrative cf. esp. Hurtado, *Mark*, p. 24.

dered fashion. Yet, for Jesus to claim the authority to forgive sin upon the earth[58] means that he is claiming for himself a power that only God himself can rightly claim, and this is quite obviously an extraordinary thing to claim. For, as far as can be determined from the extant literature, there was no expectation in ancient Judaism that the Messiah would have the power to forgive sins.[59]

Jesus' Words of Healing to the Paralytic (vv. 10b-11)

Turning, as it were, in mid-sentence, Jesus addresses the paralytic again for the first time since v. 5. The sense of dramatic build-up is intense enough, given the one-sided dialogue of Jesus with the scribes, but when attention is again directed to the paralytic, the reader quickly thinks of the expectancy of the paralytic as he now anticipates this climatic moment. Using a complementary form of address,[60] Jesus finally says the more difficult thing from v. 9, commanding the man to rise,[61] take up his cot, and go to his own house.

The Healing of the Paralytic and its Results on the Crowd (v. 12)

The effect of Jesus' command was immediate, as the one who was carried becomes the one who carries his cot before them all. The result of this miraculous healing was that all who saw it were beside themselves and glorified God, with the possible exception of the scribes[62] who may have been amazed but perhaps did not thank God for the event. The claim by the crowd that nothing like this had been seen before is especially significant, for it suggests that in the eyes of the people, this healing was even greater than the exorcism which took place during Jesus' first visit to Capernaum.[63]

---

[58] It is difficult to determine the precise significance of ἐπὶ τῆς γῆς. Cf. Cranfield (*Mark*, pp. 100-101) for a discussion of the various interpretive options.

[59] Cf. Hooker, *Mark*, p. 88.

[60] J. Coppens ['Les logia du Fils de l'homme dans l'évangile de Marc', in *L'Évangile selon Marc: Tradition et rédaction* (ed. M. Sabbe; Leuven: Leuven University Press, 1974, p. 519 n. 159] observes, 'Le σοὶ λέγω (*Mc.*, II, 11) est un indice complémentaire'.

[61] Hooker (*Mark*, p. 87) suggests that Mark's readers may very well have been aware of the implication of the use of ἔγειρε here, as it is also used in 16.6 of Jesus' resurrection.

[62] Anderson, *Mark*, p. 102; Kernaghan, 'History and Redaction in the Controversy Stories in Mark 2.1-3.6', p. 26; and Kuthirakkattel, *The Beginning of Jesus' Ministry*, p. 196.

[63] Hooker, *Mark*, p. 88.

Conclusions

Does this passage assume an explicit connection between the paralytic's sin and his condition, his forgiveness and subsequent healing? Despite the arguments to the contrary, Mk 2.1-12 does not give evidence of an explicit connection between this man' sin and his paralytic condition. In contrast to John 5, where a connection is clearly drawn between the individual's personal sin and his infirmity and where the man's healing and forgiveness take place in one moment of time, in the story of the paralytic in Mark's Gospel no explicit connection is made by Jesus, nor does the pronouncement of forgiveness heal the man of his paralysis. Rather, his healing is treated separately. This is not to say that there is no relationship between the pronouncement of forgiveness and the healing in the Marcan text. But it is to observe that the connection made by Jesus between the two is one of comparison, 'Which is easier to say?' The healing of the paralytic, then, takes place to validate Jesus' claim to have authority to forgive sins. That the paralytic is the recipient of both forgiveness and healing allows the comparison to be seen more clearly. While it is possible that a fundamental relationship exists between sin and illness for Mark, it is difficult to understand why he would make that connection on only one occasion, and there in an ambiguously articulated fashion. None of this is to deny that a healing of this nature might not serve as a powerful image of the liberating effects of sin, but that such an imagery does not appear to be foremost in the text of Mark. Therefore, despite the fact that Jesus' miraculous healings do announce the arrival of the Kingdom of God, which necessarily implies a triumph over Satan, this examination of Mk 2.1-12 suggests that on this occasion Jesus does not attribute illness directly to sin.

Mark 9.14-29 – The Demon Possessed Boy

Whereas the first passage examined in this chapter is located near the opening of the Gospel, the next Marcan text of significance for this investigation is found in the second half of the Gospel. The first half of Mark's work builds to the confession of Jesus' messianic status by Peter in 8.27-30. After this central and pivotal story, Jesus begins for the first time in the Gospel to speak plainly about the necessity of his death and resurrection (8.31-9.1). This story is followed by an account of the transfiguration of Jesus which involves Moses and Elijah, all before the eyes of Peter, James, and John. Mark says that Jesus is transformed before them (μετε-μορφώθη ἔμπροσθεν αὐτῶν) resulting in an appearance that is blinding white. After this extraordinary event, and while conversing with his three disciples about the role and function of Elijah, they make their way back to the other disciples. Given the prominence of the mountain in 9.2 (going up), 9.9 (going down), and 9.14 (at it base), it is possible that Mark may intend his readers to see a connection between these three stories.[64] This then is the context of Mk 9.14-29, the final exorcism in Mark's Gospel and the only exorcism found in the second half of the book.[65]

By way of introduction to the pericope itself, the following observations should be made. The mention of a mountain, the presence of Moses, the change in Jesus' appearance, the confusion Jesus finds upon his descent from the mountain, and the people's response to Jesus have sometimes prompted interpreters to see in these events direct allusions to the story of Moses on Sinai in Exodus 32.[66] Others have seen any intended correspondences to be intra-textual. Specifically, it has been suggested that the transfiguration (9.2-13) is meant to correspond with Jesus' baptism (1.9-11), while the healing of the demon-possessed boy (9.14-29) is said to correspond to Jesus' temptation experience in the wilderness (1.12-13).[67] Finally, one interpreter has gone so far as to argue that this story is a conspectus in that it 'alludes to at least one element of each of the previous healing/exorcism episodes before Bethsaida'.[68] While the degree of validity of each of these proposals is, no doubt, debatable, what should become clear in the course of the reading which follows is the way in which this passage is connected to that which precedes and follows it in the Marcan narrative.

---

[64] S.W.-W. Chu, 'The Healing of the Epileptic Boy in Mark 9:14-29: Its Rhetorical Structure and Theological Implications' (PhD Dissertation, Vanderbilt University, 1988), pp. 106-107.

[65] Harrington, *Mark*, p. 140.

[66] Johnson, *Mark*, p. 161 and Hurtado, *Mark*, p. 133.

[67] Cf. Lane, *Mark*, p. 329 and Harrington, *Mark*, pp. 139-40.

[68] For the suggested points of similarity cf. C. Meyers, *Binding the Strong Man: A Political Reading of Mark's Story of Jesus* (Maryknoll, NY: Orbis, 1988), p. 254.

And having come to the disciples he saw a great crowd around them and the scribes arguing with them. And immediately when the whole crowd saw him they were greatly amazed, and running to him they greeted him. And he asked them, 'What are you arguing with them about?' And one of the crowd answered him, 'Teacher, I brought my son to you, having a dumb spirit: and whenever it seizes him it throws him down, and he foams at the mouth and he grinds his teeth and he becomes rigid: and I asked your disciples in order that they might cast it out, and they could not'. And answering them he said, 'O faithless generation, how long shall I be with you? How long must I put up with you? Bring him to me.' And they brought him to him. And seeing him, immediately the spirit threw him into a convulsion, and falling upon the ground he rolled around foaming at the mouth. And he asked his father, 'How long has this happened to him?' And he said, 'From childhood; and often it both casts him into the fire and into the water in order that it might destroy him: but if you are able to do anything, help us, taking pity upon us'. And Jesus said to him, 'If you can do anything? – all things are possible for the one who believes!' Immediately crying out, the father of the child said, 'I believe! Help my unbelief!' And Jesus having seen that the crowd was gathering rapidly, rebuked the unclean spirit saying to him, 'Dumb and deaf spirit, I command you, come out of him and never enter into him again!' And having cried out and having convulsed greatly he came out. And he became as though dead, causing many to say, 'He has died'. But Jesus taking his hand, raised him up and he stood up. And when he had gone into the house his disciples privately asked him, 'Why were we not able to cast this one out?' And he said to them, 'This kind does not come out except by means of prayer'.

The pericope itself may be divided into the following outline:

a) The Arrival of Jesus and his Questioning of the Crowd (vv. 14-16)
b) The Father's Words to Jesus (vv. 17-18)
c) Jesus' Reply to the Father (v. 19)
d) The Bringing of the Boy to Jesus (v. 20)
e) Jesus' Dialogue with the Father (vv. 21-24)
f) The Exorcism of the Demon and the Healing of the Boy

(vv. 25-27)

g) Jesus in the House with his Disciples (vv. 28-29)

With this brief bit of introduction, Mk 9.14-29 is now examined.

The Arrival of Jesus and his Questioning of the Crowd (vv. 14-16)

Several helpful if not surprising bits of information are contained in the opening verse of this pericope (v. 14). Although not made explicit in the text, according to the narrative, Jesus' return to the disciples is a reunion with the nine other disciples, as Peter, James, and John have accompanied him up the mountain. In addition to the disciples, v. 14 reveals the presence of a great crowd and the scribes. Owing to the place of both crowds and scribes in the narrative to this point, the appearance of neither would normally surprise the reader, except that here the implication of the Marcan narrative is that the locale of this event is not in Galilee, as Jesus returns to Galilee only after this story (9.30), but further north in the vicinity of Caesarea Philippi (8.27). The presence of both the crowd and the scribes in this geographical location is significant. Positively, the reader is impressed with the fact that, even though Jesus has traveled so far north, his popularity has not diminished in that he continues to be sought out by the crowds. Negatively, the readers realize the scribes are so opposed to Jesus that there is no place they will not go to investigate and/or pursue him.[69] The curiosity of the reader is further heightened by the fact that there is an argument going on among the disciples, scribes, and crowd, the subject of which is not revealed until v. 17.

When the crowd sees Jesus they respond with an amazement that borders on fear.[70] Such an extreme reaction could very well be

---

[69] Such a narrative function for the scribes explains their 'odd' presence in this locale. For comments that their presence in or near Caesarea Philippi is improbable cf. Huby, *Saint Marc*, p. 230; Taylor, *Mark*, p. 397; Nineham, *Mark*, p. 246; and Mann, *Mark*, p. 369. Cranfield (*Mark*, p. 300) notes that while their appearance is surprising it is not impossible, while Swete (*Mark*, p. 195) suggests the scribes are probably rabbis from local synagogues. C. Runacher (*Croyants Incrédules: La guérison de l'épileptique Mark 9, 14-29* [Paris: Cerf, 1994], pp. 244-46) notes that the scribes consistently show up in contexts where the authority of Jesus is challenged.

[70] The other three occurrences of ἐκθαμβέομαι, a term which in the whole of the New Testament appears only in Mark, describe Jesus' agony in Gethsemane (14.33) and the reaction of the women upon entering the tomb (16.5, 6).

owing to the lingering effects of the transfiguration,[71] and might be noted by Mark to anticipate Jesus' death (14.33) and resurrection (16.5, 6).[72] At any rate, the crowd quickly makes its way to him in order to greet Jesus, whereupon Jesus inquires as to their discussion with the disciples.[73]

The Father's Words to Jesus (vv. 17-18)

Verse 17 records that one of the crowd responds to Jesus' words and explains his dilemma, perhaps revealing the content of the crowd's discussion as well. The man, who calls Jesus teacher (as the disciples had in 4.38), reveals that his son has a spirit which will not allow him to speak (ἔχοντα πνεῦμα ἄλαλον). It is not altogether clear what this phrase means. It could mean either that the demon himself refused to speak and therefore was more difficult to deal with because he would not reveal his name; or that the demon kept the boy from speaking at any time.[74] It is also possible that, given the relationship between the demonic dumbness and the seizures, the father meant that his son was unable to speak during the times of the seizures.[75] On the whole it would seem safe to assume that the father's words should be taken to mean the boy was permanently or periodically unable to speak. The father goes on to describe the 'fits' to which the boy was subject, such as falling to the ground, foaming at the mouth, grinding of the teeth, and a muscular rigidity. Scholars are nearly unanimous in identifying the condi-

---

[71] For this interpretation cf. Wesley, *Explanatory Notes*, p. 117; Waetjen, *A Reordering of Power*, p. 153; Hooker, *Mark*, p. 223; and esp. Gundry, *Mark*, pp. 487-88.

[72] Most scholars, however, reject this interpretation, preferring one which emphasizes surprise or astonishment at Jesus' sudden appearance. Cf. Gould, *Mark*, p. 167; Swete, *Mark*, p. 195; Branscomb, *Mark*, p. 166; LaGrange, *Saint Marc*, p. 238; Taylor, *Mark*, p. 396; Cranfield, *Mark*, p. 300; A. Jones, *The Gospel According to St Mark* (London: Chapman, 1963), p. 145; G. Bertram, 'ἐκθαμβέομαι', *TDNT*, III, p. 6 n. 13; van der Loos, *The Miracles of Jesus*, p. 398; Hiebert, *Mark*, p. 219; Lane, *Mark*, p. 330; and Anderson, *Mark*, p. 229. Runacher (*Croyants Incrédules*, pp. 262-67) observes that Mark intends to emphasize the epiphanic nature of the event.

[73] Chu ('The Healing of the Epileptic Boy in Mark 9:14-29', pp. 111-12) argues that Jesus' question reveals his ignorance of certain things and serves to balance his knowledge of the scribes' thoughts in 2.8.

[74] For these first two possibilities cf. LaGrange, *Saint Marc*, p. 239; Jones, *Mark*, p. 145; and Hiebert, *Mark*, p. 220.

[75] So Gundry, *Mark*, p. 488.

tion here described as some form of epilepsy.[76] The obvious implication of the father's words is that the demon was not only the
source of lack of speech, but also that of the seizures. The boy's
father concludes by informing Jesus that he brought his son to the
disciples for the purpose of exorcism, but they were not able to accomplish the task.[77] The reader may discern in these words an implicit allegation that the failure of the disciples reflects badly upon
the teacher, for there was an intimate association between Jesus and
his disciples.[78] At the very least, the words hint at the disappoint-
ment of the man over the disciples' failure and perhaps his growing
disbelief in Jesus' ability.

Jesus' Reply to the Father (v. 19)

Jesus' response in v. 19 catches the reader off guard, for it is a very
stern reprimand, even if its intended audience is not immediately
clear. The phrase 'O unbelieving generation' (Ὦ γενεὰ ἄπιστος)
introduces a set of rhetorical questions which are intended as a rebuke.[79] The use of Ὦ may be evidence of a higher literary style[80]
here used by Mark to give added emphasis to Jesus' words.[81] To
whom is this rebuke directed? Perhaps the best way to begin a response to this question is to rephrase it. Exactly what has caused
Jesus to react as he does? Is it the fact that the disciples do not have

---

[76] Gould, *Mark*, p. 168; Branscomb, *Mark*, p. 166; Huby, *Saint Marc*, p. 231; LaGrange, *Saint Marc*, p. 238; Taylor, *Mark*, p. 397; Johnson, *Mark*, p. 161; Cole, *Mark*, p. 214; Nineham, *Mark*, p. 246; van der Loos, *The Miracles of Jesus*, p. 401; Anderson, *Mark*, p. 230; Harrington, *Mark*, p. 141; J.K. Howard, 'New Testament Exorcism and its Significance Today', *ExpT* 96 (1984-85), p. 106; Waetjen, *A Re-ordering of Power*, p. 154; Juel, *Mark*, p. 131; and Hooker, *Mark*, p. 223. For an ex-tensive analysis by a medical doctor cf. J. Wilkinson, 'The Case of the Epileptic Boy', *ExpT* 79 (1967-68), pp. 39-42.

[77] Chu ('The Healing of the Epileptic Boy in Mark 9:14-29', pp. 114-15) as-serts that the use of ἰσχύω to describe the inability of the disciples to exorcise the demon is intended to remind the reader that Jesus is able to perform such acts because he is the 'mightier one' (ὁ ἰσχυρότερος) of Mk 1.7. However, given the variety of ways in which Mark uses these terms such an interpretation seems to outdistance the evidence of the text.

[78] Taylor, *Mark*, p. 398; E. Lohmeyer, *Das Evangelium des Markus* (Göttingen: Dandenhoed & Ruprecht, 1953), p. 186; Standaert, *Marc*, p. 144; Harrington, *Mark*, pp. 141-42; and Mann, *Mark*, p. 370.

[79] *BDF*, p. 81 §146 (2).

[80] J.A. Lee, 'Some Features of the Speech of Jesus in Mark's Gospel', *NovT* 27 (1985), p. 118.

[81] Gundry, *Mark*, p. 489.

enough faith to exorcise this demon?[82] If so, then why does Mark's Jesus miss the opportunity to lay this charge against the disciples when they speak privately in the house? Or is it the father's (and the crowd's) attitude toward Jesus and his disciples that has caused this response from Jesus?[83] After all, the father of the demon-possessed boy serves as a spokesperson for the crowd introduced earlier. Or is the rebuke directed to all those present, including the scribes, as a general condemnation of this world? Although similar rebukes are made in the Old Testament against Israel by Moses (Deut. 32.5) and God (Deut. 32.20) and may serve as a precedent, perhaps the most satisfactory way to settle this question is by giving attention to the way 'generation' is used in Mark to this point. Responding to the Pharisees' request for a sign in 8.12, Jesus asks, 'Why does this generation ask for a sign?', and then he goes on to say that it will not be given one. The clear implication is that this is an 'unbelieving' generation. Likewise, in his first discussion about the necessity of his death, and the warning which follows, Jesus speaks of 'this adulterous and sinful generation' (8.38). As the disciples are being warned not to deny Jesus or his words before such a generation, it is obviously in opposition to him. Given this earlier usage, the reader is predisposed not to include the disciples in this generation. As becomes apparent later (vv. 22-24), if anyone lacks faith it is the father. As the questions reveal, Jesus cannot believe the level of the unbelief. He then asks for the boy to be brought to him.

The Bringing of the Boy to Jesus (v. 20)
In accordance with Jesus' command the boy is brought to him. But as soon as the spirit sees Jesus, he begins to afflict the boy in ways the father had earlier described. Such a display of the demon's power should probably be interpreted by the reader as the demon's attempt to intimidate Jesus,[84] for although demons have spoken to Jesus in earlier exorcism accounts, there has been no display of this

---

[82] Cf. Gould, *Mark*, p. 168; Cranfield, *Mark*, p. 301; van der Loos, *The Miracles of Jesus*, p. 399; Lane, *Mark*, p. 332; Hiebert, *Mark*, p. 221; and Hooker (*Mark*, p. 223) who includes the crowd.

[83] Cole, *Mark*, p. 215; S.E. Dowd, *Prayer, Power, and the Problem of Suffering* (SBLDS 105; Atlanta: Scholars Press, 1988), p. 118 n. 109; and Gundry, *Mark*, p. 489. Taylor (*Mark*, p. 398) suggests that the rebuke is directed to the people, while Johnson (*Mark*, p. 161) identifies the whole nation as the object.

[84] Cf. Gundry, *Mark*, p. 489.

nature described by Mark. The activity also tends to heighten the sense of narrative drama as the reader awaits Jesus' encounter with this spirit.

Jesus' Dialogue with the Father (vv. 21-24)

Although sometimes viewed as unnecessary by scholars, vv. 21-24 serve to increase the narrative's sense of drama. First, just when one expects Jesus to rebuke the demon, he asks the boy's father how long his son has been so afflicted.[85] Next, the father responds, providing additional information regarding the boy's situation. The difficulty, if not impossibility, of the case is confirmed from the response that the boy had been this way from childhood. In addition, the father notes that the demon will seize his son at the most dangerous of times, especially around water and fire, which makes the boy quite susceptible to drowning or serious permanent injury or disfigurement. The father naturally concludes that the demon is out to kill his son.[86] Third, it is even sometimes suggested that while Jesus and the father discuss the boy's condition, the young man is at that moment wallowing helplessly on the ground.[87] Fourth, whether or not the boy is undergoing a seizure at the very moment of Jesus' conversation, the father's plea for Jesus' pity[88] and help underscores the fact that this boy's situation is hopeless, aside from the intervention of Jesus.

For a second time in this story Jesus reacts strongly to something the father says. Earlier in v. 18, the man implied that the disciples' inability to cast out the demon reflected poorly on Jesus. Jesus' response on that occasion has been duly noted. If the father's previous statement had indirectly implied that Jesus was unable to cast out the demon, in v. 22 the father seems to suggest that possibility

---

[85] For this interpretation of the question cf. Cole, *Mark*, p. 216; Hiebert, *Mark*, p. 222; Harrington, *Mark*, p. 142; and Hurtado, *Mark*, p. 134.

[86] Huby (*Saint Marc*, p. 232) sums up nicely, 'Dans la pensée du père, ce n'est pas simple effet du hasard que pendant ces crises l'enfant tomb fréquemment dans le feu ou l'eau: il y voit de la part du mauvais esprit l'intention expresse de causer au possédé quelque accident grave ou la mort'. Swete's interpretation (*Mark*, p. 199) that the boy has a suicidal mania in such moments seems to outdistance the evidence.

[87] For this interpretation cf. Lohmeyer, *Markus*, p. 187 and Nineham, *Mark*, p. 246.

[88] A reaction in Jesus that has always resulted in action on behalf of the ones for whom he feels this emotion. Cf. Mark 1.41; 6.34; and 8.2.

directly to Jesus,[89] although of course hoping that Jesus was indeed able to help his son.[90]

In order to make clear the specific words used by the father to which Jesus takes exception, he uses a grammatical construction to signify a direct quote (Tò) followed by 'If you are able to do anything'. The meaning of this construction results in something like – 'so far as the "if you are able" is concerned … (I say to you) …'[91] Jesus quotes the words to challenge them,[92] by stating that 'all things are possible to the one who believes'. Two things are conveyed in these words. On the one hand, Jesus implies that the problem is not with his ability but with the man's lack of faith. Perhaps Wesley best captures this aspect of the phrase when he paraphrases, 'The thing does not turn on my power, but on thy faith. *I* can do all things: canst *thou* believe?'[93] This understanding of Jesus' words is supported by the response of the man in the next verse, the way faith has functioned (5.34 and 36) and will function (10.52) in miracles within the Marcan narrative, and Jesus' future teaching about and advocacy of faith (and prayer) as found in 11.23-24. On the other hand, Jesus' words mean that nothing is impossible for the one who believes (in God or Jesus), for nothing is impossible for God, a fact which Jesus will make clearer later in the Gospel (10.27 and 14.36). These two dimensions of Jesus' words combine to challenge the father that this kind of faith sets no limits upon what God is able to accomplish.[94] The idea that *Jesus* is the one who believes is attractive[95] but has little basis in the text, as Jesus is described nowhere else in Mark as 'believing'. Jesus, then, challenges the man to greater faith, while implying that only God is able to do all things.[96]

---

[89] Runacher, *Croyants incrédules*, p. 175.

[90] Cf. Gundry (*Mark*, p. 490) on the implications of the disciples' failure for Jesus.

[91] *BDF*, p. 140 §267 (1).

[92] Cranfield, *Mark*, p. 302.

[93] Wesley, *Explanatory Notes*, p. 118. Similarly, cf. Lane, *Mark*, p. 333.

[94] Cranfield, *Mark*, p. 303; Anderson, *Mark*, p. 231; Harrington, *Mark*, p. 142; and Williams, *Other Followers of Jesus*, p. 140.

[95] As suggested by Lohmeyer (*Markus*, p. 190) and Achtemeier ('Miracles and the Historical Jesus', *CBQ* 37 [1975], p. 480).

[96] Runacher, *Croyants incrédules*, pp. 182-83.

The father's response to Jesus' stern words is immediate and apparently quite genuine. The fact that he cries out (κράξας) emphasizes the intensity of the father's passion for his son and his extraordinary desperation.[97] His cry reveals a faith that, while not yet
complete or mature, is headed in the right direction.[98] In contrast to
the unbelief of those in Nazareth (6.6), this man desires the removal of any obstacle to his faith and thus becomes a role model
for the reader.[99] The reader, who recalls the effect of such unbelief
there, now anticipates that Jesus will help the man's lack of faith.

The Exorcism of the Demon and the Healing of the Boy (vv. 25-27)

The mention of a rapidly assembling crowd in v. 25, as if there had
been no reference to the crowd earlier in this pericope, is at first
rather puzzling. Apparently, the reader is to understand that either
Jesus and the father have withdrawn somewhat from the crowd as
they discussed the boy's situation or that the existing crowd is being
enlarged by another.[100] The former option is plagued by the fact
that the crowd appears to be present in v. 20, where the boy is
brought to Jesus by some ambiguous 'they', while with the latter
option one would expect reference to 'another' crowd.[101] In terms
of the crowd's narrative function there are two points worth making. First, the reader is no doubt intended to see the father's cry as
one of the reasons for the crowd's assembling.[102] Second, consistent
with the secrecy theme in Mark, Jesus' seeing the crowd prompts
him to act before more people congregate.

In the exorcism itself, Jesus rebukes the unclean spirit, which
may imply a command to remain silent. ἐπιτιμάω often appears in
Marcan contexts where someone or something is being silenced (cf.
1.25; 3.11; 4.39; 8.30; 10.13; and 10.48). The content of the rebuke

---

[97] Lohmeyer (*Markus*, p. 188) suggests that the cry was divinely inspired.

[98] Several scholars refer to the man's belief as half faith or belief. Cf. Taylor, *Mark*, p. 400; Hooker, *Mark*, p. 224; Mann, *Mark*, pp. 370-71; and esp. Williams, *Other Followers of Jesus*, p. 140.

[99] Runacher, *Croyants incrédules*, pp. 189-91, 196-98.

[100] For this suggestion cf. Gould, *Mark*, p. 170 and LaGrange, *Saint Marc*, p. 241.

[101] Perhaps, as Lane observes (*Mark*, p. 334), the reference must remain ob-scure.

[102] So Huby, *Saint Marc*, 232.

reveals even more about this particular unclean spirit as Jesus refers to it as a dumb and deaf spirit (Tò ἄλαλον καὶ κωφὸν πνεῦμα). Such information allows the reader to know that this situation is even more difficult than previously thought[103] and heightens the reader's appreciation of Jesus' knowledge. Jesus then uses a formula (ἐγὼ ἐπιτάσσω σοι) that leaves the demon no choice but to obey.[104] Following this Jesus issues a two-fold command to the demon to come out and never enter the boy again. Such an unusual command in Mark's Gospel can be read as evidence that Jesus regarded the demonic possession to be periodic rather than permanent, coinciding with the boy's 'fits',[105] or that the double rebuke is in response to the contempt the demon had earlier shown for Jesus (v. 20).[106] However, despite its unique appearance in Mark, there is contemporaneous evidence to suggest that such a double emphasis could be part of exorcisms where no additional meaning is intended.[107] Nevertheless, the reader might be inclined to take such unparalleled language *in Mark* as additional assurance that the demon would not return.[108] It may not be without significance that, in this last exorcism described by Mark, the point is explicitly made that the demon is not to return.

In one last attempt to torment the young man the demon cried loudly and convulsed the boy. The child was left so weak that he resembled someone dead. Mark underscores this point by noting that many people in the crowd were saying that he had died. While such unconsciousness is not uncommon after such a convulsion,[109] it is clear that Mark intends for his readers to see the significance of his emphasis upon death imagery. But in a way not dissimilar to his actions with Jairus' daughter,[110] Jesus takes the boy's hand and raises

---

[103] Gundry, *Mark*, p. 491.

[104] W. Grimm, 'Ἐπιτάσσω', *EDNT*, II, p. 41.

[105] For this interpretation cf. Branscomb, *Mark*, p. 167 and Nineham, *Mark*, p. 247.

[106] Lane, *Mark*, p. 334.

[107] Cf. for example, Josephus, *Ant* 8.45 and Philostratus, *Life of Apollonius of Tyana* 4.20. Cf. also the comments by Achtemeier, 'Miracles and the Historical Jesus', p. 480.

[108] Hiebert, *Mark*, p. 224.

[109] Cf. Wilkinson, 'The Case of the Epileptic Boy', p. 42.

[110] For this comparison cf. Mann, *Mark*, p. 370.

him up so that he stands (on his own). Jesus' action of raising an apparently dead boy anticipates his own death and resurrection which is shortly to come[111] and this interpretation is in harmony with the emphasis this theme receives in the latter portion of Mark's Gospel.

Jesus in the House with his Disciples (vv. 28-29)
This story concludes with Jesus and the disciples in the privacy of a house. Based on the actions of Jesus on previous occasions when they were in the house (4.10 and 7.17), the reader has come to expect clarification and further explanation from Jesus to the disciples on the topic at hand.[112] Their question for him at this point was, 'Why were we not able to cast it out?' It is an inevitable question, because the disciples had been chosen by Jesus for the express purpose of casting out demons (3.15), they were trained by Jesus for this work (3.20-30 and 5.1-20), they were sent out by Jesus specifically to accomplish this task (6.7), and they were successful in that they cast out many demons (6.13). So, why were they unsuccessful on this occasion?

The answer to the disciples' question comes in v. 29 where Jesus notes that this kind (of demon) comes out only by prayer. Of the many intriguing aspects of this verse perhaps the place to begin is with the phrase 'this kind of demon' (Τοῦτο τὸ γένος). Despite arguments to the contrary,[113] it is difficult not to interpret that Jesus here means a specific kind or class of demon,[114] the implication being that there are various kinds or classes of demons.[115] But what does such a statement mean? Several textual indicators make a tentative answer possible. First, this kind of demon appears to be dis-

---

[111] Lane, *Mark*, p. 334; Anderson, *Mark*, p. 231; Standaert, *Marc*, p. 145; Harrington, *Mark*, pp. 142-43; Hurtado, *Mark*, p. 134; Latourelle, *Miracles de Jésus et théologie du Miracle*, p. 177; Chu, 'The Healing of the Epileptic Boy in Mark 9.14-29', p. 123; Waetjen, *Reordering of Power*, p. 156; Hooker, *Mark*, p. 225; and Gundry, *Mark*, p. 492. Runacher (*Croyants incrédules*, pp. 211-17) argues that the readers would see their own future resurrection in this imagery.

[112] Cf. esp. Lane, *Mark*, p. 335.

[113] Gould (*Mark*, p. 171) argues that the phrase should be translated as 'the genus evil spirit', not 'this kind of spirit'. Runacher (*Croyants incrédules*, pp. 168-69) proposes that '... "touto to genos" désigne l'ensemble des esprits mauvais ...'.

[114] Swete, *Mark*, p. 202; LaGrange, *Saint Marc*, p. 242; Huby, *Saint Marc*, p. 234; Taylor, *Mark*, p. 401; and Hiebert, *Mark*, p. 224.

[115] Juel, *Mark*, p. 132.

tinguished from the other kind(s) of demons described elsewhere in Mark's Gospel. Second, in the other individual exorcisms per- formed by Jesus, the demon initiates contact with him by revealing his identity. In contrast, when this demon sees Jesus he afflicts the boy before Jesus' eyes, either in an attempt to intimidate Jesus or in a show of his contempt for him. Third, another discernible textual difference between this demon and the others is that this is the only place in Mark's Gospel where an illness is ever attributed directly to demon possession. Fourth, perhaps a demon capable of inflicting the combination of these specific symptoms (deafness, dumbness, and life-threatening convulsions) belongs in a special category of demons.[116] Fifth, Mark makes clear that this boy's troubles started very early, (Ἐκ παιδιόθεν), although another child is described as being demon possessed in 7.24-30. Therefore, Jesus explains that part of the reason why the disciples were unable to cast out this demon is owing to the kind of demon which they had encountered.

Jesus goes on to answer the disciples' question by pointing out that this kind of demon can only come out by means of prayer. Al- though Jesus himself did not pray during this exorcism, he is clearly presented as a model of prayer in Mark's Gospel.[117] In 1.35, after healing many people and casting out many demons Jesus withdraws from the crowd to pray. Immediately after feeding the five thou- sand, Jesus goes up to a mountain to pray (6.46). His third major prayer is in the Garden of Gethsemane (14.32-39) just before his arrest. In addition to these major times of prayer, Jesus offers thanks or blessings on several other occasions (6.41; 8.6; and 14.22). Not only does he teach the necessity of prayer here, but he will re- turn to this topic in more detail in 11.24-25. Thus, the reader has a clear sense of the importance of prayer in Jesus' life and is not completely taken back by his words here. The implications of Jesus' words are that the disciples had not sufficiently prepared themselves in prayer for such an event as this. It is difficult to discern from the text of Mark whether or not the disciples had prayed before their previous exorcism experiences. If not, it is theoretically possible to

---

[116] For this last suggestion cf. Gundry, *Mark*, p. 493. For a somewhat similar idea cf. van der Loos, *The Miracles of Jesus*, p. 401.

[117] Cf. Pesch, *Markusevangelium*, II, p. 97; Chu, 'The Healing of the Epileptic Boy in Mark 9:14-29', pp. 199-217; and esp. Dowd, *Prayer, Power, and the Problem of Suffering*, pp. 119-21.

argue that they did not need prayer for some exorcisms but did for others. However, given that this is the last exorcism described by Mark, and the last one the disciples attempted, the message of this verse is most likely a warning that the disciples must not be deceived into believing that the ability to cast out demons resides within them, but that absolute dependence upon God for such activity is essential.[118]

At this point a large number of manuscripts include the words 'and fasting' (καὶ νηστείᾳ). Most interpreters regard the phrase as secondary, owing to the increasing emphasis in the early church upon fasting.[119] While such reasoning should not be ignored, and while two of the manuscripts which omit the phrase are impressive (ℵ* B), one wonders whether the phrase can be dismissed so easily. It is clear from Mk 2.18-22 that Jesus intended his disciples to fast after his resurrection. One would think that, given this emphasis, the inclusion of this phrase in the vast majority of manuscripts would qualify it as the more difficult reading, although some would say perhaps too difficult. In any event, it would make a great deal of sense as words of instruction for the ('future') Marcan community. If the disputed words are original, the meaning for this verse in all likelihood is to underscore the fact that an intensive consecration to God is needed in the casting out of these kinds of demons. But on balance it is probable that the phrase is secondary.

Implications

There are several implications of the examination of Mk 9.14-29 for this study of the Devil, disease, and deliverance. 1) For the first time in this investigation a physical infirmity has been unmistakably attributed to a demon or unclean spirit. 2) The demon is said to prevent the child from hearing or speaking and to cause epileptic-like seizures. 3) It appears that this unclean spirit not only desires to torment the child but also attempts to kill him. 4) Mark 9.29 suggests that there is more than one category or class of demon. 5)

---

[118] Taylor, *Mark*, p. 401; Lane, *Mark*, p. 335; and Harrington, *Mark*, p. 143. On the relationship between prayer and faith cf. Runacher, *Croyants incrédules*, pp. 169-74.

[119] Cf. esp. Metzger, *Textual Commentary on the Greek New Testament*, p. 101. For an opposing viewpoint cf. Cole, *Mark*, p. 218 n. 1.

The disciples are unable to cast out this demon, owing to a lack of prayer, which is the remedy for demons of this sort.

He Healed their Sick and Cast Out many Demons

Contrary to what is sometimes argued, Mark does not simply equate demon possession with illness in an uncritical fashion. Rather, it seems that he has been intentional in keeping the lines of demarcation drawn between the two. While it is true that on two occasions Jesus is described, in summary fashion, as healing all those who were ill and casting out demons of those possessed (1.32-34 and 3.10-12) and that the actions of the disciples are described in a similar manner (6.13),[120] it does not appear that Mark intends his readers to assume that these groups are one and the same. In addition to the fact that grammatically there are two groups in focus in these passages, the rest of the Gospel indicates that Mark is careful to distinguish between these conditions. For example, of the ten specific healing stories which Mark's Gospel contains (Mk 1.29-32; 1.40-45; 2.1-12; 3.1-6; 5.21-43; 6.54-56; 7.31-37; 8.22-26; 9.14-19; and 10.46-52)[121] only once is an illness attributed to demonic origin, Mk 9.14-19. Similarly, of the four texts where specific exorcisms are recounted (Mk 1.21-28; 5.1-20; 7.24-30; and 9.14-29)[122] none of them hints that a demon has brought on an illness except the one text examined previously, Mk 9.14-29. In other words, based upon the text of Mark itself, there is apparently little desire on his part to emphasize a connection between demonic activity and infirmities, despite the fact that Mark has a clear interest in both.

Conclusions and Implications

What might be concluded about the Devil, disease, and deliverance from this examination of the Gospel according to Mark?

---

[120] Similar activity is foretold in Mk 16.17-18. For a discussion of the textual problems surrounding Mk 16.9-20 cf. J.C. Thomas, 'A Reconsideration of the Ending of Mark', *JETS* 26 (1983), pp. 407-19.

[121] Cf. also the summary statement in Mk 6.5.

[122] Cf. also the statement regarding an exorcist unknown to the disciples in Mk 9.38-41.

1) Unlike James, Paul, and John, Mark does not directly attribute certain illnesses to sin. Although both forgiveness and healing occur in close proximity in Mk 2.1-12, there is little evidence that Mark intended a connection to be made. If such a connection did exist for Mark, he apparently does not feel under any compulsion to make this relationship obvious.

2) Mark's major contribution to the study at this point is his unambiguous attribution of an infirmity to a demon. It is clear from Mark that the only hope for the boy so afflicted was the exorcism of the demon.

3) The symptoms of dumbness and deafness, here brought on by the demon, are present in another Marcan text quite apart from demonic activity.

4) The (epileptic-like) seizures, with which the child is afflicted, appear in Mark's Gospel only in the context of demonic activity.

5) According to Jesus in Mk 9.29, there are different categories of demons. The demon in Mark 9 is apparently of a different category than the others described in the Gospel.

6) The key to the exorcism of these kinds of demons (and others it would appear) is prayer as modeled by Jesus.

7) Mark does not lump healings and exorcisms together but chooses to keep the lines drawn clearly between them, with only one instance of demonic-induced infirmity.

8) Illnesses are not attributed directly to God in Mark's Gospel.

9) If the narratives of the Gospel according to Mark are intended to serve as a paradigm for the praxis of his community, however that might be defined, one may deduce that, when faced with illness, the church would have anointed the sick with oil and prayed for healing. It is possible, though not certain, that the church also may have used discernment in sorting out illnesses which were inflicted by demons from those which were not.

5

THE GOSPEL ACCORDING TO MATTHEW

Thus far, this investigation of the New Testament documents has revealed limited interest in the role of Satan or demons in the origins of illness. Only with the examination of the Gospels does one find an unambiguous attribution of an illness to demonic influence. But as was observed in the preceding chapter, there is only one example of such an attribution in Mark.

When one turns to the Gospel according to Matthew things begin to change considerably, for not only does Matthew contain more specific examples of infirmities caused by demons than does Mark, but he even goes so far as to suggest that such maladies belong in a special category. On the face of it, this increase in numbers of demonically inspired infirmities might indicate that this association was more common within the Matthean community, although certainty on this point is difficult to determine. Yet at the same time, it would be a mistake to assume that Matthew uncritically attributes all illness to demonic origins, as he goes to great lengths to make clear that not all infirmities are caused by demonic activity. Thus, an examination of the Gospel according to Matthew should provide additional information relevant to the purposes of this enquiry.

Matthew is generally considered to have been written at some point after the destruction of Jerusalem, with estimates ranging from 72 to 85 CE. The text of Matthew suggests that it emerged at a time when the church was reflecting upon its identity in the light of the reformulation of Judaism owing to the destruction of the temple on the one hand, and what proved to be a flourishing mission to the Gentiles in the Matthean community on the other hand. The structure and content of the Gospel suggest that it was designed and utilized as a catechetical handbook for the formation of disciples.

This chapter examines the summary statements regarding healings and exorcisms (4.23-25 and 8.16-17), comments briefly upon the parallel passages found in Matthew of texts already examined in Mark (Mt 9.1-7 and 17.14-23), and examines additional relevant passages (9.27-34; 12.22-23, 36, 43-45; and 15.28). All of the above are examined in their narrative order.

Introduction

Matthew begins his Gospel with a birth narrative that seeks to answer four questions: Who? (Jesus is the Son of Abraham and Son of David.) How? (He is conceived by the Holy Spirit.) Where? (In Bethlehem, the City of David.) Whence? (He is providentially taken from Bethlehem to Egypt, to the land of Israel, to Judah, to Galilee, then to Nazareth.) From this section the reader also learns that Jesus will 'save his people from their sins' and is in effect 'God with Us'. One of the major emphases of these first two chapters is how Jesus fulfills or relives Israel's history. Through a variety of actions Jesus not only fulfills Scripture (even before he can speak!), but also exhibits a deep solidarity with his people Israel.

Chapter three opens with John the Baptist preaching a conversion baptism, condemning the sin of the religious leaders, and announcing the coming of a 'mightier one' who 'will baptize with the Holy Spirit and fire'. Jesus' coming for John's baptism and his testing in the wilderness continue the solidarity motif. With the imprisonment of John, Jesus (still fulfilling Scripture) leaves Galilee and begins to preach the same message John preached (4.17). The preaching of the Kingdom is not to be a one-person affair, so Jesus calls his first disciples to aid in that task (i.e. to become fishers of men). Just before beginning the Sermon on the Mount (5-7), Matthew offers a summary of Jesus' ministry to this point. It is to this summary passage that this examination now turns.

Matthew 4.23-25 – 'He Healed All Who Were Ill'

And he traveled in the whole of Galilee, teaching in their synagogues and preaching the gospel of the kingdom and healing
every disease and every sickness among the people. And his
reputation went out into the whole of Syria; and they brought to
him all who were ill with various diseases and suffering severe
pain and the demonized and epileptic and paralyzed, and he
healed them. And many crowds followed him from Galilee and
the Decapolis and Jerusalem and Judea and the area beyond the
Jordan.

Before examining the individual verses in detail, a word should be
offered about the passage as a whole. This is the first of several
summary statements found in Matthew.[1] While it would be outdis-
tancing the evidence to offer a single interpretation of their purpose, it is clear that the first two of these summaries are related in a
special way. First, with the exception of place of location, the actual
wording in the Greek text is identical in each summary, suggesting
that such repetition is intentional. Second, as these summaries stand
on either side of one of the first major divisions of the Gospel (the
Words of the Messiah in the Sermon on the Mount [5-7] and the
Deeds of the Messiah in a series of miracle stories [8-9]), it appears
that they are intended to function as a bracket around the section.[2]
In addition to such a larger function, the summary in 4.23-25 is
transitional in that it provides a brief overview of the ministry of
Jesus to this point and serves as an introduction to the next major

[1] Cf. 4.23-25; 9.35; 11.4-5; 12.15; 14.35; 15.30; and 19.2.

[2] M.-J. LaGrange, *Évangile selon Saint Matthieu* (Paris: Gabalda, 1948), p. 71; H.J.
Held, 'Matthew as Interpreter of the Miracle Stories', in *Tradition and Interpretation
in Matthew* (ed. G. Bornkamm, G. Barth, and H.J. Held; tran. P. Scott; Philadelphia: Westminster, 1963), pp. 249-50; D. Hill, *The Gospel of Matthew* (Grand Rapids: Eerdmans, 1981), p. 106; W.G. Thompson, 'Reflections on the Composition
of Mt. 8.1-9.34', *CBQ* 33 (1971), p. 366 n. 5; J.D. Kingsbury, 'The "Miracle Chapters" of Matthew 8-9', *CBQ* 40 (1978), pp. 566-67; J.P. Meier, *Matthew* (Wilmington, DE: Michael Glazier, 1980), p. 35; F.D. Brunner, *The Christbook: A Histori-
cal/Theological Commentary: Matthew 1-12* (Waco: Word, 1987), p. 129; U. Luz, *Matthew 1-7* (tran. W.C. Linss; Minneapolis: Augsburg, 1989), p. 203; R.A. Edwards,
Matthew's Story of Jesus (Philadelphia: Fortress Press, 1985), p. 19; D.A. Hagner,
Matthew 1-13 (Dallas: Word, 1993), p. 79; D.R.A. Hare, *Matthew* (Louisville: John
Knox, 1993), p. 33; and J.C. Anderson, *Matthew's Narrative Web: Over, and Over, and
Over Again* (JSNTSup 91; Sheffield: JSOT Press, 1994), pp. 150-51.

section. This first of many summaries puts the reader on notice that such events are typical for Jesus.[3]

Verse 23

After calling the first four disciples, Jesus systematically makes his way through the whole of Galilee. To this point in the narrative Galilee has functioned as a place of safe domicile for Jesus provided by Joseph in response to a dream warning of Herod's son Archelaus (2.22). When Jesus again appears in the story (3.13), it is from this place that he comes for John's baptism. Apparently Jesus eventually returns to Galilee after his baptism and testing, for when it is heard that John has been arrested, Jesus again leaves Galilee (4.12). In addition to the way in which Galilee is tied to Jesus in Matthew, Galilee is defined with the Gentiles in a formula of fulfillment connected to Jesus' early ministry (4.15). Finally, it is from the region of Galilee, this time the Sea of Galilee, that Jesus calls his first followers. That Jesus in 4.23 would travel throughout Galilee would come as no surprise to the reader and might even hint at the possible inclusion of Gentiles in his ministry (a theme with which the Gospel begins and will end).

The remainder of v. 23 is devoted to a summary of the content of Jesus' ministry activity which includes three aspects: teaching, preaching, and healing. It is tempting to view the activities of teaching and preaching as one enterprise, owing to the two-fold division of Jesus' actions in the following section into word (5-7) and deed (8-9), and the way in which teaching and preaching tend to overlap in Matthew's Gospel.[4] However, since Matthew *does* use three different participles to describe Jesus' activity[5] and since the reader is

---

[3] Luz, *Matthew 1-7*, p. 204.

[4] Luz, *Matthew 1-7*, pp. 206-208; J. Gnilka, *Das Matthäusevangelium*, I (Freiburg: Herder, 1986), p. 106; W.D. Davies and D.C. Allison, Jr, *Matthew*, I (Edinburgh: T. & T. Clark, 1988), p. 414; R.H. Smith, *Matthew* (Minneapolis: Augsburg, 1989), p. 73; M. Davies, *Matthew: Readings* (Sheffield: Sheffield Academic Press, 1993), p. 48; and Hagner, *Matthew 1-13*, p. 80.

[5] F.V. Filson, *A Commentary on the Gospel according to Matthew* (London: A. & C. Black, 1960), p. 74; P. Bonnard, *L'évangile selon Saint Matthieu* (Neuchâtel: Delachaux & Niestlé, 1963), p. 51; E. Schweizer, *The Good News according to Matthew* (tr. D. Green; London: SPCK, 1975), p. 77; G. Maier, *Matthäus-Evangelium*, I (NeuHausen-Stuttgart: Hänssler-Verlag, 1979), p. 92; F.W. Beare, *The Gospel according to Matthew* (Oxford: Blackwell, 1981), p. 121; Brunner, *Christbook*, p. 129; D. Patte, *The Gospel According to Matthew* (Philadelphia: Fortress, 1987), p. 57; and L. Morris, *The Gospel according to Matthew* (Grand Rapids: Eerdmans, 1992), p. 87.

not yet aware of any overlap of the concepts, it would appear premature to dispense with the text's designations just yet. A final general observation is in order about these three ministry activities of Jesus; the disciples are given authority to do all three in the inverse order of their listing here, to heal (10.1), to preach (10.7), and to teach (28.20).[6]

Initially, the reader learns that Jesus was teaching in their synagogues. Despite the fact that the teaching of Jesus is a very prominent component of this Gospel,[7] the first mention in the narrative of Jesus teaching comes here. The reader will learn that Jesus is *the* authoritative teacher in the Gospel,[8] in contrast to the scribes, and that only at the end of the narrative (28.20) are the disciples given the authority to teach.[9] Thus far the teaching takes place in 'their synagogues'. Several comments might be made on this phrase. First, on one level, Jesus' teaching in the synagogue is natural enough to understand, for visiting Jews were often given an opportunity to speak about the Scripture reading for the day.[10] Second, in terms of the narrative, it makes sense for one who has come to fulfill Scripture, as has Jesus, to go to a place where Scripture is taught.[11] Third, this approach is certainly consistent in a Gospel which, despite its openness to a gentile mission, continues to give 'the lost sheep of Israel' the primary focus in Jesus' ministry.[12]

Perhaps the most surprising part of this phrase is Matthew's reference to 'their' synagogues. Is the reader to understand a distinction here between 'their' (Jewish) synagogues and 'our' (Christian)

---

[6] J.C. Fenton, *Saint Matthew* (Baltimore: Penguin, 1963), p. 75.

[7] The fact that teaching stands first in this series does not necessarily imply that 'teaching' as such takes precedence over the other activities. *Contra* Hare, *Matthew*, p. 31.

[8] Maier, *Matthäus-Evangelium*, I , p. 92 and Meier, *Matthew*, p. 35.

[9] Fenton, *Matthew*, p. 75.

[10] Hill, *Matthew*, p. 106 and R.H. Mounce, *Matthew* (Peabody: Hendrickson, 1991), p. 34.

[11] As Bonnard (*Matthieu*, p. 51) observes, 'Ce n'est pas seulement pour des raisons pratiques que Jésus fréquent les synagogues; il y trouve le peuple des Ecritures, rassemblé pour en entendre la lecture et l'interprétation'.

[12] A.H. McNeile, *The Gospel according to St. Matthew* (London: Macmillan, 1915), p. 47; D. Senior, *Invitation to Matthew* (Garden City, NY: Image Books, 1966), p. 57; Beare, *Matthew*, p. 121; and Luz, *Matthew 1-7*, p. 205.

synagogues?[13] Or does this qualifier point to the fact that the synagogue is no longer the 'home' of Christians?[14] That Matthew intends to send some kind of message is clear from the fact that the
vast preponderance of references to synagogue in this Gospel has
the qualifier 'their' before it (cf. 4.23; 9.35; 10.17; 12.9; 13.54; 23.34)
and by the fact that the Gospel also refers to 'their' scribes (7.29)
and 'their' cities (11.1). Perhaps the reference to 'their' synagogues is
a clue to the reader that the rejection of Jesus by the Jewish leaders,
hinted at in the birth narrative, is at such a level that the synagogue
is already, at worst, alien territory for Jesus and the readers of Matthew and, at best, a reminder that the sheep of Israel are at this
point lost.

Jesus was not only teaching in their synagogues but he was also
preaching the Gospel of the Kingdom. While the reader may be
uncertain as to the content of Jesus' teaching in the synagogue
(though, based on the content of his later teaching, it is clearly connected to the coming Kingdom), there is already some knowledge
of the content of his preaching. As the Baptist before him, Jesus
comes preaching conversion owing to the nearness of the Kingdom
(4.17). Such conversion was to be validated by the fruit of conversion, without which the coming judgment could not be averted. It
will become clear later in the Gospel just how radical this message
would be.

Although the reader knows of Jesus' preaching beforehand and
of his role as savior (1.21) and a mightier one who would function
as Holy Spirit baptizer (3.11) and judge (3.12), there is no indication
until 4.23 that his ministry would involve healing.[15] However, as the
narrative unfolds it will become clear that healings were a normal
part of his ministry.[16] In fact, 16 of the 48 New Testament usages
of θεραπεύω are found in Matthew.[17] It has earlier been observed

[13] A possibility offered by Davies and Allison (*Matthew*, I, p. 414).

[14] Fenton, *Matthew*, p. 76; W. Trilling, *The Gospel according to Matthew* (London: Sheed and Ward, 1969), p. 58; B. Green, *The Gospel according to Matthew* (Oxford: Oxford University Press, 1975), p. 74; R. Schnackenburg, *Matthäusevangelium 1,1-16,20* (Würzburg: Echter, 1985), p. 43; Gnilka, *Das Matthäusevangelium*, I, p. 107; Davies and Allison, *Matthew*, I, p. 414; Luz, *Matthew 1-7*, p. 205; and D. Harring-ton, *The Gospel of Matthew* (Collegeville: Liturgical Press, 1991), p. 72.

[15] Davies, *Matthew*, p. 48.

[16] Luz, *Matthew 1-7*, p. 205.

[17] Morris, *Matthew*, p. 88.

that in the narrative Jesus' preaching has already been connected with the Kingdom of Heaven and that his teaching will also be connected to it later in the Gospel. The same is true for the relationship between miracles and the Kingdom. For it appears that his miracles of healing were signs of the in-breaking of the Kingdom[18] and, consequently, a proclamation of the Kingdom in deed, not simply the authorization of his proclamation.[19] It is perhaps significant that Matthew makes explicit reference to *every* disease (πασαν νόσον) and *every* sickness (πᾶσαν μαλακίαν) among the people (ἐν τῷ λαῷ) being healed. The same people (λαός) whom he came to save (1.21), the same people who were ruled by chief priests and scribes (2.4), the same people whom he would rule (2.6), the same people who sat in darkness (4.16) are those whom he healed. His ability to heal was more than sufficient.

Verse 24

Word of Jesus' work went out through the whole of Syria. While the mention of Syria here (its only appearance in the Gospel) might be a subtle reference to the location of Matthew's audience[20] or even to the home of the writer himself,[21] in the narrative it functions to extend the effect of Jesus' ministry far to the north[22] and may imply the presence of Gentiles among those who come to him for help.[23] On this reading Jesus both went to 'their' (Jewish) synagogues and attracted multitudes of Gentiles as well.

If word of his teaching and preaching made its way to Syria, Matthew chooses to emphasize only the fact that *all* those who were suffering from numerous maladies were brought to him. These include those afflicted with various diseases and those suffering with

---

[18] McNeile, *Matthew*, p. 47; Fenton, *Matthew*, p. 76; W.F. Albright and C.S. Mann, *Matthew* (Garden City, NY: Doubleday, 1971), p. 44; and Hill, *Matthew*, p. 104.

[19] *Contra* Bonnard, *Matthieu*, p. 52.

[20] Hill, *Matthew*, p. 107; Beare, *Matthew*, p. 122; Meier, *Matthew*, p. 36; Gnilka, *Das Matthäusevangelium*, I, p. 108; Smith, *Matthew*, p. 75; R.B. Gardner, *Matthew* (Scottdale, PA: Herald Press, 1991), p. 85; Harrington, *Matthew*, p. 73; and Hagner, *Matthew 1-13*, p. 80.

[21] Bonnard, *Matthieu*, p. 51; B. Green, *Matthew*, p. 74; and Schweizer, *Matthew*, p. 78.

[22] Davies and Allison, *Matthew*, I, p. 417.

[23] R.H. Gundry, *Matthew: A Commentary on His Literary and Theological Art* (Grand Rapids: Eerdmans, 1982), p. 64 and Davies and Allison, *Matthew*, I, p. 417.

terrible pain. It appears that Matthew's description of these suffer-
ers moves from general to specific maladies,[24] as a second, more
precise list follows the more general opening statement. In this second part of the description, three specific categories are listed:[25]
those who are demon possessed, lunatics/epileptics, and paralytics.

Several observations are in order about these infirmities. First, it
appears that each of these disorders presented extraordinary challenges: illnesses which resulted from demon possession because
their origin was supernatural; lunacy/epilepsy because the condition
was widely thought to be caused by the moon;[26] and paralysis because there was no known cure in antiquity.[27] Second, it could very
well be that mention of these three specific maladies is an anticipa-
tory summary naming infirmities that Jesus heals later in the Gospel.[28] Third, it is noteworthy that demon possession appears in a list
of physical infirmities, suggesting that demon possession is here to
be regarded as a cause of illness. At the same time, it is clear that
Matthew distinguishes between illnesses caused by demonic forces
and those that are not.[29] It is also apparent that Matthew did not
believe all demon possession resulted in illness. What will become
obvious later is that the same illness, i.e. epilepsy, may or may not
have a demonic origin. But if this is possible, the implication is that
there must have been some way to distinguish between illnesses
caused by demons and those that were not.[30] All of this is to say
that Matthew does not simply equate demon possession with illness
in an uncritical fashion, but rather, that in his first statement regarding demon possession, he lists it as a cause of illness. Whatever the
category of disorder, the observation at the end of v. 24 is that 'he
healed (ἐθεράπευσεν) them'.

---

[24] Hagner, *Matthew 1-13*, p. 81.

[25] So McNeile, *Matthew*, p. 48; LaGrange, *Matthieu*, p. 72; D.A. Carson, 'Matthew', in *The Expositor's Bible Commentary*, VIII (Grand Rapids: Zondervan, 1984),
p. 121; and Davies and Allison, *Matthew*, I, p. 418.

[26] Cf. LaGrange, *Matthieu*, p. 73; Harrington, *Matthew*, p. 73; Morris, *Matthew*,
p. 90; and esp. J.M. Roos, 'Epileptic or Moonstruck?' *Bible Translator* 29 (1978), pp.
126-28.

[27] Morris, *Matthew*, p. 90.

[28] Trilling, *Matthew*, p. 58.

[29] C.L. Blomberg, *Matthew* (Nashville: Broadman, 1992), p. 92.

[30] G. Twelftree, *Christ Triumphant: Exorcism Then and Now* (London: Hodder
and Stoughton, 1985), pp. 71-72.

Verse 25

This last verse of the section tells of the remarkable results of Jesus' ministry (with primary emphasis upon his healings). Five places are mentioned specifically: Galilee, the Decapolis, Jerusalem, Judea, and the region beyond the Jordan. Although it is possible to see in these crowds the audience for the Sermon on the Mount which follows,[31] Matthew, as he has often done before, may be telling his readers more. Jesus, the Jewish Messiah, the Son of David, the one who stands solid with his people Israel, the resident of the land of Israel (2.21), now draws crowds from the land of Israel (with Jerusalem as its capital?)[32] and beyond (with the exception of Samaria),[33] in a way not unworthy of his titles, Son of Abraham and Son of David.

Conclusions

What are the implications of Mt. 4.23-25 for the primary concerns of this enquiry? 1) In contrast to the other literature examined to this point, Matthew's first statement about demons describes them as a source of illness. This suggests that this theme will be much more prominent in Matthew's Gospel than in Mark. 2) Matthew seems careful to distinguish between infirmities that originate with the demonic and those that do not. 3) It would seem safe to assume that if some illnesses are caused by demons and some are not, there must have been some way to distinguish between the two.

Matthew 8.16-17 – 'He Took our Illnesses and Bore our Diseases'

As noted earlier, the summary offered in 4.23-25 provides a transition to the first major discourse in Matthew, the Sermon on the Mount. This carefully structured discourse expands the reader's knowledge of the Kingdom which Jesus proclaims by offering discussion of the following: Characteristics of Kingdom Members

---

[31] So Beare, *Matthew*, p. 120 and Harrington, *Matthew*, p. 75.

[32] LaGrange, *Matthieu*, p. 73; Schnackenburg, *Matthäusevangelium*, p. 44; and D.E. Garland, *Reading Matthew* (New York: Crossroad, 1993), p. 49.

[33] For various statements to that effect cf. the following: Trilling, *Matthew*, p. 59; Beare, *Matthew*, p. 122; R.T. France, *Matthew* (Grand Rapids: Eerdmans, 1985), p. 105; Gnilka, *Das Matthäusevangelium*, I, p. 109; Luz, *Matthew 1-7*, p. 206; Davies and Allison, *Matthew*, I, p. 420; Hagner, *Matthew 1-13*, p. 81.

(5.3-16), Righteousness that is Greater than that of the Pharisees (5.17-48), the Doing of Righteousness (6.1-18), Warnings (6.19-7.6), Admonitions (7.7-23), and a Call for a Response to Jesus' Words (7.24-27). The people were amazed at his teaching for he taught with authority, not as the scribes!

Following the Sermon on the Mount, Matthew continues (from 4.23-25) with his emphasis on the healing ministry of Jesus. With many crowds following him from the mountain, Jesus encounters a leper who desires healing. Ignoring the Torah prohibitions about contact with those suffering from leprosy, Jesus touches him and the man is healed. Jesus instructs the man to present himself and an offering to the priest as a testimony.

After this Jesus enters Capernaum. This observation creates in the reader an expectancy, for Jesus' earlier entry into this city prompted one of the many fulfillment passages so prominent in Matthew. Specifically, Galilee of the Gentiles is mentioned as representing those who lived in darkness who would see a great light. Upon entering the city, Jesus is met by one of these Gentiles, a centurion whose servant is suffering terribly with paralysis. Owing to the statement in 4.24, the reader anticipates the healing that is expected to follow and is not surprised at Jesus' willingness to heal. What is a bit unexpected is the faith of the centurion and Jesus' forceful statement regarding the place of such individuals at the feast with Abraham, Isaac, and Jacob.

A third healing is described in the very next pericope (8.14-15), involving Peter's mother-in-law who is ill with a fever. Like the others her healing is immediate.

These accounts are followed by another text (8.16-17) which deserves a more detailed examination.

When evening came, many who were demon possessed were brought to him and he cast out the spirits with a word and he healed many who were sick. In order that the word spoken through Isaiah the prophet might be fulfilled: 'He took our weaknesses (infirmities) and bore (our) diseases'.

Although it is possible to take 'When evening came' ('Οψίας δὲ γενομένης) as a reference to the end of the Sabbath,[34] owing to this text's Marcan parallel, it appears that Matthew wishes the reader to understand the events described in this pericope as occurring on the evening of the day on which the Sermon on the Mount takes place. If so, the remark is, no doubt, intended to reflect the pace of Jesus' ministry.[35]

At the end of this incredible day many who were demon possessed were brought to Jesus. Given the earlier reference in 4.24 to demon possession as a cause of illness, one might expect that meaning here. However, on this occasion, it appears that those suffering from demon possession are distinguished from those who were healed.[36] This interpretation is borne out by the use of 'and' (καὶ) as an additive,[37] and by the way in which this verse prepares the reader for the next reference to demon possession, the Gadarene Demoniac in 8.28-34, where there is no hint that the demoniac was suffering from an illness. Here, then, Matthew treats demon possession as distinct from illness. This observation on Matthew's part indicates that his view of demon possession is not one dimensional.

Jesus responds to the demonized by casting out the spirits with a word. Matthew's use of spirit as a synonym for demon occurs here for the first time, but will appear later in the Gospel as well (cf. 10.1; 12.43, 45). Jesus' casting out the demons with a word (λόγῳ) is most clearly reminiscent of the power of Jesus' word in the healing of the centurion's servant ('but only say the word ...' – 8.8).[38] But it is also possible to see here a subtle attempt by Matthew to point to the continuity between his authoritative word of healing and his

---

[34] For this interpretation cf. McNeile, *Matthew*, p. 107; Bonnard, *Matthieu*, p. 117; Hill, *Matthew*, p. 160; Beare, *Matthew*, p. 211; M. Green, *Matthew for Today* (London: Hodder and Stoughton, 1988), p. 98; Mounce, *Matthew*, p. 76; Blomberg, *Matthew*, p. 144; Morris, *Matthew*, p. 198; and apparently Hagner, *Matthew 1-13*, p. 209.

[35] Carson, 'Matthew', p. 204.

[36] Filson, *Matthew*, p. 112; Meier, *Matthew*, p. 85; France, *Matthew*, p. 158; Mounce, *Matthew*, p. 76; M. Green, *Matthew*, p. 98; and Hagner, *Matthew 1-13*, p. 210.

[37] *Contra* Bonnard (*Matthieu*, p. 117) who takes the καὶ as an 'explicatif'.

[38] Fenton, *Matthew*, p. 127; Brunner, *Christbook*, I, p. 310; and Harrington, *Matthew*, p. 114.

authoritative word of teaching/preaching, given his emphasis on the latter in other places throughout the Gospel (7.24, 26, 28; 13.19-23; 19.1; 24.35; 26.1).[39]

In addition to delivering the demon possessed, 'he healed all those having it bad'. The phrase 'having it bad' (κακῶς ἔχοντας) is the same one that appeared in 4.24,[40] reminding the reader of this characteristic of Jesus' ministry. Again, Matthew emphasizes that *all* were healed,[41] continuing to lift up the fact that there was nothing outside Jesus' ability.[42]

A number of things in the narrative to this point have occurred in order that Scripture might be fulfilled (1.22, 23; 2.5, 6; 2.15; 2.17-18; 3.3; 4.14-16), nearly all of which have direct reference to Jesus. Through the use of such formulae the reader is encouraged to discern the connection between the quotations and the action described in the narrative.[43] This first appearance of the formula since 4.15-16[44] indicates that the exorcisms and healings performed by Jesus are no exception. One of the interesting things about this particular formula is Matthew's decided preference for the Hebrew version of Isa. 53.4 over the more spiritualized LXX version, which specifically mentions sin in its translation. It is, of course, possible to take this citation as a proof text of sorts that undergirds the fact that Jesus took away or removed the infirmities without bearing them himself.[45] But at least in one sense Jesus does take these illnesses upon himself by his identification or solidarity with the people he touches (the leper and the woman with a fever). However, it

---

[39] Bonnard, *Matthieu*, p. 117 and W.D. Davies and D.C. Allison, *The Gospel according to Saint Matthew*, II (Edinburgh: T & T Clark, 1991), p. 36.

[40] Edwards, *Matthew's Story*, p. 37.

[41] Davies and Allison, *Matthew*, II, p. 36; Davies, *Matthew*, p. 72; Gardner, *Matthew*, p. 147; Hagner, *Matthew 1-13*, p. 210; and Hare, *Matthew*, p. 92.

[42] Morris, *Matthew*, p. 198.

[43] Anderson, *Matthew's Narrative Web*, p. 53.

[44] Edwards, *Matthew's Story*, p. 27. Whether this is the first occurrence of the formula in Jesus' public ministry, as Mounce (*Matthew*, p. 76) argues, depends upon whether or not one regards 4.15-16 as part of the public ministry.

[45] For views close to this cf. McNeile, *Matthew*, p. 108; Filson, *Matthew*, p. 112; R.V.G. Tasker, *The Gospel according to St. Matthew* (London: Tyndale, 1961), p. 90; H.-G. Link, 'Weakness', *DNTT*, III, p. 998; B. Green, *Matthew*, p. 100; Beare, *Matthew*, p. 212; and Schweizer, *Matthew*, p. 217.

would seem that there may be even more to it than that.[46] For the decision to follow the Hebrew text rather than the LXX, together with the fact that it is the narration of Jesus' exorcisms and healings that has resulted in the citation of the text in the first place, indicates that for Matthew there is a deep connection between Jesus' healing ministry and this servant song, which is noted for its emphasis on the vicarious suffering of the servant. In fact, Matthew seems to indicate that such activity is part of Jesus' atoning work. Perhaps a more Matthean way of understanding the text is to see it as an anticipation of the passion, which is foundational for that which Jesus accomplishes.[47] That Matthew considers such activity to be part of Jesus' atoning work seems to be the best reading of the Matthean text.[48]

Conclusions

How does an examination of this text contribute to the larger concerns of this investigation? 1) It indicates that Matthew not only views demon possession as a cause of illness, but also recognizes that demon possession could exist on its own, apart from its role in sickness. This conclusion serves to strengthen the intimation in 4.23-25 that Matthew makes a distinction between illnesses (and their origins) but that he does not understand all demon possession to involve infirmity. 2) It becomes clear from this passage that Matthew considers Jesus' exorcism and healing ministry to be tied to his (future) vicarious death.

Matthew 9.1-7 – 'Which Is Easier to Say?'

The next four texts are all tied together by Jesus' intention, attempt, and/or crossing of the lake. The stories include a discussion on the cost of following Jesus (8.18-22), the calming of a storm by Jesus (8.23-27), the exorcism of two demon-possessed men (8.28-34),

---

[46] As Hill (*Matthew*, p. 161) rightly notes.

[47] A. Oepke, 'νόσος', *TDNT*, IV, p. 1097; P. Benoit, *L'Évangile selon saint Matthieu* (Paris: Les Editions du Cerf, 1972), p. 72; Gundry, *Matthew*, p. 150; Brunner, *Christbook*, I, pp. 311-12; Harrington, *Matthew*, p. 115; Blomberg, *Matthew*, p. 145; Morris, *Matthew*, p. 198; and Garland, *Matthew*, p. 98.

[48] *Contra* D. Petts, 'Healing and the Atonement', *EPTA Bulletin* 12 (1993), pp. 28-29.

and the pronouncing of forgiveness upon and healing of a paralytic (9.1-8).

The pronouncing of forgiveness upon and healing of the paralytic have already received considerable attention in chapter four. Although there are a number of differences between the story as recorded in Mk 2.1-12 and its appearance in Matthew, none of the differences affect the conclusion reached earlier that there is no direct connection between the forgiveness of sin pronounced upon the man by Jesus and his subsequent healing. Although it might be possible to argue on the basis of 8.17 that Matthew sees a tie between sin and sickness, to conclude that Matthew envisions such a connection here seems to outdistance the evidence.

Matthew 9.32-34 – A Speechless Man Speaks

Following the healing of the paralytic, the author narrates the call of Matthew (9.9-13), a discussion about fasting (9.14-17), the healing of a hemorrhaging woman and the raising of a dead girl (9.18-26), and the healing of two blind men (9.27-31). Then follows the next text of relevance for this enquiry.

> And while they were going out, behold they brought to him a man who was mute because of a demon. And when the demon was cast out the mute man spoke. And the crowds were amazed saying, 'Nothing like this has ever been seen in Israel'. But the Pharisees were saying, 'He casts out demons by the ruler of demons!'

Matthew begins this pericope literally on the heels of the previous one, noting that a mute demoniac was brought to Jesus at the very time the formerly blind men were leaving. Although it is not stated who brought the man,[49] the construction conveys a sense of the rapid succession of individuals coming to Jesus for help.[50]

The text describes the individual as κωφὸν, which can mean deaf, mute, or both. Given the results of his healing, described in the next verse, it is most likely that the reader is to understand this

---

[49] Tasker (*Matthew*, p. 101) suggests that the blind men brought the first person in need they laid their eyes upon after their own healing.

[50] Bonnard, *Matthieu*, p. 139 and Hill, *Matthew*, p. 181. Hagner (*Matthew 1-13*, p. 257) suggests that it reveals the pressure on Jesus to heal.

term to mean mute in this pericope,[51] but based on the summary statement in 11.5 where it is stated that the deaf hear, the term could here mean both deaf and mute.[52] The reader would not fully understand this meaning until later when reading the summary. It is further revealed that this individual's infirmity was owing to demon possession. Despite the fact that this is the first such specific case recorded in Matthew, the idea is neither new[53] nor should it be surprising,[54] given the previous statement in 4.24. Thus far the reader has been told that demons can cause infirmities (4.24), that demons can possess individuals without necessarily being the cause of an infirmity (8.28-34), and now that a demon can cause muteness specifically. However, as the reader is to learn, all muteness is not directly attributed to demons by Matthew (cf. 15.30-31). On this occasion, Matthew gives no indication of how the demon was cast out (perhaps the reader is to assume that it was by a word as in 8.16), he says only that the demon was expelled. The exorcism results in the mute man speaking, a confirmation that his malady was demon possession, not simply the inability to speak.

The rest of the pericope is given over to a description of the reactions of the crowds and, in turn, the Pharisees. The crowds are absolutely astounded by what they have witnessed, claiming that nothing like this has ever been manifest in Israel. It is possible that their amazement was owing to the fact that a mute person speaking was unparalleled in Scripture,[55] and consequently is a new thing in Israel.[56] However, given the fact that a summary statement identical to the one in 4.23 occurs immediately after this pericope (9.35), it appears that the crowds' comments in 9.33 are a response to the whole of Jesus' healing ministry as described in chapters 8-9. On this reading, the crowds' response to Jesus' miracles in 9.33 stands

---

[51] Fenton, *Matthew*, p. 146; van der Loos, *The Miracles of Jesus*, p. 406; Smith, *Matthew*, p. 143; Harrington, *Matthew*, p. 132; and Hagner, *Matthew 1-13*, p. 257.

[52] For this translation cf. Carson, 'Matthew', p. 234; Meier, *Matthew*, p. 100; Davies and Allison, *Matthew*, II, p. 139; Gardner, *Matthew*, p. 161; and Morris, *Matthew*, p. 236.

[53] As Harrington (*Matthew*, p. 134) suggests.

[54] As France (*Matthew*, p. 173) argues.

[55] Davies, *Matthew*, p. 79.

[56] Hagner, *Matthew 1-13*, p. 257.

in parallel to their response his teaching evokes in 7.28-29.[57] It should be observed that the unfolding relationship between Jesus and Israel continues to be an emphasis of Matthew's.

In 7.29, the authority of Jesus is contrasted with the lack of scribal authority. On this occasion, the Pharisees respond to the unbridled reaction of the crowds by attributing Jesus' exorcisms to the ruler of demons, a charge that will appear three additional times in Matthew (10.25; 12.24, 27).[58] By including their response at this point, Matthew ends this major section of the Gospel with a (blasphemous) charge on the lips of the Pharisees which foreshadows the growing rejection of and opposition to Jesus that is to follow.[59] That such a response is possible, after all that Jesus has said and done in Matthew 5-9, indicates the depth of the Pharisees' opposition, in contrast to the crowd's favorable response,[60] and gives the reader a great deal to ponder.[61]

Conclusion

The primary contribution of this short pericope to the overall study is that here for the first time Matthew attributes a specific infirmity to demonic origins. So that, in addition to the general knowledge that demons can cause illness (and that demons do not always cause infirmity), the reader now learns that demons can cause muteness.

Matthew 9.35-12.21

A summary statement (identical to that in 4.23) and its following verses provide the transition to the next major discourse in Matthew's Gospel which is devoted to missionary activity. Significantly, the Twelve are first of all given authority to cast out demons and heal the sick (10.1). After being authorized to preach that 'The

---

[57] van der Loos, *Miracles*, p. 407; France, *Matthew*, p. 173; Davies and Allison, *Matthew*, II, p. 139; and Blomberg, *Matthew*, p. 163.

[58] G.H. Stanton, *A Gospel for a New People: Studies in Matthew* (Edinburgh: T & T Clark, 1992), p. 173.

[59] Meier, *Matthew*, p. 100; B.J. Malina and J.H. Neyrey, *Calling Jesus Names: The Social Value of Labels in Matthew* (Sonoma, CA: Polebridge Press, 1988), p. 59; and Stanton, *Gospel*, p. 174.

[60] Davies, *Matthew*, p. 79.

[61] For a helpful discussion of the text-critical problem in 9.34 cf. Stanton, *Gospel*, pp. 174-76.

Kingdom of Heaven is near', they are again instructed to heal and cast out demons (10.8). In both verses it appears that Matthew is careful to distinguish between healing and exorcism, although as was noted earlier, there is occasionally some degree of overlap. That Jesus fully anticipates the disciples being successful in the casting out of demons (although none are described in the Gospel itself) is indicated by his prediction that they will be called Beelzebul because he has been called this himself (10.25).

At the conclusion of the missionary discourse, Jesus again preaches in Galilee where a question regarding his messianic status comes from John the Baptist, who has been in prison since the beginning of Jesus' ministry (4.12). Jesus' reply to John includes a summary of his healing ministry (11.5). Interestingly enough, in Jesus' final words about John to the crowds he makes reference to an otherwise unknown accusation that John himself was demon possessed (11.18). Following this, Jesus begins to denounce the lack of faithful response on the part of those in the cities where so many miracles were performed (11.20-24), eventually shifting to words of comfort for the little children to whom the mysteries have been revealed.

Chapter 12 (vv. 1-12) begins with a controversy about Jesus' action on the Sabbath, in which two points are worthy of note. First, it is revealed that One greater than the Temple stands among them (12.6) who is Lord of the Sabbath (12.8). Second, Matthew at this point indicates that the Pharisees are now involved in a plot to kill Jesus (12.14). Aware of all this, Jesus withdraws again, healing all the sick in the crowd, this time instructing them not to reveal his identity. Such actions yet again fulfill Scripture (12.17-21), with still another Isaiah text being cited (Isa. 42.1-4).

Matthew 12.22-23 – A Blind and Mute Man Healed

The next passage relevant to this enquiry appears at this point in the text:

> Then a blind and mute demon-possessed man was brought to him; and he healed him, so that the mute man spoke and saw. And all the crowds were beside themselves and were saying, 'This is not the Son of David, is it?'

As has been so often the case in Matthew, the steady stream of individuals needing help from Jesus continues. Another man, who suffers infirmities owing to demonic activity, is brought to Jesus. However, this man's condition is worse than any other described to this point in Matthew, in that he is both blind and mute (κωφός should perhaps mean deaf here as well).[62] No doubt, the reader is intended to pick up on this most impressive combination of maladies.[63] Yet, before the reader has time to process the magnitude of the man's condition, the text reveals that Jesus heals him. The result being that the mute man both speaks and sees, an indication of the efficacy[64] and completeness of the cure.[65] What might be a bit surprising to the reader is that instead of narrating the expulsion of the demon, as occurs in 9.33, Matthew says that the man was healed (ἐθεράπευσεν). While perhaps a bit unusual,[66] the reader is not wholly unprepared for such a description of this miracle, in that 4.24 implies that demonically inspired illnesses are 'healed' by Jesus. Of course, it becomes clear from the dialogue which ensues (12.24-45) that Jesus has performed an exorcism.[67]

The response of the crowds to this healing is even more enthusiastic than in 9.33, for here they are literally 'out of their minds' over what Jesus has done. This Greek word (ἐξίσταντο), which occurs only here in Matthew's Gospel,[68] conveys the idea of an extraordinary state which can be described as being out of one's mind.[69] Such euphoria leads them to ask, 'This is not the Son of David, is it?' The construction of the question in the Greek text (note the use of Μήτι) indicates some degree of tentativeness or skepticism[70] in the raising of the question, if not the expectation of

---

[62] Hagner (*Matthew 1-13*, p. 342) notes, 'Only here in the four Gospels do we find reference to the healing of a man both blind and mute'.

[63] Hare, *Matthew*, p. 138.

[64] Hagner, *Matthew 1-13*, p. 342.

[65] Morris, *Matthew*, p. 314.

[66] van der Loos, *Miracles of Jesus*, p. 408 and Morris, *Matthew*, p. 314.

[67] France, *Matthew*, p. 207 and Blomberg, *Matthew*, p. 201.

[68] Meier, *Matthew*, p. 134.

[69] J. Lambrecht, 'ἐξίστημι', *EDNT*, II, p. 7.

[70] McNeile, *Matthew*, p. 174; Filson, *Matthew*, p. 149; B. Green, *Matthew*, p. 126; Beare, *Matthew*, p. 277; Carson, 'Matthew', p. 288; Blomberg, *Matthew*, p. 201; and Morris, *Matthew*, p. 314.

a negative reply.[71] But given the crowds' general sympathy with Jesus to this point in the narrative, the question should perhaps be seen as expressing hope, even if that of an uncertain kind, and as approaching the truth about Jesus.[72]

But why do they tentatively identify Jesus with the Son of David? From the very beginning of Matthew's Gospel it has been clear that Son of David is a significant title, as it appears in the book's title (1.1) where Jesus is identified as the Son of David, Son of Abraham. Also, David is given a role of emphasis in the genealogy which follows, being named twice in v. 6, where he is the only person designated as King, and twice in v. 17. Jesus' position as David's Son is confirmed when Joseph, himself the Son of David (1.20), formally names Jesus (1.25), thus legally recognizing him as his (David's) son. The next reference to the title Son of David comes in 9.27, where two blind men call upon Jesus for mercy; Jesus subsequently heals them. What the reader does not yet realize is that 9.27 is the first of several Matthean texts where the title Son of David is used in the context of healing (cf. 12.23; 15.22 and 20.30-31). In 12.3, Jesus, defending his disciples against the charge of plucking grain on the Sabbath, appeals to the actions of David and his men who ate the bread of presence located in the Tabernacle. Eventually, Jesus is hailed as the Son of David by the crowds shouting 'Hosanna' (21.9, 15). The final reference to the Son of David (22.42, 43, 45) is found in a discussion between Jesus and the Pharisees regarding the identity of David's Son. It appears then that the title Son of David functions in Matthew as one aspect of Jesus' true identity, which in his healing ministry is sometimes recognized by society's outcasts (the physically blind and the Gentiles) and the crowds, but which the Pharisees never comprehend. In terms of narrative development, the crowds seem to follow the blind men of 9.27 in making this identification. Although it is possible that the occurrence of this title in healing contexts results from reflection upon David's abilities to soothe Saul when tormented by an evil spirit (1 Sam. 16.14-23),[73] or knowledge of Solomon's alleged pow-

---

[71] LaGrange, *Matthieu*, p. 241; J.D. Kingsbury, 'The Verb akolouthein ('To Follow') as an Index of Matthew's View of his Community', *JBL* 97 (1978), p. 61; France, *Matthew*, p. 208; and Garland, *Reading Matthew*, p. 140.
[72] Trilling, *Matthew*, p. 226 and Stanton, *A Gospel for a New People*, pp. 183-84.
[73] So Garland, *Reading Matthew*, p. 140.

ers as revealed in the magical papyri,[74] their function in Matthew appears to be broader than either of these ideas alone.[75]

Conclusion

For the purposes of this enquiry this passage makes clear the connection that sometimes exists between demon possession and physical infirmity. Specifically, it clarifies that for Matthew, it is appropriate to designate such exorcisms as healing. The text also shows that this work reveals one aspect of Jesus' identity as Son of David.

Matthew 12.43-45 – 'The Final State Is Worse than the First'

As in 9.34, the enthusiasm of the crowds brings a somewhat exasperated response from the Pharisees,[76] which makes clear their own blasphemous opposition to Jesus, charging that he casts out demons by Beelzebul. The Pharisees' words provoke a stern rebuke by Jesus, in which he denies that Satan can cast out Satan (12.25-29), warns of blasphemy against the Spirit (12.30-32), and points out the continuity between that which the mouth speaks and that which is in the heart (12.33-37). Jesus then responds to the Pharisees' request for a sign by pointing to the enigmatic sign of Jonah (12.38-42). Two of the more significant items found in this section of Matthew are: 1) the revelation that some among the Pharisees practice exorcisms and 2) that just as Jesus earlier spoke of one greater than the Temple being here (12.6), he now says that one who is greater than Jonah and one who is greater than Solomon is here (12.41, 42).

At this point an intriguing but not altogether clear passage is found, one which may have relevance for this investigation:

---

[74] So L.R. Fisher, 'Can This Be the Son of David?' in *Jesus and the Historian: Written in Honor of Ernest Cadman Colwell* (ed. F.T. Trotter; Philadelphia: Westminster, 1963), pp. 82-97. Cf. also Harrington, *Matthew*, p. 182.

[75] For discussions of Matthew's use of this title cf. J.M. Gibbs, 'Purpose and Pattern in Matthew's Use of the Title "Son of David"', *NTS* 10 (1963-64), pp. 446-64; D.C. Duling, 'The Therapeutic Son of David', *NTS* 24 (1978), pp. 392-410; and W.R.G. Loader, 'Son of David, Blindness, Possession, and Duality in Matthew', *CBQ* 44 (1982), pp. 570-85.

[76] LaGrange, *Matthieu*, p. 241 and Hare, *Matthew*, p. 138.

And when the unclean spirit comes out from a man, he goes through desert places seeking rest, and he finds none. Then he says, 'I will return into my house from where I came out'. And having gone he found it empty, having been swept, and having been put in order. Then he goes and takes with him seven other spirits more evil than himself, and having entered he settles there. And the end of that man is worse than his beginning. In the same way shall it also be for this evil generation.

One of the primary problems facing the interpreter of this pericope is the question about the literary nature of these three verses. In some ways the passage resembles one of the many parables which Jesus tells in Matthew,[77] some even claim that it functions as an allegory.[78] It should be noted that neither of these literary forms would be without parallel in Matthew, as several parabolic statements have preceded these verses in chapter 12 and as there will be at least two allegorical interpretations of parables offered in chapter 13. In addition, it is clear that the verses are applied in some fashion to 'this evil generation', which in this context seems to have reference to the Pharisees, not necessarily the formerly demon-possessed persons addressed in the verses. However, despite this evidence, there is good reason to read these verses first of all as they occur within the Gospel, for as the reader quickly discerns, these verses are connected to the broader Matthean narrative in several ways. Therefore, this short passage will be read on its own terms first, before attempting to settle some of the interpretive challenges mentioned previously.

Verse 43

In v. 43 Jesus makes reference to unclean spirits which have gone out of a man. Some interpreters argue that there is no indication that the demon was cast out, preferring to understand this as a voluntary departure.[79] However, such an interpretation ignores the fact that Matthew ordinarily uses the term ἐξέρχομαι to describe de-

---

[77] Filson, *Matthew*, p. 153; Fenton, *Matthew*, p. 204; B. Green, *Matthew*, p. 129; Mounce, *Matthew*, p. 122; Smith, *Matthew*, p. 168; France, *Matthew*, p. 214; Hagner, *Matthew 1-13*, p. 356; and Hare, *Matthew*, p. 144.

[78] LaGrange, *Matthieu*, p. 251 and Gundry, *Matthew*, p. 246.

[79] McNeile, *Matthew*, p. 183; Beare, *Matthew*, p. 283; Mounce, *Matthew*, p. 122; and Morris, *Matthew*, p. 328.

mons that have been cast out of an individual. The reader has seen the term used this way once already, in 8.32, and will see it again later, in 17.18. Consequently, it is better to take the mention of the demon's departure as a reference to exorcism.[80]

Having been expelled, the unclean spirit roams through arid places, the abode of demons in popular thought,[81] seeking rest but finding none. Two observations should be made about this portion of v. 43. First, the unclean spirit is apparently unable to find rest so long as he is not tormenting another being; such would seem to be the very nature of demons.[82] Second, it appears from this wandering that a demon cannot simply enter any place desired,[83] as the failure of his search indicates.

Verse 44

At this point, the spirit decides to return to his former 'home'. In the Greek text, the phrase 'into my home' (Εἰς τὸν οἶκόν μου) stands first, indicating that the emphasis of the statement falls here. In addition to such structural emphasis, the description of the individual from whom this demon had been cast out as *'my* home' demonstrates a certain arrogance, even an imperialistic attitude on the part of the spirit.[84] This verse may also indicate that the unclean spirit regarded the human being as his natural habitat.[85]

When the spirit goes back to his former home,[86] he finds it empty, swept, and in order. It is difficult to be certain exactly what

---

[80] A.W. Argyle, *The Gospel According to Matthew* (Cambridge: Cambridge University Press, 1963), p. 99; Trilling, *Matthew*, p. 237; Gundry, *Matthew*, p. 247; and Hagner, *Matthew 1-13*, p. 357.

[81] For this identification cf. W.C. Allen, *The Gospel according to S. Matthew* (Edinburgh: T. & T. Clark, 1912³), p. 140; McNeile, *Matthew*, p. 183; Tasker, *Matthew*, p. 133; Benoit, *Matthieu*, p. 94; Hill, *Matthew*, p. 221; Schweizer, *Matthew*, p. 194; Carson, 'Matthew', p. 298; Mounce, *Matthew*, p. 122; Morris, *Matthew*, p. 328; Hagner, *Matthew 1-13*, pp. 356-57.

[82] Davies and Allison, *Matthew*, II, p. 361.

[83] Hagner, *Matthew 1-13*, p. 357.

[84] Hagner, *Matthew 1-13*, p. 357.

[85] Bonnard, *Matthieu*, p. 186.

[86] Several scholars point out that this construction is conditional, meaning, 'If he goes and finds' not 'When he goes he will find'. Cf. McNeile, *Matthew*, p. 183; H.S. Nyberg, 'Zum grammatischen Verständnis von Matth. 12, 44f.', *Coniectanea Neotestamentica* 13 (1949), pp. 1-11; Fenton, *Matthew*, p. 205; Carson, 'Matthew', p. 298; France, *Matthew*, p. 214; and Davies and Allison, *Matthew*, II, p. 361.

these words are meant to convey here. Do they mean that the occasion of the demon's departure was some half-hearted repentance,[87] or that when the demon left, the person became involved in moral reform of some type?[88] While such suggestions are *possible* explanations of the phrase, given the fact that there is nothing in the passage to this point that would confirm either possibility, perhaps it is better to look for an explanation within the text itself. If the reader is intended to understand the demon as having been expelled in the first instance, as the philological evidence would tend to indicate, then it is likely that these descriptions are the natural result of the exorcism. That is to say, the driving out of the demon itself leaves the formerly possessed person empty, swept clean, and in order. But the very fact that the person is initially described as empty (σχολάζοντα) implies that the absence of evil does not necessarily mean the presence of good. This implied message has been stated differently a bit earlier in 12.30, 'The one who is not with me is against me, and the one who does not gather with me scatters'. Apparently, an active response is necessary to avoid the return of the demon, which the state of emptiness invites.[89]

Verse 45

If the spirit finds his former home in such a condition, not only does he return, but he also brings along seven spirits more evil than himself, all of whom settle down with no intention of leaving.[90] The number seven at the very least indicates that the person is in a much more desperate circumstance now than before, as eight demons are more difficult to drive out than is one.[91] There may even be present the idea of complete or thorough domination by the demons.[92] For one who remains empty after an exorcism, it would have been better if the person had never been exorcised to begin with.[93]

---

[87] Cf. Trilling, *Matthew*, p. 237 and France, *Matthew*, p. 214.

[88] As Morris (*Matthew*, p. 329) suggests.

[89] Hill, *Matthew*, p. 221 and J.S. Wright, 'Satan', *DNTT*, III, p. 474.

[90] Morris, *Matthew*, p. 329 n. 115.

[91] Argyle, *Matthew*, p. 99; Hill, *Matthew*, p. 222; and Harrington, *Matthew*, p. 191.

[92] So Blomberg, *Matthew*, p. 208 and Hagner, *Matthew 1-13*, p. 357.

[93] Fenton, *Matthew*, p. 205.

On one level then, this pericope speaks to the many individuals who experienced the mighty delivering power of Jesus. They cannot afford to remain neutral after experiencing the deliverance brought by Jesus. They must embrace the Gospel of the Kingdom. If not, they could very well experience more dangerous domination by demonic powers. These words indicate that Jesus assumed his audience was familiar with the phenomenon described – the temporary effects of exorcism – and may even be an allegation that many exorcisms performed by others (the Pharisees in 12.27?) brought only temporary relief.[94]

The last phrase of v. 45 applies the warning of the previous verses more broadly to 'this evil generation'. The warning, which the formerly possessed receive, is extended to all his hearers. Jesus' presence among them had in effect been the equivalent of an exorcism which had driven the demons away to allow this generation an opportunity to respond favorably to his Gospel. The reader is especially appreciative of the authority of Jesus' teaching and healing ministries, as well as the ministry of John the Baptist, and understands the strategic nature of the decision facing the hearers. While some may yet respond by accepting the Gospel, many have already made clear their opposition to Jesus.

Conclusion

What are the implications of Mt. 12.43-45 for this investigation? 1) Despite the more general application of these words to the whole generation, they serve to add information about the attitude regarding the dangers of demonically inflicted illnesses, although symptoms of demon possession are not ruled out. If Matthew is comfortable attributing physical infirmities to demons, he also appears to acknowledge that unless one responds favorably to the Gospel, there is no guarantee that a healing which results from an exorcism will be lasting. 2) While clearly not the primary thrust of the passage, this text may also have implications for the knotty problem of the relationship between believers and demons. If emptiness is a sign that a person who has experienced exorcism has not gone on to receive the Gospel, so the adverse, one who is not empty has

---

[94] Cf. A. Fridrichsen, *The Problem of Miracle in Primitive Christianity* (tran. R.A. Harrisville and J.S. Hanson; Minneapolis: Augsburg, 1972), p. 109; Twelftree, *Christ Triumphant*, p. 65; and Davies and Allison, *Matthew*, II, pp. 359-60.

made the appropriate response, and this would seem to indicate that a formerly possessed person who is now a believer (and full of Christ and/or the Holy Spirit) is in no danger of being possessed a second time by demonic influences. By extension, one might even be able to say that if anyone is a believer, he/she is not in danger of being demonized.

Matthew 12.46-15.20

Before concluding this chapter two other texts should be examined briefly: Mt. 15.28 and 17.14-21. The texts which stand between 12.45 and 15.21-28 continue to build on themes developed earlier in the narrative. Following his words to this evil generation, Jesus redefines the family on the basis of the Kingdom and then gives the third major discourse of the Gospel in chapter 13, which consists of a number of parables about the Kingdom, their purpose and meaning. When Jesus finishes these words he speaks about the lack of honor a prophet receives in his own country (13.53-58), where, despite the crowd's amazement on account of his wisdom and power, they take offense at him and he does not do many miracles because of their lack of faith. After this, the death of John the Baptist is described (14.1-12). Upon hearing the report of John's death Jesus withdraws by boat but is followed by a large crowd upon whom he has compassion, eventually miraculously feeding over 5,000 of them. Then Jesus sends the disciples across the sea in a boat. When a storm develops Jesus walks toward them on the water joined by Peter, who begins to sink owing to his little faith (14.22-36). Arriving on the other shore, the crowds follow him still. In 15.1-20, Jesus rebukes and chides the Pharisees for not knowing it is that which comes from inside that defiles, not that which goes into a person.

Matthew 15.28 – 'Even the Dogs Eat the Crumbs'

Fast on the heels of the discussion about that which is clean and unclean, Jesus withdraws into 'unclean' territory and has an encounter with an 'unclean' person – a gentile woman. Although there are a number of fascinating points in this intriguing pericope, the primary aspect of interest for this study is whether or not the daughter of the Canaanite woman was sick owing to demon possession. The first clue that the girl has an infirmity is that she is described in 15.22 as κακῶς δαιμονίζεται. In all but one of the other places in Matthew's Gospel where the term κακῶς occurs (4.24; 8.16; 9.12; 14.35; 17.15), it is used to indicate an illness. In 21.41 it is used to indicate the suffering that the owner of the vineyard will inflict upon the tenants who have killed his son. Of its uses in contexts which describe physical infirmities, 17.15 alone has reference to a malady which is caused by a demon. Given its previous occurrences in Matthew, the reader is likely to pick up on this clue in v. 22.

It is v. 28, however, that seems to make clear the girl was ill as a result of demonic activity. This verse reads:

> Then Jesus answering said to her, 'Woman, great is your faith. It shall be done to you as you desire'. And her daughter was healed from that hour.

It is after an extraordinary exchange between Jesus and the woman that he utters these words. The dialogue has made clear that Jesus regards the woman as a Gentile and that, at least in the first instance, he has come (first/only?) to the lost sheep of Israel. However, her persistence reveals a faith that rivals that of another Gentile described in Matthew (8.10), the Centurion.[95] In the Greek text, emphasis is placed upon the word great (μεγάλη), as it appears first after woman. It is also interesting to note the way in which her faith is contrasted with the Pharisees' lack of 'faith' or understanding in the previous pericope,[96] and with the little faith of Peter in 14.31.[97]

In the last phrase of v. 28, Matthew makes clear that the girl has been healed from her condition. Two things are significant about the word used for 'heal' (ἰάομαι) in this passage. First, it is not the usual word Matthew uses to describe a healing (θεραπεύω). Second, the word used in 15.28 is the same as that found in 8.8, 13 to describe the healing of the Centurion's servant. Its only other appearance in Matthew is as part of an Old Testament quotation (Isa. 6.9-

---

[95] Cf. LaGrange, *Matthieu*, p. 310; Bonnard, *Matthieu*, p. 233; B. Green, *Matthew*, p. 146; Schnackenburg, *Matthäusevangelium*, p. 145; Gundry, *Matthew*, p. 316; France, *Matthew*, pp. 247-48; M. Green, *Matthew*, p. 153; Blomberg, *Matthew*, p. 244; Morris, *Matthew*, p. 405; and Gardner, *Matthew*, p. 240.

[96] Hare, *Matthew*, p. 179.

[97] Smith, *Matthew*, p. 193.

10) in Mt. 13.15. Clearly then, for the reader the appearence of ἰα-
΄ομαι in 15.28 highlights the similarity between these two (Gentile)
healings.[98]

As several other passages, this pericope is further evidence that
Matthew attributed certain illnesses to demons. In fact on this occasion, he only incidentally indicates that the girl was ill.[99]

Matthew 17.14-21 – The Epileptic Boy

The final text to be considered briefly is one whose Marcan parallel
was examined earlier in chapter 4, the healing of the demon-
possessed boy. Standing between 15.28 and this passage are several
texts. In 15.29-39, the reader is told of yet more infirm individuals
who crowd after Jesus. Their needs and interest are so great that
they stay with him for three days without food before Jesus com-
passionately and miraculously feeds over 4,000 of them. After departing by boat to Magadan, Jesus is pressed again by the Pharisees
for a sign. He points the evil and adulterous generation to the sign
of Jonah (16.1-4) given previously in chapter 12. As they again
cross the lake, Jesus warns the disciples about the yeast (teaching)
of the Pharisees and scribes (16.5-12) and chides them for their little faith (ὀλιγόπιστοι).

Having made their way to Caesarea Philippi, Peter confesses Jesus as Messiah and Jesus blesses this Spirit-inspired insight (16.13-
20). Their encounter leads to the revelation that Jesus must suffer
and die at the hands of the religious leaders. Now rebuking Peter
for his opposition to God's will, Jesus challenges the disciples to
follow him sacrificially, promising that some of them would see the
Son of Man coming in his Kingdom (16.21-28). This promise is
immediately followed by an account of the transfiguration of Jesus
before Peter, James, and John (17.1-13).

At this point in Matthew there occurs the account of the epileptic boy. The story, which is for the most part very similar to the passage found in Mark 9, does contain some distinctive material, especially as it relates to the broader Matthean narrative.

---

[98] Gundry, *Matthew*, p. 317.

[99] Davies and Allison, *Matthew*, II, p. 556.

It does not surprise the reader that as soon as Jesus reappears in public, he is greeted by another request for healing. As with the Canaanite woman, this man asks for mercy for his child, a son. That he is described as an epileptic creates in the reader the anticipation that Jesus will heal the boy, given the general statement in 4.24 that epileptics are among those Jesus heals. It is not at first apparent that the child suffers from demonic possession. When told of his disciples' failure to heal the boy, Jesus says, 'O unbelieving and perverse generation ... ' That the disciples are the likely target of this statement is indicated by their apparent lack of faith on a couple of other occasions in the Gospel (cf. 14.31 and 16.8) and by the fact that they are soon to be rebuked for this same problem later in the pericope (vv. 19-20). Calling for the boy, the demon is rebuked and cast out by Jesus. In response to a question by the disciples, Jesus makes very clear that their failure to cast out the demon was owing to their little faith (ὀλιγοπιστίαν). Not that such work requires a super abundance of faith, for even a small amount of faith will do.

Conclusions

This passage contributes several things to the larger enquiry. 1) In this text Matthew, and the reader with him, moves easily between the ideas of illness and demon possession, indicating that for Matthew demons are sometimes the origin of illness. 2) This text may indicate that on occasion discernment was needed to distinguish between those infirmities that were the result of demonic activity and those that were not. 3) Here it is indicated that a lack of proper faith can result in the failure to heal an infirmity caused by a demon.

Conclusions and Implications

What then are the conclusions and implications of an examination of the Gospel according to Matthew for this study on the Devil, disease, and deliverance?

1) Although not the primary purpose of this investigation, it is abundantly clear from the text that healing was not only a major part of Jesus' ministry, but it was also intended to be part of the disciples' ministry and, by extension, that of Matthew's readers as well.

2) Several of the Matthean summary statements with regard to healing do not include demon possession. In addition, the majority of specific healing accounts do not indicate that demonic activity was the cause of the infirmities.

3) Unlike several other strands of New Testament thought, Matthew never attributes an illness to God nor does he identify sin as a direct cause of infirmity.

4) In contrast to several other New Testament writers, Matthew makes it clear that a variety of maladies are the result of demon possession. Not only does Matthew assign certain cases of deafness, muteness, blindness, and epilepsy to demonic activity, but he can even list demon possession (his first reference to demon possession) along with epilepsy and paralysis as major infirmities which Jesus healed. At times Matthew moves easily between the concepts of healing and exorcism.

5) It is equally clear that Matthew does not regard all illness as being the result of demonic activity nor does he consider all demon possession to be connected to illness. Demon possession on its own, quite apart from illness, is described in his Gospel.

6) Since some diseases are attributed to demons but others are not, there must have been some way to distinguish between the two. In Matthew, it appears that Jesus' own discernment is the basis of some of the judgments (cf. esp. 17.14-21). If the Matthean narrative seeks to inform the praxis of his community of readers, then perhaps it is not going too far to suggest that discernment about such matters was an expected and necessary part of the community's life.

7) When exorcisms remove the cause of an infirmity, Matthew is comfortable (though not consistent) in describing such as a healing.

8) Matthew's readers are warned that unless a healing which results from exorcism is followed up by acceptance of the Gospel of the Kingdom, the healing experienced may only be temporary, owing to the person's vulnerability to the return of this and other demons.

9) If one does not remain 'empty' after an exorcism, but fills oneself with Jesus or the Gospel, it would appear that such a one is in no danger of being possessed again by demons. This may also imply that, for the Matthean community, those who have responded faithfully to the Gospel are themselves not vulnerable to such ca-

lamity. Therefore, it seems that for Matthew, the notion of a demon possessing or oppressing a believer would be an impossibility.

10) The basis of Jesus' healing ministry, and consequently, his exorcistic ministry is his atoning life and death.

11) A lack of proper faith can result in the failure to heal an infirmity caused by a demon.

12) Jesus' healing and exorcistic work is in some way related to his identity as Son of David in Matthew's Gospel.

6

THE GOSPEL ACCORDING TO LUKE

With Luke-Acts, one finds a somewhat different emphasis than that of the other New Testament documents surveyed to this point. This statement is based primarily on the fact that, whereas Mark and Matthew make clear in their summary statements the distinction between healings and exorcisms, Luke seems regularly to group such activity together. In fact, Luke uses the word 'heal' (θεραπευώ) to describe both healings and exorcisms (cf. Lk. 6.18; 7.21; and apparently Acts 5.16). In several healing stories illness or infirmity is attributed to a demonic origin (Lk. 9.37-45; 11.14; 13.10-13; Acts 5.16). Finally, in ways not dissimilar to James, Paul, and John, Luke is not reluctant to attribute the infliction of suffering as punishment or chastisement to God (Lk. 1.20; Acts 5.1-11; 9.1-18; 12.19-23; 13.6-12). Given the sheer volume of relevant information and the significant role of Luke-Acts for many in the Pentecostal and Charismatic traditions, this examination is obviously a most important one for the purposes of this study.

Although the circumstances for the writing of Luke-Acts is notoriously difficult to determine, it is generally believed that the author is a second-generation Christian, who has (perhaps) been a companion of Paul, the main subject of well over half of Luke's second volume. The composition itself suggests that the author is a Gentile believer, writing primarily for other Gentile Christians.

Given the vast amount of relevant materials in Luke-Acts, separate chapters are devoted to each of Luke's volumes.

Introduction

Luke begins his first volume with a prologue or preface, in which he states the purpose for undertaking the writing of these volumes: that the most excellent Theophilus might know of the certainty of the things he has been taught.

Unlike Matthew, Luke does not open his work with a genealogy of Jesus, although one is given later in chapter 3. Rather he tells the story of two righteous individuals, Zechariah and Elizabeth, both descendants of Aaron. However, despite their righteous standing before the Lord and the keeping of his commands, they have no children and, given their ages, have no hope for any offspring. While serving in the Temple to burn incense, Zechariah receives an angelic visitation in which he is promised a son who will be great in the sight of the Lord and will, among other things, make ready a people prepared for the Lord. The first passage relevant to the purposes of this enquiry occurs in this context.

Luke 1.18-20 – The Muteness of Zechariah

At this point the reader of Luke's narrative is caught up in the euphoria of the extraordinary event and the remarkable words concerning Zechariah and Elizabeth. The intervention of God in the lives of such godly individuals is marvelous enough, but almost staggering is the news that the removal of their personal sorrow and shame would at the same time be the vehicle for the preparation of the people of Israel for the (return of the) Lord.

> And Zechariah said to the angel, 'By what shall I know this? for *I* am an old man and my wife is well along in her days'. And answering the angel said to him, '*I* am Gabriel the one who stands before God, and I have been sent to speak to you and to preach these things to you. And behold, you will be silent and not able to speak until the day these things happen, because you did not believe in my words, which will be fulfilled in their time.'

Verse 18

With a great deal of anticipation the reader awaits the first words to be spoken in the narrative by Zechariah. In what follows it is learned that Zechariah is no less stunned than the reader by the angelic message. In words reminiscent of the great patriarch Abraham (Gen. 15.8),[1] the shaken Zechariah asks how he can be sure of all this. His request for a confirmation of these words is very much tied to the fact that Zechariah is such an old man, a point made emphatic by his use of ἐγώ εἰμι,[2] and that Elizabeth, owing to her age, is no more capable of bearing children than he is of fathering them.

Verse 19

Although Zechariah's age may cause him to request confirmation of the angel's words, the relationship between his age and the words of promise (about a son) is of no concern to the angel. The messenger counters Zechariah's emphasis upon his age by utilizing the same ἐγώ εἰμι formula to emphasize his own identity and authority.[3] The structure of the Greek text suggests that the angel's response could be rendered something like, 'You may be an old man, but *I am* Gabriel, the one who stands before God'.

Several aspects of this emphatic identification are noteworthy. First, the angel's name, Gabriel, is a transliteration of 'Man of God',[4] the meaning of which should in itself be sufficient to indicate his authority to speak the words he does to Zechariah. Second, Gabriel is the name of the angel who came to Daniel (Dan. 8.16

---

[1] Most scholars see a reference to the request of Abraham in the words of Zechariah. Cf. A. Plummer, *The Gospel according to S. Luke* (Edinburgh: T. & T. Clark, 1901), p. 16; M.-J. Lagrange, *Évangile selon Saint Luc* (Paris: J. Gabalda, 1927), p. 19; L. Morris, *The Gospel According to St. Luke* (Grand Rapids: Eerdmans, 1974), p. 70; H. Schürmann, *Das Lukasevangelium*, I (Freiburg: Herder, 1969), p. 37; F.W. Danker, *Jesus and the New Age* (St. Louis: Clayton Pub., 1972), p. 9; E. Klostermann, *Das Lukasevangelium* (Tübingen: J.C.B. Mohr, 1975), p. 9; R.E. Brown, *The Birth of the Messiah* (Garden City, NY: Doubleday, 1993), pp. 279-80; I.H. Marshall, *Commentary on Luke* (Grand Rapids: Eerdmans, 1978), p. 60; J.A. Fitzmyer, *Gospel according to Luke I-IX* (Garden City, NY; Doubleday, 1981), p. 320; L. Sabourin, *L'Évangile de Luc: Introduction et Commentaire* (Rome: Editrice Pontificia Università Gregoriana, 1987), p. 59; J. Nolland, *Luke 1-9.20* (Dallas: Word, 1989), p. 32; and C.F. Evans, *Saint Luke* (London: SCM Press, 1990), p. 151.

[2] Plummer (*Luke*, p. 16) observes that the use of ἐγώ εἰμι implies the angel had forgotten this fact.

[3] Cf. Plummer, *Luke*, p. 16; E.E. Ellis, *The Gospel of Luke* (Grand Rapids: Eerdmans, 1981), p. 69; and E. Schweizer, *The Good News according to Luke* (tran. D.E. Green; Atlanta: John Knox Press, 1984), p. 23.

[4] For this identification cf. Lagrange, *Évangile*, p. 20; A.R.C. Leaney, *The Gospel according to St. Luke* (Peabody, MA: Hendrickson, 1988), pp. 43-44; Morris, *Luke*, p. 70; Marshall, *Luke*, p. 60; and Sabourin, *Luc*, p. 59.

and again at the time of sacrifice – Dan. 9.21) in order to reveal the meaning of the visions the prophet had seen. Given his function in Daniel, here, and later in Luke (1.26-38), Gabriel is sometimes identified as a revealer.[5] Third, by identifying himself as the one who stands before God, the angel emphasizes that he is as close to God as possible.[6] Such an intimate position carries with it the obvious inference that any word which comes from Gabriel comes from God himself.[7]

In addition to his identity, Gabriel reveals that he has been sent (by God)[8] to speak to Zechariah and to bring him the good news of these things. Although use of the word εὐαγγελίσασθαι might be understood simply in terms of the Old Testament sense of the good news of salvation[9] or the good news about the messiah,[10] the reader is here introduced to a very significant Lukan theme, the preaching of the Gospel; a theme Luke uses to indicate the basic continuity of salvation history. Here, Gabriel brings the message of the Gospel, if in a somewhat proleptic sense.[11] This preaching will be continued by John (3.18), Jesus (4.18; 7.22; 20.1), and the followers of Jesus in the early church (Acts 5.42; 8.4; 10.36; 13.32). As this theme develops, it is not insignificant for the reader that the preaching of the Gospel begins with authoritative messengers from God himself (Lk. 1.19; 2.10).[12]

---

[5] Cf. W.F. Adeney, *St. Luke* (Edinburgh: T.C. & E.C. Jack, 1901), p. 134 and W. Manson, *The Gospel of Luke* (London: Hodder and Stoughton, 1930), p. 7.

[6] A. Stöger, *The Gospel according to St. Luke* (tran. B. Fahy; London: Burns & Oates, 1969), p. 12.

[7] G.B. Caird, *Saint Luke* (London: Penguin, 1963), p. 51; R.H. Stein, *Luke* (Nashville, TN: Broadman, 1992), p. 77; and D.L. Bock, *Luke* (Leicester: IVP, 1994), p. 37.

[8] According to Lagrange (*Luc*, p. 20) ἀπεστάλην '... indique une mission temperaire qui a été confiée à l'ange'.

[9] Lagrange, *Luc*, p. 20.

[10] Plummer, *Luke*, p. 17.

[11] K.H. Rengstorf (*Das Evangelium nach Lukas* [Göttingen: Vandenhoeck und Ruprecht, 1962], p. 22) states that the term means to preach the Gospel, which makes Zechariah the first person to hear it. Cf. also Sabourin, *Luc*, p. 60.

[12] L.T. Johnson, *The Gospel of Luke* (Collegeville, MN: Michael Glazier, 1991), p. 33.

Verse 20

The stern words of Gabriel in the previous verse turn into a full rebuke in v. 20. Through the use of 'behold' (ἰδου), a common expression in Luke, the angel continues his response to Zechariah but with new emphasis.[13] Zechariah is told that he will be silent[14] and unable to speak ... because of his unbelief with regard to the angel's words. Despite his inability to take in the extraordinary promise of the angel, the reader still has a rather high estimate of Zechariah, owing to his righteous standing and his implicit identification with Abraham's action in requesting confirmation of the angel's words. Consequently, Gabriel's words that Zechariah is struck mute come as quite a surprise.

Any number of reasons might be offered as an explanation of this enigmatic turn of events. On the one hand, it is possible to take this rebuke as an indication that Luke has no place for the demanding of a sign, as in Lk. 11.16, 29-30,[15] or even mild questions or demands.[16] On the other hand, perhaps despite Zechariah's following the precedent of Abraham, he is punished because a) he has a greater responsibility than his predecessor, owing to his position in salvation history,[17] or b) he did not ask in the same spirit as had Abraham,[18] or c) given the singular importance of the moment in Israel's religious history, he is held to a higher standard.[19] Such suggestions, while possible, are not wholly consistent with what the reader of the narrative would understand. What then would this story convey to its reader?

First, it is very clear that Zechariah's mute condition is the result of his failure to believe the words of his angelic messenger. How-

---

[13] Plummer, *Luke*, p. 17.

[14] Based in part on the fact that Zechariah's friends will later use sign language to communicate with him, J.G. Anderson ('A New Translation of Luke 1.20', *Bible Translator* 20 [1969], pp. 21-24) argues that σιωπῶν should be translated 'deaf'. The latter phrase 'and not able to speak' would account for his mute condition. Cf also Fitzmyer, *Luke I-IX*, p. 328; F. Bovon, *L'Évangile selon Saint Luc (1,1 – 9,50)* (Genève: Labor et Fides, 1991), p. 61; and Bock, *Luke*, p. 38.

[15] Danker, *Jesus*, p. 9.

[16] D.L. Tiede, *Luke* (Minneapolis, MN: Augsburg, 1988), p. 44.

[17] So N. Geldenhuys, *Commentary on the Gospel of Luke* (Grand Rapids: Eerdmans, 1951), p. 67.

[18] So Morris, *Luke*, p. 70.

[19] So Evans, *Luke*, p. 151.

ever one might explain the differences between Zechariah's actions and those of Abraham (Gen. 15.8), Gideon (Judg. 6.36-39), and Hezekiah (2 Kgs 20.8), the fact remains that the text attributes his condition to unbelief.[20] The reader must await the next pericope (Lk. 1.26-38) for an opportunity to compare Zechariah's response with that of Mary. Such a story at the very beginning of the narrative impresses upon the reader the important message that even righteous and blameless individuals can fall victim to unbelief.

Second, it is also evident that Zechariah's mute condition is intended to be seen as a punitive act.[21] Whereas Daniel's experience with muteness (Dan. 10.15) resulted from the impact of an extraordinary visionary experience, a condition from which he later recovered, Zechariah suffers this condition as punishment because of unbelief.[22]

Third, although the agent who causes the muteness is Gabriel, given his close proximity to God, there can be little doubt that the infliction of this condition is the result of God's own will and action. Thus, from the beginning of the narrative the reader learns that God can and will send infirmity (Acts 13.6-11) and even death (Acts 5.1-10; 12.19-21) upon certain individuals both inside and outside the community of believers.[23] In point of fact, the very first infirmity in this narrative, which will also document the removal of illnesses wrought by Satan and/or his demons, is attributed to God.

Fourth, even though Zechariah's muteness is punitive, it is at the same time a sign of God's intention to perform the mighty act of which his messenger speaks.[24] While his infirmity may not be like that of Daniel, neither does it appear on the surface to be of the same severity as the punitive affliction inflicted upon Elymus later

---

[20] Bovon (*Luc* [1,1 – 9,50], p. 60) notes, 'Dans l'Ancien Testament, on trouve souvent un signe apporté par un ange, mais exiger un signe est parfois la preuve d'une fri trop faible'.

[21] F.W. Farrar, *The Gospel according to St Luke* (Cambridge: Cambridge University Press, 1891), p. 93; J. Drury, *Luke* (London: Collins, 1973), p. 24; Fitzmyer, *Luke I-IX*, p. 328; Sabourin, *Luc*, p. 59; Bovon , *Luc (1,1 – 9,50)*, p. 61; and Stein, *Luke*, p. 77.

[22] P. Benoit, 'L'enfance de Jean-Baptiste selon Luc I', *NTS* 3 (1956-57), p. 179.

[23] Fitzmyer, *Luke I-IX*, p. 328.

[24] Plummer, *Luke*, p. 17; Geldenhuys, *Luke*, p. 68; Schürmann, *Lukas-Evangelium*, I, p. 37; G.H.P. Thompson, *The Gospel according to Luke* (Oxford: Clarendon Press, 1972), p. 51; and Nolland, *Luke 1-9.20*, pp. 32-33.

in the Lukan account (Acts 13.6-12).[25] There will be an end to Zechariah's suffering, and it will coincide with the fulfillment of the angelic/divine promise.

Gabriel's final words continue the mixture of rebuke and promise. By the use of οἵτινες instead of the usual οἱ Luke places additional emphasis upon the certainty of the angel's words: fulfillment despite Zechariah's unbelief.[26] At the same time, introduction of fulfillment language anticipates the way in which Jesus himself will fulfill the Scriptures both at Nazareth (4.21) and after his resurrection (24.44). All will be fulfilled 'in their time', a time which God has determined.[27]

Conclusions

What are the implications of Lk. 1.18-20 for the primary concerns of this enquiry? 1) In ways similar to James, Paul, and John, Luke is not afraid to attribute an illness to God. For Luke to begin his narrative with this attribution indicates that, despite the role of Satan and demonic powers as those primarily responsible for infirmities in much of what follows, the reader has been put on notice that God can and will inflict suffering when deemed necessary. 2) This text reveals that, in this case, the infliction of infirmity is the direct result of unbelief. Such an emphasis conveys to the reader the need for complete acceptance of God's words. 3) For an individual like Zechariah, who is obviously intended by Luke to be viewed in a positive light, the prospect of being inflicted in this way will caution those within the community of believers from simplistically attributing all suffering to Satan and/or demons.

Luke 4.38-41 – Jesus Rebukes the Fever of Simon's Mother-in-Law

Luke's narrative continues with the conclusion and aftermath of Gabriel's visit to Zechariah and Gabriel's visit to Mary with the news of the birth of Jesus (1.26-38). Later, Elizabeth praises Mary

---

[25] Lagrange, *Luc*, p. 21.

[26] Cf. Lagrange, *Luc*, p. 21 and J.M. Creed, *The Gospel according to St. Luke* (London: Longmans, Green, & Co., 1930), p. 12. Cf. also W. Grundmann, *Das Evangelium nach Lukas* (Berlin: Evangelische, 1934), p. 53.

[27] Thompson, *Luke*, p. 51 and esp. Fitzmyer, *Luke I-IX*, p. 328.

for believing that what the Lord has said will be accomplished (1.45), perhaps in contrast to the response of her husband Zechariah. The words elicit a (prophetic?) song of praise from Mary (1.46-56). Next the birth of John is recounted, with Zechariah's tongue being loosed and his singing a prophetic song inspired by the Holy Spirit (1.57-80). This is followed by a description of the birth of Jesus (2.1-7) and the resulting visit of the shepherds prompted by an angelic proclamation of the good news (2.8-20). Jesus' presentation at the Temple is also a time of prophecy (2.21-40) and his visit to the Temple twelve years later continues to document his spiritual and physical growth and favor before God and humankind (2.41). Chapter three describes John's public ministry and his subsequent imprisonment (3.1-20), Jesus' baptism (3.21-22), and a record of his genealogy (3.23-37).

Full of the Holy Spirit, Jesus is led by the Spirit into the wilderness to be tempted by the Devil (4.1-13). Jesus returns to Galilee in the power of the Spirit and there reads a significant text from Isaiah 61, a passage which in many ways sums up his ministry activity (4.13-20). Leaving Nazareth he teaches on the Sabbath in Capernaum and there encounters a demon-possessed man in the synagogue. Rebuking the demon, Jesus expels the unclean spirit to the amazement of all (4.31-37). At this point the next text of relevance for this enquiry occurs.

> And departing from the synagogue he entered into the house of Simon. And Simon's mother-in-law was suffering with a great fever and they were asking him concerning her. And standing over her he rebuked the fever and it left her. And at once getting up she served them. And as the sun was going down, they were bringing to him all those having various kinds of illnesses. And placing his hands upon each one of them he healed them. And demons even came out from many, crying out and saying, 'You are the Son of God'. And rebuking [them] he did not allow them to speak, because they knew that he was the Christ.

Verse 38

In some ways the transition found in 4.38 is a bit surprising, for immediately upon departing from the synagogue Jesus enters the house of Simon. This is the first mention of Simon,[28] as he is not called as a disciple until 5.1-11.[29] Does such an abrupt mention indicate that the readers would know him without an introduction?[30] In terms of the narrative world, such an explanation is a bit untenable. Rather than assuming knowledge of Peter on the part of the (implied) reader, perhaps it is more likely that this abrupt mention of Simon is a Lukan device designed to prepare the reader for the later call of this most significant character in the Lucan story.

Nearly as abrupt as the mention of Simon, is that of Simon's mother-in-law. That Luke would follow-up the account of a man in need (4.31-37) with that of a woman in need[31] is not only reminiscent of the way in which the Zechariah and Mary stories are paired in chapter 1, but also indicative of the place of women in the Lukan narrative. The reader quickly learns that Simon's mother-in-law suffered[32] (perhaps chronically)[33] from a high fever. While it is possible that Luke uses the word 'great/high' (μεγάλῳ) in a technical medical sense,[34] it is certainly the case that the reader would understand such an attributive to underscore the difficulty of the situation and the powerful act needed for its cure.[35] Given the condition of Simon's mother-in-law and what had just been witnessed in the

---

[28] Farrar, *Luc*, p. 156; Klostermann, *Lukas*, p. 67; Fitzmyer, *Luke I-IX*, p. 549; Bovon, *Luc (1,1 -9,50)*, p. 218; and Johnson, *Luke*, p. 84.

[29] Tiede, *Luke*, p. 113.

[30] So Plummer, *Luke*, p. 136 and Schürmann, *Lukas-evangelium*, I, p. 251. Nolland (*Luke 1-9.20*, p. 211) implies that this is simply the result of deviating from Markan order.

[31] Fitzmyer, *Luke I-IX*, p. 549.

[32] Lagrange (*Luc*, p. 151) takes συνέχεσθαι to be a medical term, since Luke employs it in nine of its twelve NT usages.

[33] On the basis of the phrase ἦν συνεχομένη, Farrar (*Luke*, p. 157) concludes, 'The analytic imperfect implies that the fever was chronic, and the verb that it was severe'.

[34] So W.K. Hobart, *The Medical Language of St. Luke* (London: Longmans, Green, & Co., 1882), p. 3; Farrar, *Luke*, p. 157; Adeney, *Luke*, p. 174; Plummer, *Luke*, p. 137; Ellis, *Luke*, p. 100; Thompson, *Luke*, p. 95; Morris, *Luke*, p. 110; W. Wilkinson, *The Good News in Luke* (Glasgow: Collins, 1974), p. 33; and Marshall, *Luke*, p. 195. However, cf. H.J. Cadbury's critique in 'Lexical Notes on Luke-Acts in Recent Arguments for Medical Language', *JBL* 45 (1926), pp. 194, 203, 207 n.

[35] Cf. D.G. Miller, *Saint Luke* (London: SCM Press, 1959), p. 66; Fitzmyer, *Luke I-IX*, p. 550; Twelftree, *Christ Triumphant: Exorcism Then and Now*, p. 101; C.F. Evans, *Luke*, p. 283; C.A. Evans, *Luke* (Peabody: Hendrickson, 1990), p. 81; Bovon, *Luc (1,1 -9,50)*, p. 218; and Stein, *Luke*, p. 164.

synagogue, they (probably the members of Simon's household)[36] requested that Jesus help the woman. For the reader such a petition creates a certain air of expectancy, for not only is the reader aware of the previous pericope, but also has knowledge not shared by all the characters in the narrative.

Verse 39

Jesus' response includes two somewhat unexpected actions. First, he either 'stood over her in a towering way'[37] or he 'bent over her'.[38] Both interpretations of ἐπιστὰς ἐπάνω imply that Jesus' very posture sought to convey a certain visual boldness in his action.[39] Second, in that authoritative posture Jesus 'rebuked' (ἐπετίμησεν) the fever as he had earlier rebuked the unclean spirit of a demon while in the synagogue (4.35). But, how are Luke's readers to understand the use of this term? Is the fever being treated simply as some nebulous principle hostile to humankind?[40] Is the fever a personification of evil,[41] indicating that all illness is the work of Satan?[42] Is it an indication that the fever is the result of demonic affliction?[43] Or does Jesus' rebuke indicate that Simon's mother-in-law was demon possessed?[44]

---

[36] Nolland, *Luke 1-9.20*, p. 211.

[37] So Schürmann, *Lukas-evangelium*, I, p. 251.

[38] So U. Busse, *Die Wunder des Propheten Jesus: Die Rezeption, Komposition und Interpretation der Wundertradition im Evangelium des Lukas* (Stuttgart: Katholisches Bibelwerk, 1977), p. 72 and J.D.M. Derrett, 'Getting on Top of a Demon (Luke 4.39)', *EvQ* 65 (1993), pp. 99-109.

[39] Nolland, *Luke 1-9.20*, p. 211.

[40] F. Godet, *The Gospel of St. Luke*, I (tran. E.W. Shalders; Edinburgh: T. & T. Clark, 1870), p. 248.

[41] Creed, *Luke*, p. 71; Ellis, *Luke*, p. 101; Marshall, *Luke*, p. 195; and apparently Morris, *Luke*, p. 110 and C.A. Evans, *Luke*, p. 80. For Bovon (*Luc [1,1 -9,50]*, p. 218) and Bock (*Luke*, p. 97), it is the illness that may be personified.

[42] Caird, *Luke*, p. 89.

[43] Adeney, *Luke*, p. 174; Leaney, *Luke*, p. 121; X. León-Dufour, 'La guérison de la belle-mere de Simon-Pierre', *Est Bib* 24 (1965), pp. 193-216 (207); Schürmann, *Lukas-evangelium*, I, p. 252; Danker, *Jesus and the New Age*, p. 62; Thompson, *Luke*, p. 95; Klostermann, *Lukas*, p. 67; Nolland, *Luke 1-9.20*, p. 211; and C.F. Evans, *Luke*, p. 282.

[44] E.J. Tinsley, *The Gospel according to Luke* (Cambridge: Cambridge University Press, 1965), p. 56; C.H. Talbert, *Reading Luke: A Literary and Theological Commentary on the Third Gospel* (New York: Crossroad, 1984), p. 58; F.B. Craddock, *Luke* (Louisville: John Knox Press, 1990), p. 67; Johnson, *Luke*, p. 84; and apparently Sabourin, *Luc*, p. 140.

Several things may be observed with regard to Jesus' attitude toward this fever in the Lukan narrative. From the outset it should be noted that it is very difficult not to see in this fever some sort of demonic activity. The use of ἐπιτιμάω to describe Jesus' response to the fever is by itself enough to ensure such an inference, as this same term occurs in the pericope immediately preceding and following this story in contexts where demonic activity is clearly present. Add to this the fact that, when dealing with the fever, Jesus addresses the fever and not the woman, an action consistent with the way Jesus deals with demons. Finally, the term used to describe the departure of the fever, αφίημι, is not used by Luke in any other texts to describe the casting out of a demon.

However, while it may be safe to conclude that this verse has reference to some kind of demonic activity, it is far from certain that the reader is intended to understand this event as an exorcism. Although there are similarities between this episode with Simon's mother-in-law and demon possession, there are also a number of differences. One of the most obvious differences is that Luke does not describe the woman as being demon possessed or as having a demon. Missing as well are the typical characteristics of those demon possessed – convulsions, violent reactions when the demon is cast out, and/or attempts to reveal the identity of Jesus. What is the reader to make of such mixed signals? It appears that Luke intends the reader to understand this fever as an affliction caused by demonic activity, a demonic physical oppression one might say, but not an illness resulting from demon possession in the classic sense.[45] However, as the next verses indicate, not all illness is attributed to demons in Luke's narrative.[46]

At Jesus' rebuke, the fever left. As testimony to the miraculous nature of the cure, Simon's mother-in-law arises at once and ministers to them.[47] Thus she anticipates the actions of other women

---

[45] Nolland (*Luke 1-9.20*, p. 212) concludes, 'It is perhaps better, then, to treat fever and illness generally as a Satanic oppression (Acts 10.38 and possibly Luke 13.16) comparable to demon possession but not to be identified with it: sickness itself is the demonic force'.

[46] Cf. Nolland, *Luke 1-9.20*, p. 211.

[47] Plummer, *Luke*, p. 137; Geldenhuys, *Luke*, p. 177; Morris, *Luke*, p. 110; Bovon, *Luc (1,1 -9,50)*, p. 218; and Stein, *Luke*, p. 164.

from Galilee who also minister to Jesus later in the Gospel (8.1-3; 23.49, 55).[48]

Verse 40

News of the exorcism in the synagogue and the healing of Simon's mother-in-law apparently made its way through the area, for the people could hardly wait until the Sabbath was over ('As the sun was setting')[49] until they brought all those having various kinds of infirmities to Jesus.

Jesus' response was to lay hands on each one of those who had come as a means of healing. At the least the laying on of hands indicates that Jesus has a special concern for each individual sufferer.[50] But perhaps more than that, the reader has come to appreciate the fact that in Luke's narrative the word 'hand' is a sign of authority and power. As earlier as 1.66, the reader learns that the hand of the Lord was upon the child John. Zechariah rejoices because God has brought salvation and deliverance for his people from the hand of the enemy (1.71, 74). According to John, the mightier one who follows has a winnowing fork (shovel) in his hand (3.17). In the temptation account, Jesus is told by the Devil, through a quotation from the Scripture (Ps. 91.12), that the angels have been given charge over him and will lift him up in their hands (4.11). Therefore, when the reader learns in 4.40 that Jesus lays hands on the infirm, it is no doubt taken as a sign of his power[51] and the resulting healings come as no surprise. Luke confirms this interpretation when in 6.19 he makes an explicit connection between the power of Jesus to heal and touching as the medium. While it might be appropriate to look for antecedents to this practice in Judaism and beyond,[52] Luke's emphasis here seems to underscore Jesus' power to heal,[53] an idea in much harmony with the statement in 4.18-19.

---

[48] Fitzmyer, *Luke I-IX*, p. 549 and Bovon, *Luc (1,1 -9,50)*, p. 218.

[49] Plummer, *Luke*, p. 138; Ellis, *Luke*, p. 101; and Morris, *Luke*, p. 110.

[50] Morris, *Luke*, p. 110; Danker, *Jesus and the New Age*, p. 63; and Nolland, *Luke 1-9.20*, p. 213.

[51] Bock, *Luke*, p. 97.

[52] On this cf. esp. the work of J. Tipei, 'Laying on of Hands in the New Testament', PhD thesis (2000), University of Sheffield.

[53] Stöger, *Luke*, p. 91.

Verse 41

As a result of Jesus' healing activity demons also came out of many. Several observations might be offered about the significance of this statement. First, it seems that there is for Luke at this point a very close relationship between illness and demon possession.[54] In fact, '... the form of the sentence almost makes the exorcisms incidental to the healings'.[55] At least one can say that for Luke some forms of demon possession can be included among the category of illness.[56] Second, it would appear that those to whom reference is made in v. 41 are demon possessed and not, as Simon's mother-in-law, afflicted by a demon. Both the term used to describe their departure (ἐξήρχετο) and the cries of the demons point in this direction. Third, while there may be a close connection between demon possession and infirmity in v. 41, it is equally clear that not all those who are healed suffer from demon possession. Granted, there is a large number of those so afflicted (πολλῶν), but not all. Therefore, there are at least two categories of those who come for healing: the sick and the demon-possessed sick.[57] Fourth, although it is possible to take 4.40-41 as a general description of Jesus' liberating ministry, which is divided into healing through the laying on of hands in v. 40 and exorcism by means of rebuke in v. 41,[58] the sentence structure suggests that these are two parts of one activity.[59] Despite the fact that this may be the only place in the Scripture where the laying on of hands is explicitly associated with exorcism,[60] the reader of Luke's narrative would find such a connection here natural, given the relationship between hand and power to this point in the story.[61]

---

[54] E. LaVerdiere, *Luke* (Collegeville, MN: Michael Glazier, 1980), p. 72.

[55] Marshall, *Luke*, p. 196.

[56] Nolland, *Luke 1–9.20*, p. 213.

[57] Godet, *Luke I*, p. 251; Plummer, *Luke*, p. 137; Miller, *Luke*, p. 67; and LaVerdiere, *Luke*, p. 72.

[58] So Sabourin, *Luc*, p. 141; M. Green, *I Believe in Satan's Downfall* (London: Hodder & Stoughton, 1995), p. 127 and S.H.T. Page, *Powers of Evil: A Biblical Study of Satan & Demons* (Grand Rapids: Baker, 1995), p. 167.

[59] Bovon (*Luc [1,1 –9,50]*, p. 218-19) notes that these are distinct activities and yet here 'des échantillons d'une activité plus intense'.

[60] Page, *Powers of Evil*, p. 167.

[61] Apparently exorcism accompanied by the laying on of hands was known at Qumran, cf. 1QapGen 20.16-17.

Thus, it appears that during (or through) the process of the laying on of hands the demonic manifestations occurred.

As the demons came out they were crying out/screaming and saying to Jesus, 'You are the Son of God'. From a variety of texts, the reader knows that the demons' exclamation is accurate, for Jesus is the Son of God (cf. 1.32; 2.49; 3.22; 3.37; 4.3, 9, 34). However, it is not altogether clear as to why the demons make such proclamations. Are their cries attempts to control Jesus' actions, owing to their knowledge of his true identity?[62] Or are these involuntary exclamations which demonstrate Jesus' superior powers?[63] For the reader, these confessions serve to underscore Jesus' identity and to emphasize his superiority over the demonic forces,[64] who know his identity but are still vulnerable before him. Jesus will have none of their testimony and rebukes them, as he had earlier rebuked the demon in the synagogue and the fever afflicting Simon's mother-in-law. The last clause in v. 41 indicates that the reason for their silencing is that they knew he was the Christ, a knowledge the reader shares (2.12; 2.26) but which the people generally did not (3.15). Such a rationale suggests that Jesus did not want the demons revealing his identity; this was his work not theirs.

Conclusions

This examination of Lk. 4.38-41 has a number of important implications for this enquiry. 1) This text reveals that for Luke there is an extremely close connection between illness and demonic activity. 2) The story of Simon's mother-in-law indicates that one can be afflicted by a demonic power, in this case fever, without being demon possessed. This is the first Gospel text to suggest that a demon could inflict an illness upon an individual without it implying that the sufferer is demon possessed. 3) To this point, the Gospel of Luke has assigned the origin of infirmities to God, demonic affliction, demon possession, and unattributed causes (the others healed in v. 40). 4) In appears that at least on this occasion (v. 41) Jesus may have used the laying on of hands in some exorcistic activity in addition to his healing activity. 5) Both the healing of disease and the

---

[62] So Stöger, *Luke*, p. 92 and suggested as a possibility by Marshall, *Luke*, p. 197.

[63] Godet, *Luke*, p. 231; Plummer, *Luke*, p. 139; and Tinsley, *Luke*, p. 56.

[64] León-Dufour, 'La guérison de la belle-mere de Simon-Pierre', p. 215.

casting out of demons is attributable to the power (of the Holy Spirit) resident in Jesus. 6) It appears that Jesus' own discernment is the basis of distinguishing between the different origins of the various infirmities.

Luke 6.18-19 – 'Those Troubled by unclean Spirits were Healed'

Following this period of healing, Jesus continued preaching in the synagogues of Judea. The narrative then fills the lacuna created by the apparently premature mention of Simon in 4.38 by recounting his call and that of his partners, James and John the sons of Zebedee (5.1-11). After this Jesus heals a man with leprosy by touching him (5.12-16) and restores a paralytic to health (5.17-26). The story about the pronouncement of forgiveness upon and healing of the paralytic has already received considerable attention in chapter four. While Luke's treatment of the story is not considerably different from Mark's, Luke does make a point of emphasizing that 'the power of the Lord was present for him to heal the sick', continuing the theme of Jesus' power (4.14). The call of Levi follows (5.27-32), as do questions about fasting (5.33-39) and the Sabbath, and then comes still another healing (6.1-10). Verses 12-15 of chapter 6 are devoted to the choosing of the Twelve. The healing stories mentioned in this section provide additional evidence that not all sickness is regarded as being the result of demonic or Satanic activity. While it is tempting to conclude that almost all diseases are expressions of evil for Luke,[65] in these accounts the infirmities are treated in an unattributed fashion with regard to origins.

Verses 17-19 introduce Luke's Sermon on the Plain (vv. 20-49), but they are of special interest, owing to the way they speak of demons and healing. This study focuses on vv. 18-19.

And coming down with them he stood upon a level place, and a great crowd of his disciples, and a great assembly of people from all over Judea and Jerusalem and the coastal district of Tyre and Sidon, those who came to hear him and to be healed from their diseases; and those who were troubled by unclean spirits

---

[65] As does J. Green, *The Theology of the Gospel of Luke* (Cambridge: Cambridge University Press, 1995), p. 96.

> were healed. And the whole crowd was seeking to touch him, because power was going out from him and healing all.

Large crowds from various regions, both near and far, come to Jesus. Their purpose in coming is two-fold: to hear him teach and to be healed. By observing that they come to hear him, Luke continues to develop the theme of Jesus' teaching, which could produce rage on the part of the hearers (4.28) but often is an indication of the people's desire to hear the 'word of God' (5.1; cf. also v. 15). The mention of their coming to hear him in 6.18 also prepares the reader for the Sermon on the Plain which follows.[66] The mention of their coming 'to be healed from their diseases' continues the, by now, familiar theme of Jesus' healing powers. The specific appearance of the word used here for disease (νόσων) connects this text in an explicit fashion with 4.40, where similar ideas are present. Only here in the New Testament is the expression 'troubled by unclean spirits' used.[67] It is not altogether clear exactly what Luke has in mind when he uses this phrase. Is it simply another way of describing demon possession,[68] in which case Luke again treats demon possession as a form of illness[69] and exorcism as a form of healing?[70] Or does Luke intend for this phrase to be understood in ways comparable to the demonic affliction of Simon's mother-in-law? If the former, then here Luke uses θεραπεύω to describe exorcism, as 4.40 seems to indicate. If the latter, Luke may be using this term to describe the curing of a demonic affliction, rather than describing exorcism of a demon-possessed person. Although the latter option is a possibility, given the connection in 4.40 (and what will appear in 7.21) it appears that the former option is more likely. If this is the case, Luke is not unlike Matthew in describing exorcisms as healing.

Several aspects of v. 19 merit exploration. The reader learns that the crowd was (continually?) seeking to touch Jesus, perhaps less an

---

[66] Marshall, *Luke*, p. 242.

[67] Nolland, *Luke 1–9.20*, p. 276. However, cf. also Acts 5.16 which utilizes a very similar expression.

[68] So Page, *Powers of Evil*, p. 168.

[69] Marshall, *Luke*, p. 242.

[70] Nolland, *Luke 1–9.20*, p. 276 and Bovon, *Luc (1,1 -9,50)*, p. 281. Klostermann (*Lukas*, p. 77) goes so far as to say '… bei dem stark zusammenziehenden Lc besteht die Trennung der gewöhnlichen Kranken und Dämonischen nicht'.

emphasis on the crowd's superstitious beliefs[71] than a reference to the reader's (and the crowd's) knowledge of Jesus' utilization of the laying on of hands in healing (4.40; 5.13).[72] In order to make this point clear, the reader is informed that the crowd sought his touch, because 'power (δύναμις) was coming out of his body and all were healed'. But what is the reader to make of this reference? No doubt this text develops the idea that Jesus' messianic anointing of the Spirit at his water baptism (3.22) continued to be manifested throughout Jesus' ministry to empower him to accomplish mighty things. For example, Jesus is said to be 'full of the Holy Spirit' when he enters the temptation period in the wilderness (4.1), 'in the power of the Spirit' when he returns to Galilee (4.14), cognizant of the Lord's Spirit being upon him in the synagogue sermon at Nazareth (4.18), and that 'the power of the Lord was with him to heal' (5.17).[73] Clearly this last text is the closest to the idea expressed in 6.19, but here the reader is told not only of the power present to heal, but also that it goes out of his body to heal, an idea Luke develops further in 8.43-48 where Jesus acknowledges that (healing) power has left his body. Although it is possible to take these references as an indication that the power of the Spirit to heal was especially present on certain occasions and that the effect of Jesus' healing activity would have left him drained,[74] it seems more in keeping with Luke's overall portrait of Jesus to take these statements as pointing to the fact that Jesus was continually full of the power of the Spirit to heal. Despite the fact that this healing power left his body during individual healings,[75] the reader is less likely to see this as leaving Jesus depleted as to assume that access to this power is never ending, for it comes from an inexhaustable source, the Spirit of God himself. The result is that all are healed.

---

[71] So Marshall, *Luke*, p. 243 and Schweizer, *Luke*, p. 116.

[72] Sabourin, *Luc*, p. 157.

[73] Cf. Schürmann, *Lukas-evangelium*, I, p. 322.

[74] An idea assessed by E. May, '... for Power Went forth from Him', *CBQ* 14 (1952), pp. 93-103.

[75] E. Nestle ('Luke vi. 19', *ExpT* 17 [1905-1906], p. 431) and A. Bonus ('Luke vi. 19', *ExpT* 18 [1906-1907], pp. 187-88) appear correct to argue that the Greek text implies *he* cured them rather than *it* (the power) cured them.

Conclusion

The primary contribution of this Lukan text is that it offers additional support for the idea that Luke can regard certain kinds of demonic activity (possession) as a category for which healing is needed. As in 4.40-41, it is implied that there may have been some contact between Jesus and those 'troubled by unclean spirits', for the whole crowd (πᾶς ὁ ὄχλος) sought to touch him.

Luke 7.21-23 – The Report to John the Baptist

The Sermon on the Plain follows 6.18-19 and is itself followed by an account of a Centurion's faith which results in the healing of his nearly dead servant without Jesus ever seeing the servant (7.1-10). This gives way to an even more extraordinary story, the raising of a widow's only son from the dead (7.11-17). On the heels of this most remarkable event, disciples of John come relaying a question of their master for Jesus, 'Are you the coming one or should we expect another?' Jesus' answer to John is of some relevance for this enquiry.

> In that hour he healed many from diseases and illnesses and evil spirits, and many blind he caused to see. And answering he said to them, 'Going tell John what you have seen and heard: the blind receive their sight, the lame are walking, lepers are cleansed and the deaf hear, the dead are raised, to the poor the Gospel is being preached. And blessed is the one who is not scandalized in me'.

Verse 21

No sooner had John's disciples relayed the question than Jesus performs, before their eyes, the kinds of work that he has done throughout the narrative. To underscore the importance of the moment, Luke employs a phrase 'at that very hour' (ἐν ἐκείνῃ τῇ ὥρᾳ), which along with similar ones, are often used in his Gospel to signal particularly important moments in the narrative (i.e. 2.38; 10.21; 12.12; 13.31; 20.19; 22.53; 24.33).[76] On this occasion, Jesus heals those suffering from diseases, illness (μαστίγων) of a particu-

---

[76] Johnson, *Luke*, p. 123.

larly distressing nature,[77] and evil spirits. Once again, the reader comes to regard demon possession as, in some sense, closely connected with disease,[78] even if Luke seems to distinguish between the two as well.[79] In addition, Jesus opens blinded eyes.

Verse 22

In response to John's enquiry, Jesus places emphasis upon what John's disciples have both heard (in terms of his teaching?) and seen (in terms of his healings). Earlier the shepherds had glorified and praised '... God for all the things they had heard and seen' (2.20). On the day of Pentecost Peter appeals to what his listeners had seen and heard (Acts 2.33). In the face of the Sanhedrin's wrath, Peter and John appeal to what they have seen and heard as the driving factor behind their preaching (cf. Acts 4.20). In Samaria, hearing (Philip's preaching) and seeing the signs which he did (exorcisms and healings) produce great joy in the city (8.6). In Paul's testimony before the Jews in Jerusalem he bears witness to the fact that God called him to know his will, to see the Righteous One and to hear a voice from his mouth. In turn, he is to be a witness to all people of what he has seen and heard (Acts 22.14-15). Finally, Luke closes his second volume with a quotation from Isa. 6.9, 10:

> Go to this people and say,
> Hearing you hear and never understand,
> and seeing you see but never perceive;
> for the heart of this people has become calloused,
> and with their ears they hardly hear,
> and they have closed their eyes;
> Otherwise they might see with their eyes
> and hear with their ears
> and understand with their heart
> and turn and I would heal them.

Clearly, the theme of seeing and hearing as the basis for belief and proclamation is an extremely important one for Luke-Acts. It might

---

[77] The word literally means 'lash'. Plummer (*Luke*, p. 202) suggests, 'The notion that troubles are Divine chastisements is implied in the word'.

[78] Cf. Fitzmyer, *Luke I-IX*, p. 667 and Johnson, *Luke*, p. 122.

[79] Stein, *Luke*, p. 226 and Page, *Powers of Evil*, p. 168.

not be going too far to say that here the disciples of John are being invited to believe and testify of these things to John.

Jesus' answer to John's rather straightforward question is to point to his own actions.[80] While all of these activities may be explained on the basis of Jesus' actions in the Lukan narrative (with the exception of the deaf hearing, which will occur later in the story – 11.14), they also correspond to a remarkable degree with citations from the book of Isaiah, a book which has informed Jesus' ministry from the beginning (4.18-19).[81] A deliberate hearkening back to Isaiah 61 may be indicated by the fact that the first and last of the six works Jesus mentions are mentioned in Isaiah 61. This may even suggest that all six works are intended to be interpreted in the light of the Isaiah passage.[82] The fact that 'preaching to the poor' stands last in this list not only indicates that it is the most important and encompasses the rest,[83] but is also a way in which Luke can make an explicit connection with the Isaiah quote in Lk. 4.18-19. John is to be told that Jesus is doing what he set out to do from the beginning.

Verse 23

Jesus' last words for John in this pericope are a warning of sorts. The reader must have some idea by this time that John's expectations about 'the mightier one who is to come' is somewhat different than the way in which Jesus carries out his ministry. Now those suspicions are confirmed as John is given a sensitive warning.[84]

The first indication that these words are significant is the use of καὶ to join this sentence with what precedes,[85] thereby connecting

---

[80] J. Dupont, 'L'Ambassade de Jean-Baptiste (Matthieu 11, 2-6; Luc 7, 18-23)', *NRT* 83 (1961), p. 943.

[81] Farrar, *Luke*, p. 200; Plummer, *Luke*, p. 203; Grundmann, *Lukas*, p. 164; Leaney, *Luke*, p. 145; W.G. Kümmel, *Promise and Fulfillment: The Eschatological Message of Jesus* (tran. D.M. Barton; London: SCM Press, 1961), p. 110; Schürmann, *Lukas-evangelium*, I, p. 411; Marshall, *Luke*, pp. 291-92; Fitzmyer, *Luke I-IX*, p. 664; Sabourin, *Luc*, p. 175; Tiede, *Luke*, p. 155; Nolland, *Luke 1-9.20*, p. 330; and C.F. Evans, *Luke*, p. 352. For an excellent discussion of these individual activities cf. esp. Dupont, 'L'Ambassade de Jean-Baptiste', pp. 943-51.

[82] So Stein, *Luke*, p. 227.

[83] Dupont, 'L'Ambassade de Jean-Baptiste', p. 948; Danker, *Jesus and the New Age*, p. 96; and Nolland, *Luke 1-9.20*, p. 330.

[84] Geldenhuys, *Luke*, pp. 226-27 and Caird, *Luke*, p. 112.

[85] Fitzmyer, *Luke I-IX*, p. 668.

the one who is blessed with the messianic work of Jesus.[86] For Luke the term μακάριος is closely associated with the Kingdom of God. It has been used to describe Mary's belief of what the angel had said (1.45) and more recently in the story the term has appeared in the Sermon on the Plain. The first beatitude, 'Blessed are the poor for theirs is the Kingdom of God' (7.20), is particularly relevant at this point in that it directly connects with what Jesus has just stated in 7.22 about his activity of 'preaching to the poor'.[87] All of this is to say that the introduction of the term 'blessed' brings the idea of the Kingdom of God into view. The beatitude is pronounced on the one who is not scandalized by Jesus and his ministry. The impression left is that refusal to accept the kind of ministry Jesus fulfills leads to falling into a snare of unbelief or sin.[88] How one responds to what has been seen and heard is as extraordinarily important for John as it will be for others later in the narrative.

Conclusion
The importance of this short text for this enquiry is the way in which it continues the Lukan emphasis on the close identification of demon possession as an illness.

Luke 8.24 – Jesus Rebukes the Wind
After John's disciples leave, Jesus makes clear to the crowd (and the reader) that John indeed is more than a prophet - he is the messenger who prepares the Lord's way. There is none greater than John, yet the least in the Kingdom of God is greater than he! Jesus likens to children those who do not receive John's message (7.24-35). A Pharisee, perhaps one of those who had rejected the purposes of God by not receiving John's baptism (7.30), invites Jesus to dinner. While there a sinful woman comes and washes Jesus' feet with her tears and dries them with her hair. Jesus defends her actions as the result of her great love, owing to much forgiveness of sin; he then pronounces forgiveness upon her (7.36-50).

Following this episode, the reader learns that Jesus continues to preach the Kingdom of God and that several women who had been healed of evil spirits and illnesses follow Jesus and support his work

---

[86] Dupont, 'L'Ambassade de Jean-Baptiste', p. 952.

[87] Dupont, 'L'Ambassade de Jean-Baptiste', p. 952.

[88] C.F. Evans, *Luke*, p. 352

out of their means (8.1-3). Jesus, continuing his proclamation of the Kingdom, tells two parables, of the sower and of the lampstand (8.4-18), and identifies those who hear and practice God's word as his mother and brothers (8.19-21).

At this point occurs another brief text of relevance for this enquiry, the calming of the storm. The primary focus of this four-verse pericope is v. 24, where Jesus responds to the disciples' pleas for intervention:

> And getting up he rebuked the wind and the raging water and they subsided and it became calm.

The issue of primary concern relates to the meaning of Jesus' rebuke of the wind and water. Is the reader to infer from this language that an exorcism is being described?[89] Is the sea/storm to be thought of in personal terms?[90] Is the reader to see here the presence of demonic activity[91] or the evil one himself?[92] Or are the elements of nature themselves in view?[93]

Although it is quite possible that in this rebuke Luke simply has in mind Jesus' power over the elements, which in the Old Testament is seen as the prerogative of God (cf. Pss 65.7; 77.16; 89.9; 104.7; 107.23-29; Job 26.12; Jer. 5.22),[94] two things suggest that the reader is to see some sort of allusion to the powers of evil, demonic or otherwise, in this story. First, the reader has come to understand that the language of rebuke in the Lukan narrative has come to have associations with Jesus' activity over against the demonic. For the reader, this idea is at least in the background. Second, this story is followed immediately by Jesus healing a demon possessed man (8.26-38). While certainty on this point is difficult to achieve, perhaps the thought in v. 24 is not of an exorcism *per se*,[95] but as with Simon's mother-in-law a case where the forces of evil

---

[89] Craddock, *Luke*, p. 114 and apparently Miller, *Luke*, p. 91.

[90] Creed, *Luke*, p. 119.

[91] Farrar, *Luke*, p. 220; Tinsley, *Luke*, p. 91; Morris, *Luke*, p. 155; Danker, *Jesus and the New Age*, p. 106; and C.F. Evans, *Luke*, p. 381.

[92] Geldenhuys, *Luke*, p. 252.

[93] Ellis, *Luke*, p. 127; Schürmann, *Lukas-evangelium*, I, p. 476; Nolland, *Luke 1-9.20*, p. 400; and apparently Plummer, *Luke*, p. 226.

[94] On this point cf. Nolland, *Luke 1-9.20*, p. 401.

[95] Cf. Marshall, *Luke*, p. 334.

work in a way to harm or destroy individuals – on this occasion through the use of nature itself.

Conclusion

This reading of Lk. 8.24 suggests that in addition to the presence of demonic activity in some illnesses, sometimes the elements of nature may be used by evil powers in a malevolent way. Although this pericope does not add much new information to an understanding of origins of disease, it does contribute to the Lukan picture of the ways in which the demonic powers seek to oppose and harm the work and people of God.

Luke 10.17-20 – 'I Saw Satan Fall'

As mentioned earlier, the calming of the storm is followed by the transformation of a demon-possessed man (8.26-39). Upon Jesus' return from Gerasenes and on his way to see Jairus' daughter, who was deathly ill, Jesus is touched by a woman who had been bleeding for twelve years. Through her contact with Jesus, 'power' left his body and the woman was healed. Despite word that Jairus' daughter was dead, Jesus goes to his house and raises the little girl from death (8.40-56). In chapter nine the reader learns of the sending of the Twelve who 'preach the Gospel and heal people everywhere' (9.1-6). Upon their return, Jesus feeds the five thousand (9.10-17), Peter confesses that Jesus is the Christ, whereupon Jesus begins to reveal the cost of following him (9.18-27). Eight days later the transfiguration takes place (9.28-36).

At this point in the narrative, Luke recounts the healing of a boy with an evil spirit (9.37-43), a parallel passage that has received extensive consideration in chapter four of this study. What in Matthew and less clearly in Mark is a story of a boy who suffers with epilepsy caused by a demon, in Luke is the story of a boy who suffers from demon possession. Since no infirmity is mentioned in this pericope, it does not merit additional attention here.

Immediately after warning his disciples of his impending betrayal (9.43-45), there is a dispute among them concerning who is the greatest (9.46-49). Later they are reproved for prohibiting the work of an exorcist whom they did not know (9.49-50) and rebuked for their attitude to the Samaritans who opposed Jesus because he is going to Jerusalem (9.51-56). The chapter closes with a discussion between Jesus and some would-be followers (9.57-62).

The next text of relevance to this enquiry occurs upon the return of the Seventy[-Two] who have been sent out by Jesus to heal and proclaim the Kingdom of God. Jesus makes especially clear the connection between him and his messengers - to receive or reject them is to receive or reject him.

> And the Seventy[-Two] returned with joy saying, 'Lord, even the demons submit to us in your name'. And he said to them, 'I was watching Satan fall as a star out of heaven. Behold I have given to you the authority to walk upon snakes and scorpions, and over all powers of the nations, and nothing will ever be able to harm you. However, do not rejoice in this, that the demons submit to you, but rejoice because your names have been written in heaven'.

Verse 17

The Seventy[-Two] return with joy from their mission to preach and heal. The reason for their joy is soon expressed – 'even the demons submit' to them in the name of Jesus. In the Greek text, emphasis is placed upon 'the demons', for Τὰ δαιμόνια stands near the beginning of the sentence. It is perhaps significant that the casting out of demons was not part of the commission received by the Seventy[-Two],[96] who were to preach and heal. What is one to make of their obvious emphasis upon exorcism? It is possible to take exorcism as an understood (though unspoken) part of their commission, owing to its presence in Jesus' ministry and the commission of the Twelve,[97] in which case the Seventy[-Two] express joy at the fact that the demons were indeed subject to them. Conversely, the reader could take such language to mean that this reference has in view the demonic opposition to their mission with no mention of

---

[96] Adeney, *Luke*, p. 243; Plummer, *Luke*, p. 277; Thompson, *Luke*, p. 162; Morris, *Luke*, p. 185; Marshall, *Luke*, p. 428; Schweizer, *Luke*, p. 179; Sabourin, *Luc*, p. 222; C.F. Evans, *Luke*, p. 453; and G.H. Twelftree, *Jesus the Exorcist: A Contribution to the Study of the Historical Jesus* (Peabody: Hendrickson, 1993), p. 125.

[97] Fitzmyer, *Luke X-XXIV* (Garden City, NY: Doubleday, 1983), p. 861; Twelftree, *Christ Triumphant*, p. 108; Nolland, *Luke 9.21-18.34*, p. 562; and Stein, *Luke*, p. 309.

the sick intended.[98] Another possibility is to see in exorcism a reference to the Seventy[-Two]'s full range of ministry activities. However, given the emphasis placed upon exorcism in this verse, it seems more likely that the subjection of demons to them was more than they expected.[99] While there is some ambiguity in their report, on the basis of the narrative to this point, the reader is probably to understand reference to the subjection of demons as including exorcisms and the healing of those suffering from demonically inflicted infirmities.

The Seventy[-Two] go on to say that the subjection of the demons to them is the direct result of the authoritative use of Jesus' name. This is the first such use of Jesus' name by his disciples in Luke (or any of the Gospels for that matter),[100] though in the Acts narrative this practice will become frequently performed by followers (3.6; 4.10, 17-18, 30; 5.40; 9.27) and would-be exorcists (19.13-14) alike.[101] The authoritative use of Jesus' name is grounded in the solidarity that exists between Jesus and his disciples (cf. Lk. 10.16) and is evidence of the equivalency of the authorized agents' ministry with the ministry of Jesus himself.[102]

Verse 18

Jesus goes on to say that he '... was watching Satan fall like a star from heaven'. Such language sounds very much like the description of a prophetic visionary experience.[103] This experience not only introduces what follows in this verse but prepares the reader for the visions which will occur in Acts (7.56; 10.11). Given the context of this vision, Satan's fall undoubtedly has some connection to the mission of the Seventy[-Two], which focuses entirely on exorcisms

---

[98] Lagrange, *Luc*, p. 301.

[99] Plummer, *Luke*, p. 277.

[100] C.F. Evans, *Luke*, p. 454.

[101] Fitzmyer, *Luke X-XXIV*, p. 861.

[102] Nolland, *Luke 9.1-18.34*, p. 512. Cf. also Ellis, *Luke*, p. 157.

[103] So Creed, *Luke*, p. 147; Grundmann, *Lukas*, p. 212; Kümmel, *Promise and Fulfillment*, pp. 113-14; Caird, *Luke*, p. 143; Thompson, *Luke*, p. 165; Wilkinson, *Luke*, p. 65; Sabourin, *Luc*, p. 222; C.F. Evans, *Luke*, p. 454; and especially S.R. Garrett, *The Demise of the Devil: Magic and the Demonic in Luke's Writings* (Minneapolis, MN: Fortress, 1989), pp. 49-50.

(at least in their report to Jesus).[104] Whether Jesus saw the fall of Satan in the exorcisms that were taking place at that time,[105] or saw the mission of the Seventy[-Two] pointing to the mission of the church in a proleptic fashion,[106] or saw it pointing to the ultimate fall of Satan through Jesus' death and resurrection,[107] or as an anticipation of the eschatological fall of Satan, the exorcisms are powerful reminders of the victory which is being won over Satan and the demons.

Verses 19-20

The reference to Satan's fall is bounded on either side by descriptions of the disciples' authority. Verse 19 begins with ἰδού, which draws attention to the importance of the statement that follows. Jesus, as if to clarify his earlier instructions and the disciples' apparent surprise that the demons are subject to them, makes explicit that he has given them (perfect tense) authority over all sorts of foes. His charismatic power has been transferred to them,[108] reinforcing his earlier language of solidarity. Such authority extends to (absolute?) protection from well-known sources of evil,[109] whether human or non-human. However, instead of rejoicing over subjection of demons to them, they are to rejoice over their names having been written in heaven. Such a statement does not minimize the importance of their authority over demons, which is a major motif in the Lukan narratives, but rather underscores that of greatest importance – salvation.[110]

Conclusion

This text (perhaps) adds additional weight to the emerging Lukan picture of the relationship of the demonic to some infirmities. Al-

---

[104] Adeney, *Luke*, p. 244; Morris, *Luke*, p. 185; Danker, *Jesus and the New Age*, p. 128; and Fitzmyer, *Luke X-XXIV*, p. 860.

[105] Plummer, *Luke*, p. 278; Manson, *Luke*, p. 126; Caird, *Luke*, p. 143; Marshall, *Luke*, p. 428; Stöger, *Luke*, p. 199; Stein, *Luke*, p. 309; and Bock, *Luke*, p. 192.

[106] Miller, *Luke*, p. 103 and Craddock, *Luke*, p. 147.

[107] Garrett, *The Demise of the Devil*, pp. 50-55.

[108] C.F. Evans, *Luke*, p. 455.

[109] Fitzmyer, *Luke X-XXIV*, p. 863 and Tiede, *Luke*, p. 205.

[110] Garrett, *The Demise of the Devil*, p. 57.

though not an explicit statement in this regard, it seems safe to deduce this conclusion from the pericope.

Luke 11.14 – Jesus Drives out a Mute Demon

Reflection upon what has just transpired (the mission of the Seventy[-Two] and Jesus' vision) causes Jesus to rejoice in the Spirit and to emphasize the solidarity the disciples share with him in terms of what they have seen and heard (10.21-24). This pericope is followed by the parable of the Good Samaritan (10.25-37), Mary's (the sister of Martha) affirmation for choosing 'what is better' (10.38-42), and Jesus teaching the disciples to pray (11.1-13). At this point another relevant text appears, Lk. 11.14.

> And Jesus was casting out a demon that was mute; and after the demon had gone out the mute man spoke. And the crowds were amazed.

This brief account serves primarily to introduce the Beelzebub controversy which immediately follows.[111] But despite its brevity, the story is important to this study, for it is an explicit example of an occasion where Luke attributes a specific illness to a demon. Here Jesus was casting out a demon which caused the man afflicted to be mute,[112] a situation remedied when the demon came out. At the beginning of the Lukan narrative it was God (or his angel) who inflicted muteness upon Zechariah; here the infirmity is attributed to a demon. The text does not make clear how contact was first made between Jesus and the mute man, or how Jesus knew the mute condition in 11.14 was a demonic affliction. The speech of the formerly mute individual resulted in the amazement of the crowds.

Conclusion

What are the implications of this brief account for the purposes of this study? First, as with a number of passages before it, there is an attribution of infirmity to a demon. On this occasion it is clear that

---

[111] Stein (*Luke*, p. 330) notes, 'The transition from the preceding account is abrupt. The tense of the verb (an imperfect periphrastic) throws us immediately into the present story'.

[112] Plummer, *Luke*, p. 301; Ellis, *Luke*, p. 167; and Schürmann, *Lukasevangelium*, II, p. 227.

when the demon is cast out, the infirmity is gone as well. Second, since earlier in the narrative God, not a demon, had afflicted an individual with muteness, there is present here the idea that the cause of such an illness must be discerned. In 11.14, the discernment is, no doubt, on the part of Jesus. The implication of such a situation for the readers of the Lukan narrative might very well be that discernment on their part is needful in distinguishing between origins of illness.

Luke 13.1-5 – 'Do You Think These Were Worse Sinners?'

Following fast on the heels of this account of exorcism is the story of the Beelzebub controversy (11.15-23). Closely related to this is the Lukan version of the demon's desire to return to his former home if it is unoccupied (11.24-26). As noted in chapter five of this study, these verses add information about the attitude regarding the dangers of demonically inflicted illnesses, although symptoms of demon possession are not ruled out. As with Matthew, Luke appears to acknowledge that unless one responds favorably to the Gospel, there is no guarantee that a healing which results from an exorcism will be lasting. As with its Matthean parallel, this text may also have implications for the knotty problem of the relationship between believers and demons. If emptiness is a sign that a person who has experienced exorcism has not gone on to receive the Gospel, so the adverse, that one who is not empty has made the appropriate response, would seem to indicate that a formerly possessed person who is now a believer (and full of Christ and/or the Holy Spirit) is in no danger of being possessed again by demonic influences. By extension, one might even be able to say that if anyone is a believer, he/she is not in danger of being demon possessed.

The next section of Luke's Gospel is devoted to discourses about the Sign of Jonah (11.29-32), the eye as the lamp of the body (11.33-36), the Pharisees (11.37-12.12), warnings about riches (12.13-21), worry (12.22-34), watchfulness (12.35-49), and divisions inherent in receiving the Gospel (12.49-53). Just before the next passage of particular interest for this pericope is a text which focuses upon interpreting the times, judging of self, and the need for reconciliation (12.54-59).

And there were some arriving at that time telling him about the Galileans whose blood Pilate had mingled with their sacrifices. And answering he said to them, 'Do you think that these Galileans are greater sinners than all the Galileans, because they suffered these things? No, I say to you, but if you do not repent, in like manner you will all perish. Or those eighteen men upon whom the tower in Siloam fell and killed them, do you think that these were greater debtors than all the other men living in Jerusalem? No, I say to you, but if you do not repent you will all perish in the same way.'

At first glance this text does not seem to be of special significance for this enquiry for it says nothing about illness and its origin. However, the value of this passage is what it may reveal about the relationship between sin and calamity either human or natural.

Verse 1

The first thing of significance about this text is how closely related it is to the passage that precedes it,[113] which emphasizes reconciliation. Standing there as Jesus spoke were individuals who either, just arriving, bring word of a catastrophe in Jerusalem,[114] or mention the event with the hope of evoking messianic retribution on the part of Jesus.[115] Given the fact that Jesus has just spoken of discerning the time, perhaps these individuals hope for a discerning response from him about this recent terrible event.[116]

The event itself concerned a group of Galileans who were apparently in Jerusalem to celebrate a Jewish feast, probably Passover.[117] Three things may be deduced from the mention of the Galileans. First, it reminds the reader of Jesus' particularly close associa-

---

[113] Creed, *Luke*, p. 180; Lagrange, *Luc*, p. 378; H.G. Wood, 'Interpreting this Time', *NTS* 2 (1955-56), p. 262; Marshall, *Luke*, p. 553; Danker, *Jesus and the New Age*, p. 156; F.W. Young, 'Luke 13.1-9', *Int* 31 (1977), p. 60 and Fitzmyer, *Luke X-XXIV*, p. 1004.

[114] J. Blinzler, 'Die Niedermetzelung von Galiläern durch Pilatus', *NovT* 2 (1957), p. 25.

[115] Farrar, *Luke*, p. 283.

[116] Tiede, *Luke*, p. 246.

[117] Marshall (*Luke*, p. 553) observes that Passover is the only feast at which the laity killed their own sacrifices. Cf. also, Blinzler, 'Die Niedermetzelung', p. 32; Ellis, *Luke*, p. 184; Fitzmyer, *Luke X-XXIV*, p. 1006; and C.A. Evans, *Luke*, p. 204. *Contra* Plummer (*Luke*, p. 338), who identifies the feast as Tabernacles.

tion with Galilee to this point in the Gospel and may anticipate the fact that both Peter and Jesus will themselves be referred to as Galileans later in the narrative (22.59 and 23.6 respectively). Such an association might suggest to the reader that Jesus would be especially sensitive to the fate of these (fellow) Galileans. Second, mention of the Galileans may also be a subtle reference to the anti-Roman and/or Zealot attitudes on the part of some Galileans,[118] a specific example of which the text itself will later provide (cf. Acts 5.37). Third, reference to the Galileans in v. 1 and those living in Jerusalem in v. 4 may be Luke's way of emphasizing that the need for conversion, one of the primary themes of vv. 1-5, applies to all of Israel.[119]

Specifically, Pilate is said to have mixed the blood of these Galileans with their sacrifices. While Josephus does not mention this particular event, and there is no reason to believe that he intended to record all such events,[120] this action is in keeping with what is known of Pilate from Josephus' account.[121] The imagery of the metaphor suggests that at the very time these individuals were preparing to offer their sacrifices, Pilate spilled their own blood.[122] Whether or not this metaphor was to be taken literally,[123] it does convey to the reader an especially gruesome idea.[124]

Verses 2-3

At this point, Jesus raises a rhetorical question[125] which reflects the commonly held view that tragedy is the measurement of one's sinfulness.[126] Were these Galileans worse sinners than others because they suffered in this way? Before allowing any of his hearers to an-

---

[118] Danker, *Jesus and the New Age*, p. 136.

[119] So O.C. Edwards, Jr., *Luke's Story of Jesus* (Philadelphia: Fortress Press, 1981), p. 65 and C.F. Evans, *Luke*, pp. 546-47.

[120] Blinzler, 'Die Niedermetzelung', pp. 39-40.

[121] Farrar, *Luke*, p. 284; Plummer, *Luke*, p. 337; Manson, *Luke*, p. 162; Leaney, *Luke*, p. 206; Stöger, *Luke*, p. 248; and Fitzmyer, *Luke X-XXIV*, p. 1007.

[122] Plummer, *Luke*, p. 338 and Nolland, *Luke 9.21-18.34*, p. 718.

[123] C.F. Evans, *Luke*, pp. 546-47.

[124] Marshall, *Luke*, p. 533.

[125] Ellis, *Luke*, p. 185.

[126] Miller, *Luke*, p. 113; Danker, *Jesus and the New Age*, pp. 156-57; Marshall, *Luke*, p. 553; Fitzmyer, *Luke X-XXIV*, p. 1007; Talbert, *Reading Luke*, p. 145; and Bock, *Luke*, p. 237.

swer this rhetorical question, Jesus emphatically denies that these individuals suffered because they were more deserving of punishment owing to greater sinfulness. Jesus' strong response is introduced by οὐχί[127] and is based on his own authority (λέγω ὑμῖν), perhaps an indication that he saw a connection between the report of this tragedy and discerning the times. Rather than perceiving in this calamity the sinfulness of the ones who suffered, Jesus sees it as a warning of the impending destruction that awaits all those who do not convert (μετανοῆτε), receiving forgiveness for their sins (cf. 3.3, 8; 5.32; 10.13; 11.32). It is difficult to avoid seeing a reference to the destruction of Jerusalem in Jesus' words.[128] At any rate, he turns the attention away from the sinfulness of the Galileans to the sinfulness of the hearers.

Verses 4-5

A second calamity is now mentioned by Jesus, one with which he assumes his hearers are familiar, although again Josephus does not record it. This event occurred in Jerusalem at a tower (on the city wall)[129] named Siloam, near the angle where the eastern and southern walls come together.[130] The tower collapsed killing 18 men. It is sometimes argued that the tower was part of an aqueduct building program which was partially financed by Pilate's misappropriation of temple funds.[131] On this view, Jesus' hearers would perhaps see the death of these individuals (construction workers?) as divine retribution for the violation of the Temple treasury. However, the reader is not in a position to know these things, so perhaps it is best to see in the tower's fall a natural calamity paired with the earlier human calamity. As before (v. 2), Jesus asks a rhetorical question. Were these people greater debtors (to God)[132] than anyone else living in Jerusalem? Again, Jesus responds with an emphatic (οὐχί) and authoritative (λέγω ὑμῖν) no, as he calls for conversion on the

[127] Fitzmyer, *Luke X-XXIV*, p. 1007.

[128] So Marshall, *Luke*, p. 554; R. Maddox, *The Purpose of Luke-Acts* (Edinburgh: T. & T. Clark, 1982), p. 17; and Stein, *Luke*, p. 370.

[129] Johnson, *Luke*, p. 211.

[130] Geldenhuys, *Luke*, p. 371.

[131] Cf. Thompson, *Luke*, p. 193; Wilkinson, *Luke*, p. 85; and C.F. Evans, *Luke*, p. 547.

[132] For this definition of ὀφειλέται cf. Lagrange, *Luc*, p. 381 and Danker, *Jesus and the New Age*, p. 157.

hearers' part. Unless such conversion takes place, the hearers face the same fate (note the use of ὡσαύτως)[133] as that of these unfortunate men. Again there seems to be more than a hint that destruction awaits Jerusalem itself (19.44)[134] (just as the Tower of Siloam fell, so the towers of Jerusalem will fall)[135] and perhaps an allusion to the eschatological judgment as well.[136]

Conclusion

It is evident that the primary emphasis of this passage is to encourage repentance in the light of judgment. However, it is also clear that this text says something about the relationship between misfortune and sinfulness. In both the examples described, Jesus specifically denies that the calamities were the result of greater culpability on the part of those who were killed. Pressed too far, Jesus' words could be interpreted to mean that there is no relationship between misfortune, in these cases death, and one's sinfulness. However, the reader is keenly aware that God has already punished sin with an infirmity (i.e. Zechariah – Lk. 1.20) and will learn that on occasion God even takes the lives of those who commit (certain kinds of?) sin (i.e. Ananias and Sapphira in Acts 5.1-11 and Herod in Acts 12.19-24). Thus, Luke (13.1-5) challenges the notion that calamity is (generally?) the direct result of one's sinfulness, but at the same time he does not imply that God is inactive in the punishment of sin even in this life. Such an emphasis periodically recurs in Luke's two-volume work.

Luke 13.10-17 – The Woman with a Spirit of Infirmity

A third warning about impending judgment comes in the form of a parable in 13.6-9, the parable of the barren fig tree. Following these three admonitions to conversion stands the last major text of significance for this enquiry.

And he was teaching in one of their synagogues on one of the Sabbaths. And behold (there was) a woman having a spirit of in-

---

[133] Plummer, *Luke*, p. 339.
[134] Wood, 'Interpreting the Times', p. 263 and Danker, *Jesus and the New Age*, p. 157.
[135] Creed, *Luke*, p. 181.
[136] Leaney, *Luke*, p. 206.

firmity for eighteen years, and she was stooped over and unable to straighten up at all. And seeing her Jesus called and said to her, 'Woman, you are loosed from your infirmity', and he laid hands upon her; and at once she straightened up, and glorified God. And the ruler of the synagogue, indignant that Jesus healed on the Sabbath, said to the crowd, 'There are six days in which it is necessary to work; therefore, on one of these come and heal and not on the Sabbath'. And the Lord answered him and said, 'Hypocrite! Which of you on the Sabbath does not loose his ox or donkey from the stall and leading (it), it drinks? And is it not necessary for this daughter of Abraham, whom Satan has bound, behold, for eighteen years, to be loosed from that bondage on this Sabbath?'

Verse 10

This story finds Jesus teaching in one of their synagogues on one of the Sabbaths. It is significant that again Jesus' mighty works are found in the context of teaching,[137] teaching being a major emphasis in this section of Luke's narrative.[138] Also of significance is the fact that this is the last time in the Gospel that Jesus will be found in a synagogue,[139] which in many ways has become identified as a source of opposition to him.[140]

Verse 11

The appearance of ἰδοὺ alerts the reader that something important is about to transpire. The focus of the verse is upon a woman. At this point all that is known about her is her presence in the synagogue, which might imply that she was a devout person, but even a demoniac was earlier found in a synagogue (4.31-37). The reader quickly learns that this woman had a spirit of infirmity (πνεῦμα ἔχουσα ἀσθενείας) for eighteen years. What is the reader to understand by this phrase? Does it mean that the woman's condition

---

[137] Tiede, *Luke*, p. 249.

[138] Fitzmyer, *Luke X-XXIV*, p. 1012.

[139] Plummer, *Luke*, p. 341; Geldenhuys, *Luke*, p. 374; Morris, *Luke*, p. 222; Marshall, *Luke*, p. 557; Laverdiere, *Luke*, p. 182; Fitzmyer, *Luke X-XXIV*, p. 1012; Nolland, *Luke 9.21-18.34*, p. 723; C.F. Evans, *Luke*, p. 550; and J.B. Green, 'Jesus and a Daughter of Abraham (Luke 13.10-17): Test Case for a Lukan Perspective on the Miracles of Jesus', *CBQ* 51 (1989), p. 647.

[140] C.A. Evans, *Luke*, p. 207.

was the result of demon possession[141] and she was, therefore, in need of exorcism?[142] Such a meaning would certainly make sense, given the ease with which Luke is able to attribute a variety of infirmities to demonic possession. However, there are certain indicators in the text which suggest this is not what the reader is intended to understand. First, the symptoms usually associated with demon possession are absent from this pericope.[143] Second, Jesus does not treat it as an exorcism; it looks rather much like how he treats healings in Luke's Gospel.[144] Third, there is no description of an exorcism nor the leaving of a demon.[145] It is, therefore, more likely that something other than demon possession is here described.[146] But what?

It is clear from the text that this woman's infirmity is the direct result of demonic and/or Satanic influence, as indicated here and in v. 16. Yet, it is equally clear that the normal signs of demon possession, the loss of control over personality, etc., are missing here. Rather than an internal assault of the person, as with demon possession, here the assault comes from the outside. Therefore, while this woman is afflicted (bound) by Satan, she is not demon possessed, as that term is normally understood in Luke.

The reader learns the duration of the presence of the spirit of infirmity, eighteen years. The number conveys two ideas. First, it connects this text with that which precedes it, the eighteen men

---

[141] Johnson, *Luke*, p. 212 and Bock, *Luke*, p. 241.

[142] Twelftree, *Christ Triumphant*, p. 100; J.T. Squires, *The Plan of God in Luke-Acts* (Cambridge: Cambridge University Press, 1993), pp. 92-3; and T.K. Seim, *The Double Message: Patterns of Gender in Luke-Acts* (Edinburgh: T. & T. Clark, 1994), p. 41.

[143] Manson, *Luke*, p. 164.

[144] Adeney, *Luke*, p. 282; J. Wilkinson, 'The Case of the Bent Woman in Luke 13.10-17', *EvQ* 49 (1977), p. 201; and Nolland, *Luke 9.21-18.34*, p. 724.

[145] Wilkinson, 'The Case of the Bent Woman', p. 201 and Marshall, *Luke*, p. 557.

[146] Lagrange, *Luc*, p. 302; Ellis, *Luke*, p. 186; van der Loos, *The Miracles of Jesus*, p. 520; Wilkinson, 'The Case of the Bent Woman', p. 203; Marshall, *Luke*, p. 557; Sabourin, *Luc*, p. 261; C.A. Evans, *Luke*, p. 207; and Page, *Powers of Evil*, p. 119. R.F. O'Toole ('Some Exegetical Reflections on Luke 13, 10-17', *Bib* 73 [1992], p. 93) argues that on the basis of Acts 10.38, it does not really matter whether the spirit of infirmity is identified as demon possession or caused by the Devil. Cf. also M.D. Hamm ('The Freeing of the Bent Woman and the Restoration of Israel: Luke 13.10-17 and Narrative Theology', *JSNT* 31 [1987], pp. 32-33) who takes the spirit of infirmity as a generic end-time reference.

who were killed by the tower's fall,[147] and it indicates the long-standing nature of the infirmity,[148] which suggests the extraordinary power needed to heal this woman. The long-term nature of the affliction resulted in the woman's inability to rise from her stooped position. Her condition has generally been identified as spondylitis ankylopoietica,[149] a type of bone fusion.

Verses 12-13

There is no indication in the text that the woman had come for healing.[150] The initiative lies wholly with Jesus,[151] an unusual occurrence in the Gospel.[152] When he saw her, he called her (the same word used for the calling of the disciples is used here [προσφωνέω], but cf. also its use in 7.32) and spoke to her. Although the reader might expect some interaction with the spirit, it is significant that Jesus speaks to the woman, not to the spirit of infirmity,[153] certainly a sign that exorcism is not in view here.[154] His words to her indicate that she has been set free from her infirmity. The use of the perfect tense verb (ἀπολέλυσαι) indicates that the cure is permanent.[155] The word spoken to her is accompanied by the laying on of hands,[156] which in the Gospel is a sign of power through which healings (and exorcisms?) are wrought. Her healing is described as immediate (παραχρῆμα), a term which has often accompanied healings in Luke's Gospel (cf. 1.64; 4.39; 5.25; 8.44, 47, 55). The immediate nature of the cure stands in stark contrast to the long duration of the infirmity.[157] Understandably enough, the healing

---

[147] Johnson, *Luke*, p. 212 and Stein, *Luke*, p. 372. *Contra* Marshall (*Luke*, p. 557) and Sabourin (*Luc*, p. 265), who see the appearance of the same numbers as a coincidence.

[148] Danker, *Jesus and the New Age*, p. 158 and Thompson, *Luke*, p. 194.

[149] Wilkinson, 'The Case of the Bent Woman', p. 197. *Contra* Grundmann (*Lukas*, p. 279), who identifies the condition as skoliosis hysterica.

[150] Morris, *Luke*, p. 223.

[151] Danker, *Jesus and the New Age*, p. 158; Fitzmyer, *Luke X-XXIV*, p. 1013; Tiede, *Luke*, p. 250; and Nolland, *Luke 9.21-18.34*, p. 724.

[152] Adeney, *Luke*, p. 282.

[153] Wilkinson, 'The Case of the Bent Woman', p. 201; C.F. Evans, *Luke*, p. 551; and Page, *Powers of Evil*, p. 119.

[154] *Contra* Morris, *Luke*, p. 223.

[155] Marshall, *Luke*, p. 558.

[156] So Marshall, *Luke*, p. 558 and Stein, *Luke*, p. 373.

[157] Stein, *Luke*, p. 373.

results in the woman glorifying God, an activity which often accompanies healings in Luke (cf. also 5.25, 26; 7.16).

Verse 16

The next verse in this pericope of significance for the purposes of this enquiry is v. 16, which follows a rather sharp exchange between the ruler of the synagogue and Jesus over appropriate conduct on the Sabbath. In this verse, Jesus contrasts the woman with animals who are loosed on the Sabbath for the purpose of watering. It is in this context that Jesus refers to the woman as a 'Daughter of Abraham'. While the use of this phrase may simply be a way of underscoring the aforementioned contrast[158] or a means of establishing her nationality,[159] it appears that a more significant identification is being made. A true Israelite,[160] one of God's chosen people,[161] is, of course, part of its meaning here. But, the woman's description as a 'Daughter of Abraham' is quite unusual with few, if any, true parallels.[162] This extraordinary title seems to be a way of emphasizing the fact that this woman, too, was part of Abraham's lineage and, consequently, an heir to the promises of the oath sworn to him.[163] Given the other occurrences of Abraham in Luke (cf. esp. 1.54-55; 3.7-9; 16.22-32; 19.9-10) and those with whom he is identified, the reader is left with the impression that these are individuals in (special?) need of God's mercy.[164] Such ones have a special claim on salvation, if they believe. On this view, Jesus identifies her as one especially entitled to the benefits of salvation.

Jesus not only identifies the woman as a 'Daughter of Abraham', but he also makes clear that her infirmity had been from the hand of Satan, underscoring the length of the condition by use of ἰδού.

---

[158] Plummer, *Luke*, p. 343; Adeney, *Luke*, p. 283; Manson, *Luke*, p. 164; and Geldenhuys, *Luke*, p. 375.

[159] Drury, *Luke*, p. 143.

[160] Wilkinson, *Luke*, p. 196; Klostermann, *Lukas*, p. 145; C.F. Evans, *Luke*, p. 551.

[161] Thompson, *Luke*, p. 195; Marshall, *Luke*, p. 559; Fitzmyer, *Luke X–XXIV*, p. 1013; Nolland, *Luke 9.21-18.34*, p. 724.

[162] Cf. the discussion in Seim (*The Double Message*, p. 44) for the similarities and differences between this description and those in 4 Maccabees 14.20; 15.28; 17.6; and 18.20.

[163] Danker, *Jesus and the New Age*, p. 159; Hamm, 'The Freeing of the Bent Woman', p. 34; Seim, *The Double Message*, p. 48-49; and Bock, *Luke*, p. 242.

[164] Cf. esp. Green, 'Jesus and a Daughter of Abraham', p. 651.

Two additional aspects of this verse are deserving of comment. First, while it is clear that Jesus attributes this infirmity to Satan,[165] is the reader to surmise that for Luke all infirmities have a Satanic or demonic dimension?[166] Although Luke blurs the lines between healing and demonic activity more than any other New Testament writer, the reader is also aware that the very first infirmity recounted in the Gospel has its origin attributed to God. Therefore, not all illness has a Satanic dimension. In addition, a number of healings described by Luke are treated as unattributed with regard to origins. Consequently, while Luke may place greater emphasis on the demonic/Satanic dimension of infirmities, the text itself gives some cause for caution before drawing blanket conclusions. Second, despite the fact that the woman has been bound in this stooped condition by Satan for eighteen years, the text does not imply that she is sinful or in any other way culpable.[167] As far as the reader can tell, it is the infirmity that is evil, not the woman.[168] On this view her situation might be similar to that of Paul's thorn.[169]

Conclusions

There are several implications of this reading of Lk. 13.10-17 for the purposes of this enquiry. 1) This text gives perhaps the clearest evidence in the New Testament of an individual who, apparently in good standing before God, is afflicted by an infirmity that has a demonic origin. 2) The condition of this woman is quite distinct from demon possession, sharing none of its characteristics and being treated by Jesus as a healing. 3) In the healing of the woman, Jesus does not rebuke the spirit, speak to it, or acknowledge it in any way. 4) It is possible that the Lukan readers would see in this woman the possibility that a person in right standing before God (a believer) might be afflicted by a spirit by means of an infirmity, although Acts does not offer corroborating evidence.

---

[165] Adeney, *Luke*, p. 283 and Wilkinson, 'The Case of the Bent Woman', pp. 204-205.

[166] Nolland, *Luke 9.21-18.34*, p. 724; Twelftree, *Christ Triumphant*, p. 104; Green, *The Theology of the Gospel of Luke*, pp. 78-79; and Page, *Powers of Evil*, p. 119.

[167] Lagrange (*Luc*, p. 384) notes, 'L'intervention de Satan ne prouve pas que cette femme ait été coupable, non plus que Job'.

[168] Morris, *Luke*, p. 224.

[169] Wilkinson, 'The Case of the Bent Woman', p. 304-305.

Luke 13.32 – 'Tell Herod that Fox'

A final brief text should be mentioned in this examination of Luke's Gospel. In 13.32, Jesus responds to a warning that Herod wished to kill him (13.31) by pointing to his continued exorcistic and healing ministry. For the reader such a mention keeps this aspect of Jesus' work in view. In this text there appears to be a distinction made between exorcisms and healings, though a certain blurring of distinctions for the reader is inevitable by this point in the narrative.

Conclusions and Implications

Before proceeding to an examination of the relevant texts in Acts, a drawing together of the several conclusions and implications of this reading of Luke might prove helpful.

1) In ways similar to James, Paul, and John, Luke is not reluctant to attribute an infirmity to God. In fact, as the first infirmity attributed to any source in the Gospel is attributed to God, Luke sends a message to the reader about God's ability and willingness to afflict.

2) Unbelief in response to a (prophetic) word from God is the reason for the affliction God sends upon Zechariah, an otherwise upright individual. That such a devout person could be punished in this way cautions the reader to be very careful to respond to a word from God in an appropriate manner.

3) There is an extremely close connection between infirmity and demonic/Satanic activity. In point of fact, of all the NT writers, Luke tends to blur the lines of distinction between illness and demonic activity the most, meaning that the reader cannot always be as certain of the origins of a given illness, as is the case with the other New Testament writers examined to this point.

4) As with Mark and Matthew, Luke is comfortable with attributing infirmity to demon possession, even commonly using healing vocabulary to describe what otherwise would be described as an exorcism.

5) A number of healings are recounted which give no indication as to the origin of the illness. It would appear that such a 'neutral' assessment indicates Luke did not always see the hand of Satan and/or demons involved in such conditions.

6) In Luke for the first time, with the possible exception of Paul's thorn, there is evidence of an infirmity inflicted by a spirit upon an otherwise devout individual. Luke seems to distinguish between this condition and those produced by demon possession.

7) In the clearest case of a non-possessed person being afflicted by Satan, Jesus did not address the spirit/Satan, he did not rebuke or even acknowledge him; he simply acted as he normally did in his healing ministry. Such an example might have something to contribute to some aspects of certain deliverance ministries.

8) In Luke's Gospel Jesus denies that calamities are always a gauge of one's sinfulness. Although his words are offered in the context of human and natural disasters, it may not be going too far to apply this to infirmities as well.

9) Healings and the casting out of demons are the result of Jesus' power, which is sometimes described as leaving his body during certain periods of healing.

10) The fact that the same infirmity (muteness) can be attributed to God on one occasion and a demon on another occasion indicates the need for discernment on the part of Jesus and, consequently, his followers. The theme of discernment continues to be of significance across the spectrum of NT writings examined in this study.

7

THE ACTS OF THE APOSTLES

This study continues with an examination of the relevant texts in
Luke's second volume, the Acts of the Apostles. Although it is pos-
sible to treat Acts on its own, certain indicators in the text suggest
that this volume is to be read as a companion piece to the Gospel.
The opening lines of the work remove any doubts for the reader.
First, reference is made to the Gospel as 'the first Book' (τὸν μὲν
πρῶτον λόγον), implying that this is the second λόγον. Second,
Acts is addressed to the same person as is the Gospel, a certain
Theophilus. Third, the reader next learns that the contents of the
Gospel were devoted to 'all Jesus began to do and to teach', suggesting that in the account which follows the reader will discover
what Jesus continued to do and teach. Fourth, two aspects of the
Gospel's concluding section, Jesus' final instructions to the disciples
and the ascension, are taken up afresh at the beginning of Acts with
some expansion. It is difficult to believe the reader would miss such
obvious hints that Acts is to be read in conjunction with the Gospel. Such clues indicate that while there may, no doubt, be some
variation in emphases, the reader should draw upon a knowledge of
Luke's Gospel when reading Acts. Therefore, the reader is prepared
for some degree of continuity between the two volumes.

After the ascension and in accordance with Jesus' earlier instruction (Lk. 24.49), the disciples are found in Jerusalem. Here, Peter
and the others, numbering about 120, choose a replacement for Judas. The lot falls to Matthias (1.12-26). While still in Jerusalem, the
promise of the Father, the Holy Spirit, falls upon all those gathered
and they are all filled with the Holy Spirit and speak in tongues as
the Spirit enables them. This empowerment is immediately observ-
able in Peter's prophetic preaching which results in 3,000 converts.

In the aftermath of this spiritual outpouring and initial success, the group of believers give themselves to the teaching of the apostles, to fellowship, to the breaking of bread, and to prayer (2.42). All the while the Lord adds to their numbers on a daily basis. These activities are described in the first of three summary statements which appear in Acts 2-5.

Acts 3.2 and 4.22 – A Man Crippled from Birth

The first text of some significance for this study occurs at this point in the narrative. At a time when many wonders and signs are being performed by the apostles (2.43) and the believers are continuing to meet together in the Temple courts (2.46), Peter and John make their way to the Temple at three in the afternoon.

> And a certain man lame from his mother's womb was carried, whom they placed every day at the gate of the Temple called Beautiful so that he could ask for alms from those going into the temple.... For the man was more than forty years old upon whom this sign of healing had been accomplished.

Inasmuch as this, the first miracle of healing described in Acts, does not directly attribute the condition of this man to a specific cause, it might have been appropriate to mention it only in passing. The text comes no closer to suggesting a cause for his condition than to describe the man as 'lame from his mother's womb'. Rather than revealing a direct cause of the man's infirmity, which appears to have been an affliction of the feet, ankles, knees, or hips,[1] it appears that this phrase underscores the gravity of the man's plight and the greatness of the healing that will be performed.[2] The mention of

---

[1] Cf. P.W. van der Horst, 'Hellenistic Parallels to Acts (Chapters 3 and 4)', *JSNT* 35 (1989), p. 37.

[2] E. Haenchen, *The Acts of the Apostles: A Commentary* (tran. B. Noble, G. Shinn, H. Anderson, and R.Mcl. Wilson; Philadelphia: Westminster, 1971), p. 198 n. 8; I.H. Marshall, *The Acts of the Apostles* (Grand Rapids: Eerdmans, 1980), p. 87; D.J. Williams, *Acts* (Peabody, MA: Hendrickson, 1990), p. 64; L.T. Johnson, *The Acts of the Apostles* (Collegeville, MN: Liturgical Press, 1992), p. 64; J.B. Polhill, *Acts* (Nashville: Broadman, 1992), p. 126; C.K. Barrett, *The Acts of the Apostles*, I (Edinburgh: T&T Clark, 1994), pp. 178-79; and W.J. Larkin, Jr., *Acts* (Leicester: IVP, 1995), p. 64.

his age in 4.22 serves the same function.[3] The primary implication of this text for the broader purposes of this study is to give additional support to the idea that for Luke, not all infirmities are attributed to God or Satan.

The healing of the man becomes the occasion for another sermon by Peter, which like the Pentecost sermon results in thousands of converts, as now their numbers swell to more than 5,000. The sermon also results in the first of several confrontations between Peter and others with the religious authorities. Responding to their question, Peter preaches yet again, prompting bewilderment on the part of the authorities as to how they might respond to these uneducated, but bold men. Upon their release, Peter and John return to the community of believers and pray for boldness in their speaking the word and for God's intervention through healing, miraculous signs, and wonders in the name of Jesus. That their prayer meets with divine approval is confirmed by the fact that the place where they gathered was shaken, they were all filled with the Holy Spirit, and they spoke the word of God boldly (4.31).

The unity of this group of believers becomes apparent in the second summary statement of the section (4.32-35) by the fact that even the possessions of individual members were put at the disposal of the community. Periodically, those who owned houses or lands sold them and placed them at the feet of the apostles for distribution. This summary is expanded by offering examples of this activity.[4] One particular individual, who will figure prominently later in the narrative, is identified as contributing in just this way; Joseph, whom the apostles called Barnabas – the Son of Encouragement, a Levite from Cyprus.

---

[3] E. Jacquier, *Les Actes des Apôtres* (Paris: Gabalda, 1926), p. 136; F.F. Bruce, *Commentary on the Book of the Acts* (Grand Rapids: Eerdmans, 1954), p. 104; Haenchen, *Acts*, p. 220; Marshall, *Acts*, p. 103; Polhill, *Acts*, pp. 146-47; and Barrett, *Acts*, I, p. 239.

[4] On the significance of the summary statements for this section of the narrative cf. S.J. Noorda, 'Scene and Summary. A Proposal for Reading Acts 4, 32-5,16', in *Les Actes des Apôtres* (ed. J. Kremer; Paris-Gembloux: Duculot, 1979), pp. 475-83 and D. Marguerat, 'La mort d'Ananias et Saphira (Ac 5.1-11) dans la stratégie narrative de Luc', *NTS* 39 (1993), pp. 209-26.

Acts 5.1-11 – Ananias and Sapphira

With the knowledge of Barnabas' action still in mind the reader quickly comes upon a second episode which expands upon the previous summary statement. Nothing in the narrative to this point prepares the reader for what follows. This text is of special relevance for the purposes of this broader enquiry.

> And a certain man named Ananias, with Sapphira his wife, sold a piece of property and kept back from the price, and with the knowledge of his wife, and bringing a part of it placed it at the apostles' feet. And Peter said, 'Ananias, why has Satan filled your heart to lie to the Holy Spirit and to keep back from the price of the land? While it remained unsold did it not remain yours and after it was sold, did you not have authority over it? Why was this plan conceived in your heart? You have not lied to men but to God.' And hearing these words Ananias falling down, died. And great fear came upon all those who heard these things. And raising up, the young men wrapped him and carrying him out they buried him.
>
> And there was about a three-hour interval and his wife, not knowing what had happened, came in. And Peter answered her, 'Tell me, did you receive so much for the land?' And she said, 'Yes, so much'. And Peter said to her, 'Why have you agreed to test the Spirit of the Lord? Behold the feet of those who buried your husband at the door and they will bury you'. And at once she fell to his feet and died. And entering the young men found her dead, and carrying her out they buried her with her husband. And great fear was upon the whole church and upon all those who heard these things.

Verse 1

With the reader perhaps wanting to know more about this Barnabas, a desire that will be met later in the narrative, another man and his wife are introduced who also sold a piece of property. What will become clear to the reader is that this story functions as a sequel to the mention of Barnabas and is to be understood in the context of the preceding summary about community life.[5] It is possible that the appearance of δέ would alert the reader to the contrast which follows.[6]

Ananias, whose name ironically means 'the Lord is gracious',[7] and his wife Sapphira[8] do, at least on the surface of things, what others in the community have done. He sells a possession (κτῆμα), a piece of land.[9] Perhaps all actions such as those described in this section are intended to be seen as in accordance with the words of Jesus spoken in Lk. 12.33, to sell possessions and give to the poor.[10]

Verse 2

However, the reader quickly learns that there is a marked difference between the actions of Barnabas and those of Ananias. He had 'kept back' part of the price which he received from the sell of the property. While the reader might be prepared to take such an action as entirely legitimate, the appearance of the term ἐνοσφίσατο alerts the reader that such conduct is far from appropriate. For this word is far from the neutral translation 'kept back' but conveys the idea of embezzlement. In point of fact, this is the same term used in the LXX to describe Achan's action in Josh. 7.1, where in violation of

---

[5] Cf. J.D.M. Derrett, 'Ananias, Sapphira, and the Right of Property', *Downside Review* 89 (1971), p. 226; R. Pesch, *Die Apostelgeschichte*, I (Zurich: Benziger Verlag, 1986), p. 1; and R.C. Tannehill, *The Narrative Unity of Luke-Acts A Literary Interpretation volume two: The Acts of the Apostles* (Minneapolis, MN: Fortress, 1990), p. 79. *Contra* A. Harnack (*The Acts of the Apostles* [tran. J.R. Wilkinson; New York: Putnam's Sons, 1909], p. 154) who does not see the story as a necessary link with the rest of the Acts narrative, but standing by itself.

[6] Jacquier, *Actes*, p. 150; Marshall, *Acts*, p. 111; Polhill, *Acts*, p. 156; and Barrett, *Acts*, I, p. 264.

[7] Jacquier, *Actes*, p. 150 and Barrett, *Acts*, I, p. 264.

[8] It has been suggested that the Sapphira mentioned in this verse is to be identified with the name ΣΑΦΕΙΡΑ which appears on a beautifully decorated ossuary discovered in Jerusalem. For this suggestion cf. J. Klausner, *From Jesus to Paul* (New York: Menorah, 1979), p. 289 n. 13.

[9] Jacquier, *Actes*, p. 150; F.J.F. Foakes-Jackson and K. Lake, *The Beginnings of Christianity Part I: The Acts of the Apostles*, IV (Grand Rapids: Baker, 1965), p. 49; C.W. Carter and R. Earle, *The Acts of the Apostles* (Grand Rapids: Eerdmans, 1959, 1973), p. 69; Haenchen, *Acts*, p. 237; H. Conzelmann, *Acts of the Apostles* (tran. J. Limburg, A.T. Kraabel, and D.H. Juel; ed by E.J. Epp with C.R. Matthews; Philadelphia: Fortress Press, 1987), p. 37; Johnson, *Acts*, p. 88; and Barrett, *Acts*, I, p. 265.

[10] J.W. Packer, *Acts of the Apostles* (Cambridge: Cambridge University Press, 1966), pp. 42-43.

the Lord's command not to 'keep back' any of the plunder, Achan took some. The utilization of this term may imply that Ananias' action was of the same kind as Achan's.[11] In addition, the reader learns that Sapphira is in agreement that part of the price should be kept back.[12] Taking only part (μέρος) of the price, Ananias lays it at the apostles' feet. By laying the money at the apostles' feet, Ananias is in conformity with the actions of others (4.35), especially Barnabas (4.37).[13] But what does such an act signify?

In Luke-Acts the feet often serve as a symbol of power or authority. Shaking the dust off the feet is a sign of contempt or rejection (Lk. 9.5; 10.11; Acts 13.51). Sitting at the feet of an individual indicates that the individual is considered an authoritative teacher (Lk. 10.39; Acts 22.3) and/or Lord (Lk. 8.35). Weeping (Lk. 7.38, 44) or falling at one's feet (Lk. 8.41; 17.16; Acts 10.25) at the least suggests that such a one is capable of meeting a significant need in the life of the supplicant. Psalms which mention a footstool for the feet (whether enemies or the earth) are cited by Luke on three occasions (Lk. 20.43; Acts 2.35; 7.49).

In the Lukan narrative, for the believers to place money at the feet of the apostles could very well indicate that they held a position of authority and respect within the group.[14] But to see this as the only or even primary meaning of the act is to overlook two clues

---

[11] Foakes-Jackson and Lake, *Beginnings*, IV, p. 50; Bruce, *Acts*, p. 110; C.S.C. Williams, *The Acts of the Apostles* (London: Adam & Charles Black, 1964), p. 88; J. Munck, *The Acts of the Apostles* (New York: Doubleday, 1967), p. 40; Carter and Earle, *Acts*, p. 71; Haenchen, *Acts*, pp. 237 and 239; Marshall, *Acts*, p. 111; Schneider, *Die Apostelgeschichte*, I, p. 373 n. 30; D. Williams, *Acts*, p. 96; Pesch, *Die Apostelgeschichte*, I, p. 198; Conzelmann, *Acts*, p. 37; F.L. Arrington, *The Acts of the Apostles* (Peabody, MA: Hendrickson, 1988), p. 55; J.R.W. Stott, *The Message of Acts* (Leicester: IVP, 1990); Johnson, *Acts*, p. 88; Polhill, *Acts*, p. 156; S.H.T. Page, *Powers of Evil: A Biblical Study of Satan and Demons* (Grand Rapids: Baker, 1995), p. 132; and Larkin, *Acts*, p. 84. In contrast, Marguerat ('La mort d'Ananias et Saphira [Ac 5.1-11] dans la stratégie narrative de Luc', pp. 222-25) argues that this verbal parallel is insufficient evidence that Luke wishes to draw the reader's attention to the Achan story in a primary way.

[12] Barrett, *Acts*, I, p. 265.

[13] But to conclude with A.C. Winn (*The Acts of the Apostles* [Richmond: John Knox, 1960], p. 51) that the action of laying the money at the feet of the apostles was in imitation of Barnabas may be to outdistance the evidence in that from the narrative this appears to be the generally accepted practice of the community.

[14] B.J. Capper, 'The Interpretation of Acts 5.4', *JSNT* 19 (1983), p. 125; Johnson, *Acts*, p. 91; and Marguerat, 'La mort d'Ananias et Saphira (Ac 5.1-11) dans la stratégie narrative de Luc', p. 219.

given in the text of Acts itself that there is more than authority here. First, while the idea of the apostles' authority is, no doubt, present in this action, it is not the case that they were occupying a position or positions on the order that Jesus had in Luke, for later in the narrative Peter is clearly uncomfortable with Cornelius falling at his feet. On that occasion (Acts 10.26) Peter immediately urges him to rise, stating rather emphatically, καὶ ἐγὼ αὐτὸς ἄνθρωπός εἰμι. Whatever authority is implied in laying money at the apostles' feet, it is clearly not the same authority as that of Jesus in the Gospel. Second, there appears to be a close parallel to this action in the book of Acts itself. In 7.58 the text reveals that at the stoning of Stephen those involved laid their garments at the feet of a young man named Saul. While it is true that Saul will exercise a certain authority in his zeal to persecute members of the Christian community, the idea expressed in 7.58 seems to be that Saul is entrusted with the garments until the act of stoning is complete. These two clues suggest that when members of the believing community lay money at the feet of the apostles they understand it to be held in trust until such time it is dispensed to those in need of assistance.[15]

Verse 3

The reader's suspicion that something is amiss in Ananias' keeping back part of the money is immediately confirmed as v. 3 opens. Peter asks three rhetorical questions in rapid-fire fashion disclosing the grave nature of Ananias' action.[16] His first question reveals a number of things. First, by the occurrence of the words διὰ τί the question suggests that the deed need not have happened.[17] Second, Peter implies that behind this deed is Satan, filling Ananias' heart. In the Gospel the reader has learned that Satan entered into Judas, prompting the betrayal of Jesus (Lk. 22.3), and desires to sift Peter as grain (Lk. 22.31).[18] Consequently, his action here hardly takes the

---

[15] For this interpretation cf. Derrett, 'Ananias, Sapphira, and the Right of Property', p. 227; Marshall, *Acts*, p. 111; Schneider, *Die Apostelgeschichte*, I, p. 373 n. 32; and D. Williams, *Acts*, p. 95.

[16] J. Roloff, *Die Apostelgeschichte* (Göttingen: Vandenhoeck & Ruprecht, 1981), p. 94.

[17] D. Williams, *Acts*, p. 96.

[18] Cf. Schneider, *Die Apostelgeschichte*, I, p. 373 n. 34; Johnson, *Acts*, p. 88; Polhill, *Acts*, p. 157; and Marguerat, 'La mort d'Ananias et Saphira (Ac 5.1-11) dans la stratégie narrative de Luc', p. 220.

reader by surprise. Third, the fact that Satan has filled (ἐπλήρωσεν) Ananias' heart stands in stark contrast to the rest of the community which is filled (ἐπλήσθησαν) with the Holy Spirit (Acts 4.31)[19] and shares one heart and soul (4.32). While Peter treats Ananias as fully responsible for his action, the idea that Satan has filled his heart indicates that Satan helps control him.[20] It is perhaps noteworthy that this first mention of Satan in Acts deals with his influence over members of the believing community.[21] Fourth, Peter's question also reveals that Ananias' Satan-inspired action entails lying to or falsifying/counterfeiting the Holy Spirit. While ψεύσασθαι can mean 'to lie to' its occurrence here with the accusative can result in the translation 'to falsify or counterfeit' the Holy Spirit. Such a translation fits the context nicely, for in Ananias' placing at the feet of the apostles only part of the price, he is attempting to counterfeit what the Holy Spirit is doing in the community.[22] The falsification itself is the 'embezzlement' of part of the proceeds from the sale price.[23] Fifth, it is clear that although the money is laid at the feet of the apostles, the offense itself is against the Spirit. Ananias' action transcends a 'keeping back' from a human community and becomes part of a cosmic confrontation. In his attempt to deceive the church he becomes an instrument of Satan, an enemy of the church.[24] In one sense, in lying to the Spirit-filled apostles[25] and the Spirit-filled community[26] Ananias lies to the Holy Spirit. But to say only this runs the risk of missing the fact that Ananias seeks to

---

[19] J. Crowe, *The Acts* (Wilmington, DL: Michael Glazier, 1979), p. 32; G.A. Krodel, *Acts* (Minneapolis, MN: Augsburg, 1986), p. 120; and M. Turner, *Power from on High: The Spirit in Israel's Restoration and Witness in Luke-Acts* (JPTSup 9; Sheffield: Sheffield Academic Press, 1996), p. 406.

[20] Cf. Barrett, *Acts*, I, p. 265.

[21] Page, *Powers of Evil*, p. 132.

[22] Cf. esp. Johnson, *Acts*, p. 88 and Polhill, *Acts*, p. 157.

[23] Barrett (*Acts*, I, p. 266) notes that the double clause is dependent on ἐπλήρωσεν. 'The second infinitive supplies the content of the first'. For a similar conclusion cf. R. Pesch (*Die Apostelgeschichte*, I [Zurich: Benziger Verlag, 1986], p. 199 n. 19) who takes the καί as epexegetical, with the meaning 'that is to say....'

[24] Marguerat, 'La mort d'Ananias et Saphira (Ac 5.1-11) dans la stratégie narrative de Luc', p. 221.

[25] Cf. Jacquier, *Les Actes*, p. 152; Haenchen, *Acts*, p. 237; and Marshall, *Acts*, p. 112.

[26] R.B. Rackham, *The Acts of the Apostles* (London: Methuen & Co., 1901), p. 66; Haenchen, *Acts*, p. 237; Krodel, *Acts*, p. 120; and Barrett, *Acts*, I, p. 266.

counterfeit what the Spirit himself is doing. By counterfeiting the Spirit's activity he lies to God. This is not to drive too much of a wedge between the actions of the Spirit and the actions of the community, for in many regards they are identical. Rather it is an attempt to keep the focus upon the activity of the Spirit despite the prominent role played in this regard by the apostles and the community, and not overplay the function of the human characters.

Verse 4

While uncertain of the details, the reader at this point understands that there was something wrong in Ananias keeping back part of the money. Nothing in Acts 4 indicates that such acts were anything but voluntary and Peter's second rhetorical question[27] reinforces this understanding. Specifically, Peter states in his question that before the sale, the land remained in Ananias' possession and after the sale he had authority over it. While it is possible that this question points to a two-stage process of joining the community by divesting oneself of one's goods (stage one: the sale, stage two: the handing over of the goods to the community for safe keeping until a period of initiation is over),[28] nothing else in the text suggests such a process. In fact, the question seems to underscore the point that throughout the process of selling and deciding what to do with the proceeds, the money was at the disposal of Ananias.[29] It is tempting to look for something extra-textual that would explain how, if the money is entirely at Ananias' disposal, he counterfeits the Spirit's activity by bringing only part of the sale price.[30] Perhaps the closest the text comes to revealing the rationale behind this issue is the implication that when one sells a piece of property and decides to give it to the community for the benefit of all, to keep back part of the

---

[27] Schneider, *Die Apostelgeschichte*, I, p. 374 and Pesch, *Die Apostelgeschichte*, I, p. 199.

[28] So Capper, 'The Interpretation of Acts 5.4', pp. 117-31.

[29] Cf. the discussions in Bruce, *Acts*, p. 113; J. Dupont, 'L'Union entre les premières chretiennes dans les Acts des Apôtres', *NRT* 91 (1969), p. 901; Krodel, *Acts*, p. 121; Johnson, *Acts*, p. 88; and Barrett, *Acts*, I, p. 267.

[30] Derrett ('Ananias, Sapphira, and the Right of Property', pp. 228-29) suggests that a vow is implied.

money is a sign of a lack of trust in the ability of the Spirit and the community to meet one's material needs.[31]

Peter's third rhetorical question makes clear that this is no mere mistake on the part of Ananias but rather is the result of a plan in his very heart. The only other occurrence of the term πρᾶγμα in the Lukan writings (Lk. 1.1) suggests that Ananias' plan was carefully prepared. At the least, the question indicates that Ananias is culpable in this matter. Peter returns at the end of v. 4 to his initial point – Ananias has lied, not to men, but to God. By seeking to counterfeit the work of the Spirit, Ananias lies to God.[32]

Verse 5

And as Ananias hears these words[33] he falls down and dies. Several things might be noted about the nature of the words which Peter spoke. To this point in the narrative, the reader has grown accustomed to Peter serving as the spokesperson for the Twelve. Specifically, he has been filled with the Holy Spirit and as a result speaks the word of God boldly before the people and the authorities alike. He is also an instrument of God's healing power. When he speaks to Ananias in 5.3-4, the reader understands these words to come from an individual especially gifted by the Holy Spirit and able to discern matters pertaining to the Spirit.[34] In Luke's Gospel Jesus often discerns what is in the heart of friend and foe alike (5.21-22; 6.8; 9.46-47; 20.14; 24.38). Here Peter is able to reveal and rebuke the deceptive heart.[35] It is not altogether clear from the narrative

---

[31] Johnson (*Acts*, p. 92) notes, 'They were hoping that by counterfeiting the gesture, they could both partake of the community life and "hold back something of their own".'

[32] Foakes-Jackson and Lake (*Beginnings* IV, p. 51) go so far as to say, 'Because the Apostles were filled with the Holy Spirit they were not merely representatives of God – but actually God'.

[33] The present participle ἀκουών expresses simultaneity. It was during the hearing of these words that Ananias falls down and dies. Cf. Jacquier, *Les Actes*, p. 152 and Haenchen, *Acts*, p. 237 n. 9.

[34] Munck (*Acts*, p. 43) observes, 'He who lies to the Spirit can be detected by men filled with the Spirit'. For the idea that Peter receives this knowledge from the Spirit cf. Jacquier, *Les Actes*, p. 151; Carter and Earle, *Acts*, p. 71; and Marshall, *Acts*, pp. 111-12. Schneider (*Die Apostelgeschichte*, I, p. 374) sees Peter functioning as a prophet in the Lukan sense.

[35] Tannehill, *The Narrative Unity of Luke-Acts A Literary Interpretation volume two: The Acts of the Apostles*, p. 79. Cf. also R.C. Tannehill, *The Narrative Unity of Luke-*

whether Peter in his words anticipates the death of Ananias. Whether or not he was surprised by Ananias' death,[36] it is obvious that while Peter does not pronounce a curse upon him,[37] the Apostle's words are used to carry out the judgment of God.[38]

The divine nature of Ananias' death is revealed in part by the appearance of ἐξέψυξεν to describe it. This term, which appears only three times in Acts, occurs in contexts where the divine nature of the death is either implicit (5.5, 10) or explicit (12.23). It is also used in the LXX for the death of Sisera at the hands of Jael (Judg. 4.21).[39] Whether the death is attributed to shock,[40] the conviction felt by means of the Spirit,[41] or the hand of God directly,[42] it is hard to avoid the conclusion that Ananias' death is the result of divine judgment upon him.[43]

In the Lukan narrative it is not unusual for the term φόβος to appear in contexts of the miraculous. It can accompany angelic visitations (Lk. 1.12; 2.9), healings or other signs (Lk. 1.65; 5.26; Acts 2.43), exorcisms (Lk. 8.37) or botched ones (Acts 19.17), and a resurrection (Lk. 7.16).[44] It comes as no surprise to the reader then that the immediate result of Ananias' demise is great fear coming upon all those hearing - additional evidence that the hand of God is at work in this death. It is not clear whether the reader is to under-

---

Acts A Literary Interpretation volume one: The Gospel according to Luke (Minneapolis, MN: Fortress, 1990), pp. 43-44. Polhill (*Acts*, p. 157) likens Peter's actions to the prophetic insight of Elisha with Gehazi in 2 Kgs 5.26. Johnson (*Acts*, p. 88) also attributes to Peter the abilities of a prophet.

[36] A possibility suggested by G.T Stokes, *The Acts of the Apostles*, II (New York: A.C. Armstrong and Son, 1891), p. 223 and A.W.F. Blunt, *The Acts of the Apostles* (Oxford: Clarendon Press, 1923), p. 153.

[37] Winn, *Acts*, p. 51 and Johnson, *Acts*, p. 88.

[38] Cf. Conzelmann, *Acts*, pp. 37-38.

[39] Johnson, *Acts*, p. 88.

[40] So Derrett, 'Ananias, Sapphira, and the Right of Property', p. 229 and J.D.G. Dunn, *Jesus and the Spirit* (Philadelphia: Westminster, 1975), p. 166.

[41] Rackham, *Acts*, p. 67 and C.H. Rieu, *Saint Luke: The Acts of the Apostles* (Edinburgh: Penguin Books, 1957), p. 123.

[42] Foakes-Jackson and Lake, *The Beginnings of Christianity Part I: The Acts of the Apostles*, IV, p. 51; W. Neil, *The Acts of the Apostles* (Grand Rapids: Eerdmans, 1981), p. 95; and C.E. Faw, *Acts* (Scottdale, PA: Herald Press, 1993), p. 70.

[43] Marshall, *Acts*, p. 112; D. Williams, *Acts*, p. 98; Arrington, *Acts*, p. 57; Stott, *Acts*, p. 110; and Polhill, *Acts*, p. 158.

[44] Cf. Jacquier, *Les Actes*, p. 153.

stand 'all those hearing' as a reference to those within the community who heard (and saw?) what Peter said or whether this has reference to those outside the group among whom word like this would quickly spread.

Verse 6

Apparently there is a group of young men sitting there observing the whole episode, who, no doubt, sharing in the great fear, rise up. Although it is possible to take the term νεώτεροι as having reference to an office,[45] it is likely a reference to a group of young men fit for such a task,[46] not an official designation,[47] as Luke can use another term to describe the same group later in this story (v. 10). Wasting no time, these young men wrap the body and bury it straightway. While it is possible to appeal to the climate of Palestine as making an immediate burial necessary,[48] the reader no doubt sees in this hasty burial, which departs from the normal pattern of including a period of mourning (not to mention notification of the deceased's spouse), an additional indication that God has struck down this individual. In such a case, a prompt burial is the only appropriate response.[49]

Verse 7

After an interval of about three hours the scene continues. Although three hours could simply be a temporal indicator, given the frequency with which the group of believers prays, there could be a reference to the next time of prayer.[50] Since v. 2 Sapphira has not been mentioned and has not been named since v. 1. Here she is simply his wife. In v. 2 she had knowledge with her husband of the plan to 'keep back' part of the money (note that the verbs which

---

[45] As do Rackham, *Acts*, p. 67 and Blunt, *Acts*, p. 153.

[46] Carter and Earle, *Acts*, p. 72 and Neil, *Acts*, p. 95.

[47] Foakes-Jackson and Lake, *The Beginnings of Christianity Part I: The Acts of the Apostles*, IV, p. 51; Haenchen, *Acts*, p. 238; Marshall, *Acts*, p. 112; D. Williams, *Acts*, pp. 98-99; Conzelmann, *Acts*, p. 38; Arrington, *Acts*, p. 55; Johnson, *Acts*, pp. 88-89; Polhill, *Acts*, p. 158; Faw, *Acts*, p. 70; and Barrett, *Acts*, I, p. 268.

[48] As do Jacquier, *Les Actes*, p. 154 and Bruce, *Acts*, p. 114.

[49] Derrett, 'Ananias, Sapphira, and the Right of Property', p. 230; Marshall, *Acts*, p. 113; D. Williams, *Acts*, p. 98; and Larkin, *Acts*, p. 86.

[50] Cf. Capper, 'The Interpretation of Acts 5.4', p. 121; Conzelmann, *Acts*, p. 38; D. Williams, *Acts*, p. 99; and Marguerat, 'La mort d'Ananias et Saphira (Ac 5.1-11) dans la stratégie narrative de Luc', p. 218.

describe this action are all third person singular, not plural, implying that this was Ananias' plan for the most part); now she comes with no knowledge of her husband's fate or God's plan![51] In such a state, she comes in.

Verse 8

Peter greets Sapphira's entry with an answer in the form of an enquiry. In contrast to the questions Peter raised with Ananias in vv. 3-4, which appear to be rhetorical in nature, his question to Sapphira expects and receives an answer. This is borne out by his instruction Εἰπέ μοι. As such his question could be taken as an opportunity to confess/repent.[52] By the same token, his words can also be taken as a means of making '… her complicity plain to the reader',[53] not an opportunity to repent.[54] In particular, he enquires into the price of the land by means of the term τοσούτου, which means '… a specific but unspecified number' as in Lk. 15.29,[55] or amount in this case. Quite obviously, emphasis is placed on this word as it stands near the beginning of the Greek sentence.[56] The reader is not certain whether Peter mentions the actual price[57] or the part that Ananias brought. In either case, Sapphira gave a positive answer to his question; 'τοσούτου' is the amount.

---

[51] To observe as does Haenchen (*Acts*, p. 238) that she comes unsuspecting misses the play on words between συνειδυίης in v. 2 and εἰδυῖα in v. 7.

[52] So John Calvin, *Commentary on the Acts of the Apostles*, I (tran. C. Fetherstone; ed. by H. Beveridge; Grand Rapids: Eerdmans, 1949), p. 200; E.M. Knox, *The Acts of the Apostles* (London: MacMillan, 1908), p. 68; Bruce, *Acts*, p. 115; Marshall, *Acts*, p. 113; D. Williams, *Acts*, p. 99; and Stott, *Acts*, p. 110. Derrett ('Ananias, Sapphira, and the Right of Property', p. 231) argues that both Ananias and Sapphira confessed in a manner consistent with Josh. 7.19: Ananias by his silence, Sapphira in v. 8.

[53] Haenchen, *Acts*, p. 238. For a similar idea cf. G. Schneider, *Die Apostelgeschichte*, I (Freiburg: Herder, 1980), p. 377.

[54] P.H. Menoud, 'La Mort d'Ananias et de Saphira (Actes 5.1-11)', in *Aux sources de la Tradition chrétienne: Mélanges offerts à M. Maurice Goguel* (Neuchâtel & Paris: Delachaux & Niestlé, 1950), p. 147 and Roloff, *Die Apostelgeschichte*, p. 94.

[55] Barrett, *Acts*, I, p. 270.

[56] Jacquier, *Les Actes*, p. 154.

[57] A possibility mentioned by Marshall, *Acts*, p. 113; D. Williams, *Acts*, p. 99; and Polhill, *Acts*, p. 159.

Verse 9

Whatever her answer, it revealed the harmony she and her husband shared, which makes a mockery of the community's unity of the Spirit (4.32). Earlier the reader learned that Ananias, through his attempt to counterfeit the Holy Spirit, had lied to God. Here it is revealed that the couple's actions test the Spirit of the Lord. The reader knows from the words of Jesus to the Devil in the Gospel that the Lord is not to be put to the test (4.12). From that passage such testing involves seeing how far one could go, how much one could get away with and still rely upon the protection of God. Such a meaning is present in this verse as well,[58] only here to test the Spirit takes on the idea of going '… against the direction the Spirit has already clearly indicated',[59] an idea that will reappear in Acts 15.10.

By means of 'Behold', a common term throughout Luke-Acts, the reader is alerted that even more is to come. If earlier it was un-clear whether or not Peter expected Ananias to die, here it is very clear that he not only anticipates but utters the prophecy of divine judgment upon Sapphira.[60] The verbal imagery is graphic. It appears that at just this time the young men who were burying Ananias ar-rive back. Perhaps the reader takes Peter's mention of the young men's feet being at the door as a deliberate means of drawing Sap-phira's attention to the spot where their sin remains (at the feet of the apostles). With this, she learns of her husband's death and of her own impending demise. Once again Peter functions in the pro-phetic role which in the Gospel characterized Jesus' ability to dis-cern the hearts of others.

Verse 10

The effect of Peter's words upon Sapphira are the same as they had been earlier on her husband. The result is immediate death. Only here the reader discovers that she falls at Peter's feet, perhaps an

---

[58] For this interpretation cf. Marshall, *Acts*, p. 113; Stott, *Acts*, p. 110; Polhill, *Acts*, p. 159; and Barrett, *Acts*, I, p. 270.

[59] Turner, *Power from on High*, p. 406.

[60] Rackham, *Acts*, p. 67; Neil, *Acts*, p. 95; Haenchen, *Acts*, p. 239; Schneider, *Die Apostelgeschichte*, I, p. 377; Pesch, *Die Apostelgeschichte*, I, p. 201; Krodel, *Acts*, p. 121; Marguerat, 'La mort d'Ananias et Saphira (Ac 5.1-11) dans la stratégie narra-tive de Luc', p. 219; Faw, *Acts*, p. 70; Barrett, *Acts*, I, p. 270; and Larkin, *Acts*, p. 87.

ironic unintended obeisance.[61] The same term is used to describe her death as her husband's; it is from the hand of God.[62] The young men (νεανίσκοι) come in at just this time, find her dead, and carry her out to bury her with her husband.

Verse 11

As with the death of Ananias, so the death of Sapphira creates a sense of holy fear among the whole church and upon all those who were hearing these things. In all likelihood, this last category includes those outside the church.[63] It is interesting that no one who is part of the church is excluded from this fear.[64] The emphasis on such fear begun in 2.43 thus continues at the close of this story as well.[65] It is also noteworthy that this is the first time the reader sees ἐκκλησία in Luke-Acts, a term which will figure prominently later in the narrative. Several observations might be made as to its significance here. First, the mention of church in 5.11 together with the reference to the group of believers in 4.32 serves to put brackets around the section 4.32-5.11.[66] Second, it may be significant that the first mention of church occurs in an inauspicious context.[67] Third, the reader may experience this reference as indicating a growing sense of unity, identity, and development among the believers to this point in the narrative.[68] This growing sense of definition no doubt involves the eventual claim of being the true people of God.[69]

---

[61] Johnson, *Acts*, p. 89.

[62] Jacquier, *Les Actes*, p. 155 and D. Williams, *Acts*, p. 99.

[63] Haenchen, *Acts*, p. 239.

[64] Cf. the following summary observation by Krodel (*Acts*, p. 122), 'The reports of the deaths of Judas, Ananias, and Sapphira tell of three final judgments on disciples before the end in order to warn the reader that God is not mocked.... Just as miracle stories are signs of the salvation that is yet to come, so the story of Ananias and Sapphira is a solemn warning of the future judgment on unforgiven sin within the people of God.'

[65] Polhill (*Acts*, p. 160) makes the point that such repetition is not by chance but is the whole point of the story.

[66] Johnson, *Acts*, p. 90.

[67] Marshall, *Acts*, p. 113.

[68] Jacquier, *Les Actes*, p. 154.

[69] Marshall, *Acts*, p. 113; D. Williams, *Acts*, p. 100; and Larkin, *Acts*, p. 87.

Conclusion

What are the implications of Acts 5.1-11 for the broader concerns of this enquiry? 1) As might be expected from the analysis of the Gospel, Luke is not reluctant to assign the cause of an infirmity, in this case death, to God. 2) As in the case of Zechariah, the recipients of God's judgment in Acts 5.1-11 are identified as part of the believing community. 3) On this occasion, an attempt to counterfeit the work of the Holy Spirit, which involved lying to God, precipitated the punishment. 4) Satan is involved in the episode, but God is clearly the one who brings judgment in the form of death. 5) Coming as early in the narrative as it does, this story functions to caution the readers that even those within the believing community can suffer judgment at the hands of God if the sin is serious enough. Zechariah was made mute owing to unbelief; Ananias and Sapphira died because they lied to (and tested the Spirit of) God. 6) It is very clear that Peter discerned the plan that was in the heart of Ananias and Sapphira. In this regard, his discerning action is reminiscent of Jesus' own discernment evidenced in the Gospel.

Acts 5.12-16 – Peter's Shadow

The next text of importance for this study follows fast on the heels of the Ananias and Sapphira story.

> Through the hands of the apostles many signs and wonders were performed among the people. And they were all in one accord in Solomon's Portico. And none of the rest dared to join them, but the people magnified them. And more were being added believing in the Lord, a multitude of men and women, so that they even brought the sick out into the streets and placed them upon small beds and cots, in order that as Peter would come at least his shadow might fall upon them. And there also came together the multitude of the surrounding cities of Jerusalem, carrying the sick and those tormented by unclean spirits, who were all healed.

This is the third of three summary statements which mark chapters 2-5,[70] and it exhibits links both to the immediate and broader literary context.

Verse 12

The reader next learns that the prayer of 4.30 for God to stretch forth his hand to perform healings, signs, and wonders is being answered here in 5.12.[71] In fact, from the reader's vantage point the fulfillment of the prayer may be rather more spectacular than the request.[72] Such miraculous feats come through the hands of the apostles (Διὰ δὲ τῶν χειρῶν τῶν ἀποστόλων). No doubt the reader understands there to be a link here between the hand of God mentioned in the prayer of 4.30 and the hands of the apostles. But there may be more to the phrase than this imagery alone, powerful though it is. The reader will recall that in the Gospel Jesus himself sometimes either laid hands upon an individual for healing (Lk. 4.40; 13.13) or took them by the hand (5.13; 8.54), and the reader will discover that in Acts the hands are used in acts of healing (Acts 3.7; 9.12, 17, 41; 28.8), anointing/consecrating (6.6; 13.3), and occasionally in reception of the Spirit (8.17; 19.6). Thus, it very well may be that the reader sees in Διὰ δὲ τῶν χειρῶν τῶν ἀποστόλων a reference to the literal laying on of hands.[73] However, two clues in the text suggest that this phrase, while including the laying on of hands, should not be limited to this act. First, the construction found here, διὰ plus the hands, occurs in several other places in Acts with the meaning of 'through the agency of' (2.23; 7.25; 11.30; 14.3; 15.23; 19.11). In all likelihood the statement in 5.12 would have a similar meaning. Second, the text will later reveal that some of those healed through the hands of the apostles were healed when Peter's shadow fell upon them. Therefore, while the reader might see the practice of the laying on of hands in this phrase, it would certainly not be restricted to that meaning. The image the reader receives is one where the miracles are occurring time

---

[70] Bruce, *Acts*, p. 117.

[71] Haenchen, *Acts*, p. 242; Neil, *Acts*, p. 95; Crowe, *Acts*, p. 32; Marshall, *Acts*, p. 114; Schneider, *Die Apostelgeschichte*, I, p. 379; and Conzelmann, *Acts*, p. 39.

[72] Johnson, *Acts*, p. 95.

[73] For this idea cf. G. Stählin, *Die Apostelgeschichte* (Göttingen: Vandenhoeck & Ruprecht, 1966), p. 86 and D. Williams, *Acts*, p. 104.

after time,[74] the healing of the paralytic being repeated ten to a hundred times over.[75]

It is also disclosed in v. 12 that 'they were all in one accord in Solomon's Portico (in the temple)'. Several aspects of this sentence are noteworthy. First, the appearance of the term ὁμοθυμαδὸν indicates that, despite the tragedy involving Ananias and Sapphira, the church continues to be characterized by its essential unity. This unity has been present from the beginning (cf. the use of ὁμοθυμαδὸν in 1.14; 2.46; 4.24)[76] and will continue in the future (15.25), but will increasingly be contrasted with the ὁμοθυμαδὸν of the church's opponents (7.57; 18.12; 19.29).[77] Second, as was earlier revealed (2.46), the context of their unity is the temple, with Solomon's Portico (cf. 3.11) becoming a regular meeting place for the believers.[78] Third, it is not altogether clear who is included in the word 'all'. Is the reader to see this term in a restrictive sense with reference to the immediate antecedent, meaning all the apostles?[79] Or does 'all' include the entire group of believers? It would appear that the latter meaning is here in view, as it would be quite unusual, after having stressed the ὁμοθυμαδὸν of the group of believers in 1.14, 2.46, and 4.24, now to exclude them while emphasizing the ὁμοθυμαδὸν of the apostles only.

Verse 13

While it is possible to take the λοιπῶν of v. 13 as all the Christians except the apostles,[80] if in v. 12 ἅπαντες has reference to the entire group of believers, then λοιπῶν here would likely be understood as those who are not believers.[81] The immediate effect of the deaths

[74] Jacquier, *Les Actes*, p. 159.

[75] So Haenchen, *Acts*, p. 245.

[76] The one heart and soul of 4.32 conveys the same idea.

[77] G. Haufe, 'ὁμοθυμαδόν', *EDNT*, II, p. 511.

[78] Neil, *Acts*, p. 95 and Barrett, *Acts*, I, p. 274.

[79] So Johnson, *Acts*, p. 95.

[80] Rackham, *Acts*, p. 68; Pesch, *Die Apostelgeschichte*, I, p. 206; and Johnson, *Acts*, p. 95.

[81] Jacquier, *Les Actes*, p. 159; Bruce, *Acts*, p. 118; Carter and Earle, *Acts*, p. 74; Winn, *Acts*, p. 52; Haenchen, *Acts*, p. 242; J. Jervell, *Luke and the People of God* (Minneapolis, MN: Augsburg, 1972), p. 47; Marshall, *Acts*, p. 115; Schneider, *Die Apostelgeschichte*, I, p. 381; H. Fendrich, 'λοιπός', *EDNT*, II, p. 360; D. Williams,

of Ananias and Sapphira as well as the extraordinary miracles wrought by the disciples is to make those outside the church afraid to approach the believers.[82] Yet, despite such apprehensions, the people at large praised them.[83] The occurrence of the word 'people' (λαός) reminds the reader of the division to this point in the Acts narrative between the negative response of the Jewish leaders and the more positive response of the people in general.[84] (Such a pre-disposition on the part of the people begins to change with the Stephen story.) But at this point, the people are 'over the top' in their praise of the believers, specifically the apostles.

Verse 14

Even though such fear keeps 'the rest' away, more and more were being added to the church. The imperfect tense of the verb (προσετίθεντο) suggests that people kept on being added, its passive voice implies that God is the one adding these believers.[85] A whole multitude responds to the work of God – believing,[86] both men and women. The mention of women along with men at this point is probably not so much an indication that Luke had only been counting men up to this point,[87] but rather it continues Luke's emphasis on the role of women in the community (cf. Lk. 8.2-3; 23.49, 55; 24.10; Acts 1.14; 5.14; 8.3, 12; 9.2; 12.12; 16.13; 17.4, 12;

Acts, p. 102; Krodel, *Acts*, p. 123; Conzelmann, *Acts*, p. 39; and Barrett, *Acts*, I, p. 274. Cf. also the discussion by D.R. Schwartz, 'Non-Joining Sympathizers (Acts 5,13-14)', *Bib* 64 (1983), pp. 550-55.

[82] J. Roloff, *Die Apostelgeschichte* (Göttingen: Vandenhoeck & Ruprecht, 1981), p. 97.

[83] Cf. Barrett [*Acts*, I, 275] who notes that the verb μεγαλύνειν '... is practically a synonym for *praise*'.

[84] Cf. J. Kodell, 'Luke's Use of *Laos*, "People," Especially in the Jerusalem Narrative (Lk 19,28-24,53)', *CBQ* 31 (1969), pp. 327-43; Jervell, *Luke and the People of God*, p. 54; and H. Frankemölle, 'λαός', *EDNT*, II, pp. 340-41.

[85] D. Williams, *Acts*, p. 103.

[86] Given the context of signs and wonders, it is particularly difficult to make sense of Krodel's (*Acts*, p. 124) comment that 'The church's growth, in Luke's opinion, was not the result of miracles'. In this passage, the growth of the church is at least in part attributable to the fear and praise wrought through such acts! Luke, one must assume, was aware of the implication of this portion of his narrative.

[87] A question asked by Haenchen (*Acts*, p. 143 n. 1) to which Schneider (*Die Apostelgeschichte*, I, p. 381 n. 24) offers a resounding 'No'.

22.4),[88] and is perhaps a subtle counterbalance to the story of Sapphira still fresh in the reader's mind.

Verse 15

The result (ὥστε) of all this activity[89] is that the sick are brought into the wide streets upon couches and cots. The combination of πλατείας, which indicates broad city streets, with words for couches (κλιναρίων) and cots (κπαβάττων)[90] suggest to the reader that the response was enormous. The identity of those who bring the sick is somewhat ambiguous. In all likelihood though they are part of the λοιπῶν of v. 13.[91]

The most spectacular aspect of the verse still awaits the reader. In the latter part of v. 15 it is disclosed that the hope of those who brought the sick is not that Peter should lay hands upon them, which might be expected from v. 12, but that perhaps even his shadow might fall upon them. Clearly, such action indicates the extent to which the people ἐμεγαλύνεν the believers, especially Peter. It is possible, of course, to take this detail as highlighting the superstition of the people[92] and/or attempt to shield Luke from the embarrassment of affirming this view himself.[93] However, to do so ignores the ideas surrounding the power of the shadow in the Graeco-Roman world,[94] the fact that Luke does indicate in the very next verse that numbers of healings and exorcisms take place (some

---

[88] Jacquier, *Les Actes*, p. 160; D. Williams, *Acts*, p. 103; and Barrett, *Acts*, I, p. 275.

[89] Schneider, *Die Apostelgeschichte*, I, p. 381. Barrett (*Acts* I, p. 276) notes, '... ὥστε looks back to the whole paragraph'.

[90] Foakes-Jackson and Lake (*The Beginnings of Christianity Part I: The Acts of the Apostles*, IV, p. 55) indicate that the two terms are probably synonyms. Jacquier (*Les Actes*, p. 161) believes the two terms convey different meanings. 'Luc veut dire qu'on apportait des malades riches et des pauvres'.

[91] Non-Christian Jews according to Haenchen, *Acts*, p. 243.

[92] E.M. Blaiklock, *The Acts of the Apostles* (Grand Rapids: Eerdmans, 1959), p. 71; Winn, *Acts*, p. 52; Dunn, *Jesus and the Spirit*, pp. 165-66; and D. Williams, *Acts*, p. 103.

[93] Some scholars observe either that it is not clear whether Luke approved of this belief or that Luke does not record the outcome of such a belief. Cf. Carter and Earle, *Acts*, p. 75; Neil, *Acts*, p. 96; Marshall, *Acts*, p. 116; and Polhill, *Acts*, p. 164.

[94] P.W. van der Horst, 'Peter's Shadow: The Religio-Historical Background of Acts V. 15', *NTS* 23 (1976-77), pp. 204-12.

presumably through precisely this means),[95] and that Luke does not see healing by physical means to be illegitimate[96] but assigns such action to Jesus (Lk. 8.43)[97] and later to Paul (Acts 19.12). Such misgivings also ignore the significance of the verb ἐπισκιάσῃ which in the Lukan writings means 'to overshadow'. In Lk. 1.35, this term is used when Mary is told by the angel, 'The power of the Most High will overshadow (ἐπισκιάσει) you'. In Lk. 9.34, the verb reappears to describe the cloud which overshadows (ἐπεσκίαζεν) the three disciples during the Transfiguration.[98] As its previous occurrences in Luke have conveyed a sense of the divine presence and power, so the reader is here likely to understand the appearance of ἐπισκιάσῃ in the very same way. While technically it is Peter's shadow with which the sick want contact, the reader understands this overshadowing as very closely connected if not representative of the power of God.[99]

Verse 16
In addition to the activity described in v. 15, the reader learns that a multitude of people from the cities surrounding Jerusalem evidently hear and bring their own in need of healing. The disclosure that people are coming from outside Jerusalem informs the reader that the promise of 1.8 is in a small way already beginning to be fulfilled. Both the sick (ἀσθενεῖς) and those troubled (ὀχλουμένους) by unclean spirits are brought for help. Throughout the Gospel the reader has learned of the close connection between illness and demonic activity. While ordinarily some distinction is preserved between them,[100] on occasion the categories overlap.[101] Here, the reader is presented with two distinct groups of afflicted individuals.

[95] Arrington, *Acts*, p. 60.

[96] Rackham, *Acts*, p. 69.

[97] Stott, *Acts*, p. 113; Faw, *Acts*, p. 71.

[98] C. Williams, *Acts*, p. 89; Arrington, *Acts*, p. 60; and Stott, *Acts*, p. 113.

[99] Neil, *Acts*, p. 96; G.W.H. Lampe, 'Miracles in the Acts of the Apostles', in *Miracles: Cambridge Studies in their Philosophy and History* (ed. by C.F.D. Moule; London: Mowbray, 1965), p. 175; and Krodel, *Acts*, p. 125.

[100] W. Barclay's (*The Acts of the Apostles* [Philadelphia: Westminster, 1976], p. 96) conclusion that all diseases were attributed to demons by the ancients is clearly wide of the mark.

[101] Despite the claims of D. Williams (*Acts*, p. 104) and Page (*Powers of Evil*, p. 174) that a clear distinction is always maintained.

It is not clear whether the phrase 'troubled by unclean spirits' is to be taken as a reference to demon possession or to physical infirmities caused by them. It appears similar to the thought of Lk. 6.18, where the term ἐνοχλούμενοι appears. There the reader will likely have seen a reference to demon possession. In all likelihood, the reader will conclude the same here. The end result is the same. Whatever their affliction, all of them are healed.[102]

Conclusion

There are several implications of Acts 5.12-16 for the broader concerns of this enquiry. 1) As in the Gospel according to Luke, illness and being troubled by unclean spirits (i.e. demon possession) can be spoken of in the same breath. 2) Again in continuity with the Gospel, healing language is used with reference to exorcism. 3) It appears that healings are attributed to contact with the shadow of Peter. Does this imply that unclean spirits are expelled by means of his shadow as well? 4) The fear which results from the death of Ananias and Sapphira results in numerous individuals coming to faith and the healings of large numbers.

Acts 8.4-8 – Philip in Samaria

On the one hand, the many signs and wonders performed through the apostles result in numerous additions to the church. On the other hand, these activities result in the arrest and persecution of the apostles. Such opposition is not able to hinder the church's proclamation that Jesus is the Christ (5.17-42). Internally, the church responds to a dispute about the inadequate care of the hellenist widows by appointing seven ministers (apparently all hellenists) who are filled with the Holy Spirit to oversee the distribution of the community's goods (6.1-7). Two of this number figure prominently in the later narrative: Stephen and Philip.

The preaching and miraculous works of Stephen, one of the seven, creates a great deal of opposition among certain members of the Synagogue of the Freedmen. This antagonism results in Stephen being put on 'trial' on which occasion he delivers a powerful sermon. The consequence of his words and actions is his death by

---

[102] Jacquier (*Les Actes*, p. 162) suggests that the imperfect tense of the verb ἐθεραπεύοντο indicates that the healings were multiplied continually.

stoning (6.8-8.1). The story of Stephen's death introduces two significant details. For the first time, the reader is introduced to Saul,
who will be both the church's persecutor and servant (7.58; 8.1).
Through this agent, a severe persecution of the church, except for
the apostles, ensues. At this point in the narrative occurs the next
text to receive detailed attention.

> Those who were scattered went about preaching the word. And
> Philip, going down into a city of Samaria, preached to them the
> Christ. And the crowds paid careful attention with one accord to
> the things being said by Philip when they heard and saw the
> signs which he did. For many having unclean spirits came out
> crying with a loud voice, and many of the paralytics and lame
> were healed. And there was great joy in that city.

Verse 4

With the μὲν οὖν of v. 4 a new scene begins,[103] but one that is connected with what has come before in several ways. Specifically, mention of those who are scattered, literally 'the dispersed ones' (Οἱ ...
διασπαρέντες), connects these individuals to the persecution described in 8.1. Therefore, the reader immediately learns the fate of
some of these scattered ones. At the same time, this reference anticipates the future missionary work in Antioch which also results
from this persecution (11.19).[104] This term, which occurs only three
times in Acts, may be a subtle hint that already the church is taking
the Gospel into all the world.[105] These dispersed ones go out
preaching. The introduction of the term διέρχομαι at this point is
strategic, for it becomes almost a technical term for missionary
travel later in the book.[106] As they make their way through, they are
described as preaching the word. The persecution is transformed

---

[103] Foakes-Jackson and Lake (*The Beginnings of Christianity Part I: The Acts of the
Apostles*, IV, p. 88) note that μὲν οὖν is a usual sign of transition. Cf. also Carter
and Earle, *Acts*, p. 111 and Haenchen, *Acts*, p. 301.

[104] Haenchen, *Acts*, p. 301; Crowe, *Acts*, p. 53; Roloff, *Die Apostelgeschichte*, p.
133; A. Weiser, *Die Apostelgeschichte*, I (Würzburg: Gütersloh und Echter Verlag,
1981), p. 199; and Barrett, *Acts*, I, p. 400. For an excellent discussion of the links
of 8.4 in the Acts narrative cf. esp. F.S. Spencer, *The Portrait of Philip in Acts*
(JSNTSup 67;Sheffield: JSOT Press, 1992), pp. 33-34.

[105] Cf. Schneider, *Die Apostelgeschichte*, I, p. 479 n. 65.

[106] U. Busse, 'διέρχομαι', *EDNT*, I, p. 323; Spencer, *The Portrait of Philip in
Acts*, p. 36; and Barrett, *Acts*, I, p. 401.

into a missionary tour, not by a specific guidance of the Spirit, but rather such a course of action appears to be the natural thing to do.[107] The appearance of εὐαγγελίζομαι continues for the reader an emphasis on preaching as a prominent occurrence in the Lukan narratives.[108] It may not be without significance that the heaviest concentration of εὐαγγελίζομαι terminology is found in Acts 8.4-40. This vocabulary places the anonymous missionaries in the tradition of Zechariah (Lk. 1.19), the angel (2.10), John the Baptist (3.18), Jesus (4.18, 43; 7.22; 8.1; 16.16; 20.1), and the Twelve (9.6; Acts 5.42). Their message, the word, is clearly the message about Jesus.

Verse 5

Here it is learned that one of the dispersed ones is Philip, one of the Seven. From Jerusalem, Philip makes his way down to a city of Samaria. Suggestions for the possible identity of this city include Sebaste (Samaria),[109] Gitta,[110] Shechem,[111] and Sychar.[112] However, attempts to identify the city precisely run the danger of missing the significance of the fact that Luke does not name the city. By mentioning one of the cities of Samaria, the reader's attention is drawn to the fact that the church has now moved into the region of Samaria just as Jesus had prophesied (1.8). The reader also knows from the Gospel that Jesus had sent messengers into a village of Samaria (Lk. 9.52), but they were not received. Despite that fact, Jesus' own teaching could cast a Samaritan in a complimentary light (10.30-36) and his healings included that of a Samaritan leper, who alone gave thanks (17.16). While the reader knows that the Gospel will be preached in Samaria, perhaps there is some question about the nature of the response that awaits Philip in Samaria.

---

[107] Marshall, *Acts*, p. 153.

[108] According to Jacquier (*Les Actes*, p. 250) the term appears 10 times in the Gospel and 15 times in Acts.

[109] Rackham, *Acts*, p. 114; F.J.F. Foakes-Jackson, *The Acts of the Apostles* (London: Hodder and Stoughton, 1931), p. 70; Neil, *Acts*, p. 121; Carter and Earle, *Acts*, p. 112; and Arrington, *Acts*, p. 87.

[110] C. Williams, *Acts*, p. 115.

[111] Apparently Haenchen, *Acts*, p. 302.

[112] Jacquier, *Les Actes*, p. 251.

The content of Philip's preaching is 'the Christ'.[113] The reader is not told whether Philip couched his message about Jesus in Taheb terminology or not. While various scholars suggest that this was his starting point,[114] the reader of the Acts narrative is left with the same general impression as the reader of John 4 and Justin Martyr's First Apology 53.6, that the Samaritans '... shared a general messianic consciousness with other Jewish groups'.[115]

Verse 6

Given the Spirit-inspired activity of Stephen, one of the Seven, the reader is somewhat expectant that Philip too will do mighty things. Such expectations are not to be disappointed. In ways reminiscent of the response to Jesus' teaching, the preaching of Philip draws the crowds.[116] Rather than being rejected, as had the messengers Jesus earlier sent to a Samaritan village, Philip's preaching receives the close attention of all. So genuine is the interest of the Samaritans that they are said to be in one accord as they give his message their attention. The appearance of ὁμοθυμαδὸν, a term which often describes the unity of those who comprise the church, suggests to the reader that the response of the Samaritans will be positive. In that sense, it might be proper to speak of ὁμοθυμαδὸν as having an incipient meaning in this verse.[117] The Samaritans both hear (the words) and see the signs which Philip did. Just as with Jesus[118] and the Apostles,[119] so signs accompany the preaching of Philip.[120] Thus the anointing of the Spirit extends even to members of the Seven.

---

[113] ὁ Χριστός for Luke is a designation of his function and is rarely for him a proper name. Cf. Jacquier, *Les Actes*, p. 252 and Spencer, *The Portrait of Philip in Acts*, p. 38.

[114] Bruce, *Acts*, p. 177; Neil, *Acts*, p. 121; Marshall, *Acts*, p. 154; D. Williams, *Acts*, p. 154; Polhill, *Acts*, p. 215; Barrett, *Acts*, I, p. 403; and Larkin, *Acts*, p. 126.

[115] Spencer, *The Portrait of Philip in Acts*, p. 38.

[116] For the significance of οἱ ὄχλοι in the Lukan narratives cf. Haenchen, *Acts*, p. 302 n. 2.

[117] Barrett, *Acts*, I, p. 403.

[118] Tannehill, *The Narrative Unity of Luke-Acts A Literary Interpretation volume two: The Acts of the Apostles*, p. 104.

[119] Marshall, *Acts*, p. 154.

[120] Munck, *Acts*, p. 73 and Pesch, *Die Apostelgeschichte*, I, p. 273.

Verses 7-8

The reader learns several things in v. 7. First, some indication of the extent of Philip's Spirit-enabled activity is suggested by the double πολλοὶ which appears. In point of fact, the first word the reader sees after 'the signs which he did' is 'many'. Second, the signs which Philip performs are divided into two categories: exorcisms and healings,[121] both preceded by πολλοὶ.

Unclean spirits come out of many with loud cries.[122] This description is reminiscent of the demon-possessed man whom Jesus liberates in Lk. 4.31-37, who also cries out with a loud voice.[123] Such an echo might again encourage the reader to see continuity between the ministries of Jesus and Philip.[124] These activities show classic signs of exorcism, and aside from the healing of those troubled by unclean spirits in 5.16, are the first exorcisms described in Acts.[125]

In addition to the expulsion of many unclean spirits, many (πολλοὶ) paralytics and lame are healed. It is significant that on this occasion a clear line of demarcation is drawn between demon possession and ordinary illness.[126] The mention of these two particular categories of infirmity reminds the reader yet again of the basic continuity of the ministries of Jesus (Lk. 5.18, 24; 7.22), Peter (Acts 3.2; 9.33), Philip, and Paul (Acts 14.8).[127] Earlier, in his response to the enquiry of John's messengers, Jesus appealed to the healing of the lame as evidence of the presence of the messianic kingdom (Lk. 7.22).[128] Adding to this emphasis is the fact that in the parable of the great banquet, it is the χωλοὶ in particular that are to be invited. Such points are not lost on the reader.

Just as many unclean spirits come out and many are healed, so there is much (πολλὴ) joy in this Samaritan town owing to the

---

[121] As Jacquier (*Les Actes*, p. 253) notes, 'Luc a soin de distinguer les maladies naturelles des possessions démoniaques'.

[122] For a discussion of the grammatical problems in v. 7a cf. the discussions in Haenchen, *Acts*, p. 302 and Barrett, *Acts*, I, p. 404.

[123] Spencer, *The Portrait of Philip in Acts*, p. 45.

[124] Johnson, *Acts*, p. 146.

[125] Faw, *Acts*, p. 103.

[126] Schneider, *Die Apostelgeschichte*, I, p. 488 and D. Williams, *Acts*, p. 154.

[127] Spencer, *The Portrait of Philip in Acts*, p. 45.

[128] Cf. the comments of D. Williams, *Acts*, p. 154.

words and actions of Philip.[129] In the Lukan narratives joy is particularly tied to the word that brings salvation and deliverance (Lk. 1.14; 2.10; 8.13; 10.17; 15.7, 10; Acts 15.3). Along with the appearance of ὁμοθυμαδὸν in v. 6, the mention of joy may imply that the Samaritans are at this point more than just favorably disposed toward the Gospel, but may suggest that they are very close to belief if not already converted.

Conclusion

There are at least two primary implications of this text for the broader concerns of this enquiry. 1) Yet again Luke distinguishes between demon possession and infirmity which appears to result from 'unattributed causes'. Therefore, Luke does not attribute all illness to the direct influence of the Devil or demons. 2) This text along with other Lukan texts indicates that there is some means by which Luke and/or Philip in the narrative discerns the difference between various categories of affliction.

Acts 9.8-9, 17-18 – The Conversion of Saul

Following Philip's initial success, the reader learns of a magician named Simon who (apparently) with a number of the Samaritans believe the gospel preached by Philip and are baptized in the name of Jesus (8.9-13). The apostles in Jerusalem send Peter and John down to Samaria where they lay hands on the believers who are then filled with the Holy Spirit. Simon seeing this offers money to purchase this ability and is rebuked by Peter (8.14-24). Meanwhile, Philip through supernatural direction preaches to a eunuch from Ethiopia. The eunuch comes to faith and is baptized. Philip is then on his way (supernaturally moved), preaching his way to Caesarea (8.26-40), justly earning him the name εὐαγγελιστής in Acts 21.8.

At this point in the narrative is the first of three accounts of Saul's conversion. Although terribly significant for the overall Acts story, four verses in chapter nine merit special consideration in this study.

---

[129] Tannehill, *The Narrative Unity of Luke-Acts A Literary Interpretation volume two: The Acts of the Apostles*, p. 104.

And Saul getting up from the ground, opening his eyes saw nothing. And he was not able to see for three days, and did not eat or drink.... And Ananias departed and entered into the house, and placing hands upon him he said, 'Brother Saul, the Lord sent me, Jesus the one who appeared to you on the way on which you traveled, in order that you might receive your sight and be filled with the Holy Spirit. And immediately something like scales fell from his eyes, he received his sight, and rising he was baptized....

Verse 8

Falling down as a result of his encounter with the risen Jesus, Saul seeks to get up but as the passive voice of the verb (ἠγέρθη) may indicate, he is probably lifted to his feet by those with him.[130] When he opens his eyes he is unable to see. It is clear from the text that the reader understands what transpires in this verse, including the blindness as a supernatural sequence of events.[131] Although it is possible to minimize or deny altogether the punitive aspect of the blindness,[132] the reader is keenly aware that in the Lukan narratives God sends infirmity and death to bring about his purposes. If God would work in such a way with Zechariah, it is difficult not to see a similar thrust in Paul's blindness.[133] As a result of his condition, rather than entering Damascus breathing out murderous threats (9.1), Saul is led by the hand, much like a little child, completely dependent upon others.[134]

Verse 9

The blindness lasted for three days. The number three appears to be a standard Lukan designation for passage of time whether it be hours (Acts 5.7), days (Lk. 2.46; Acts 9.9; 25.1; 28.7, 17), months (Lk. 1.56; 4.25; Acts 7.20; 19.8; 20.3; 28.11), or years (Lk. 13.7). Not only is Paul unable to see for this period, but also he neither eats nor drinks. While it is possible that this fast may be attributed to

---

[130] Haenchen, *Acts*, p. 323.

[131] Marshall, *Acts*, p. 170 and Barrett, *Acts*, I, p. 452.

[132] As do Roloff, *Die Apostelgeschichte*, p. 150; Conzelmann, *Acts*, p. 72; Polhill, *Acts*, p. 235; Barrett, *Acts*, I, p. 452; and Larkin, *Acts*, p. 141.

[133] Jacquier (*Les Actes*, pp. 286-87) calls it '... un châtiment de son incrédulité'.

[134] Haenchen, *Acts*, p. 323; Neil, *Acts*, p. 129; Schneider, *Die Apostelgeschichte*, II, p. 28; Crowe, *Acts*, pp. 63-64; Faw, *Acts*, p. 111; and Barrett, *Acts*, I, p. 452.

shock (as a result of the vision),[135] penance,[136] or preparation for additional revelation, the reader of the Lukan narratives has a slightly different vantage point.[137] By not eating or drinking Paul identifies with the attitude of John the Baptist toward food and drink (Lk. 7.33) and is the diametric opposite to the attitude of those controlled by such things (Lk. 12.19, 29; 17.27-28). The nearest parallel is Jesus' action in the wilderness just after his own visionary experience (Lk. 4.2).[138] The reference to prayer in v. 11 underscores this general idea. Mention of this three-day period without sight, food, or drink also indicates to the reader that the story is not yet at its resolution.

Verse 17

During the intervening verses the reader is introduced to another Ananias, whom the Lord addresses in a dream to go to Saul, lay hands on him to restore his sight, and tell him of his future role as an instrument of the Lord. After a bit of resistance, Ananias consents.

Upon Ananias' departure and entry into the house he does as he has earlier been told, placing his hands on Saul. This act appears from v. 12 to be in connection with the recovery of sight[139] and as such is in keeping with the practice of Jesus (Lk. 4.40; 13.13) and Paul (Acts 28.8). The act does not here seem to be connected with the gift of the Holy Spirit, although such cannot be ruled out altogether.[140] Accompanying the laying on of hands are the first words Paul hears from a believer after his Damascus Road experience,

---

[135] Foakes-Jackson and Lake, *The Beginnings of Christianity Part I: The Acts of the Apostles*, IV, p. 102; Rieu, *Acts*, p. 134; C. Williams, *Acts*, p. 123; Neil, *Acts*, p. 129; Marshall, *Acts*, p. 170; Krodel, *Acts*, p. 176; Polhill, *Acts*, p. 236; Barrett, *Acts*, I, p. 452; and Larkin, *Acts*, p. 141.

[136] Carter and Earle, *Acts*, p. 127; Haenchen, *Acts*, p. 323; Marshall, *Acts*, p. 170; Pesch, *Die Apostelgeschichte*, I, p. 305; Krodel, *Acts*, p. 176; and Barrett, *Acts* I, p. 452.

[137] Johnson, *Acts*, p. 164.

[138] Rackham, *Acts*, p. 131.

[139] Jacquier, *Les Actes*, p. 291; J.H.E. Hull, *The Holy Spirit in the Acts of the Apostles* (London: Lutterworth Press, 1967), pp. 102-103; Marshall, *Acts*, p. 172; D. Williams, *Acts*, p. 172; Polhill, *Acts*, p. 238; Barrett, *Acts*, I, p. 457; and Turner, *Power from on High*, pp. 375-76.

[140] For this suggestion cf. Calvin, *Acts*, I, p. 382; Krodel, *Acts*, p. 177; and Johnson, *Acts*, p. 165.

'Brother Saul'.[141] Such a greeting, no doubt, indicates Saul's reception into the community,[142] but does it say more? Specifically, does this address indicate that Ananias already considers Saul to be a 'Christian' brother? There is a certain ambiguity to the term in the Lukan narrative being used both for Christians and for those of the family of Abraham.[143] It is utilized especially by Jewish Christian missionaries in speaking to fellow Jews.[144] But here it is used by a Christian to an individual whom the Lord has identified in a vision as one who is praying and is a chosen instrument. These considerations suggest that the reader would understand Ananias' usage as indicating that Paul is already a believer.[145] In addition to this action and greeting, Ananias informs Saul about the divine nature of his mission. In addition to the aspects already known from the previous narrative, Ananias informs Saul that he will be filled with the Holy Spirit, an event which is not described in this passage. Both Ananias and the reader understand that the work of God as described in Acts necessitates such empowerment by the Spirit.

Verse 18

The effects of Ananias' action and words result in the instantaneous recovery of sight by Saul.[146] The supernaturally inflicted infirmity is miraculously cured.[147] The actual recovery of sight is said to be the result of something like scales falling from Saul's eyes. Although it is possible to take λεπίδες in a metaphorical or figurative sense,[148] it is unlikely that readers, who earlier have been told the

---

[141] Stott, *Acts*, pp. 175-76.

[142] Johnson, *Acts*, p. 165. Rackham (*Acts*, p. 135) suggests that this address is tantamount to words of forgiveness.

[143] Krodel, *Acts*, p. 177 and Turner, *Power from on High*, p. 375.

[144] J. Jervell, *The Theology of the Acts of the Apostles* (Cambridge: Cambridge University Press, 1996), p. 51.

[145] So Foakes-Jackson and Lake, *The Beginnings of Christianity Part I: The Acts of the Apostles*, IV, p. 104; C. Williams, *Acts*, p. 124; Carter and Earle, *Acts*, p. 129; Haenchen, *Acts*, p. 325; Schneider, *Die Apostelgeschichte*, II, p. 30; H.M. Ervin, *Conversion-Initiation and the Baptism in the Holy Spirit* (Peabody, MA: Hendrickson, 1984), pp. 41, 46, 48; J.B. Shelton, *Mighty in Word and Deed* (Peabody, MA: Hendrickson, 1991), p. 131; Polhill, *Acts*, p. 238; Barrett, *Act*, I, p. 456; and Larkin, *Acts*, p. 143.

[146] Haenchen, *Acts*, p. 325.

[147] *Contra* Blunt (*Acts*, p. 172) who inexplicably argues there is '... nothing necessarily supernatural in the temporary blindness or the recovery'.

[148] Neil, *Acts*, p. 131 and Johnson, *Acts*, p. 165.

Spirit descended upon Jesus in bodily form, would understand the scales in any way other than a literal sense. The scales seem to be a flaky substance or film of some sort.[149] Receiving his sight, he arose, this time under his own power, and was baptized, completing the process of Christian initiation (cf. Acts 2.38).

Conclusion

What are the implications of Acts 9.8-9 and 17-18 for the broader concerns of this enquiry? 1) Primarily, this text confirms that, for Luke, infirmity sometimes comes from God in working his purposes. In ways not dissimilar to Zechariah's experience, Saul is struck with a temporary infirmity. In Zechariah's case, the mute state was the result of unbelief and served as a sign to the old man. With Saul, the blindness appears to have been the result of his persecution of the church and a means by which he is brought to faith in Jesus. 2) In this case, the infirmity is removed at the appointed time through the prayer of a fellow believer. On other occasions in the Lukan narratives the cause or origin of an infirmity is sometimes discerned; here such knowledge comes via supernatural revelation in the form of a dream. 3) In ways reminiscent of James 5, the effects of the prayer are immediate.

Acts 10.38 – 'Healing All of Those Dominated by the Devil'

The impact of his conversion is dramatic for Saul, for he immediately goes to the synagogues in Damascus preaching that 'Jesus is the Son of God'. Such activities soon result in his departure from Damascus (9.19b-22) and initial journey to Jerusalem, where Barnabas intercedes with the apostles on Saul's behalf (9.26-31). At this point in the Acts narrative, Peter again takes center stage as he heals a paralytic named Aeneas (9.32-35) and restores to life a Christian woman named Dorcas (9.36-43). Following these miraculous acts, the reader is told about Cornelius, a Roman centurion who fears God and is filled with the Holy Spirit. Through visions, both Cornelius and Peter are prepared for this most strategic encounter.

---

[149] The nearest ancient analogy seems to be Tob. 3.7 and 11.12-13. Aside from this there appear to be no ancient medical parallels, although such flakes were sometimes described on the skin. Cf. Haenchen, *Acts*, p. 325.

The next text to receive a more detailed examination is found in Peter's sermon to Cornelius in Acts 10.38.

> ... Jesus from Nazareth, how God anointed him with the Holy Spirit and power, who went about doing good and healing all those under the tyranny of the Devil, because God was with him.

Rehearsing some of the things that Cornelius knows (ὑμεῖς οἴδατε), Peter puts special emphasis upon Jesus, placing the name first in the Greek text of v. 38.[150] In this verse the reader is given a brief overview of the origins and ministry of Jesus. That his origins are in view is made clear by reference to Nazareth, which appears only here in Acts but five times in the Gospel where it is confined to passages which speak of Jesus' physical origin and the beginning of his ministry. It is the place where Gabriel tells Mary about the birth of Jesus (Lk. 1.26). It is Joseph's home, from which he returns to Bethlehem (2.4), and Jesus' home, in that the birth narrative describes Jesus' family as returning there on two occasions (2.39, 51). In 4.16, Nazareth is named as the location where Jesus, near the beginning of his ministry, reads from the Isaiah scroll (61.1-2), a text which largely defines his ministry in the Lukan narrative. Therefore, Peter takes Cornelius (and the reader) back to Jesus' origins by the mention of Nazareth at this point.

A reference to his origins naturally leads to the statement, 'God anointed him with the Holy Spirit and power'. For the reader the most natural referent to such anointing is the baptism of Jesus,[151] for there the Spirit comes down upon him in bodily form (3.22), he goes to the wilderness full of the Holy Spirit (4.1), returns to Nazareth in the power of the Spirit (4.14), and in the synagogue acknowledges that the Spirit of the Lord is upon him (4.18).[152] Given the occurrence of the phrase ἐν τῇ δυνάμει τοῦ πνεύματος in Lk. 4.14, it could very well be that in Acts 10.38 the words πνεύματι ἁγίῳ καὶ δυνάμει should be understood as a hendiadys,

---

[150] Haenchen, *Acts*, p. 352.

[151] Rackham, *Acts*, p. 157; Neil, *Acts*, p. 140; Roloff, *Die Apostelgeschichte*, p. 172; D. Williams, *Acts*, p. 193; Page, *Powers of Evil*, p. 133; and Barrett, *Acts*, I, p. 524.

[152] Bruce, *Acts*, pp. 226-27; Haenchen, *Acts*, p. 352; Marshall, *Acts*, p. 192; Roloff, *Die Apostelgeschichte*, p. 172; J. Dupont, *Nouvelles Études sur les Acts des Apôtres* (Paris: Cerf, 1984), p. 67 n. 16; and Johnson, *Acts*, p. 192.

meaning 'with the power of the Spirit'.[153] The reader is also keenly aware of the fact that the presence of the Spirit in Jesus' life and mission does not go back only to his baptism, but all the way back to his birth (Lk. 1.34).[154]

This Holy Spirit anointing empowers the activity of Jesus, which is spoken of in two ways, both of which build off the Lukan missionary verb διῆλθεν, 'he went about'. First, his ministry is described in terms of continuous benefaction.[155] In point of fact, the verb which here appears (εὐεργετῶν) will remind the reader of what Jesus had earlier said (Lk. 22.25) about rulers who fancied themselves as benefactors (εὐεργέται)[156] and as such would be an intentional play on words.[157] In all likelihood the reader would understand this as a general description of Jesus' healing ministry, which was such a prominent part of his mission generally. Such a reading seems confirmed by the fact that in Acts 4.9 the related word εὐεργεσία is used to describe the healing of the man lame from his mother's womb. Second, Jesus' ministry is described in terms of the continuous healing of πάντας τοὺς καταδυναστευομένος ὑπὸ τοῦ διαβόλου. What exactly is the reader to make of this claim? It is possible to take this phrase as having reference to all those whom Jesus healed, including those with physical infirmities and the demon possessed. On this view, Jesus' healing activity is seen as liberating the diseased and possessed from the power of evil, the realm of the Devil.[158] One implication of such an interpretation is it suggests that in the Lukan narrative all illness has a Satanic character.[159] On the surface, this interpretation has much to

---

[153] Barrett, *Acts*, I, p. 524 and Turner, *Power from on High*, p. 263.

[154] Barrett, *Acts*, I, p. 524.

[155] Note the appearance of the present participles εὐεργετῶν and ἰώμενος, indicating continuous action. Cf. Barrett, *Acts*, I, p. 525. Roloff (*Die Apostelgeschichte*, pp. 172-73) suggests that his action of doing good is contrasted with the actions of the Jews in Acts 2.22-23.

[156] Marshall, *Acts*, p. 192.

[157] Foakes-Jackson and Lake, *The Beginnings of Christianity Part I: The Acts of the Apostles*, IV, p. 121; Haenchen, *Acts*, p. 353; Marshall, *Acts*, p. 192; Dupont, *Nouvelles Études sur les Acts des Apôtres*, p. 67 n. 18; Krodel, *Acts*, p. 197; Polhill, *Acts*, p. 262 n. 103; and Barrett, *Acts*, I, p. 525.

[158] Marshall, *Acts*, p. 192; Johnson, *Acts*, p. 192; Barrett, *Acts*, I, p. 525; Page, *Powers of Evil*, p. 133; and Turner, *Power from on High*, p. 264.

[159] Cf. esp. the discussion in Page, *Powers of Evil*, p. 133.

commend it. 1) One of Luke's favorite words for healing appears in this phrase. 2) It is clear that for Luke the lines of demarcation between illness and demon possession are sometimes blurred. 3) In the Lukan narrative, the activity of Jesus and the church is seen within the context of the invasion of the domain of Satan by the Kingdom of God, with healings and exorcisms being signs of such an invasion.

However, when this phrase is examined in more detail, this interpretation appears less than convincing. 1) It has become evident to the reader that in the Lukan narratives illness/infirmities are attributed to a variety of sources. To be sure, illness can be and is attributed to Satan or demons, but on a number of occasions the text presents those in need of healing in a rather neutral light with regard to the origin of illness. Add to this the fact that Luke, more than any other New Testament writer, attributes infirmities and even death to the direct intervention of God, and it becomes clear that such an understanding of the phrase in question in Acts 10.38 may be a bit too simplistic in terms of the narrative itself. 2) It could very well be the case that the reader would see in the appearance of the term καταδυναστευομένος not reference to Jesus' healing ministry in general, but rather reference to those individuals in the narrative who have been described as being especially under the domination of the Devil. On such a view the phrase πάντας τοὺς καταδυναστευομένος ὑπὸ τοῦ διαβόλου would be translated 'those being under the tyranny of the Devil'.[160] In particular the reader would associate such a description with individuals described in the narrative as demon possessed, those troubled by unclean spirits, and those afflicted with various infirmities by means of the Devil or demons.

The last phrase in v. 38 makes explicit how it was that Jesus could do such mighty things – 'because God was with him'. In a sense this statement, along with 'God anointed him with the Holy Spirit and power', serves as an inclusio around the description of the ministry itself. By this means the reader is reminded that divine enablement accounts for Jesus' miraculous ministry.

---

[160] *BAG*, p. 411.

Conclusion

What does a study of Acts 10.38 contribute to the primary purposes of this enquiry? This reading suggests that Acts 10.38 is not evidence that all illness is regarded as owing its origin to the Devil, as is sometimes argued, but rather that Jesus' ministry can be spoken of as two-fold: a ministry of benevolence through healing various illnesses and a ministry of healing those under the tyranny of the Devil. At this point in the narrative, there seems to be a differentiation between infirmity from 'unattributed causes' and a whole category of malevolence attributed directly to the Devil.

Acts 12.21-23 – Herod's Death

During Peter's sermon, the Holy Spirit falls upon all those who are listening and they all speak with tongues and magnify God. Following this demonstrable sign, they are baptized in water (Acts 10.37-48). After this, Peter is called upon to give a report to the church in Jerusalem with regard to the conversion of these Gentiles (11.1-18). At this point the story of the dispersed hellenist Christians is taken back up. The reader learns of a mission in Antioch, to which Barnabas is sent by the church in Jerusalem. Straightway, he goes to Tarsus and finds Saul who works alongside Barnabas in the Antiochene church. Through a prophetic utterance by Agabus, Barnabas and Saul are set aside to deliver an offering to the Jerusalem church with regard to a famine which is also prophesied (11.19-30).

In chapter twelve the story shifts back to Jerusalem where the death of James at the hands of Herod is recounted. Peter, who has been thrown into prison by Herod, is miraculously delivered and himself leaves Jerusalem (12.1-19a). Having been mentioned at the beginning of chapter twelve, Herod's activities again become the focus of the story. The reader learns that Herod and the people of Tyre and Sidon had been quarreling, and in an attempt to stabilize their food supply the people ask for peace.

> And on an appointed day, Herod having clothed himself in kingly apparel and having sat upon the judgment seat made a speech to them. And the crowd kept crying, 'A voice of God and not of man!' And at once an angel of the Lord struck him

because he did not give glory to God, and being eaten by worms he died.

Verse 21

On an appointed day Herod came out to make a speech to the people of Tyre and Sidon. The reader learns that Herod has left no stone unturned as he seeks to convey a sense of power and authority. Herod had been introduced to the reader as a king in 12.1 and true to form dresses in a 'royal' fashion for this occasion. Not only is his dress impressive, but he also sits on the βήματος, the seat of judgment. One of the great ironies of this detail is that as Herod prepares to sit in judgment upon his audience, God is about to judge Herod for his persecution of the church. Herod then begins to deliver his public address.

Verse 22

But as he spoke the crowd keeps on shouting, 'A voice of God and not of man'. The imperfect tense of the verb (ἐπεφώνει) may indicate that this chant began and did not subside.[161] This action could very well be in accord with the courtly style, where one goes 'over the top' in praise in order to obtain the thing requested.[162]

Verse 23

The reader learns that before the crowd can stop its chant, an angel of the Lord struck Herod. In the Lukan narrative angels have been very prominent and their significance in the text may be described in the following ways. In Luke-Acts they: function primarily as emissaries from God, communicating his divine message (Lk. 1.11, 13, 18, 19, 16, 18, 30, 34, 35, 38; 2.9, 10, 13, 15, 21; 4.10; 22.23; Acts 7.30, 35, 38, 53; 8.26; 10.3, 7, 22; 11.13) and serving as a sign of encouragement (Acts 27.23-24); are sometimes mentioned as in the company of God (Lk. 9.26; 12.8, 9); greatly rejoice when one sinner converts (Lk. 15.10); intervene, at God's bidding, in the affairs of humankind in benevolent (Lk. 16.22; Acts 5.19; 12.7-11) and malevolent (Lk. 1.20; Acts 12.23) ways; and are a point of contention between the Pharisees, who believed in their existence, and the Sadducees, who did not (Acts 23.8-9).

---

[161] D. Williams, *Acts*, p. 218.

[162] Conzelmann, *Acts*, p. 96. Cf. also the discussion in Rackham, *Acts*, p. 182 and Pesch, *Die Apostelgeschichte*, I, p. 367.

The appearance of an angel of the Lord at this point calls all this to the reader's mind, most immediately the role of the angel of the Lord in the liberation of Peter from prison. One anticipates that the angel here appears in a similarly powerful way. The angel's intentions are made clear in the Greek text where the verb (ἐπάνταξεν) stands first before the subject (ἄγγελος κυρίου). The verb 'strike' is known to the reader from its appearance in Lk. 22.49-50, where the disciples ask if they should strike those who come to arrest Jesus and one of them does, though not in a lethal way. It also occurs in Acts 7.24 to describe Moses' killing of an Egyptian. The term is also used in a gentler way to denote a 'nudge' which Peter received from the angel in Acts 12.7. Here, however, it is very clear that the Angel of the Lord strikes Herod in a mortal fashion which conveys the judgment of God upon him.[163] In this usage, it is very similar to the Old Testament idea of the Angel of the Lord.[164]

The reason for this divine punishment is clearly stated in the text: 'he did not give the glory to God'. The reader has several bits of information to draw on in coming to an understanding of this explanation. 1) The most immediate referent in the passage is the praise of the people. Not only does the imperfect tense of the verb indicate that the crowd kept shouting, 'The voice of God and not of man', but there is also no indication in the text itself that Herod sought to rebuke or even to stop such idolatrous flattery.[165] The appearance of the term παραχρῆμα appears to underscore this connection. Instead of giving glory to God, as had the Samaritan leper (Lk. 17.18), Herod received the glory unto himself.[166] 2) The reader also knows that Herod both dresses as a king and sits upon the seat of judgment. These two details serve to highlight the fact that in some ways Herod induced this response from the people. 3) It is very clear from Acts 12 that Herod is a major opponent of the work of God, persecuting strategic members of its leadership. God in this case will have no rivals and will remove certain opponents who impede the spread of the Gospel.

---

[163] Rackham, *Acts*, p. 182; Neil, *Acts*, p. 152; Marshall, *Acts*, p. 212; and Johnson, *Acts*, p. 215.

[164] Rackham, *Acts*, p. 182; Roloff, *Die Apostelgeschichte*, p. 191; Johnson, *Acts*, p. 215; and Faw, *Acts*, p. 138.

[165] Blunt, *Acts*, p. 186 and Neil, *Acts*, p. 152.

[166] Blaiklock (*Acts*, p. 100) calls the episode a case of hubris.

The angel's punitive action in particular is that Herod dies as a result of being eaten by worms. Attempts to identify the precise nature of his infirmity[167] or even to explain it as the kind of death that came to many great men who opposed God[168] may miss the Lukan point that Herod dies from his acts of taking glory away from God. In the eyes of Luke it is a most fitting end. As if anything else were needed to emphasize the fact that Herod's demise comes from the hand of God, the same word used to describe the deaths of Ananias and Sapphira (ἐξέψυξεν) appears in describing the death of Herod as well.

Conclusion

A study of this text reveals that Luke is very comfortable in attributing punitive affliction, and in this case death, upon a given individual to God. Earlier, an upright man was made mute owing to a lack of faith (Lk. 1.20), then two members of the believing community dropped dead because they had lied to God by trying to counterfeit the work of the Spirit (Acts 5.1-11), and then a persecutor of the church is made blind in an affliction which facilitated his conversion (9.8-9, 17-18). Now an enemy of the church is struck down for his failure to give God the glory, which no doubt involved his aggressive opposition to the church. This story, coming as it does after the statement found in Acts 10.38, reminds the reader that not all affliction comes from the Devil.

---

[167] Bruce (*Acts*, p. 256) suggests the rupture of a hydotid cyst, while Larkin (*Acts*, p. 188) calls it '… peritonitis from a perforated appendix, combined with intestinal roundworms, ten to sixteen inches long'. D. Williams (*Acts*, p. 218) notes that it '… should be taken as a medical description rather than the stereotyped description of the death of a tyrant'.

[168] Jacquier, *Les Actes*, p. 374; Foakes-Jackson and Lake, *The Beginnings of Christianity Part I: The Acts of the Apostles*, IV, p. 140; Munck, *Acts*, p. 115; Haenchen, *Acts*, p. 387 n. 3; Roloff, *Die Apostelgeschichte*, p. 191; Conzelmann, *Acts*, p. 97; Arrington, *Acts*, p. 127; Pesch, *Die Apostelgeschichte*, I, p. 368; Krodel, *Acts*, p. 223; Johnson, *Acts*, p. 216; and Barrett, *Acts*, I. p. 591. Cf. also the amazing similarities between Acts 12 and Ezekiel 28 pointed out by M.R. Strom, 'An Old Testament Background to Acts 12.20-23', *NTS* 32 (1986), pp. 289-92. On Isaiah 14 and Ezekiel 28-32 as a possible Old Testament background to Acts 12 cf. the discussion by S.R. Garrett ('Exodus from Bondage: Luke 9.31 and Acts 12.1-24', *CBQ* 52 [1990], esp. pp. 676-77).

Acts 13.4-12 – Elymas the False Prophet

In contrast to the death of Herod, the church continues to increase and spread (12.24). Meanwhile, Barnabas and Saul fulfill their ministry in Jerusalem and return to Antioch with John Mark (12.25). At Antioch, a community with numerous prophets and teachers, Barnabas and Saul are set aside through the Holy Spirit, and after fasting and prayer, hands are laid upon them and the community sends them off. The next passage of special significance for this study is found at this point.

> Therefore, they, being sent out by the Holy Spirit, went down to Seleucia; from there they went to Cyprus. And having arrived at Salamis they were proclaiming the word of God in the synagogues of the Jews. And they had John as a servant. And going through the whole island as far as Paphos, they found a man, a certain magician false prophet Jew by the name of Bar-Jesus, who was with the proconsul Sergius Paulus, a man of intelligence. This one called Barnabas and Saul, seeking to hear the word of God. And Elymas the magician (for that is what his name being interpreted means), opposed them, seeking to turn the proconsul from the faith. And Saul, who is also Paul, filled with the Holy Spirit, fixing his eyes upon him said, 'O full of all guile and all unscrupulousness, son of the Devil, enemy of all righteousness, will you not stop trying to make crooked the straight paths of the Lord? And now behold the hand of God upon you, and you will be blind not seeing the sun for a time.' At once mist and darkness fell upon him, and going about he sought someone to lead him by the hand. Then, the proconsul, seeing what had happened, believed, being amazed at the teaching of the Lord.

Verse 4
By means of μὲν οὖν the reader is both introduced to a new episode[169] and, at the same time, encouraged to see the following as connected to what has just transpired.[170] Somewhat emphatically,

---

[169] Haenchen, *Acts*, p. 396.
[170] Barrett, *Acts*, I, p. 610.

attention is directed to Barnabas and Saul, identified by αὐτοι.[171] Underscoring the divine initiative of this mission, the reader is told again that Barnabas and Saul have been sent by the Holy Spirit. Such repetition indicates that this point is an important one. Their actions come not through human but divine direction.[172] Being so sent by the Holy Spirit, they make their way from Antioch to the coastal town of Seleucia and then on to Cyprus. Such a move, aside from its divine guidance, makes good sense to the reader, owing to the fact that Cyprus is the birthplace of Barnabas (Acts 4.36) and that believers from Cyprus were at the forefront of the mission in Antioch (11.19-20).

Verse 5

Having arrived at Salamis, the island's largest town, they were preaching. Although the term κατήγγελλον has occurred earlier in Acts on one occasion with reference to the preaching of Peter (4.2), it becomes increasingly identified with the preaching of Paul in Acts (13.5, 30; 15.36; 16.17, 21; 17.3, 13, 23; 26.23), appearing for the first time with such a meaning in the context of Paul's first mission-ary preaching. The content of their preaching is identified as the word of God, a phrase used regularly in Acts as the content of preaching the Gospel. The context of such preaching is the syna-gogues of the Jews. The reader is aware by this point that those most receptive to the Gospel have been at the fringe of Judaism, to include the Samaritans, the Ethiopian Eunuch, Cornelius (who feared God), and numbers of converts in Antioch. That Barnabas and Saul would begin their missionary activity by preaching in Jew-ish synagogues fits with this picture well, as those loosely connected will make some of the best candidates for conversion. This pattern frequently follows in Acts (13.14, 46; 14.1; 16.13; 17.1, 10; 18.4, 19;

---

[171] So Jacquier, *Les Actes*, p. 381 and Barrett, *Acts*, I, p. 610. *Contra* Haenchen, *Acts*, p. 396.

[172] Jacquier, *Les Actes*, p. 381; Haenchen, *Acts*, p. 396; Neil, *Acts*, p. 154; Mar-shall, *Acts*, p. 217; Schneider, *Die Apostelgeschichte*, II, p. 199; D. Williams, *Acts*, p. 224; Johnson, *Acts*, p. 221; Barrett, *Acts*, I, p. 610; and Larkin, *Acts*, p. 192.

19.8; 28.17).[173] Of course, the statement here suggests that there were a significant number of Jews in this city.[174]

Almost as an afterthought, it is revealed that in the company of Barnabas and Saul as a servant is John. The reader knows of John from his first mention earlier in the narrative (Acts 12.12). From this text it is learned that John is also called Mark. His mother Mary, who hosts the members of the church in her home, is apparently to be understood as a women of means and some spiritual commitment. John Mark, it might be deduced, is no novice in the faith but heir to a rather rich Christian heritage. Acts also indicates that John Mark had accompanied Barnabas from Jerusalem to Antioch (12.25). Given his earlier identification with Barnabas and Saul, his presence with the two missionaries now does not come as too much of a surprise.

His mention at this point in the present pericope raises a couple of issues for the reader. It is interesting that John is not mentioned in regard to the commissioning of Barnabas and Saul by the Holy Spirit. Such an omission at the least conveys the idea that John is to be seen in a secondary role,[175] but may also indicate that the reader ought not to expect the same sense of missionary commitment from him that may rightly be expected from Barnabas and Saul. Given the fact that John Mark will later leave the group to return to Jerusalem (13.13), such a subtle hint at this point ought not be ignored.[176] Interestingly, later in the narrative, when Paul refuses to agree to allow John Mark to accompany himself and Barnabas on another missionary expedition (15.37), it is Barnabas who takes Mark to Cyprus (15.39), an act which brings some degree of closure to this aspect of the story for the reader.

The other thing the reader learns about John in this verse is that he travels in the capacity of a ὑπηρέτην. The precise meaning of

---

[173] As noted by Marshall, *Acts*, p. 217. In comparing Luke's account to Paul's own words, Barrett (*Acts*, I, p. 611) observes, '... what was to Luke little more than a missionary technique ... is to Paul a theological principle...'.

[174] For which there is some extra-biblical support. Cf. C. Williams, *Acts*, p. 136; Haenchen, *Acts*, p. 396; and Neil, *Acts*, p. 154.

[175] D. Williams, *Acts*, p. 224.

[176] Blunt, *Acts*, p. 188; Haenchen, *Acts*, p. 397; Schneider, *Die Apostelgeschichte*, II, p. 120; and Marshall, *Acts*, p. 218.

the term is not obvious[177] and can be taken to mean that Mark simply serves as a servant or functionary to Barnabas and Saul, performing whatever menial tasks are needed.[178] However, it should be observed that Luke's narratives give some hint as to the meaning of the term in this passage. From the very beginning of the Gospel, the reader learns of a group called 'ministers of the word' (ὑπηρέται τοῦ λόγου), upon whom Luke depends in drawing up his own account. In Lk. 4.20, upon the conclusion of his reading from the Isaiah scroll, Jesus hands it back to the synagogue attendant (τῷ ὑπηρέτῃ), who was apparently given charge over the scrolls. In Acts (5.22, 26) this same term is used to describe those who go on behalf of the Sanhedrin to check on the whereabouts of Peter and John. In addition, as Paul defends himself before King Agrippa (26.16) he relates that during his conversion, Christ said that Paul would be a witness and ὑπηρέτην. Such Lukan usage, together with Mark's background as provided in Acts 12, suggests that his role is more than that of a servant, although he would no doubt have a share in the menial duties such a journey would entail. Rather, given the use of this term in the Lukan narratives, Mark's family in the Jerusalem church, and the meaning of the term in secular literature (where in the preponderance of its occurrences it is related in some way to scrolls or documents),[179] it appears that Mark served in some type of ministerial assistant role to the two missionaries. Perhaps this involved attending to the formational needs of new converts and preaching or teaching on some occasions.[180] The reader would also assume that John Mark is involved with more mundane duties as well.

---

[177] Several commentators are content to say that the meaning is unclear. Cf. Marshall, *Acts*, p. 218; Conzelmann, *Acts*, p. 99; and Stott, *Acts*, p. 219.

[178] So Munck, *Acts*, p. 118; Carter and Earle, *Acts*, p. 177; D. Williams, *Acts*, p. 225; Johnson, *Acts*, p. 222; and Polhill, *Acts*, p. 292.

[179] For this evidence cf. B.T. Holmes, 'Luke's Description of John Mark', *JBL* 54 (1935), p. 68 and C. Williams, *Acts*, p. 156.

[180] Rackham, *Acts*, p. 199; Jacquier, *Les Actes*, p. 383; R.O.P. Taylor, 'The Ministry of Mark', *ExpT* 54 (1942-43), pp. 136-38; Bruce, *Acts*, p. 263; Roloff, *Die Apostelgeschichte*, p. 198; C. Williams, *Acts*, p. 156; Neil, *Acts*, p. 155; Arrington, *Acts*, p. 133; Barrett, *Acts*, I, p. 611; and Larkin, *Acts*, p. 193 n.

Verse 6

Although the reader is not told of any preaching activity in v. 6, the appearance of the verb διελθόντες, typically used for missionary journeys, suggests that the preaching continues throughout the island. Upon arrival in Paphos, a city on the western coast of Cyprus, they find a man. The reader is told five things in rapid-fire succession about this man. First, he is called a magician. Although this is the first appearance of the term μάγος in Acts, the term calls to the reader's mind an earlier individual who was said to have practised magic (μαγεύων) and amazed the populace with his magic (μαγείαις), Simon the Sorcerer. The reader would bring to Acts 13 the knowledge that an individual like this possessed certain powers and is not to be regarded simply as a charlatan or quack.[181] The appearance of this term here would also create in the reader a sense of anticipation with regard to the inevitable conflict which is sure to ensue. From the episode involving Simon, the reader knows that magic is no match for the power of the Spirit and that belief on the part of a magician is possible (8.13) albeit difficult (8.18-24).

Second, in addition to being described as a magician, this man is called a false prophet. The theme of prophecy is a major one in the Lukan narratives, with the vast preponderance of references being to the Old Testament prophets, as individuals or writers of Scripture.[182] John the Baptist (Lk. 1.76; 7.26; 20.6), Jesus (Lk. 4.24; 7.16, 39; 13.33; 24.19; Acts 3.22, 23; 7.37), and David (Acts 2.30) have also been designated as prophets in the narrative. Most recently, the reader has learned of the presence of certain prophets in Antioch (11.27; 13.1) and will discover still others later in the story (Judas and Silas in 15.32 – Agabas in 21.10). It is the mention of the prophets in Antioch and the exalted view of prophecy, which comes from the narrative generally, that make the designation 'false prophet' so very significant. If the reader has come to regard prophecy as God-inspired and revelatory to the point of initiating this missionary trip, then false prophecy is understood to lay claim to the same sort of phenomena falsely. While this man may have

---

[181] Cf. Jacquier, *Les Actes*, p. 383 and Haenchen, *Acts*, p. 397. *Contra* Bruce, *Acts*, p. 264 and Krodel, *Acts*, p. 229.

[182] Cf. Lk. 1.70; 3.4; 4.17, 27; 6.23; 9.8, 19; 10.24; 11.47; 13.28, 34; 16.16, 29, 31; 18.31; 24.25, 27, 44; Acts 2.16; 3.18, 21, 24, 25; 7.42, 48, 52; 8.28, 30, 34; 10.34; 13.15, 20, 27, 40; 15.15; 24.14; 26.22, 27; 28.23, 25.

possessed certain power as a magician, his claims of being a medium of divine revelation are said to be blatantly false.[183]

Third, the reader next learns that this man is a Jew. Given the previous descriptions, this revelation must be surprising to the reader. The practice of magic is bad enough, but for a Jew either to turn his back on the religion of Israel or to accommodate it to the practice of magic is especially abhorrent.[184] It does begin to explain the previous description, as false prophets, mentioned in Lk. 6.26, are conceived of as saying things which are pleasing to hear and not the true word of God. In the Gospel text the reference is no doubt to Jewish false prophets. This title also has the effect of moving the attention of the reader to the boundary between Judaism and paganism.[185]

Fourth, the name of this man is finally given, and, though the reader might not think it could get worse, it does. For this magician-false prophet-Jew bears in his name that of the Christ, Bar-Jesus! Given the previous revelations about this man, his name could not fit any better, for it accentuates the fact that this man is not at all who he claims to be.

Verse 7

The fifth aspect of this man's identity is revealed in v. 7. He in some ways serves at the court of a Roman proconsul, perhaps as a court astrologer,[186] a position commonly utilized by Roman dignitaries.[187] That he is considered worthy of a place at the court of an intelligent man like the proconsul says something positive about the abilities of Bar-Jesus.[188]

The proconsul himself is now introduced to the reader, a certain Sergius Paulus. Aside from filling out the details with regard to Bar-

---

[183] Cf. Bruce, *Acts*, p. 264 and Neil, *Acts*, p. 155. Arrington (*Acts*, p. 132) goes so far as to attribute his inspiration to demons. Similarly, Larkin (*Acts*, p. 194) calls him a court astrologer with demonic powers.
[184] Cf. the comments by S.R. Garrett, *The Demise of the Devil: Magic and the Demonic in Luke's Writings* (Minneapolis: Fortress, 1989), p. 81.
[185] Barrett, *Acts*, I, p. 613.
[186] Haenchen, *Acts*, p. 398; Stott, *Acts*, p. 219; and Larkin, *Acts*, p. 194.
[187] Cf. Neil, *Acts*, p. 155.
[188] So W.M. Ramsay, *The Bearing of Recent Discovery on the Trustworthiness of the New Testament* (London: Hodder and Stoughton, 1915), p. 135 and Jacquier, *Les Actes*, p. 384.

Jesus' identity, the introduction of Sergius Paulus is important in that this is Paul's first appearance before a Roman official,[189] a sign of things to come, and to this point in the narrative he is the highest ranking Roman to come into contact with the Gospel. The proconsul is described as a man of understanding (ἀνδρὶ συνετῷ), which is more likely to reflect positively on his desire to hear the gospel[190] than to be an indication that he was not 'taken in' by Bar-Jesus,[191] as Bar-Jesus served at his court.[192]

It seems that the reader is to understand that news of this missionary team's preaching came to the attention of Sergius Paulus, for inviting them he sought to hear the word of God. It may be just coincidence but the reader does not miss the fact that just as Barnabas and Saul had earlier been called (προσκέκλημαι) by the Holy Spirit to do this work (preach the word of God), they are now called (προσκαλεσάμενος) by one who wants to hear precisely that. In contrast to Herod who sought (ἐπιζητήσας) a messenger of the Gospel (Peter) in order to do that messenger harm (12.19), Sergius Paulus sought (ἐπεζήτησεν) messengers of the Gospel in order to hear the word of God. Thus, in this first encounter with a Roman authority, the reader finds a remarkable openness to the Gospel.[193] The word of God, of course, is that which has been preached in the Jewish synagogues (v. 5).

Verse 8
Opposition to this invitation is immediate, with the word ἀν-θίστατο standing first in the Greek sentence for emphasis. In fact,

[189] Rieu, *Acts*, p. 142.

[190] Haenchen, *Acts*, p. 398; Neil, *Acts*, p. 155; and Barrett, *Acts*, I, p. 613.

[191] Marshall, *Acts*, p. 219 and D. Williams, *Acts*, p. 226. Schneider (*Die Apostelgeschichte* II, p. 121) notes that this description of Segius contrasts him with the magician.

[192] There are at least two pieces of epigraphical evidence which indicate the existence of a Roman official by this name. The significance of these inscriptions for this text has been much debated. For a discussion cf. W.M. Ramsay, *The Bearing of Recent Discovery on the Trustworthiness of the New Testament*, pp. 150-72; Bruce, *Acts*, p. 264; B. Van Elderen, 'Some Archaeological Observations on Paul's First Missionary Journey', in *Apostolic History and the Gospel* (ed. W. Gasque and R.P. Martin; Paternoster Press, 1970), pp. 151- 61; Neil, *Acts*, p. 155; Marshall, *Acts*, p. 219; Johnson, *Acts*, p. 222; F.F. Bruce, 'Chronological Questions in the Acts of the Apostles', *BJRL* 68 (1986), pp. 279-80; and Barrett, *Acts*, I, p. 613.

[193] Johnson, *Acts*, p. 222.

the reader is not even told whether Barnabas and Saul make a presentation before it is countered perhaps point by point[194] by Elymas the magician. Although the narrative makes clear that Elymas and Bar-Jesus are to be understood as one and the same, there is a very unexpected introduction of a second name for the magician. There are numerous etymological debates as to the origin and meaning of the name Elymas, for Luke states that it is a translation /interpretation. It is unclear whether the translation/interpretation is from Bar-Jesus or μάγος. In fact, there is no consensus at all in this etymological debate.[195] Perhaps the best way forward on this point is to take μεθερμηνεύεται '... in a broad and non-technical sense ...' with the translation 'was understood to mean'.[196] However, in terms of the narrative itself, the reader would be struck by the fact that before this pericope concludes all five of the main characters will be people with two names: Barnabas – the Son of Encouragement (4.36), John Mark (12.25), Sergius Paulus (13.7), Bar-Jesus – Elymas (13.6-7), and Saul who is Paul (13.9). There may also be an intended contrast between the first person in the narrative with a 'translated name' (Barnabas) with the last person in the narrative with a 'translated name' (Bar-Jesus).

While the emphasis upon the opposition of Elymas is clear, it probably serves to heighten the reader's sense of anticipation for the narrative has revealed something that the character Elymas has no way of knowing. Jesus has earlier promised, 'For I will give to you a mouth and wisdom which they will not be able to oppose (ἀντιστῆναι) or your adversaries can speak against' (Lk. 21.15). This promise has already been fulfilled once in the narrative of Acts when none of Stephen's opponents were able to oppose (ἀντισ-

---

[194] Jacquier (*Les Actes*, p. 386) says the opposition was doctrine by doctrine.

[195] Among the suggestions are that Elymas: (1) comes from a semitic word meaning sage or skilful one, (cf. Jacquier, *Les Actes*, p. 386: Foakes-Jackson and Lake, *The Beginnings of Christianity Part I: The Acts of the Apostles*, IV, p. 144; Barclay, *Acts*, p. 100; Bruce, *Acts*, p. 264; D. Williams, *Acts*, p. 225; Stott, *Acts*, p. 219; and Larkin, *Acts*, p. 194 n.); (2) means dreamer or interpreter of dreams (cf. L. Yaure, 'Elymas – Nehelamite – Pethor', *JBL* 79 [1960], pp. 297-314; Schneider, *Die Apostelgeschichte*, II, p. 122; and Krodel, *Acts*, p. 229); (3) should be emended to read 'that pertinent fellow' (cf. F.C. Burkitt, 'The Interpretation of *Bar-Jesus*', *JTS* 4 [1903], pp. 127-29); (4) is simply a textual error (cf. C. Williams, *Acts*, p. 157 and Barrett, *Acts*, I, p. 615); (5) is too difficult to decide (cf. Carter and Earle, *Acts*, p. 179; Neil, *Acts*, p. 155; Arrington, *Acts*, p. 132; and Polhill, *Acts*, p. 293).

[196] Johnson, *Acts*, p. 223.

τῆναι) him, for he 'spoke with wisdom and with the Holy Spirit' (Acts 6.10). The reader, then, anticipates that the promise of Jesus will be fulfilled yet again.

The reason for Elymas' opposition becomes clear in the last portion of this verse: he is 'seeking to turn the proconsul from the faith'. In contrast to Sergius Paulus, who was seeking to hear the word of God, Elymas seeks to turn him away from it. Given its earlier Lukan uses (Lk. 9.41; 23.2), διαστρέψαι carries with it the sense of perverting something. Thus in his attempt to turn Sergius from the faith there is the hint that such an attempt involves perversion. While faith (πίστεως) here in some ways appears to be the equivalent to the Christian movement,[197] its nearest parallel being Acts 6.7,[198] this distinct aspect of meaning should not be pressed too far, for in v. 12 the reader is told that Segius believed or had faith (ἐπίστευσεν). It might be best then to take faith here as the equivalent of the Christian message.[199]

Verse 9

At this point Saul reappears. The reader learns two things about him in this verse. First, the reader discovers that, as everyone else in this pericope, Saul also has two names. Saul is also Paul. The name Saul, which has obvious links to Israel's first king, has been used to this point in the narrative to show his deep roots in Judaism.[200] From the reader's standpoint, there can be no question about his heritage, a point which receives additional attention later (Acts 22.3). For a different name to be introduced at this point coincides with Saul's transition into Gentile territory,[201] his first encounter with a Roman official (also named Paul),[202] and an occasion when he is filled with the Spirit in the face of a challenge to the word of God.[203] While it is possible that a name change accompanies a

---

[197] Johnson, *Acts*, p. 223.

[198] Haenchen, *Acts*, p. 399.

[199] Schneider, *Die Apostelgeschichte*, II, p. 121.

[200] Barrett, *Acts*, I, p. 616.

[201] Neil, *Acts*, p. 155; Marshall, *Acts*, p. 220; and Larkin, *Acts*, p. 195 n.

[202] D. Williams, *Acts*, p. 227. Cf. also G.A. Harrer's suggestion ('Saul Who Also Is Called Paul', *HTR* 33 [1940], pp. 19-34) that Saul received counsel from Sergius Paulus with regard to his future ministry in Asia Minor.

[203] Crowe, *Acts*, p. 98.

change in status,[204] it is difficult to believe that this is the case here, as everyone seems to have two names without a particular change in status implied. Second, the reader is also told that Saul is filled with the Holy Spirit. Especially in the light of the commissioning by the Holy Spirit in 13.2 and the empowerment by the Spirit for this journey (13.4), the reader is not surprised by the fact that Saul is filled with the Holy Spirit on this occasion. This is especially true in the light of Jesus' promise in Lk. 21.15. Despite the constant emphasis upon the Spirit's role, the reader is likely to take this comment as indicating a sudden filling of the Spirit reminiscent of Peter in 4.8,[205] perhaps indicating that he is a genuine prophet[206] in sharp contrast to Elymas. In addition, this note also prepares the reader for the description of Elymas in v. 10. In such a Spirit-filled state Saul fixes his eyes upon him. The verb ἀτενίζω, which appears often in Luke-Acts, conveys the sense of a riveted gaze and ordinarily alerts the reader that an extraordinary thing is about to happen (Lk. 4.20; 22.56; Acts 1.10; 3.4, 12; 6.15; 7.55; 10.4; 11.6; 14.9; 23.1). In this case it prepares the reader for Paul's seeing into the heart of Elymas.[207]

Verse 10

For the first time in this pericope the reader hears Paul speak. His words are marked by completeness (note the three uses of 'all')[208] and reveal the clear contrast between Elymas and Paul. In fact, Paul's words expose the difference between what Elymas claims and his true nature. As this man was introduced with a series of terms in rapid-fire succession, so is he exposed by Paul in the same rapid-fire style.

Paul, the one full of the Holy Spirit, reveals that Elymas is also full, but he is full of all guile and all unscrupulousness.[209] In the first charge Paul uses a term (δόλος) that in the Old Testament wisdom tradition is commonly used of the godless person who is deceit-

---

[204] So Garrett, 'Exodus from Bondage: Luke 9.31 and Acts 12.1-24', p. 85.
[205] Rackham, *Acts*, p. 201; and Winn, *Acts*, p. 80.
[206] Roloff, *Die Apostelgeschichte*, p. 199 and Johnson, *Acts*, p. 226.
[207] Rackham, *Acts*, p. 201; Haenchen, *Acts*, p. 403; Schneider, *Die Apostelgeschichte*, II, p. 122; and Pesch, *Die Apostelgeschichte*, II, p. 25.
[208] Jacquier (*Les Actes*, p. 387) observes, 'La triple répétition de l'adjectif, παντὸς … πάσης … πάσης est emphatique'.
[209] Rackham, *Acts*, p. 201 and Krodel, *Acts*, p. 229.

ful.[210] The modifier 'all' (παντὸς) suggests that for Paul there is
room for nothing which opposes guile in Elymas. Paul extends this
idea by identifying the other thing that filled Elymas, unscrupulousness. This term (ῥᾳδιουργία), which is found only here in the
Greek Bible, adds the idea of fraud.[211] Again, the accompanying
modifier (πάσης) conveys the idea that there is room for nothing
which opposes fraud in Elymas. Paul has begun with a contrast of
fullness; he now continues with an identification related to sonship.

While earlier in the text (v. 6) Elymas is named Bar-Jesus, Paul
now reveals that far from being a 'son of salvation' Elymas is in
reality a 'son of the Devil'.[212] Certainly it is possible to take this accusation to mean that opposition to the Gospel is to side with the
Devil.[213] However, the reader sees even more in this description of
Elymas as a son of the Devil. One of the ideas that the concept of
sonship conveys is that a son resembles the father, bearing many of
his traits. In opposing the word of God Elymas is acting precisely
as the Devil is said to act in Jesus' explanation of the Parable of the
Sower. In Lk. 8.11-12, Jesus explains,

> The seed is the word of God. Those along the path are those
> who hear, then the Devil comes and takes away the word from
> their heart, in order that not believing they might not be saved.

The reader would understand that Elymas' actions parallel those of
the Devil in the Parable of the Sower exactly. Therefore, the title,
'son of the Devil', fits perfectly.

Elymas is also called an enemy of all righteousness. To be an enemy of righteousness seems here to be one opposed to that which
is appropriate in terms of proper action,[214] the ethical dimension of
δικαιοσύνη being prominent.[215] Given the fact that righteousness is
that which God accepts (Acts 10.35) and that which characterizes
his own judgment (17.31), for Elymas to be revealed as an oppo-

---

210 L. Oberlinner, 'δόλος', *EDNT*, I, p. 344.

211 Barrett, *Acts*, I, p. 617.

212 Jacquier, *Les Actes*, p. 387; Bruce, *Acts*, p. 265; Rieu, *Acts*, p. 142; C. Williams, *Acts*, p. 157; Carter and Earle, *Acts*, p. 180; Neil, *Acts*, p. 155; Roloff, *Die
Apostelgeschichte*, p. 199; Johnson, *Acts*, p. 224; and Barrett, *Acts*, I, p. 617.

213 So Page, *Powers of Evil*, p. 131.

214 K. Kertelge, 'δικαιοσύνη', *EDNT*, I, p. 330.

215 Barrett, *Acts*, I, p. 617.

nent of righteousness indicates his true state and final fate. The reader who knows that Jesus has given all authority and power to his followers over their enemies (Lk. 10.19)[216] anticipates Paul's next move.

Verse 10 ends this barrage with a question, which makes a powerful statement. By attempting to turn (διαστρέψαι) Sergius from the faith (v. 8), Elymas has, in effect, made crooked (διαστρέφων) the straight ways of the Lord.[217] Perhaps this charge above all strikes at the heart of Elymas' role as a false prophet, for his actions are the opposite of those by a true prophet, John the Baptist, who in accord with the words of another prophet prepared the way of the Lord by making straight his path. In the final analysis, Elymas is diametrically opposed to God.

Verse 11

With language vaguely reminiscent of the LXX (Gen. 12.9), Paul moves from his discerning description of Elymas to a word of judgment for him. To this point in the narrative, the hand of the Lord has been a sign of divine blessing (Lk. 1.66; Acts 11.21). Therefore, for Paul to say that the hand of the Lord is upon Elymas, might at first not appear to fit with the reader's expectations with regard to Elymas' fate. However, the reader quickly discovers that the hand of the Lord can bless and curse, can heal and afflict.[218] In Elymas' case, divine judgment[219] comes in the form of temporary blindness. Given the previous account of Herod's death (not to mention Ananias and Sapphira!), it is perhaps striking that the magician's punishment is not more severe.[220] Rather than death, he is to experience blindness, like Paul. The reader, who is not told why the affliction is only 'for a time', must be content to think that

---

[216] Johnson, *Acts*, p. 224.

[217] While Barrett (*Acts* I, p. 617) may technically be correct in noting the differences between the two uses of the verb διαστρέφω, there is a clearly intended play on the terms with the latter building off the first.

[218] Rackham, *Acts*, p. 201.

[219] Bruce, *Acts*, p. 265; Munck, *Acts*, p. 119; and Packer, *Acts*, p. 103.

[220] Haenchen, *Acts*, p. 403.

perhaps this affliction will result in belief for Elymas, in a fashion not dissimilar to Paul's own experience.[221]

At once that which Paul speaks happens to Elymas. A mist and darkness fall upon him, a phrase that perhaps accurately describes both his physical condition and his spiritual situation.[222] Later in the narrative (Acts 26.18) darkness will be identified as the domain of Satan.[223] Now the one who earlier sought to turn Sergius away from the faith and claimed to have numerous powers must seek for someone to lead him by the hand in order to find his way.[224] This outcome of an opponent of the Gospel, then, is additional testimony for the folly of such a course of action.

Verse 12

The reader learns that when the proconsul saw this series of events he believed. The appearance of τότε at the beginning of the sentence makes explicit the connection between what he saw and his faith. Although there is no mention of Sergius' baptism, it is clear that the reader would understand Sergius' conversion to be genuine.[225] As for the fact that his baptism is not described, it should be remembered that not all the conversions described in Acts recount a subsequent baptism.[226] The amazement which Sergius expresses at

---

[221] Rackham, *Acts*, p. 201; E.R. Knox, *Acts*, p. 199; Foakes-Jackson, *Acts*, p. 112; Foakes-Jackson and Lake, *The Beginnings of Christianity Part I: The Acts of the Apostles*, IV, p. 146; Packer, *Acts*, p. 103; Neil, *Acts*, p. 156; Schneider, *Die Apostelgeschichte*, II, p. 123; Marshall, *Acts*, p. 219; Krodel, *Acts*, p. 230; and Barrett, *Acts*, I, p. 617. However, there are differences as well, for which cf. Garrett, *The Demise of the Devil*, p. 84.

[222] Polhill, *Acts*, p. 294.

[223] Garrett, *The Demise of the Devil*, p. 83.

[224] Garrett, *The Demise of the Devil*, p. 84.

[225] Jacquier, *Les Actes*, p. 389; Munck, *Acts*, p. 119; Packer, *Acts*, p. 103; Carter and Earle, *Acts*, p. 181; Haenchen, *Acts*, p. 400; Krodel, *Acts*, p. 230; Stott, *Acts*, p. 220; Polhill, *Acts*, p. 295; Barrett, *Acts*, I, p. 619; and Larkin, *Acts*, p. 192 n. On the basis of epigraphical information Ramsay argues that Sergius was converted (*The Bearing of Recent Discovery on the Trustworthiness of the New Testament*, pp. 150-72). Cf. also J. Foster ('Was Sergius Paulus Converted?: Acts xiii. 12', *ExpT* 60 [1948-49], pp. 354-55) who finds evidence for the historicity of Sergius' conversion in the fact that Julian the Apostate states that Cornelius and Sergius were the only men of standing to become Christians. For the view that Sergius was not converted cf. Rackham, *Acts*, p. 202; Rieu, *Acts*, p. 142; Blaiklock, *Acts*, p. 104; and Neil, *Acts*, p. 156.

[226] Jacquier, *Les Actes*, p. 389; C. Williams, *Acts*, p. 158; and Barrett, *Acts*, I, p. 619.

the teaching of the Lord is no doubt a response to both the miracle and the word, although the reader is probably to understand these holistically.[227] Thus, the results of this first missionary enterprise give evidence for the spread of the Gospel throughout the Roman world.

Conclusion

What is the contribution of a study of Acts 13.4-12 for this study on the Devil, disease, and deliverance? 1) Above everything else, this text gives yet additional support that the Lukan narratives are very comfortable attributing responsibility for the cause of affliction to God. In this case Paul, filled with the Holy Spirit, announces the punishment which comes as a result of the hand of the Lord. 2) In this passage, the punitive affliction is clearly the result of complete opposition on the part of Elymas to the word of God. 3) In addition to punishment for opposing the word of God, in some ways it appears that this affliction may also be redemptive in purpose: its temporary nature perhaps offering an opportunity for repentance and conversion on the order of Saul's. 4) When added to the stories of Zechariah, Ananias and Sapphira, and Herod, the account of Elymas underscores the fact that not all illness is attributable to the Devil.

Acts 14.8 – A Man Lame from Birth

Following this encounter with Sergius, Paul and those with him (the reader notes that Paul – no longer Saul – is regarded as the group's leader), sail to Perga on the south coast of Asia Minor. Making their way north to Antioch of Pisidia, their preaching in the synagogue results in the spread of the word of God throughout the region and opposition by the Jewish leaders who incite a persecution which cause their expulsion from the city. Shaking the dust off their feet, they go to Iconium filled with joy and with the Holy Spirit (13.13-52). Facing extraordinary hostility in Iconium, they preach boldly, performing many signs and wonders. A plot among the Gentiles

---

[227] D. Daube, *The New Testament and Rabbinic Judaism* (New York: Arno Press, 1973), p. 207. Krodel's comment (*Acts*, p. 231) that Sergius Paulus interpreted the miracle and this interpretation led him to faith does not bear a lot of resemblance to the verse itself.

and Jews to stone Paul and Barnabas is discovered, so they leave for Lystra and Derbe, continuing to preach the gospel (14.1-7). At this point occurs another text of significance for this enquiry.

> And there was a certain crippled man in Lystra, lame from his mother's womb, who had never been able to walk.

A couple of things are of particular interest in this verse. First, the reader is reminded of a similar situation in Acts 3.2 involving Peter and John and a man lame from his mother's womb. Whether or not there is an intentional parallel drawn between Peter and Paul at this point,[228] it will certainly not escape the reader's attention that Paul does the same miraculous works as did Jesus (Lk. 7.22) and Peter (Acts 3).[229] Second, the three-term description of the man's condition makes clear that his situation is congenital and beyond hope,[230] thus preparing the reader for the extraordinary miracle which follows.[231] Third, it is significant for this study that although the infirmity is described in considerable detail, the reader is given no indication as to the cause of the lame state. Absent is any reference to the Devil or demons. Luke seems to treat this affliction as neutral with regard to origin as it is unattributed.

Acts 19.11-12 – Handkerchiefs and Aprons of Paul

The next text of particular significance for this enquiry stands at a considerable distance from 14.8 in terms of the narrative. The reader learns a number of extraordinary things with regard to Paul's missionary activity. Two things perhaps bear special mention. The only healing account during this interval is that of the lame man in Acts 14, which causes such a stir that the people of Lystra take Paul and Barnabas to be the gods Hermes and Zeus. There is also one account of an exorcism. In Philippi, Paul and Barnabas are followed around by a young woman with a πνεῦμα πύθωνα, who kept shouting, 'These men are servants of the most high God, they are

---

[228] So C. Williams, *Acts*, p. 170; Crowe, *Acts*, p. 108; Stott, *Acts*, p. 230. For an opposing view cf. Munck, *Acts*, p. 131.

[229] Neil, *Acts*, p. 163 and Johnson, *Acts*, p. 247.

[230] Jacquier, *Les Actes*, p. 421; Foakes-Jackson, *Acts*, pp. 125-26; C. Williams, *Acts*, p. 170; Bruce, *Acts*, p. 290; and Barrett, *Acts*, I, p. 674.

[231] Carter and Earle, *Acts*, p. 195 and Haenchen, *Acts*, p. 430.

proclaiming to you the way of salvation'. One day Paul turns upon her and, speaking to the spirit, casts it out in the name of Jesus (Acts 16.16-18).

Upon arriving in Ephesus Paul discovers certain disciples who, like Apollos, know only the baptism of John. After hearing Paul they are baptized in the name of the Lord Jesus. When Paul lays hands upon them the Holy Spirit comes on them and they speak in tongues and prophesy (19.1-6). Paul's preaching activity, which begins in the synagogue, eventually moves to the lecture hall of Tyrannus and results in the word of God being heard by the Jews and Greeks who live in Asia.

> God did unusual deeds of power through the hands of Paul, so that even upon those who were sick were brought handkerchiefs and aprons which had touched him and the diseases departed from them, and the evil spirits came out.

Verse 11

The reader learns that accompanying the preaching of the word of God are extraordinary miracles. Nearly every aspect of v. 11 serves to underscore the remarkable nature of the events. First, the Greek sentence begins with the word δυνάμεις, a term that to this point in the Lukan narrative is used to describe the mighty works which Jesus (Lk. 10.13; 19.37; Acts 2.22), Stephen (Acts 6.8), and Philip (8.13) have performed. The appearance of this term indicates to the reader something of the powerful nature of Paul's ministry. Second, these mighty works are said to be unusual (οὐ τὰς τυχούσας).[232] In other words, although mighty works are unusual enough, the reader is told that Paul's (unusual) mighty deeds are unusually unusual. Third, it is clearly stated that God did these things, an observation that in some cases in Acts is merely assumed. Finally, these deeds are said to come through the hands of Paul. As observed earlier in Acts (5.12), the reader is likely to understand this phrase to mean that Paul is the channel through whom God does mighty acts. It may include the idea that Paul laid hands on those who were in

---

[232] G. Haufe ('τυγχάνω', *EDNT*, III, p. 372) observes that this meaning results from the adjectival use of the intransitive participle with negation. For a similar usage cf. Acts 28.2.

need,[233] but perhaps should not be limited to this means of healing alone, as v. 12 indicates. Nevertheless, the statement does convey the idea that Paul is especially used by God in this fashion.

Verse 12

However, this extraordinarily emphatic description of Paul's mighty works looks understated when it is compared to what is revealed in v. 12. Paul's mighty works were so extraordinary that (ὥστε καὶ) even pieces of cloth that touched his body were taken to the sick and demon possessed, and the diseases and evil spirits left. The reader learns that these clothes are the handkerchiefs (σουδάρια) and aprons (σιμικίνθια) a tent maker would normally use in the course of his or her work.[234] The powerful presence of God in Paul's ministry is so pervasive that direct contact is not any more required with him than with Jesus (Lk. 6.19; 8.44) or Peter (Acts 5.15-16).[235] Observations about the superstitious nature of such a practice[236] and questions about whether or not Paul gave his approval to this action[237] miss the point that for the reader these events indicate the powerful presence of God in Paul's ministry. When he comes up against illness or the work of demons the totality of God's victory is demonstrated.[238]

The expulsion of evil spirits accompanies the healing of the sick in this verse. It is not altogether clear whether or not the reader is to understand the healing of the sick and the expulsion of the evil spirits as two separate events. Although Luke can blur the lines between the two conditions, on this occasion, given the fact that two different infinitives are used to describe the results of diseases leav-

---

[233] For this interpretation cf. Foakes-Jackson and Lake, *The Beginnings of Christianity Part I: The Acts of the Apostles*, IV, p. 239; Barclay, *Acts*, p. 143; Haenchen, *Acts*, p. 561 n. 2; and Neil, *Acts*, p. 204.

[234] Cf. Bruce, *Acts*, p. 389. However, cf. T.J. Leary, 'The Aprons of St. Paul – Acts 19.12', *JTS* 41 (1990), pp. 527-29, for evidence that σιμικίνθια is a belt rather than a leather-worker's apron.

[235] Foakes-Jackson and Lake, *The Beginnings of Christianity Part I: The Acts of the Apostles*, IV, p. 240; Munck, *Acts*, p. 192; Packer, *Acts*, p. 161; Neil, *Acts*, p. 204-205; Crowe, *Acts*, p. 146; Tannehill, *The Narrative Unity of Luke-Acts A Literary Interpretation volume two: The Acts of the Apostles*, p. 237; and Johnson, *Acts*, p. 340.

[236] Rackham, *Acts*, p. 353; Foakes-Jackson, *Acts*, p. 179; Blaiklock, *Acts*, p. 156; Dunn, *Jesus and the Spirit*, p. 168; and Marshall, *Acts*, p. 310.

[237] E. Knox, *Acts*, p. 306 and D. Williams, *Acts*, p. 333.

[238] Garrett, *The Demise of the Devil*, p. 91.

ing and evil spirits going out, it would appear that Luke here has two distinct categories in mind.[239] Such is the extent of God's presence with Paul that exorcisms appear to be accomplished, not through direct contact with Paul, but by clothes which had contact with his skin.

Conclusion

Although it is possible to read Acts 19.11-12 as indicating a connection between illness and evil spirits, this text seems to make a distinction between the two. In that sense, it continues to indicate that not all illness is from the Devil and/or demons.

Acts 19.13-16 – The Sons of Sceva

The mention of the evil spirits in the previous verse provides a natural lead-in to the next story.

> And some of the wandering Jewish exorcists attempted to name the name of the Lord Jesus over those having evil spirits, saying, 'I command you by Jesus whom Paul preaches'. And there were seven sons of a certain Sceva, a Jewish high priest, doing this. And answering, the evil spirit said to them, 'I know Jesus and I know Paul, but who are you?' And the man, in whom the evil spirit was, jumped upon them, mastering them all he overpowered them, so that naked and wounded they fled out of that house.

Verse 13

Despite the fact that only two texts to this point in Acts testify of Paul's involvement with the expulsion of spirits, his reputation as an exorcist is apparently great enough to invite imitation. Although there is no mention of Paul's use of the name of Jesus in 19.11-12, the reader knows that in casting out a πνεῦμα πύθωνα from the girl in Philippi Paul had said, 'Παραγγέλλω σοι ἐν ὀνόματι Ἰησοῦ Χριστοῦ ἐξελθεῖν ἀπ' αὐτῆς'. In v. 13 the reader learns of the existence of Jewish exorcists who were seeking to imitate Paul by naming the name of Jesus in their exorcism rituals. The idea behind such a use is that the more powerful the name, the more suc-

---

[239] Jacquier, *Les Actes*, p. 573.

cessful the exorcism.[240] From the Lukan narratives there is no question about the power of the name of Jesus. This is the only occurrence of the word exorcist (ἐξορκιστής) in the entire New Testament. It does not seem to be a term of derision here, but rather another example of Paul's encounter with persons of 'power' in antiquity. The statement that there were some (τινες) exorcists implies that there were others as well.[241] In point of fact, the reader already knows of the existence of Jewish exorcists from Jesus' words in Lk. 11.19. Perhaps the reader is intended to pick up on the difference between Paul's use of Jesus' name and the exorcists' use of it by the different phrase used to describe their exorcistic formula. Instead of παραγγέλλω the exorcists say Ὁρκίζω.[242] Instead of 'Jesus Christ' the exorcists say 'Jesus'. There is clearly a dependence upon Paul in their words and an indirect knowledge of Jesus at best.[243]

Verse 14

The reader not only learns that there are some Jewish exorcists, but also is quickly introduced to specific Jewish exorcists who attempt to use the name of Jesus. Although the subject of v. 14 is the seven sons, the emphasis in the Greek sentence is upon a certain Sceva, a Jewish high priest. The reader can hardly avoid being struck by the sense of irony here present.[244] Throughout the narrative of Luke-Acts the role of the high priests has for the most part been that of adversaries to Jesus. In a surprising turn of events, the sons of a high priest (i.e. adversary) are now attempting to use a name that the high priests as a group have opposed. That Sceva is described as a high priest also heightens the reader's sense of expectation with regard to the abilities of these Jewish exorcists.[245] The fact that

---

[240] Bruce, *Acts*, p. 389.

[241] Garrett, *The Demise of the Devil*, p. 91 and Johnson, *Acts*, p. 340. Origen (*Contra Celsus* 1.6) states that demons have been exorcised even by bad (Jewish) men by use of the name of Jesus. Cf. also the discussion in Schneider, *Die Apostelgeschichte*, II, p. 269.

[242] Garrett (*The Demise of the Devil*, p. 92) notes that ὁρκίζω is never used by Jesus, but in extra-biblical texts it is used by demons. Jesus never uses this term, only the Sons of Sceva. Cf. also Roloff, *Die Apostelgeschichte*, p. 286.

[243] Cf. Tannehill, *The Narrative Unity of Luke-Acts A Literary Interpretation volume two: The Acts of the Apostles*, p. 237.

[244] Crowe, *Acts*, p. 146.

[245] B.A. Mastin, 'Scaeva the Chief Priest', *JTS* 27 (1976), p. 412.

there are seven sons also heightens the sense of expectancy.[246] It is perhaps worth observing that the reader is never told whether or not Sceva himself is present in Ephesus.[247]

Verse 15

Oddly, the scene develops, not with the words of the sons but with an answer from the evil spirit. That an answer is given indicates to the reader, along with v. 14, that the sons were making use of the same formula as that recorded in v. 13. This spirit, like those described in Lk. 4.34, 41 and 8.28, exhibits a (supernatural?) knowledge of Jesus and also of Paul.[248] The spirit also exhibits some wit.[249] The contrast between Jesus and Paul on the one hand and the would-be exorcists on the other is brought out by a μὲν ... δὲ construction. In the latter part of the sentence, emphasis is placed upon the sons both by the use of the personal pronoun ὑμεῖς and by the fact that this pronoun stands first in the clause. It is not enough that these would-be exorcists know the name; they must know Jesus, that is, be invested with his authority,[250] anointed by the Holy Spirit.

Verse 16

While the spirit in the man speaks, the man himself leaps upon the sons. The term ἐφαλόμενος appears only here in Luke-Acts, but three times in the LXX (1 Sam. 10.6; 11.6; 16.13), where all the references describe the Spirit of the Lord leaping upon an individual for empowerment.[251] Instead of the demon being subdued, as in a

---

[246] Conzelmann, *Acts*, p. 165. Foakes-Jackson [*Acts*, p. 179 n. 1] suggest that these were not Sceva's sons but members of a guild of exorcists.

[247] Attempts to explain the absence of Sceva's name in lists of high priests from that period include suggestions that Sceva: (1) is a purely legendary figure (Conzelmann, *Acts*, p. 164), (2) was high priest of the local (pagan) temple – in effect a renegade Jew (B.E. Taylor, 'Acts xix. 14', *ExpT* 57 [1945-46], p. 222 and though slightly different C. Williams, *Acts*, p. 222), (3) simply claimed to be a high priest for professional purposes (Bruce, *Acts*, p. 390; Rieu, *Acts*, p. 156; Neil, *Acts*, p. 205; and Polhill, *Acts*, p. 404), (4) was a priest serving at a local synagogue (Rackham, *Acts*, p. 35), (5) was a member of a high priestly family though not high priest himself (D. Williams, *Acts*, p. 333).

[248] Marshall, *Acts*, p. 311 and Page, *Powers of Evil*, p. 177.

[249] Rieu, *Acts*, p. 157.

[250] Garrett, *The Demise of the Devil*, p. 93.

[251] The irony of this situation should be obvious according to Johnson, *Acts*, p. 341.

successful exorcism, this spirit became all the more violent,[252] mastering (κατακυριεύσας) them all. It is not altogether clear to the reader whether the spirit attacked all seven of the sons or only two of them as the term ἀμφοτέρων, which appears here, ordinarily means 'both'. It is possible to take ἀμφοτέρων as having reference to Jesus and Paul, the last two names mentioned in the text, in the sense that the spirit mastered the sons' use of the two names.[253] However, since the term is also sometimes used in the sense of all,[254] the reader probably takes it to mean all seven of the sons were mastered. The result of this encounter is that the sons were left naked,[255] terribly beaten (cf. Lk. 20.12), and fled from the house as if to save their lives (cf. Lk. 21.36 and Acts 16.27). The reputation of the high priest's sons' power is left in rags, as it were.

Conclusion

The primary contribution of a reading of this text for the purposes of this enquiry is that here is an example of physical suffering that is the result of demonic activity, if only indirectly. While the text does not say that the evil spirit attacked the men, given the spirit's earlier words to the sons and the fact that one man, in whom the evil spirit was, overpowered seven others is an indication that the superhuman strength is evidence of demonic activity.

Acts 20.7-12 – Eutychus

Fear fell upon Jews and Greeks in Ephesus and the name of the Lord Jesus was held in high regard. In fact, numbers of those who believed brought numerous books of magic and burned them (19.17-20). As a result of so many conversions the silversmith, Demetrius, stirs up a riot against Paul and his associates. However, the city clerk intervenes to reason with the people of Ephesus. After he speaks the crowd breaks up (19.23-41). Eventually, Paul and some

---

[252] Neil, *Acts*, p. 205.

[253] For this view cf. C. Lattey, 'A Suggestion on Acts xix. 16', *ExpT* 36 (1924-25), pp. 381-82.

[254] H.G. Meecham, 'Acts 19.16', *ExpT* 36 (1924-25), p. 478.

[255] This detail may be designed to reflect on the haste of their departure; cf. Foakes-Jackson and Lake, *The Beginnings of Christianity Part I: The Acts of the Apostles*, IV, p. 242. According to Haenchen (*Acts*, p. 565 n. 6) they were clothed only in their undergarments.

of his companions travel to Troas (20.1-6), at which point occurs another text of some significance for this enquiry.

> And on the first day of the week when we gathered together to break bread, Paul spoke to us, since he was about to leave on the next day, he prolonged the word until past midnight. And there were many lamps in the upper room where we were gathered. And a certain lad named Eutychus was sitting upon the window, being overcome by a deep sleep as Paul continued to speak longer, overcome by sleep he fell from the third storey and was lifted up dead. Coming down Paul fell upon him and embracing him said, 'Do not be troubled, his life is in him'. And getting up and breaking bread and eating and preaching a little longer until daylight he departed. And they led the boy away alive, and they were comforted not a little.

Verse 7

After a seven-day stay at Troas, Paul and the others (note the use of 'we' by the narrator) are planning to leave on their way to Jerusalem. On the first day of the week the believing community of Troas assembles for a last time together with Paul. It is clear to the reader that the meeting is taking place on Sunday.[256] What is not so clear is whether the meeting is on Sunday by Jewish (Saturday night)[257] or Roman reckoning (Sunday night).[258] A Jewish reckoning would preserve the parallels with the resurrection.[259] However, it appears that elsewhere Luke uses the Roman reckoning[260] (Acts 3.1), and that would be what the reader would expect here. Part of the reason given for the gathering is 'to break bread'. While it is conceivable

---

[256] Rackham, *Acts*, p. 377; Knox, *Acts*, p. 322; Jacquier, *Les Actes*, p. 598; Foakes-Jackson and Lake, *The Beginnings of Christianity Part I: The Acts of the Apostles*, IV, p. 255; Bruce, *Acts*, p. 407; Winn, *Acts*, p. 111; Blaiklock, *Acts*, p. 164; H. Riesenfeld, 'Sabbat et Jour du Seigneur', in *New Testament Essays: Studies in Memory of Thomas Walter Manson* (ed. A.J.B. Higgins: Manchester: Manchester University Press, 1959), p. 211; Schneider, *Die Apostelgeschichte*, II, p. 285; Conzelmann, *Acts*, p. 169; and Arrington, *Acts*, pp. 207-208.

[257] Blunt, *Acts*, p. 230 and Rieu, *Acts*, p. 159.

[258] C. Williams, *Acts*, p. 230; Neil, *Acts*, p. 211; Marshall, *Acts*, pp. 325-26; Krodel, *Acts*, p. 378; D. Williams, *Acts*, p. 347; Stott, *Acts*, p. 319; and Polhill, *Acts*, p. 418.

[259] Cf. Rieu, *Acts*, p. 159.

[260] Marshall, *Acts*, pp. 325-26.

that the breaking of bread is a reference simply to a fellowship meal,[261] the reader knows that the breaking of bread to this point in the narrative has Eucharistic overtones. The verb or noun form of the Greek term has appeared at the last supper (Lk. 22.19), with the disciples on the Road to Emmaus (Lk. 24.30, 35), and in the earliest Christian gatherings (Acts 2.42, 46). It is hard to miss the connection between such meals in Luke-Acts. Consequently, the reader most likely takes κλάσαι ἄρτον here as a reference to the Lord's Supper.[262] Although it is apparent that Paul does a lot of the talking on this occasion, the term used to describe his speaking (δι-ελέγετο) often appears in contexts which involve some degree of dialogue (Acts 17.2, 17; 18.4, 19; 19.8, 9; 20.7, 9; 24.12, 25), and this idea may be included here as well.[263] Owing to his imminent departure (μέλλων ἐξιέναι τῇ ἐπαύριον), Paul speaks until past midnight. From its other appearances in the narrative (Lk. 11.5; Acts 16.25), μεσονυκτίου is understood by the reader as indicating an unusual time.

Verse 8

Two aspects of v. 8 are important to note. First, mention of the many lamps in the place confirm the just-learned detail that the meeting is going on until past midnight. At this point in the story the detail contributes little more than that. Attempts to see the reference as a response to accusations of the claim of immortality, which were often made against the church,[264] fail to convince both in terms of the narrative and by the fact that the date for most of these accusations is relatively late in comparison to the date of Luke-Acts. The idea of burning lamps, though not identical vocabulary, has already appeared in Luke (12.35) where the idea of

[261]Foakes-Jackson and Lake, *The Beginnings of Christianity Part I: The Acts of the Apostles*, IV, p. 256; and Blaiklock, *Acts*, p. 165.

[262] Calvin, *Acts*, II, p. 235; Stokes, *Acts*, II, p. 398; Rackham, *Acts*, p. 377; Blunt, *Acts*, p. 230; Foakes-Jackson, *Acts*, p. 187; Bruce, *Acts*, p. 408; Rieu, *Acts*, p. 159; Crowe, *Acts*, p. 152; D. Williams, *Acts*, p. 347; Arrington, *Acts*, p. 206; Stott, *Acts*, p. 319; Krodel, *Acts*, p. 377; Dupont, *Nouvelles Études sur les Acts des Apôtres*, p. 134; Polhill, *Acts*, p. 418; and Larkin, *Acts*, p. 289.

[263] Carter and Earle, *Acts*, p. 305.

[264] Blunt, *Acts*, p. 230; Packer, *Acts*, p. 169 and esp. Haenchen, *Acts*, p. 585.

readiness is emphasized.[265] If anything is to be made of such a similar idea, it may suggest that Paul's speech is one about readiness. Perhaps a bit closer to the mark is the idea that the lamps underscore the 'light' which is characteristic of the Christian community.[266] However, this detail may not be fully comprehensible until later in the narrative, where it may be seen as a contributing factor in Eutychus' slumber, owing to the heat and fumes such a number of lamps would emit.[267] The second aspect of this verse which merits comment regards the location of the meeting. It is in an upper room. It is interesting that both the contexts in which ὑπερῷον earlier appears contain references to the theme of death: that of Judas (Acts 1.13) and Dorcas (9.37, 39) in particular. Perhaps such a mention here alerts the reader to the 'death' that is to come in this passage.

Verse 9

At this point the reader learns of a young man[268] named Eutychus[269] who is sitting on the window opening. Perhaps this detail indicates that the crowd is large, so that people were sitting wherever they could,[270] or perhaps the reader understands this detail to be connected to the earlier comment about the many lamps. On this latter view, Eutychus is seeking some fresh air, owing to the heat and fumes of the lamps. Whatever the reason for his location, it soon becomes apparent that Eutychus is being overcome by sleep. What is the reader to make of the repetitive nature of the description of Eutychus' battle with sleep? It is, of course, possible to take the

[265] Tannehill, *The Narrative Unity of Luke-Acts A Literary Interpretation volume two: The Acts of the Apostles*, p. 249.
[266] Schneider, *Die Apostelgeschichte*, II, p. 286.
[267] Rackham, *Acts*, p. 380; Foakes-Jackson and Lake, *The Beginnings of Christianity Part I: The Acts of the Apostles*, IV, p. 256; Barclay, *Acts*, p. 149; Bruce, *Acts*, p. 408; C. Williams, *Acts*, p. 230; Carter and Earle, *Acts*, p. 306; Blaiklock, *Acts*, p. 165; Winn, *Acts*, p. 112; Neil, *Acts*, p. 211; Marshall, *Acts*, p. 326; D. Williams, *Acts*, p. 348; Conzelmann, *Acts*, p. 169; Arrington, *Acts*, p. 208; Stott, *Acts*, p. 320; Pesch, *Die Apostelgeschichte*, II, p. 191; Polhill, *Acts*, p. 419; Faw, *Acts*, p. 232; and Larkin, *Acts*, p. 290.
[268] Probably between the ages of eight and fourteen, so Marshall, *Acts*, p. 326; D. Williams, *Acts*, p. 348; and Stott, *Acts*, p. 320.
[269] As Johnson (*Acts*, p. 356) points out, it may simply be coincidental that Eutychus' name means 'lucky'.
[270] Carter and Earle, *Acts*, p. 306.

words of v. 9 as casting Eutychus in a bad light,[271] especially given the earlier negative connotations which sleep has in the Gospel (9.32; 22.45-46).[272] However, several things make such an interpretation unlikely. First, aside from the appearance of ὕπνος in Luke 9.32, the vocabulary in these passages is significantly different. Second, the idea of sleep does not always carry a negative meaning in the Gospel, as this action is also ascribed to Jesus (8.23). Third, rather than presenting Eutychus in an uncomplimentary fashion, the reader is led to be in some degree of sympathy with the character by the mention of the many lamps and the emphasis on the length of Paul's speech. The result of his deep sleep is that he falls from the third storey and is taken up dead. Although v. 10 is taken by some as somewhat ambiguous on this point, from v. 9 the reader can conclude nothing else but that the lad is dead.[273] Among other things, the description of Eutychus' death ties this upper room to the others mentioned previously in the narrative. The appearance of the passive ἤρθη underscores the fact that the lad is unable to raise himself.

Verse 10

Immediately, Paul comes down from the upper room and falls upon the boy and embraces him. This action, which is reminiscent of the actions of Elijah and Elisha in 1 Kgs 17.21 and 2 Kgs 4.34-35 respectively,[274] is similar to the actions of the father upon the return of the son in the Parable of the Lost Son (Lk. 15.20), where he falls upon his neck and embraces him. Calming those gathered together, Paul declares that the boy's life is in him. Although it is possible to

---

[271] So B. Trémel, 'A propos d'Actes 20,7-12: Puissance du thaumaturge ou du témoin?' *RTP* 112 (1980), p. 361.

[272] Tannehill, *The Narrative Unity of Luke-Acts A Literary Interpretation volume two: The Acts of the Apostles*, pp. 249-50.

[273] E.M. Knox, *Acts*, p. 323; Blaiklock, *Acts*, p. 165; Munck, *Acts*, p. 201; C. Williams, *Acts*, p. 230; Neil, *Acts*, p. 212; Marshall, *Acts*, p. 326; D. Williams, *Acts*, p. 348; Conzelmann, *Acts*, p. 169; Stott, *Acts*, p. 320; Polhill, *Acts*, p. 419; and Larkin, *Acts*, pp. 290-91 n.

[274] Rackham, *Acts*, p. 380; Jacquier, *Les Actes*, p. 600; Foakes-Jackson and Lake, *The Beginnings of Christianity Part I: The Acts of the Apostles*, IV, p. 257; Bruce, *Acts*, p. 408; C. Williams, *Acts*, p. 231; Munck, *Acts*, p. 200; Lampe, 'Miracles in the Acts of the Apostles', p. 178; Haenchen, *Acts*, p. 585; Neil, *Acts*, p. 212; Schneider, *Die Apostelgeschichte*, II, p. 287; Crowe, *Acts*, p. 152; Roloff, *Die Apostelgeschichte*, p. 298; Conzelmann, *Acts*, p. 169; Stott, *Acts*, p. 320; Polhill, *Acts*, p. 419; Faw, *Acts*, p. 232; and Larkin, *Acts*, p. 290.

take this statement to mean his life is still in him[275] or to leave open the question of his previous 'death',[276] the reader would have little reason not to take this as a resurrection.[277] In this event, Paul's actions once again parallel those of Jesus (Lk. 8.49-56) and Peter (Acts 9.39-41).[278]

Verses 11-12

Making his way back up to the meeting place, the (long-awaited) breaking of bread occurs. The meal which appears to at least include the Eucharist, resembles and in some ways functions as a farewell meal.[279] Having eaten, Paul continues his discussion (for this meaning of ὁμιλήσας cf. Lk. 24.14-15 and Acts 24.26) until daylight, at which point he departs. The boy is led home living, and they are greatly comforted.[280]

Conclusion

Although this text does not relate to this study as directly as some of the other passages which have been examined, it does serve to underscore the fact that some afflictions (even death!) are not attributed directly to God or the Devil. While it is possible to read this text in a fashion which suggests that Eutychus may be in spiritual danger, nothing in the text itself attributes his death to a particular agency. Other texts have made the point that death may be the result of divine judgment; this one presents the death of Eutychus as an unfortunate accident.

---

[275] D. Williams, *Acts*, p. 348.

[276] M. Dibelius, *Studies in the Acts of the Apostles* (tran. M. Ling and P. Schubert; ed. by H. Greevan; London: William Clowes and Sons, 1956), p. 18 and Dunn, *Jesus and the Spirit*, p. 165.

[277] Bruce, *Acts*, p. 408; Conzelmann, *Acts*, p. 169; Arrington, *Acts*, p. 288; Stott, *Acts*, p. 320; Krodel, *Acts*, p. 379; and Faw, *Acts*, p. 233.

[278] Crowe, *Acts*, p. 152.

[279] Tannehill, *The Narrative Unity of Luke-Acts A Literary Interpretation volume two: The Acts of the Apostles*, p. 251 and Faw, *Acts*, p. 232.

[280] It should perhaps be observed that there are a number of resemblances between this story and the Easter story. For the details cf. Johnson, *Acts*, p. 358 and Polhill, *Acts*, p. 419. Cf. also the discussion by Trémel ('A propos d'Actes 20,7-12: Puissance du thaumaturge ou du témoin?' p. 364), who interprets this story symbolically as having reference to the rupture between belief and unbelief and the prospect that members of the community of faith might fall from the sphere of light into darkness. However, the power of the word is sufficient to enable the transgressor to return to life.

Acts 28.1-6 – Paul's Snakebite on Malta

A final text which might have some bearing on this enquiry is found near the end of the Acts narrative.

> And having been brought safely through, we found that the island is called Malta. And the natives showed us unusual kindness, for lighting a fire they welcomed us all on account of the rain which had set in and the cold. And when Paul had gathered a bundle of sticks and put them upon the fire, a viper from the heat coming out fastened upon his hand. And as the natives saw the snake hanging from his hand, they were saying to one another, 'This man is certainly a murderer who, escaping from the sea, Dikē would not allow to live'. Therefore, shaking the snake off into the fire he suffered nothing bad. And they were expecting him to swell up or fall over dead. And after a long while they were expecting but nothing bad happened to him; changing their minds they were saying he is a god.

Verses 1-2

Chapter 28 continues the sea voyage portion of Luke's narrative. Through an angel, God revealed to Paul that no one would be lost in the shipwreck (27.23). Just as he was told, all arrived safely on the island of Malta, southwest of Sicily. The reception by the natives[281] of those from the ship, particularly Paul and his companions (upon whom the narrative focuses), was extraordinarily kind (παρεῖχον οὐ τὴν τυχοῦσαν φιλανθρωπίαν), including the provision of heat from a much needed fire.

Verses 3-4

In the process of gathering wood for the fire (the image of Paul as one who works hard with his own hands is very much in view), a viper is driven out of the sticks and attaches itself to Paul's hand. The natives who witness this event are certain Paul will soon die, meaning that the snake is poisonous, and they assume that he is guilty of an especially horrible crime (murder), for after surviving

---

[281] Given the kind reception it is hard to take βάρβαροι in any other way than native, i.e. non-Greek speaking. For this interpretation cf. Jacquier, *Les Actes*, p. 746; Barclay, *Acts*, p. 187; Blaiklock, *Acts*, p. 192; Neil, *Acts*, p. 253; Schneider, *Die Apostelgeschichte*, II, p. 401 n. 9; Marshall, *Acts*, p. 416; and Arrington, *Acts*, p. 264.

the ship wreck, he is now felled by a snake. In point of fact, the natives see in this event the hand of the divine; Dikē the goddess of justice, daughter of Zeus,[282] will not allow him to live.[283] Very clearly their assumption is that this snakebite is the result of divine punishment.

The reader is thus presented with a very interesting set of indicators. In one sense the natives are right about Paul being involved in murder, for the reader knows that Paul is guilty of breathing out murderous (φόνου) threats in his persecution of Christians (Acts 9.1). The reader is also well aware that God does sometimes inflict judgment, even death, upon those whom he deems deserving. So the natives' response is not a throw away for the reader, but rather an intriguing possibility, if only a fleeting one. But while there may be some element of truth in the natives' assumptions, the reader knows that they are not fully informed. For not only would it be exceedingly difficult for the reader to believe that the goddess Dikē would do the bidding of the God of Acts, but the reader also knows that Paul has earlier been instructed by the Lord that he must testify in Rome (Acts 23.11). Therefore, the reader, while interested in the response of the natives, knows something they do not and is prepared for the resolution of this aspect of the story.

But this leads to yet another interesting issue: would the reader regard the snakebite as an attack of an enemy in the light of Jesus' words in Lk. 10.18-19?[284] At the very least, one can say that the snakebite is viewed as yet another obstacle which threatens to keep Paul from offering his testimony in Rome. But perhaps in the natives' attribution of the bite to Dikē, the reader sees still another confrontation between the Christian faith and the 'powers' of its environment. On this view, Dikē is seeking to oppose the will of God, which earlier had been opposed by magicians, kings, silver-

---

[282] D. Williams, *Acts*, p. 413.

[283] There is a somewhat similar story found in the *Greek Anthology* 7.290. 'The shipwrecked mariner had escaped the whirlwind and the fury of the deadly sea, and as he was lying on the Libyan sand not far from the beach, deep in his last sleep, naked and exhausted by the unhappy wreck, a baneful viper slew him (ἔκτανε λυγρὸς ἔχις). Why did he struggle with the waves in vain, escaping then the fate that was his lot on the land?' Cited according to the translation of W.R. Paton, *The Greek Anthology*, II (London; Heinemann, 1917), p. 159. For the idea that Dike keeps watch even over the deep cf. 9.269.

[284] It is possible that this verse lies behind the origin of Mk 16.18.

smiths, Jewish authorities, etc. Consequently, the reader could very well see a more sinister opposition behind the bite of the snake.

Verses 5-6
The structure of these two verses is governed by a μὲν ... δὲ construction, where the reactions of Paul and the natives are contrasted. On the one hand, v. 5 reveals that far from being overly concerned, Paul merely shakes the snake off into the fire. On the other hand, in v. 6 the natives watch for symptoms of the deadly bite. None follow. The natives quickly reverse their earlier estimate of Paul. He is no murderer but a god. The similarity between this verse and the reaction to Paul and Barnabas in 14.11-13 is not lost on the reader.[285] Instead of dying, Paul lives. The hand of God is no doubt seen as preserving the life of Paul yet again in accordance with the words of Jesus.

Conclusion
The most significant implication of Acts 28.1-6 for this enquiry has to do with the question of how the snakebite is interpreted. If the bite is seen simply as an event that just takes place, then the text is more evidence that Luke is happy to leave some infirmities unattributed. However, a couple of indicators in the text suggest that in the snakebite the reader sees the activity of the Devil, at least implicitly. In this light, the text suggests that for those who follow a divine commission, even attacks which come from sinister forces cannot hamstring the work of God, the witness of the Gospel. This adds yet another dimension to Luke's overall view of the Devil, disease, and deliverance.

Conclusions and Implications

There are a number of conclusions and implications of this reading of Acts for the broader purposes of the present enquiry.

1) In a way quite different from the other New Testament narratives, Luke is not reluctant in Acts to attribute death to the hand of God. At least three deaths in the narrative are viewed as the direct action of God: that of Ananias, Sapphira, and Herod. The closest New Testament parallel to these activities may be found in 1 Cor.

---

[285] Munck, *Acts*, p. 255.

11.30, where it is said that some have fallen asleep because they have abused the Lord's table.

2) Acts continues the idea that infirmity can also come from the hand of God. Given that the first infirmity recorded in the Gospel is such an affliction, such attributions in Acts are not surprising. Both Saul and Elymas are made blind as a result of an encounter with God and/or his servant. Interestingly, Paul is involved in both cases.

3) The reasons for afflictions sent by God include an attempt to counterfeit the activity of the Holy Spirit (Ananias and Sapphira), opposition to the Gospel (Herod, Elymas, and Saul?), and redemption (Saul).

4) When an infirmity is sent by God for redemptive purposes, it is sometimes removed by prayer. On such an occasion the result is immediate.

5) Those afflicted by God in one way or another can be within the believing community.

6) Such events can produce a holy fear, both inside and outside the believing community, and thereby serve to caution the reader with regard to his or her own conduct.

7) Although there is often a rather clear line of demarcation drawn between demonic activity and physical infirmity (Acts 8.4-8; 19.11-12) in ways not unlike that found in the Gospel, the lines are a bit more blurred between these two categories in Acts than in other New Testament documents. In the case of Acts, the idea that the Devil and/or demons cause infirmities must be deduced.

8) However, aside from some occasional summary statements that treat demonic activity and physical infirmity together, it is rather significant that there is no concrete example in all of Acts where an illness is attributed directly to demonic activity. In this, Acts is quite different from Luke's Gospel.

9) On at least one occasion, healing language is used to describe the results of exorcism (5.16), indicating some degree of continuity with the Gospel on this point.

10) Healings and exorcisms are attributed to the power of God as it comes upon both Peter (5.12-16) and Paul (19.11-12) in ways reminiscent of the Lukan description of Jesus.

11) There is an instance of suffering indirectly being ascribed to an evil spirit on one occasion in Acts. A man in whom there was an

unclean spirit is said to have overpowered the sons of Sceva, beating them severely. Nothing quite like this observation has been seen to this point in the study.

12) In the passage which describes Paul's snake bite on Malta, there is at least an allusion to an attack by sinister forces upon an agent of God. On this reading, God stymies the attempt on the life of Paul in a way that fulfills the words of Jesus spoken in the Gospel.

13) In addition to afflictions which result from divine and demonic origins, there appears in Acts to be a category of infirmities and/or death that are unattributed appearing to result from neutral or natural causes. In this way too, Acts stands in continuity with the Gospel.

14) Although not as pronounced as in the Gospel, discernment appears to be the basis for some of the distinctions between natural infirmities, demonic afflictions, and the activity of God. Such discernment is exhibited by Luke, but perhaps as well by those within the narrative (Peter, Philip, and Paul), underscoring the need for such practice among the community of readers.

8

TOWARD A NEW TESTAMENT THEOLOGY OF THE DEVIL, DISEASE, AND DELIVERANCE

This investigation has sought to discover New Testament thinking and attitudes about origins of illness by examining the various New Testament writings on their own terms. By proceeding in this fashion, this study has attempted to allow the different New Testament voices to be heard in all their variety and diversity. Consequently, to this point there has been no attempt to read one writer in the light of another with only occasional references to the differences and similarities that exist. However, at this juncture the question arises as to the feasibility of placing the various voices into dialogue with one another in order to push toward the possible construction of a New Testament theology of the Devil, disease, and deliverance.

It is, of course, possible to take a minimalist approach to this issue. In such a case the enquiry is complete with the examination of the last set of New Testament writings. On this view the most one can hope for is a better understanding of the distinctive voices contained in the New Testament. To go farther is to violate the integrity of the documents themselves, which were not necessarily written with an eye on the others, with the possible exception of the Synoptics and perhaps James and Paul. In the instances where such is the case, part of the purpose may very well have been to correct rather than to confirm.

However, at least two things suggest that pushing beyond a hearing of the various voices is not an altogether illegitimate enterprise. First, even for those who might be called minimalists, there is an acknowledgment of an essential unity of thought in the New Testament as a whole even if it be ever so slight.[1] In the case of the origins of illness, this examination has revealed that on a number of issues there is a fair amount of overlap of thought. In other words, this examination suggests that a certain unity of thought does exist on this issue in the New Testament itself. Second, although to push in this direction may go beyond what some New Testament writers would have themselves envisioned, the fact that these documents are part of the New Testament canon and as a result have been and continue to be read within that broader context suggests that such an interpretive move is not inappropriate but may be a necessary one.[2] Therefore, despite the risk of leaving some readers behind at this point, this enquiry continues with the attempt to draw upon the various New Testament voices in working toward a New Testament theology of the Devil, disease, and deliverance.

Origins of Illness in NT Thought

The foregoing examination of relevant texts reveals that the New Testament identifies three primary causes of illness and/or infirmities: God, the Devil and/or demons, and what might most appropriately be called unattributed causes. This section attempts to construct a tentative New Testament theology on the origins of illness based on the readings of the pertinent New Testament texts in the previous chapters.

God as Source of Infirmity and/or Death

One of the points on which there is a great deal of agreement in the New Testament materials is that God is often attributed a role in the origins of illness. In fact, God is described as the direct or indirect source of infirmity by the majority of writers examined, the lone exceptions being Mark and Matthew. Generally speaking, the New Testament writers show little of the reluctance many modern students of the New Testament exhibit in assigning to God an active role in the affliction of individuals with disease and/or death.

---

[1] For example, cf. J.D.G. Dunn, *Unity and Diversity in the New Testament* (London: SCM Press, 1990), pp. 369-88.

[2] On this approach cf. esp. J. Goldingay, *Theological Diversity and the Authority of the Old Testament* (Grand Rapids: Eerdmans, 1987). Cf. also J. Reumann, *Variety and Unity in New Testament Thought* (Oxford: Oxford University Press, 1991).

God's involvement in the origins of illness is not presented in a monolithic fashion but as multi-faceted. Specifically, infirmity and/or death can be used by God as a pedagogical device, an instrument of punishment, a source of sanctification, as a means of spreading the Gospel, or as an instrument of salvation. Each of these dimensions is explored briefly.

Infirmity and Death as Pedagogical Device

On more than one occasion and by more than one writer, God is described as sending an illness or death in an attempt to teach those identified as part of the Christian community that sin must not be tolerated but dealt with in an appropriate manner. On such occasions the affliction appears as God's way of calling the believers' attention to their sin. In these situations it is clear that a causal relationship exists between sin and affliction. However, unlike later theological reflection on the subject, there is no suggestion in these texts that the affliction is inherent in the sin. Rather, it is either implied or stated explicitly that the affliction comes directly from God himself as a result of the sin. For both James and Paul, in cases where God is the origin of an affliction the purpose is to draw the attention of the individual or community to the sin in question and the need for repentance. While James does not indicate the precise nature of the sin which results in illness, other writers disclose the reason for the affliction. Paul makes clear in 1 Corinthians 11 that abuses at the Lord's table have resulted not only in illness but even death. Luke's description of Zechariah's mute condition is attributed to the unbelief he exhibits in response to the divine promise spoken by the angel Gabriel. Each passage implies that discernment on the part of the individuals and/or the community involved would result in avoidance of such culpable behavior. Consequently, had such discernments taken place these afflictions would not have occurred in the first place. In James 5 removal of such afflictions is assured by a combination of confession and intercessory prayer. The communal dimension is evident in at least the Jaocbian and Pauline texts.

On one occasion an affliction sent by God plays some role in the salvation of an individual. In the well known story of Saul's conversion, the encounter with the risen Christ leaves Saul blind, evidenced by the fact that the former persecutor of the church must now be led by the hand in order to find his way (Acts 9.8-9). While it could be argued that the blind condition was simply a by-product of the brilliance of the Christophany, as noted earlier it would be odd indeed for the reader not to see the hand of God actively at work in this event. The blindness serves to provide Saul with a sufficiently solitary experience in which the significance of his encounter with Jesus might be adequately pondered. In that sense it might be appropriate to describe this affliction as a pedagogical tool by which Saul is brought to faith.

Infirmity and Death as Punishment

Closely related to the idea of affliction as pedagogical device is that of affliction as punishment by God. In cases where illness or death are the result of divine punishment, they are said to have resulted in relation to a variety of reasons. John 5.14 indicates that the infirmity of the man at the pool of Bethesda is the result of sin and that the continuation of sin might result in a worse physical calamity. While Jesus' warning about 'something worse' might serve a pedagogical function, there is no suggestion that the previous infirmity played such a role. On this occasion, the nature of the man's sin is not disclosed. The Book of Acts tells of three deaths attributed to the hand of God. The first two deaths are the result of attempts to counterfeit the work of the Holy Spirit within the early Christian community (Acts 5.1-11). Such punishment is all the more significant because it comes to those within the believing community, Ananias and Sapphira. In this passage the only pedagogical value comes through the fear in the community and beyond – fear evoked from knowledge of their deaths. God's hand of judgment is certain.

Opposition to the Gospel also can result in divine punishment. Both Herod (Acts 12.19b-23), who is killed by the Angel of the Lord, and Elymas the magician (Acts 13.6-12) are smitten by God. In the case of Herod, the affliction primarily functions as a punitive act, while Elymas' blindness may carry with it the hope of salvation for the magician, as Paul's own blindness serves as a catalyst in his move toward faith in Jesus. It may be significant that most of the examples of God's punitive acts occur in the book of Acts.

Affliction and the Spread of the Gospel

God is presented not only as one who sends affliction as a teaching or punitive device, but also as one who can use affliction to further the spread of the Gospel. Two New Testament texts present God as using infirmity in precisely this manner. Both the blind man in John 9 and Paul, who suffers from a weakness in the flesh in Galatians 4, experience infirmity in order that God might accomplish his purpose through the revelation of his message. With the blind man the reader is told that this condition exists in order that the works of God might be revealed. Such a statement is a response to the disciples' question about the origin of the man's condition and at the same time a sign that such an action on God's behalf is not viewed as something distasteful by John. Clearly this statement conveys the sense that God may send (or use) affliction to suit his purpose, in this case the manifestation of his works, in order to generate the faith that leads to eternal life. In similar fashion, Paul's illness described in Galatians 4 results in the preaching of the Gospel to the Galatians. This illness, which could have proven to be a stumbling block or obstacle to the Galatians, turns out to be the very occasion for them to hear the message of salvation about Jesus Christ. The implication is that God's hand can be seen even in this illness, for it serves his ultimate purpose.

Affliction and Sanctification

A final category of affliction attributed to God concerns Paul's thorn in the flesh (2 Cor. 12.7-10). If, as suggested earlier, the thorn is understood to be a physical ailment rather than a reference to Paul's opponents, it becomes a clear reference to God's use of affliction to work his purpose in the life of his servant. Specifically, Paul explains that the thorn, which comes from a messenger of Satan, is for his ultimate good. Despite Paul's petitions for it to be removed, the thorn is an instrument of sanctification in Paul's life, as it is designed to keep Paul from being conceited, owing to the greatness of the revelations disclosed to him. In this case, then, an infirmity, even one which has Satanic connections, can be sent by God and used by him to accomplish his desire in his messenger.

Conclusion

Far from being viewed simply as a source of healing, God, in the view of most of the New Testament writers consulted in this investigation, can be depicted as the origin of infirmity or death. When he is described in such a way there always seem to be specific reasons for his actions. Thus, God is seen to be sovereign, one who may act in ways that will achieve his will, a God who is to be approached with a (holy) fear. Such evidence suggests that the New Testament writers did not always attribute infirmity to Satan, but worked with a more dialectical world-view - a world where God could also afflict. Such an understanding suggests that God is not only able to use suffering indirectly to accomplish his purposes, but he can also take a direct role in this activity.

The Devil and/or Demons as Source of Infirmity

It comes as little surprise that several New Testament writers attribute infirmity to the Devil and/or his demons. What is somewhat unexpected is that not all writers make such attributions, and some who do offer fewer examples than one might be led to expect. While there is a certain amount of diversity in views on the role of the Devil and demons in the sending of affliction, one might attempt to put the evidence together in the following manner.

The Nature of the Evidence

The attribution of infirmity to the Devil or demons is primarily confined to three New Testament documents, Matthew and Luke-Acts. Neither James nor John give any hint that the Devil or demons have a role to play in the infliction of infirmity. In Paul, where there appears to be one attribution, the thorn in the flesh, it is perhaps not insignificant that, despite the close connection between the thorn and the messenger of Satan, God is identified as the ultimate origin of the thorn. The only other attribution of an infirmity to a demon, outside Matthew and Luke-Acts, is found in Mark 9, where a demon-possessed boy is afflicted by a 'dumb' spirit which, among other things, seeks to kill him. While this text is similar to some of those found in the other Synoptic Gospels, it is at least noteworthy that Mark does not make such a connection clear in other places where its synoptic counterparts do.

The Relationship of Demon Possession to Infirmity

There are numerous accounts in the New Testament of demon possession as a malady. The victims of demon possession are described as being dominated by the demon or unclean spirit to the extent that they lose the ability to control or perform normal bodily functions. At times, the convulsions and other body or motor responses prove to be so violent and uncontrollable that they place both the victims and those near them in danger of physical harm.

In contrast to claims made both at the scholarly and popular levels, the New Testament writers generally make a clear distinction between demon possession and illness. For example, Mark is very careful to keep the lines of demarcation between the categories distinct, with Mark 9 being the only occasion where demon possession and infirmity converge. This cautious approach, along with the attribution of several infirmities to God and the fact that many accounts of healing in the Synoptics give no hint as to the origin of the infirmity (let alone attribute the illness to a demon), suggests that for the New Testament writers there was no simple equation between infirmity and the demonic. To make such a dubious equation the starting point for an explanation of the origins of illness in the New Testament errs methodologically by not paying sufficient attention to the New Testament documents themselves. On such a view, pride of place is given to a worldview or Sitz-im-Leben constructed from evidence outside the New Testament itself, against which the New Testament documents are then read. The result is a reading predetermined by the 'historical' construct. Unfortunately, when such an approach is taken, the New Testament documents are not heard on their own terms but often are forced to fit the construct, thus denying a hearing to the distinctive thought of the New Testament writers.

In addition to the numerous cases of demon possession in which infirmity does not play a role, there are a number of occasions in the Synoptics and Acts in which infirmities of various kinds are attributed to demon possession. These maladies include deafness, muteness, blindness, and epilepsy. It may not be insignificant that some of these very same infirmities also appear in contexts with no connection to demonic activity. A reading of the New Testament texts reveals that, while not all demon possession is directly related to infirmity, there is a connection at several places in Matthew and Luke in particular. In these accounts, it is evident that there would be no infirmity if not for the demon possession. On occasions such as these, the remedy for the malady is brought through exorcism. In this regard, it should be observed that Mark 9 suggests the existence of different classes of demons, some of whom are more difficult to exorcise than others.

Although careful to distinguish between demon possession and illness, Matthew seems to regard certain forms of demon possession as a category of illness, in that he lists demon possession alongside epilepsy and paralysis as major infirmities which Jesus healed (Mt. 4.24). As such, Matthew occasionally uses healing language where one might expect the vocabulary of exorcism. Luke blurs the lines of demarcation further, not only failing to distinguish between demon possession and infirmity but also leaving the reader unable to be as certain about the origins of illness as do other New Testament writers. However, it is interesting that in Acts, while the lines continue to be occasionally blurred in summary statements, there is not a single concrete example of an illness being directly attributed to demonic activity.

However the evidence is read, there can be little disagreement about the fact that the Synoptics and Acts regard a number of infirmities as being the direct result of demon possession.

Demonic Affliction Distinct from Demon Possession

In addition to the attribution of infirmity to demon possession there are also two or three occasions where an infirmity is attributed to demonic activity without any suggestion that the afflicted person is under the (complete) control of the unclean spirit or is regarded as demon possessed. These specific cases include Paul's thorn in the flesh (which is identified with a messenger from Satan), Luke's account of Simon's mother-in-law, and Luke's account of the woman with a spirit of infirmity. In each of these accounts the individual sufferer is afflicted by a spirit but the signs of demon possession are absent. In fact, aside from the affliction, there is nothing in the texts to suggest that the reader is to view the sufferer in anything but a positive light. Thus the reader is led to the conclusion that there is a category of demonically inflicted infirmity separate from demon possession proper. Individuals who suffer in this way are not described as being in need of exorcism (or deliverance) as much as healing, which would involve the removal of the cause of the affliction.

In the case of the woman with a spirit of infirmity Jesus simply pronounces her well, laying his hands upon her, and she immediately straightens up (Lk. 13.10-16). When encountering Simon's mother-in-law (Lk. 4.38-39), he rebukes the fever and it leaves. If the fever is to be viewed as demonically induced (as appears likely), it is significant that Jesus does not engage the demon in conversation, as he had done in the previous pericope, but simply rebukes it. That the remedy in cases such as these is not as clear cut as in those of demon possession is demonstrated by the case of Paul whose petitions for the thorn's removal are met with a revelation that the thorn is there to stay; the messenger of Satan will continue his work, for in this messenger, God is himself working on Paul's behalf. Thus, the New Testament knows of a category of demonic activity separate from demon possession in which individuals who appear to be in a positive relationship with God suffer infirmity.

Attack by Sinister Forces

A final observation should be offered before concluding this section. There is some evidence within the New Testament that a messenger of God could be attacked by sinister forces in an attempt to thwart the preaching of the Gospel. The place in the Acts narrative which describes Paul's snakebite on Malta (28.1-6) suggests that the reader of Acts would see more than coincidence in this event, especially given the previous promises by Jesus about the protection and authority of his followers who encounter all manner of opposition. Despite this attack, God's messenger is preserved from harm in order to complete the mission to which he is called.

Infirmity and Unattributed Causes

A number of infirmities in the New Testament might best be described as owing their origin to neutral or natural causes. This observation is based on several facts. First, the vast majority of NT references to infirmities do not give any indication as to the origin of the particular malady in question. Such references occur in every New Testament writing surveyed in this investigation. While it is theoretically possible to attribute all these infirmities to the Devil, or a world estranged from God, or the effects of sin in the world, etc., the texts themselves do not explicitly offer support for such a view. In point of fact, despite the frequent appearance of such views in contemporary theological explanations of the origins of illness, it is interesting that in New Testament discussions about the origins of illness the writers never explain the presence of infirmity as being simply the result of living in a fallen sinful world. Second, on more than one occasion it is explicitly stated that sin is not the cause of certain infirmities (cf. esp. John 9 and James 5). James 5 leaves open the prospect of the origin of illnesses which are not the result of sin. Third, in two Lukan texts (13.1-3, 4-5) Jesus makes clear that calamities are not necessarily a gauge of one's spirituality. Fourth, in discussing Paul's co-workers who are ill (Phil. 2.25-30; 1 Tim. 5.23; 2 Tim. 4.20), the Pauline literature never suggests that there is anything sinister behind their condition. This attitude suggests that Paul regards such illness in a somewhat neutral fashion. Therefore, it is fair to say that certain, if not the majority of, infirmities are treated by New Testament writers as somewhat neutral in terms of origin.

Responses to Illness

Given the various origins of and purposes for infirmity in the New Testament, it comes as no surprise that responses to illness take a variety of forms. However, here too one finds a significant amount of overlap in the responses to infirmity as recounted in the New Testament writings examined. This portion of chapter eight is devoted to a presentation of the various New Testament responses to infirmity based upon the previous reading of the relevant texts.

Prayer

One of the more common responses to infirmity in the New Testament is prayer. Not only does the evidence of James 5 indicate that prayer plays an integral role in the healing of the sick, but Paul's practice in 2 Corinthians 12 also indicates that prayer may have been his own habit in the face of infirmity. In fact, the evidence from this latter passage suggests that it may have been Paul's habit to continue in prayer about a specific infirmity until either healing occurred or one 'heard from God' (as Paul says that he did) that the malady is not to be removed but is to serve a purpose in keeping with the divine will. It may not be going too far to suspect that prayer had a place in the ministry of those with the gifts of healings and perhaps accompanied the practice of the laying on of hands. Mark 9 indicates (as does much of the Marcan narrative) that prayer plays a crucial role in the casting out of demons, as the disciples are there told that 'this kind of demon' comes out only by prayer. The idea of prayer in the face of infirmity is also found in

Luke-Acts. Thus, it is fair to say that part of the New Testament response to infirmity ordinarily includes some form of prayer.

Discernment

Given the diverse origins of infirmity and the fact that the same malady may be attributed to as many as three separate causes respectively on different occasions in the New Testament, it is clear that discernment plays a crucial role in the process of responding to infirmity. This point may be illustrated by the two attested categories: 1) infirmity that results from sin and 2) infirmity that results from demon possession.

In cases of sin as the cause of an illness several things are said. a) James 5 seems to assume that when sin is the cause of an illness such a sin would be readily known to the individual sufferer. This same assumption appears to be present in Jn 5.14, where Jesus warns the recently healed man to 'stop sinning lest something worse come upon you'. b) At least one text reveals the role of the community in the discernment of sin. Paul's admonition to the Corinthians with regard to the illness and death in the community (1 Corinthians 11) shows that members of the community should be active in discerning the reason for the presence of such in the church. If they had discerned (judged) themselves, the Corinthians would not have come under the judgment of the Lord as they had. It is not clear whether Paul's words apply to individual as well as corporate conduct, although it is difficult to distinguish between the two on this occasion. The discernment advocated in this text might well have been expected to come from those in the community with the gift of discernment. c) Several texts testify to the fact that a vital role in the discernment process is played by leaders in the community. Of course, one of the primary examples of such discernment is the role played by Jesus. He is not only able to detect when the presence of sin is behind an infirmity (Jn 5.14) but he is also able to discern when this is not the case (Jn 9.3; Lk. 13.1-5). In addition to Paul's ability in this regard, mentioned earlier, Peter also detects (through the Holy Spirit) the presence of sin among those in the community when he prophesies judgment upon Ananias and Sapphira in Acts 5. From the reader's vantage point, another leader – the narrator of Luke's Gospel – displays the ability to discern the presence of sin in the account of Zechariah's unbelief and resulting punishment.

In the discernment of demonic activity standing behind an infirmity, the New Testament discloses two primary categories. a) Demon possession seems to be readily identifiable by most anyone close to the individual so afflicted. This observation is based on the comments made by the father of the demon-possessed boy in Mark 9, the mother of the demon-possessed girl in Matthew 15, and the actions of those who bring to Jesus demon-possessed individuals who suffer infirmities owing to the presence of demons (cf. esp. Mt. 9.32; 12.23). b) In addition to discernment of this more general nature, the New Testament also testifies to the ability to discern the presence of demonic activity behind an infirmity which might not otherwise be known. Such appears to be the case with Paul's knowledge of the Satanic nature of his thorn, as well as Jesus' disclosure about Satan's role (through a spirit of infirmity) in the affliction of a woman who for eighteen years had not been able to stand up straight (Lk. 13.11, 16). To these examples might be added the narrators who often inform the readers as to which infirmities are from demonic sources and which are from other sources.

While other observations could be made with regard to this topic, these examples are enough to indicate that discernment is extraordinarily important in the New Testament responses to infirmity. Given the various references to the practice of discernment in the New Testament, it is probably safe to assume that the practice of discernment within the various New Testament communities was informed by the examples contained in the narratives and letters examined. In other words, it is likely that the New Testament communities implied by these documents made similar distinctions with regard to origins of infirmity.

Confession and Intercession

When sin stands behind an infirmity in the New Testament, one of the responses called for is confession. Although implied in other texts, this response is made explicit in James 5. In this text, when it is determined that sin is the cause of an illness, those individuals are called upon to confess their sin. This confession is to be made to one another (other members of the community) for the express purpose of intercession. The implication of this admonition is that such confession is to result in forgiveness and healing. In fact, it is probably fair to say that when sin is viewed as the cause of an illness, confession would normally be thought to end in healing.

It is significant that confession does not stand alone in James 5 but is to be accompanied by intercession. Intercessory prayer is described as efficacious and has roots deep in the New Testament spirituality, which is filled with admonitions which presuppose mutual accountability among believers as a given in the early Christian world view. Of course, it almost goes without saying that intercession is not possible without confession.

Exorcism

When an infirmity is the result of demon possession, the only response found in the New Testament texts examined here is exorcism. It is perhaps significant that the exorcisms examined in this study are performed only upon those 'outside' the believing community.[3] There is no account of an exorcism within the church itself. The picture of Paul that emerges from the letters which bear his name and from the book of Acts illustrates this point. In the letters Paul never makes reference to exorcism, while in Acts exorcisms are attributed to him. While it is possible to explain this situation as simply the difference between Luke's Paul and the Paul of the Pauline literature, it may also be that the context determines the content. That is to say, perhaps there is no mention of exorcism in the letters because there is no evidence that exorcisms occurred inside the believing community, while Luke's account of Paul focuses on Paul's missionary activity outside the believing community where exorcisms are said to have taken place. This observation may be supplemented by the fact that there is no mention of exorcisms in the New Testament outside the Synoptics and Acts. Such evidence might suggest that in New Testament thought exorcism occurred solely in a missionary or evangelistic context.

The nearest New Testament analogies to the occurrence of an exorcism inside the community of faith are found in that category of infirmity caused by demons but distinct from demon possession proper. In these few cases it is true that the affliction is attributed to Satan or a demon, but there are significant differences as well. Only in the story of Simon's mother-in-law is there anything remotely resembling an exorcism and there the resemblance is simply the rebuke of the fever and its departure. In the case of the woman in

---

[3] By 'believing community' I mean those whom the early Christians themselves would have viewed as being in a right relationship with God.

Luke 13, the condition (aside from its description as a spirit of infirmity – a binding by Satan) and healing (the laying on of hands – no speech directed to the spirit) resemble what is seen in other non-demonic infirmities and cures. With Paul's thorn, it is extraordinary that if exorcism were needed to expel this messenger of Satan, God's response is that Paul can live with the condition. As with the other two texts, this passage bears little resemblance to demon possession and none to exorcism. Thus, even with this additional category of infirmities inflicted by Satan and/or his demons, the New Testament evidence for the presence of exorcisms within the believing community is very slim if not non-existent.

As for the methods of exorcism,[4] it would seem that prayer, at least before the event, is essential. The disciples experience failure at just this point (cf. Mark 9). In the New Testament accounts of exorcism there is little if any physical contact between the deliverer (Jesus, the Twelve, Philip, or Paul) and the possessed. Aside from the possibility that the laying on of hands occasionally accompanied exorcism, a point that is not altogether clear, the closest one comes to such is the account of contact with pieces of cloth that had touched Paul's body being used to effect healings and exorcisms (Acts 19). Instead of physical contact the New Testament texts depict a conversation, at most, between the deliverer and the demon or unclean spirit. Ordinarily such conversations include the cry of the demon, in which there is an acknowledgment of Jesus' true identity (and authority). On one occasion, Jesus asks an evil spirit to reveal its name (Mk 5.9), but ordinarily Jesus simply silences the demons, refusing to let them speak, and drives them out with a word. On most every occasion, the effect is immediate.[5] Judging from Mt. 12.43-45 and Lk. 11.24-26, those delivered from demons are expected to follow up their exorcism with acceptance of the gospel in order to ensure that the expelled demons would not return, for such a return would result in a condition worse than the former state.

---

[4] On this topic cf. esp. Twelftree, *Jesus the Exorcist* (Peabody, MA: Hendrickson, 1993), pp. 143-56.

[5] The account of the Gerasene demoniac in Mk 5.1-20 is one example of an exorcism that does not seem to be successful on the first attempt.

Medicine

In addition to the responses just described there is one indication in the New Testament texts that medicine might also be viewed as an appropriate response to an infirmity in certain situations. This comment is based on 1 Tim. 5.23 where Timothy is admonished to take a little wine for his stomach's sake on account of his frequent illness. The context, which is concerned with Timothy's health, makes clear that the wine is here being prescribed as a medicinal aid. Thus, while perhaps representing only a small strand in New Testament thought, the use of medicine as a response to infirmity cannot be ignored altogether.

9

IMPLICATIONS FOR PENTECOSTAL THEOLOGY AND MINISTRY

The foregoing study of the Devil, disease, and deliverance has offered a careful reading of the relevant New Testament texts and has proposed one way in which the various writings might be drawn upon in the construction of a New Testament theology on this topic. In what follows a set of reflections are offered about the implications of this investigation for Pentecostal theology and ministry. Such a move may be justified in several ways. First, the current hermeneutical and theological environments are calling for readings and theologies which allow the voices of those at the margins to be heard in ways that are consistent with the dynamics of the communities from which they come. For Pentecostals, the thought and praxis of the tradition has been and continues to be informed directly by the biblical texts themselves. Therefore, for those working within the tradition, this move is a wholly legitimate and (many would feel) necessary one.

Second, the need for interdisciplinary theological reflection is becoming more and more apparent to a number of scholars working within a variety of theological traditions. While this study has obviously been undertaken within the boundaries of New Testament studies, it seeks to make some overtures to those working within theology proper, whether it be systematic, historical, or practical theology. While there *is* more to doing theology than a detailed reading of the New Testament texts, the doing of constructive theology *can* benefit not a little from a careful examination of the biblical texts. The incredible magnitude of the theological task should be clear to most and the need for interdisciplinary approaches apparent. Therefore, some of the reflections which follow should be read as an invitation to dialogue about this most important topic across a variety of theological disciplines.

Third, the recent decades have witnessed a tremendous surge in the productivity of Pentecostal theologians which reveals the desire of many to construct and articulate a 'Pentecostal theology' which addresses the broader theological task as well as those numerous issues of special significance for the tradition. Given the prominence of 'Jesus as Healer' within the Pentecostal fivefold gospel, it is natural that a number of individuals are now giving attention to this topic. Perhaps the results of this investigation may be of some use in the construction of a comprehensive theology of healing. Specifically, my hope is for one or more Pentecostal theologians to enter into serious dialogue with the results of this study and, if the results are deemed worthy, to utilize them in the construction of a theology of healing proper. The very helpful response of Frank D. Macchia to my earlier study on Footwashing suggests how the fruit of biblical studies may contribute to the theological task, while at the same time indicating how a more decidedly theological approach can enrich, challenge, and envelop the results of a biblical enquiry.[1]

Fourth, many within the Pentecostal and charismatic traditions not only believe in healing as a point of faith, but also participate in a variety of activities designed to bring about physical healing in the lives of those to whom they minister. In addition, most academic Pentecostal theology is closely connected to practical theology, in that its constructive orientation almost demands that the results of academic endeavors be placed into dialogue with the practice of ministry in Pentecostal and charismatic communities. Consequently, the results of this enquiry may be of relevance for the on-going life and ministry of the church. Such an observation is not intended to suggest a paternalistic attitude that would posit, 'Since the scholarly work has been done, the practitioners should now conform'! But rather, the reflections on the implications of this study for Pentecostal praxis are also intended to function as an invitation for dialogue about this most vital aspect of Pentecostal ministry.

---

[1] Cf. F.D. Macchia, 'Is Footwashing the Neglected Sacrament? A Theological Response to John Christopher Thomas', *Pneuma* 19.2 (1997), pp. 239-49.

In what follows, then, one finds not a comprehensive discussion of healing and its voluminous secondary literature, but rather reflections on the implications of this study for Pentecostal theology and ministry.

The Theology and Ministry of Healing

The area of Pentecostal theology and ministry to which the results of this study might make some contribution is, quite obviously, that element of the fivefold gospel which focuses upon Jesus as Healer. There are several specific issues that could well benefit from additional reflection in the light of this study. Perhaps the following comments might serve to facilitate this process.

The Role of Prayer

This investigation suggests that prayer, one might even say fervent prayer, is always an appropriate response to infirmity. This observation is based upon the admonition of James 5 which gives explicit directives to the church when there are those in the community who are ill. It is further supported by Paul's apparent practice when faced with the thorn in the flesh and the example of Jesus and others within the narratives of the Gospels and Acts. It appears that such prayer should, in most cases, precede any other action, with the possible exception of anointing with oil.[2] The fact that the cause or origin of a specific infirmity may be unknown should result in no hesitancy about whether or not fervent prayer is appropriate. On the basis of a variety of New Testament texts, such prayer - whether offered by a leader, one who possesses the gifts of healings, a group of elders, or other members of the community - should be offered with the full expectation that the infirm person will receive healing. While it is clear that not all are healed in all cases cited in the New Testament literature, it is difficult to ignore the impression that emerges from reading the texts themselves that in the vast majority of cases the writers (and readers with them) exhibit an extraordinary expectancy with regard to healing.

---

[2] When Pentecostals rethink and construct their theology from the ground up, it is very likely that anointing with oil will come to be viewed as a sacrament: (apparently) instituted by Jesus (Mk 6.13), practised by the church (Jas 5.14), tied (through healing) to the atonement (Mt. 8.17).

Although the majority of New Testament cases suggests that healings were immediate, there is some evidence to suggest that one is to keep praying for healing until one hears from God. Such an idea may appeal for support to Mk 8.22-26 where Jesus twice lays hands upon a blind man before the man receives complete healing. Additional support for this suggestion may be found in Paul's own approach when faced with the thorn in the flesh. The fact that Paul prayed not once but three times for its removal may imply that the apostle would have kept on praying if he had not heard from God as to its 'permanent' nature. Thus, rather than becoming overly discouraged or embarrassed in those cases where the sick are not healed, it appears that individual and community alike are on good grounds to continue in prayer for healing.

The Role of Discernment

The suggestion that one should continue in prayer until the infirmity is removed or one hears from God leads rather naturally to the next major implication of this study. Although it is always appropriate to respond to any infirmity with prayer, it is also clear from this study that discernment plays a crucial role in the ministry of healing especially as it relates to the Devil, disease, and deliverance. Not only do the New Testament documents indicate that discernment is a part of many situations described, but they also imply that the readers of these documents are to have a place for discernment as an on-going part of their community life. How might such evidence inform Pentecostal theology and ministry?

It almost goes without saying that discernment is a topic which is very difficult to define, as it at first glance seems to be an almost entirely intuitive process. Yet, despite the unique challenges which such a task presents, it is possible to gain some understanding of the process by identifying the things discerned in the New Testament and those who are shown discerning them. In order to accomplish this goal, attention is given to the dynamics of the discerning process as it relates to the origins of illness.

The Discernment of Sin

As noted earlier, sin is depicted in several New Testament documents as an origin of illness. Several significant factors emerge from an examination of those contexts. On each occasion (James 5, 1 Corinthians 11, and John 5), there is the clear assumption expressed that the individual who suffers an infirmity owing to sin would know of the presence of sin and its nature. Despite the fact that someone else (a leader of some sort) indicates a knowledge of the presence of sin, none of the texts examined suggests that the sufferer would be unaware of the sin or surprised by such an identification. Rather, the individual who bears the infirmity would appear to know full well the nature of the sin and, consequently, would play a crucial role in the discernment process. Thus, the admonitions of James to confess, of Paul to examine, and of Jesus to stop sinning reveal that the first step in discerning the origin of an illness on the part of a believer is an examination of self to discern whether sin may be the origin of a particular infirmity.

Another part of this discernment process is played by leaders in the community. Often in contexts where sin is identified as the origin of an infirmity, the presence of sin is known or alluded to by an individual portrayed as in an authoritative position. In the case of James, the author merely mentions the possibility that sin may lie behind some illness, while Paul, Jesus, and Peter (Acts 5) appear to know of sin's presence by the revelatory work of the Holy Spirit and/or the supernatural knowledge of Jesus. While the role of leadership in the discernment process is important, it should not be forgotten that in the New Testament, the discernment of leaders tends to confirm that which should already be known by the individual sufferer. It does not appear that the discernment of leaders ordinarily reveals something otherwise unknown to the believer who is afflicted, although the admonitions of the leader might cause the individual to act upon what he or she knows.

The community itself also plays a role in the discernment process as it relates to sin. Here there appear to be two primary functions. The community offers the context for the discerning judgment for which Paul calls, and the community provides an appropriate context for confession of sin and the resulting intercession. Thus, the community provides the support and balance necessary for the process of discernment.

The Discernment of Divine Chastisement

Closely related to the discernment of sin is the discernment of the hand of God in affliction, for in the vast majority of New Testament cases there is a clear connection between sin as origin of illness and God as the one who afflicts. If sin as the origin of an infirmity can be discerned by the individual believer, then it follows that the presence of the hand of God in infirmity can also be discerned in those cases. In addition to what has been said about the discernment of sin generally, a few other observations might be offered.

First, on those occasions in the New Testament where an infirmity is deemed to be the result of sin, the implication is that God stands behind the affliction(s). Interestingly enough, sin does not appear to function as an autonomous force as an origin of illness. Rather, in those cases reference is made in an explicit or implicit way to God and/or his agents. Second, often divine affliction is accompanied by a revelation of its origin. This revelation may come through an angelic visitation, prophetically spoken words, words from Jesus, or a Christophanic message from the risen Christ. Third, on occasion the divine origin of an affliction is discerned only after sufficient time has passed to allow for an assessment of the results of the infirmity for the Gospel's sake, as in the case of Paul's preaching to the Galatians on account of a weakness in the flesh and the case of the blind man in John 9. In addition, the purpose of Paul's thorn is discerned by means of a divine word from the risen Christ only after a period of prayerful intercession.

The Discernment of the Demonic

The discernment of a demonic origin of infirmity is also described in the New Testament documents. For this study, two aspects of the discernment process are most significant. First, it is clear that on certain occasions the discernment of a demonic presence in an infirmity is based primarily upon observation of the person afflicted. For example, when the father of the demon-possessed boy comes to the disciples and then Jesus for help, it is the father who informs of the boy's condition. From the text it is apparent that the father's assessment is based upon the convulsions which endanger the boy's life. Other similar diagnoses of the demonic origin of certain illness in the New Testament are probably best viewed as in line with the case of this father. However, it is also clear that the same kind of infirmity could be attributed to the demonic on one occasion, God on another occasion, and treated in an unattributed fashion on still another occasion. Thus, while the observation of various phenomena may be a part of the discernment process with regard to the demonic, it is certainly not the whole process.

The second aspect of the discernment process with regard to the demonic includes what might be called an intuitive dimension. This dimension has special reference to those immediate diagnoses on the part of Jesus and others where an infirmity is attributed without delay to the demonic. Such discernment is the result of a special or supernatural knowledge which appears to be attributable to the Holy Spirit's activity. This ability to discern, as with the ability to discern sin as an origin of illness, is primarily confined to those who are regarded as leaders in a given community. Perhaps the Pauline 'gift of discernment' is the means by which the discernment of demonic afflictions is possible (cf. 1 Cor. 12.10). If so, then others in the community would be able to operate in this fashion, while the need for this gift among leaders would be especially crucial.

Conclusion

The role of discernment in the healing ministry of the church is crucial and should work to supplement the prayer of the believing community. Although there may be occasions where the Holy Spirit instantaneously reveals the origin and/or purpose of a given infirmity, ordinarily it appears that the process of discernment may take some time to operate. The New Testament picture suggests that discernment requires a communal context, the involvement of the individual sufferer (except perhaps in the case of certain infirmities brought on by demon possession), as well as the leaders of the believing community. There is also a role for other believers to play a part in this process, particularly those with the gift of discernment.

The Role of Confession

When an infirmity is the result of sin in the life of a believer, the appropriate response is confession. Such confession is to be made to the believing community in order that intercession might be made on behalf of the one who has sinned. It appears that in some New Testament communities public confession was practised. The fact that there is no place for such confession in many contemporary churches within Pentecostal and charismatic circles is more an indication of the church's superficiality and fragmentation than it is a sign of the early church's naiveté or lack of sophistication. Part of the problem with appropriating such a practice today is that in many parts of the world churches (within the Pentecostal/charismatic tradition) are no longer communities, but rather collections of individuals. It would appear that the church has paid the price for failing to provide an opportunity for confession as a regular and on-going part of the community's worship. Confession on the New Testament order where community does not exist would, no doubt, prove to be foolhardy. Therefore, the challenge which faces those in the tradition is not to give up forever on this vital dimension of community life, but rather to work for the construction of communities where believers are loved and nurtured in a familial fashion. Perhaps a first step in the re-appropriation of regular confession would be to make a place for the regular practice of footwashing, given its prominent emphasis on forgiveness and the community's involvement in the act.

The Role of Exorcism, Deliverance, and Sanctification

Given the current preoccupation with exorcism and deliverance in some circles within the tradition, it is especially important to make clear any implications of this study for this dimension of Pentecostal theology and ministry. The following observations are tentatively offered:

First, in the light of the fact that in the New Testament only a small percentage (perhaps 10%) of infirmities are attributed to the demonic, it would seem wise to avoid the temptation of assuming that in most cases an infirmity is caused by Satan and/or demons. Such a realization and in some cases adjustment in thinking could serve to bring a degree of moderation through biblical critique to an area that has been and continues to be sorely abused. As the New Testament texts are not guilty of indiscriminate attributions of infirmities to the demonic, Pentecostal and charismatic ministers of healing would seem obliged to show a similar restraint and caution in the attribution of origins of illness.

Second, the fact that in the New Testament there is no evidence that exorcisms took place within the church but rather seem to have occurred outside in evangelistic contexts suggests that the current specialization in exorcisms by some in the church is misdirected at best. This statement should not be taken to mean that exorcisms have no place in the church at all, but to point out that the current practice of many within the tradition is at odds to some extent with the Scriptures, texts which most practitioners treat as authoritative guides in their theology and ministry.

Third, even though the New Testament gives some evidence that believers may suffer from infirmities in which Satan or demons are involved, these texts give no evidence that believers may be demon possessed or oppressed to an extent that the sufferer loses control of his/her faculties. Speaking to this issue is complicated by the ambiguity which surrounds the meaning of the word Christian in many contexts today. If one wishes to include within the category of believer 'nominal' Christians or those who may no longer consider themselves to be believers but are part of traditions which still regard them as Christian, owing to a previous profession of faith or baptism, then perhaps one can argue for the domination of such 'Christians' by demons. However, such modern ways of defining the term 'Christian' do not take seriously enough the lines of demarcation which the New Testament draws between believers and unbelievers. Thus, while the New Testament makes clear the reality of the demonic, and few working within the Pentecostal and charismatic traditions would wish to dispute this reality, there is precious little evidence in the New Testament to support many of the claims that come from those in the 'deliverance ministry'. In point of fact, the very New Testament texts that might be appealed to as support for the view that it is theoretically possible for Christians to suffer an infirmity brought by a demon do not even hint that such believers are in need of exorcism but either treat the removal of the infirmity as an 'ordinary' healing or indicate that the infirmity is to remain, in accordance with the divine will.

Fourth, Pentecostals have long had an appreciation for the fact that the Christian journey includes a struggle against the flesh. In fact, it has not been uncommon for phrases like 'the Devil has a hold' on a particular individual to describe the extent of the struggle. However, even where such language has been employed there has been little or no suggestion that the person was possessed by the Devil or a demon. Rather, these battles were understood in the context of the pursuit of holiness of life. Perhaps one way forward is for theologians and practitioners working within the tradition to re-appropriate the doctrine and practice of sanctification. Such a re-appropriation might accomplish at least two things: 1) It would provide an opportunity for serious self examination which acknowledges the reality of the struggle against the Devil, sin, and flesh but in a way that is much more at home with the biblical texts. 2) It would facilitate an appropriate use of exorcism language by restricting its usage to those occasions where demon possession is clearly present.

Fifth, it appears that part of the confusion over exorcism and deliverance has resulted from an uncritical application of exorcism language to describe the spiritual and Scriptural experience of sanctification. Since exorcism (often called deliverance) has become for many the paradigm for dealing with any number of spiritual problems, it is not surprising that similar expected phenomena have accompanied times of 'deliverance'. If sanctification again finds a place in the vocabulary and life of the tradition's spirituality, perhaps those in the tradition may find a way past this current controversial impasse.

The Role of Doctors

Given the ambiguous nature of the relationship between Pentecostalism and medicine, it may not be unwise to include a final observation about the implications of this study for Pentecostals and doctors. It probably comes as no surprise that some of the suspicion that some in the tradition have at times shown to the use of doctors is in some ways a response to the fact that the New Testament presents doctors as not being able to heal the sick nearly as effectively as are Jesus and his followers. However, the fact that in the Pastorals the medicinal use of wine can be prescribed suggests that a total rejection of the use of doctors outdistances the New Testament teaching and thus may do much to harm rather than help.

A Final Word

It should perhaps be restated that the purpose of this monograph is not to answer all the questions on this very difficult topic. Rather it is an invitation to further research, prayer, critical reflection, and discernment. If this study can aid in a better understanding of any of the challenging issues facing students of the New Testament or those interested in healing generally, then the effort will have been worth it.

BIBLIOGRAPHY

Achtemeier, P., 'Miracles and the Historical Jesus', *CBQ* 37 (1975), pp. 471-91.

Adeney, W.F., *St. Luke* (Edinburgh: T.C. & E.C. Jack, 1901).

Albertz, M., *Die synoptischen Streirgespräche* (Berlin: Trowitzsch & Sohn, 1921).

Albright, W.F., and C.S. Mann, *Matthew* (Garden City, NY: Doubleday, 1971).

Alexander, L., 'Hellenistic Letter-Forms and the Structure of Philippians', *JSNT* 37 (1988), pp. 87-101.

Alexander, W.M., 'St. Paul's Infirmity', *ExpTim* 15 (1903-1904), pp. 469-73, 545-48.

Allen, W.C., *The Gospel According to S. Matthew* (Edinburgh: T. & T. Clark, 3rd edn, 1912).

Allo, E.-B., *Première épître aux Corinthiens* (Paris: J. Gabalda, 1956).

—*Saint Paul; seconde épître aux Corinthiens* (Paris: J. Gabalda, 1956).

Anderson, J.C., *Matthew's Narrative Web: Over, and Over, and Over Again* (JSNTSup 91; Sheffield: JSOT Press, 1994).

Anderson, H., *The Gospel of Mark* (London: Oliphants, 1976).

Anderson, J.G., 'A New Translation of Luke 1:20', *Bible Translator* 20 (1969), pp. 21-24.

Aquinas, Thomas, *Commentary on the Four Gospels Collected out of the Works of the Fathers: St. John* (Oxford, 1844).

Argyle, A.W., *The Gospel According to Matthew* (Cambridge: Cambridge University Press, 1963).

Armerding, C., 'Is Any among You Afflicted?', *BibSac* 95 (1938), pp. 195-201.

Arrington, F.L., *The Ministry of Reconciliation* (Grand Rapids: Baker Book House, 1980).

—*Divine Order in the Church* (Grand Rapids: Baker Book House, 1981).

—*The Acts of the Apostles* (Peabody, MA: Hendrickson, 1988).

Aune, D., 'Magic in Early Christianity', in W. Haase (ed.), *Aufstieg und Niedergang der römischen Welt* (Berlin: de Gruyter, 1980), II.23.2, pp. 507-57.

Babbitt, F.C. (trans.), *Plutarch's Moralia,* II (London: Heinemann, 1971).

Baker, D., 'The Interpretation of 1 Corinthians 12-14', *EvQ* 46 (1974), pp. 224-34.

Balz, H., 'ἐκπτύω', *EDNT,* I, p. 421.

Band, S., 'Reincarnation (Matthew xi. 14 and John ix. 2)', *ExpTim* 25 (1913-14), p. 474.

Barclay, W., *The Gospel of John,* I (St Andrews: St Andrews Press, 1955).

—*The Letters of James and Peter* (Philadelphia: Westminster Press, 1960).

—*The Acts of the Apostles* (Philadelphia: Westminster Press, 1976).

Barnett, P., *The Message of 2 Corinthians* (Leicester: IVP, 1988).

Barre, M.L., 'Qumran and the Weakness of Paul', *CBQ* 42(1980), pp. 216-27.

Barrett, C.K., *A Commentary on the First Epistle to the Corinthians* (London: A. & C. Black, 1968).

—*The Gospel According to St. John* (Philadelphia: Westminster Press, 1978).

—*The New Testament Background: Selected Documents* (New York: Harper & Row, 1987).

—*The Acts of the Apostles,* I (Edinburgh: T. & T. Clark, 1994).

Barrett, M.P.V., 'Lessons in Patience and Prayer', *Biblical Viewpoint* 14 (1980), pp. 52-58.

Beare, F.W., *The Epistle to the Philippians* (San Francisco: Harper & Row, 1959).

—*The Gospel According to Matthew* (Oxford: Basil Blackwell, 1981).

Beasley-Murray, G.R., *The General Epistles* (London: Lutterworth Press, 1965).

—*John* (Waco, TX: Word Books, 1987).

Beecher, E., 'Dispensations of Divine Providence toward the Apostle Paul', *BibSac* 12 (1855), pp. 499-527.

Beeckman, P., *L'Evangile selon Saint Jean* (Paris: Beyaert-Bruges, 1951).

Beernaert, P.M., 'Jésus controversé: structure et théologie de Mark 2, 1-3, 6', *NRT* 95 (1973), pp. 129-49.

—*Saint Marc* (Brussels: Lumen Vitae, 1985).

Beet, J.A., *A Commentary on St. Paul's Epistle to the Corinthians* (London: Hodder & Stoughton, 1882).

—*A Commentary on St. Paul's Epistle to the Galatians* (London: Hodder & Stoughton, 1885).

—'Epaphroditus and the Gift from Philippi', *Exp* (Third Series) 9 (1889), pp. 64-75.

Bennett, W.H., *The General Epistles* (New York: Henry Frowde, 1900).

Benoit, P., 'L'enfance de Jean-Baptiste selon Luc I', *NTS* 3 (1956-57), pp. 169-94.

—*L'Evangile selon Saint Matthieu* (Paris: Cerf, 1972).

Béraudy, R, 'Le sacrement des malades: Etude historique et théologique', *NRT* 96 (1974), pp. 600-11.

Berkhof, H., *The Doctrine of the Holy Spirit* (London: Epworth Press, 1965).

Bernard, J.H., *The Pastoral Epistles* (Cambridge: Cambridge University Press, 1899).

—*The Gospel According to St. John*, I (Edinburgh: T. & T. Clark, 1928).

Bertram, G., 'ἐκθαμβέομαι', *TDNT*, III, pp. 4-7.

Betz, H.D., *Galatians* (Philadelphia: Fortress Press, 1979).

Bietenhard, H., 'ὄνομα', *TDNT*, V, p. 278.

Bittlinger, A., *Gifts and Graces* (trans. H. Klassen; London: Hodder & Stoughton, 1967).

Blackburn, B., *Theios Aner and the Markan Miracle Traditions* (Tübingen: J.C.B. Mohr [Paul Siebeck], 1991).

Blackman, E.C., *The Epistle of James* (New York: Macmillan, 1957).

Blaiklock, E.M., *The Acts of the Apostles* (Grand Rapids: Eerdmans, 1959).

Blair, H.J., 'Spiritual Healing: An Enquiry', *EvQ* 30 (1958), pp. 147-51.

Bligh, J., 'The Man Born Blind', *HeyJ* 7 (1966), pp. 129-44.

—*Galatians* (London: St Paul's Publications, 1969).

Blinzler, J., 'Die Niedermetzelung von Galiläern durch Pilatus', *NovT* 2 (1957), pp. 24-49.

Blomberg, C.L., *Matthew* (Nashville: Broadman, 1992).

Blunt, A.W.F., *The Acts of the Apostles* (Oxford: Clarendon Press, 1923).

Bock, D.L., *Luke* (Leicester: IVP, 1994).

Bogle, A.N., 'I Corinthians 11:23-34', *ExpTim* 12 (1900-1901), p. 479.

Boismard, M.E., and A. Lamouille, *L'Evangile de Jean* (Paris: Cerf, 1977).

Bonnard, P., *L'Evangile selon Saint Matthieu* (Neuchâtel: Delachaux & Niestlé, 1963).

—*L'Epître de Saint Paul aux Galates* (Paris: Delachaux & Niestlé, 1972).

—*Les Epîtres johanniques* (Geneva: Labor et Fides, 1983).

Bonus, A., 'Luke vi. 19', *ExpTim* 18 (1906-1907), pp. 187-88.

Boobyer, G.H., 'Mark 2, 10a and the Interpretation of the Healing of the Paralytic', *HTR* 47 (1954), pp. 115-20.

Bornkamm, G., 'πρεσβύτης', *TDNT*, VI, pp. 651-83.

Borse, U., *1. und 2. Timotheusbrief Titusbrief* (Stuttgart: Katholisches Biblewerk, 1985).

Bovon, F., *L'Evangile selon Saint Luc (1,1-9,50)* (Geneva: Labor et Fides, 1991).

Branscomb, B.H., *The Gospel of Mark* (London: Hodder & Stoughton, 1937).

Brockhaus, U., *Charisma und Amt* (Wuppertal: R. Brockhaus, 1972).

Brodie. T.L., 'Jesus as the New Elisha: Cracking the Code', *ExpTim* 93 (1981-82), pp. 39-42.

Brooks, J.A., *Mark* (Nashville: Broadman Press, 1991).

Brown, C., *That You May Believe* (Grand Rapids: Eerdmans, 1985).

Brown, E.F., *The Pastoral Epistles* (London: Methuen, 1917).

Brown, M.L., *Israel's Divine Healer* (Grand Rapids: Zondervan, 1995).

Brown, R.E., *The Gospel According to John,* I (Garden City, NY: Doubleday, 1966).
—*The Epistles of John* (Garden City, NY: Doubleday, 1982).
—*The Birth of the Messiah* (Garden City, NY: Doubleday, 1993).
Brox, N., *Die Pastoralbriefe* (Regensburg: Friedrich Pustet, 1969).
Bruce, F.F., *Commentary on the Book of the Acts* (Grand Rapids: Eerdmans, 1954).
—*The Epistles of John* (London: Pickering & Inglis, 1970).
—*1 and 2 Corinthians* (London: Oliphants, 1971).
—*The Epistle to the Galatians* (Grand Rapids: Eerdmans, 1982).
—*The Gospel of John* (Grand Rapids: Eerdmans, 1983).
—*Philippians* (New York: Harper & Row, 1983).
—*The Pauline Circle* (Grand Rapids: Eerdmans, 1985).
—'Chronological Questions in the Acts of the Apostles', *BJRL* 68 (1986), pp. 273-95.
Brunner, F.D., *The Christbook: A Historical/Theological Commentary: Matthew 1-12* (Waco, TX: Word Books, 1987).
Buchanan, C.O., 'Epaphroditus' Sickness and the Letter to the Philippians', *EvQ 36* (1964), pp. 157-66.
Bucher, O., *Dämonenfurcht und Dämonenabwehr* (Stuttgart: Kohlhammer, 1970).
—*Christus Exorcista* (Stuttgart: Kohlhammer, 1972) .
—*Das Neue Testament und die damonischen Machte* (Stuttgart: Katholisches Bibelwerk, 1972).
Buchsel, D.F., *Die Johannesbriefe* (Leipzig: Deichert, 1933).
Budesheim, T.L., 'Jesus and the Disciples in Conflict with Judaism', *ZNW* 62 (1971), pp. 190-209.
Bultmann, R., *Theology of the New Testament,* II (trans. K. Grobel; New York: Charles Scribner's Sons, 1955).
—*The Gospel of John* (trans. G.R. Beasley-Murray; Philadelphia: Westminster Press, 1971).
—*The Johannine Epistles* (ed. R.W. Funk; trans. R.P. O'Hara, L.C. McGaughty, and R.W. Funk; Philadelphia: Fortress Press, 1973).
—*The Second Letter to the Corinthians* (trans. R.A. Harrisville; Minneapolis: Augsburg, 1985).
Bürki, H., *Der ewe Brief des Paulus an Timotheus* (Wuppertal: R. Brockhaus, 1974).
Burkitt, F.C., 'The Interpretation of *Bar-Jesus'*, *JTS* 4 (1903), pp. 127-29.
Burton, E.D., *The Epistle to the Galatians* (Edinburgh: T. & T. Clark, 1921).
Bussche, H. van den, 'Guérison d'un paralytique à Jerusalem la jour du Sabbat: Jean 5, 1-18', *Bible et vie chrétienne* 61 (1965), pp. 18-28.
Busse, U., *Die Wunder des Propheten Jesus: Die Rezeption, Komposition und Interpretation der Wundertradition im Evangelium des Lukas* (Stuttgart: Katholisches Bibelwerk, 1977).
—'διέρχομαι', *EDNT,* I, pp. 322-23.
Cabaniss, A., 'A Fresh Exegesis of Mark 2:1-12', *Int* II (1957), pp. 324-27.
Cadbury, H.J., 'Lexical Notes on Luke-Acts in Recent Arguments for Medical Language', *JBL* 45 (1926), pp. 190-209.
Caird, G.B., *Saint Luke* (London: Penguin, 1963).
Calloud, J., 'Toward a Structural Analysis of the Gospel of Mark', *Semeia* 16 (1980), pp. 133-65.
Calvin, J., *Commentary on the Epistles of Paul the Apostle to the Corinthians* (Edinburgh: Calvin Translation Society, 1843).
—*Commentaries on the Epistles of Paul to the Galatians and Ephesians* (trans. W. Pringle; Edinburgh: Calvin Translation Society, 1864).
—*Commentaries on the Catholic Epistles* (Grand Rapids: Eerdmans, 1948).
—*Commentary on the Acts of the Apostles* (2 vols.; trans. C. Fetherstone; ed. H. Beveridge; Grand Rapids: Eerdmans, 1949).
—*The Gospel According to St. John,* I (Grand Rapids: Eerdmans, 1959).
Cantinat, I., *De Saint Jacques et de Saint Jude* (Paris: J. Gabalda, 1973).
Capper, B.J., 'The Interpretation of Acts 5.4', *JSNT* 19 (1983), pp. 117-31.

Carpus, 'The Strength of Weakness', *Exp* (First series) 3 (1876), pp. 174-77.

Carson, D.A., 'Understanding Misunderstanding in the Fourth Gospel', *TynBul* 33 (1982), pp. 59-91.

—'Matthew', in *The Expositor's Bible Commentary,* VIII (Grand Rapids: Zondervan, 1984).

—*From Triumphalism to Maturity* (Grand Rapids: Baker Book House, 1984).

—*Showing the Spirit* (Grand Rapids: Baker Book House, 1987).

—*The Gospel According to John* (Grand Rapids: Eerdmans, 1990).

Carter, W.C., and R. Earle, *The Gospel According to St. John,* I (Grand Rapids: Eerdmans, 1957).

—*The Acts of the Apostles* (Grand Rapids: Eerdmans, 1973).

Chaine, B., *Les Épîtres catholiques* (Paris: J. Gabalda, 1939).

Chaine, J., *L'Epître de Saint Jacques* (Paris: J. Gabalda, 1927).

Chappell, P.G. 'Healing Movements', *DPCM*, pp. 353-74.

Charlesworth, J.H. (ed.), *The Old Testament Pseudepigrapha,* II (Garden City, NY: Doubleday, 1985).

Chenderlin, F., *Do This as my Memorial* (Rome: Biblical Institution Press, 1982).

Chu, S.W.-W., 'The Healing of the Epileptic Boy in Mark 9:14-29: Its Rhetorical Structure and Theological Implications' (PhD Dissertation; Vanderbilt University, 1988).

Cole, R.A., *Mark* (Grand Rapids: Eerdmans, 1989).

—*Galatians* (Grand Rapids: Eerdmans, 1989).

Collange, J.-F., *The Epistle of Saint Paul to the Philippians* (trans. A.W. Heathcote; London: Epworth Press, 1979).

Colson, F.H., and G.H. Whitaker, *Philo,* V (London: Heinemann, 1988).

Condon, K., 'The Sacrament of Healing', *Scripture* 11.14 (April 1959), pp. 33-42.

Conzelmann, H., *1 Corinthians* (trans. J.W. Leitch; Philadelphia: Fortress Press, 1975).

—*Acts of the Apostles* (trans. J. Limburg, A.T. Kraabel and D.H. Juel; ed. E.J. Epp and C.R. Matthews; Philadelphia: Fortress Press, 1987).

Coppens, J., 'Les logia du Fils de l'homme dans l'évangile de Marc', in M. Sabbe (ed.), *L'Evangile selon Marc: Tradition et rédaction* (Leuven: Leuven University Press,1974), pp. 487-528.

—'Jacq. v, 13-15 et l' onction des malades', *ETL* 53 (1977), pp. 201-207.

Cosgrove, C.H., *The Cross and the Spirit: A Study in the Argument and Theology of Galatians* (Macon, GA: Mercer University Press, 1988).

Craddock, F.B., *Luke* (Louisville: John Knox, 1990).

Cranfield, C.E.B., *The Gospel According to St Mark* (Cambridge: Cambridge University Press, 1959).

—*The Gospel According to Saint Mark* (Cambridge: Cambridge University Press, 1972).

Creed, J.M., *The Gospel According to St. Luke* (London: Longmans, Green & Co., 1930).

Crowe, J., *The Acts* (Wilmington, DE: Michael Glazier, 1979).

Cullis, C., *Faith Cures; or, Answers to Prayer in the Healing of the Sick* (Boston: Willard Tract Repository, 1879).

Culpepper, R.A., 'Co-Workers in Suffering: Philippians 2:19-30', *RevExp* 77 (1980), pp. 349-58.

—'The Gospel of John and the Jews', *RevExp* 84 (1987), pp. 273-88.

—'Un exemple de commentaire fondé sur la critique narrative: Jean 5,1-18', in *La communauté johanniques et son historie: La trajectoire de l'évangile de Jean aux deux premiers siècles* (Geneva: Labor et Fides, 1990), pp. 135-51.

Dana, H.E., and J.R. Mantey, A *Manual of the Greek New Testament* (Toronto: Macmillan, 1957).

Danker, F.W., *Jesus and the New Age* (St Louis: Clayton Publishing, 1972).

—*II Corinthians* (Minneapolis: Augsburg, 1989).

Daube, D., *The New Testament and Rabbinic Judaism* (New York: Arno Press, 1973).

Dautzenberg, G., 'διακρίνω', *EDNT*, I, pp. 305-307.

Davids, P.H., *The Epistle of James* (Grand Rapids: Eerdmans, 1982).

Davies, M., *Matthew: Readings* (Sheffield: Sheffield Academic Press, 1993).

Davies, W.D., and D.C. Allison, Jr., *The Gospel According to Saint Matthew, I-II* (Edinburgh: T. & T. Clark, 1988, 1991).

Dayton, D.W., *Theological Roots of Pentecostalism* (Grand Rapids: Zondervan, 1987).

Deissmann, A., *Light from the Ancient East* (trans. L.R.M. Strachan; Grand Rapids: Baker Book House, 1978).

Denny, J., *The Second Epistle to the Corinthians* (London: Hodder & Stoughton, 1894).

Derrett, J.D.M., 'Ananias, Sapphira, and the Right of Property', *Downside Review* 89 (1971), pp. 225-32.

— 'Getting on Top of a Demon (Luke 4:39)', *EvQ* 65 (1993), pp. 99-109.

Dewey, J., 'The Literary Structure of the Controversy Stories in Mark 2:1-3:6', *JBL* 92 (1973), pp. 394-401.

—*Mark and Public Debate* (SBLDS, 48; Chico, CA: Scholars Press, 1980).

Dibelius, M., *Studies in the Acts of the Apostles* (trans. M. Ling and P. Schubert; ed. H. Greevan; London: William Clowes & Sons, 1956).

—*James* (ed. H. Koester; trans. M.A. Williams; Philadelphia: Fortress Press, 1976).

Dibelius, M. and H. Conzelmann, *The Pastoral Epistles* (Philadelphia: Fortress Press, 1972).

Dodd, C.H., *The Johannine Epistles* (London: Hodder & Stoughton, 1946).

—*The Interpretation of the Fourth Gospel* (Cambridge: Cambridge University Press, 1953).

Dods, M., *The Gospel of St. John* (New York: Armstrong & Son, 1903).

Donley, D., 'The Epilepsy of Saint Paul', *CBQ* 6 (1944), pp. 358-60.

Dornier, P., *Les Epîtres pastorales* (Paris: J. Gabalda, 1969).

Doughty, D.J., 'The Authority of the Son of Man', *ZNW* 74 (1983), pp. 161-81.

Dowd, S.E., *Prayer, Power, and the Problem of Suffering: Mark 11:22-25 in the Context of Markan Theology* (SBLDS, 105; Atlanta: Scholars Press, 1988).

Drury, J., *Luke* (London: Collins, 1973).

Duling, D.C., 'The Therapeutic Son of David', *NTS* 24 (1978), pp. 392-410.

Dunn, J.D.G., *Jesus and the Spirit* (Philadelphia: Westminster Press, 1975).

—'Mark 2.1-3.6: Between Jesus and Paul', *NTS* 30 (1984), pp. 395-415.

—*Unity and Diversity in the New Testament* (London: SCM Press, 1990).

Dupont, J., 'L' Ambassade de Jean-Baptiste (Matthieu 11, 2-6; Luc 7, 18-23)', *NRT* 83 (1961), pp. 943-59.

—'L'Union entre les premières chrétiennes dans les Actes des Apôtres', *NRT* 91 (1969), pp. 898-915.

—*Nouvelles études sur les Actes des Apôtres* (Paris: Cerf, 1984).

Dupont-Sommer, A., 'Exorcismes et guérisons dans les écrits de Qoumrân', in G.W. Anderson *et al.* (eds.), *Congress Volume, Oxford 1959* (VTSup 7; Leiden: E.J. Brill, 1960).

Duprez, A., *Jésus et les dieux guérisseurs* (Paris: J. Gabalda, 1970).

Easton, B.S., *The Epistle of James* (Nashville: Abingdon Press, 1957).

Ebrard, J.H.A., *The Epistles of St John* (Edinburgh: T. & T. Clark, 1860).

Edwards, O.C., Jr., *Luke's Story of Jesus* (Philadelphia: Fortress Press, 1981).

Edwards, R.A., *Matthew's Story of Jesus* (Philadelphia: Fortress Press, 1985).

Ellis, E.E., *Paul and his Recent Interpreters* (Grand Rapids: Eerdmans, 1961).

—*The Gospel of Luke* (Grand Rapids: Eerdmans, 1981).

—*Pauline Theology* (Grand Rapids: Eerdmans, 1989).

Ellis, P., *The Genius of John: A Composition-Critical Commentary on the Fourth Gospel* (Collegeville, MN: Liturgical Press, 1984).

Ervin, H.M., *Conversion-Initiation and the Baptism in the Holy Spirit* (Peabody, MA: Hendrickson, 1984).

Evans, C.A., *Luke* (Peabody, MA: Hendrickson, 1990).

Evans, C.F., *Saint Luke* (London: SCM Press, 1990).

Falconer, R., *The Pastoral Epistles* (Oxford: Clarendon Press, 1937).

Farrar, F.W., *The Gospel According to St Luke* (Cambridge: Cambridge University Press, 1891).

Farrer, A., 'The Eucharist in 1 Corinthians', in *Eucharistic Theology Then and Now* (London: SPCK, 1968), pp. 15-26.

Faw, C.E., *Acts* (Scottdale, PA: Herald Press, 1993).

Fee, G.D., 'On the Inauthenticity of John 5:3b-4', *EvQ* 54 (1982), pp. 207-18.

—*The First Epistle to the Corinthians* (Grand Rapids: Eerdmans, 1987).

—*1 and 2 Timothy, Titus* (Peabody, MA: Hendrickson, 1988).

Fendrich, H., 'λοιπός', *EDNT*, II, p. 360.

Fenton, J.C., *Saint Matthew* (Baltimore: Penguin, 1963).

Feuillet, A., 'L'exousia du fils de l'homme (d'après Mc. II, 10-28 et parr.)', *RSR* 42 (1954), pp. 161-92.

Filson, F.V., *A Commentary on the Gospel According to Matthew* (London: A. & C. Black, 1960).

Fisher, L.R., 'Can This Be the Son of David?', in F.T. Trotter (ed.), *Jesus and the Historian: Written in Honor of Ernest Cadman Colwell* (Philadelphia: Westminster Press, 1963), pp. 82-97.

Fitch, W.O., 'The Interpretation of St. John 5,6', in F.L. Cross (ed.), *Studia Evangelica, IV* (Berlin: Akademie-Verlag, 1968), pp. 194-97.

—*1 and 2 Timothy, Titus* (Peabody, MA: Hendrickson, 1988).

Fitzmyer, J.A., *Gospel According to Luke I-IX, X-XXIV* (Garden City, NY: Doubleday, 1981-83).

Foakes-Jackson, F.J.F., *The Acts of the Apostles* (London: Hodder & Stoughton, 1931).

Foakes-Jackson, F.J.F., and K. Lake, *The Beginnings of Christianity Part I: The Acts of the Apostles, IV* (Grand Rapids: Baker Book House, 1965).

Fortna, R.T., *The Gospel of Signs* (Cambridge: Cambridge University Press, 1970).

Foster, J., 'Was Sergius Paulus Converted?: Acts xiii. 12', *ExpTim* 60 (1948-49), pp. 354-55.

France, R.T., *Matthew* (Grand Rapids: Eerdmans, 1985).

Frankemolle, H., 'λαός', *EDNT*, II, pp. 339-44.

Fridrichsen, A., *The Problem of Miracle in Primitive Christianity* (trans. R.A. Harrisville and J.S. Hanson; Minneapolis: Augsburg, 1972).

Fung, R.Y.K., *The Epistle to the Galatians* (Grand Rapids: Eerdmans, 1988).

Furnish, V.P., *II Corinthians* (Garden City, NY: Doubleday, 1984).

Gardner, R.B., *Matthew* (Scottdale, PA: Herald Press, 1991).

Garland, D.E., '"I Am the Lord Your Healer": Mark 1:21-2:12', *RevExp* 85 (1988), pp. 327-43.

—*Reading Matthew* (New York: Crossroad, 1993).

Garrett, S.R., *The Demise of the Devil: Magic and the Demonic in Luke's Writings* (Minneapolis: Fortress Press, 1989).

—'Exodus from Bondage: Luke 9:31 and Acts 12:1-24', *CBQ* 52 (1990), pp. 656-80.

Geldenhuys, N., *Commentary on the Gospel of Luke* (Grand Rapids: Eerdmans, 1951).

Getty, M.A., *Philippians and Philemon* (Wilmington, DE: Michael Glazier, 1980).

Gibbs, J.M., 'Purpose and Pattern in Matthew's Use of the Title "Son of David"', *NTS* 10 (1963-64), pp. 446-64.

Gnilka, J., 'Das Elend vor dem Menschensohn (Mk. 1, 1-12)', in R. Pesch *et al.* (eds.), *Jesus und der Menschensohn* (Freiburg: Herder, 1975), pp. 196-209.

—*Das Evangelium nach Markus,* I (Zürich: Benziger Verlag, 1978).

—*Das Matthäusevangelium,* I (Freiburg: Herder, 1986).

Godet, F., *The Gospel of St. Luke,* I (trans. E.W. Shalders; Edinburgh: T. & T. Clark, 1870).

Goedt, M. de, 'Un schème de Révélation dans le quatrième évangile', *NTS* 8 (1961-62), pp.142-50.

Goguel, M., *L'Eucharistie: Des origins à Justin Martyr* (Paris: Librairie Fischbacher, 1910).

Goldingay, J., *Theological Diversity and the Authority of the Old Testament* (Grand Rapids: Eerdmans, 1987).

Gould, E.P., *The Gospel According to Mark* (Edinburgh: T. & T. Clark, 1896).

—*A Critical and Exegetical Commentary on the Gospel According to Saint Mark* (New York: Charles Scribner's Sons, 1907).

Gourgues, M., 'L'aveugle-né (Jn 9). Du miracle au signe: typologie des réactions à l'égard du Fils de l'homme', *NRT* 104 (1982), pp. 381-95.

Grabe, P.J., 'The All-surpassing Power of God through the Holy Spirit in the Midst of our Broken Earthly Existence: Perspectives on Paul's Use of ΔΥΝΑΜΙΣ in 2 Corinthians', *Neot* 28 (1994), pp. 147-56.

Grayston, K., *The Letters of Paul to the Philippians and the Thessalonians* (Cambridge: Cambridge University Press, 1967).

—*The Johannine Epistles* (Grand Rapids: Eerdmans, 1984).

—*The Gospel of John* (London: Epworth Press, 1990).

Greek Anthology, II (ed. W.R. Paton; London: Heinemann, 1917).

Green, B., *The Gospel According to Matthew* (Oxford: Oxford University Press, 1975).

Green, J.B., 'Jesus and a Daughter of Abraham (Luke 13:10-17): Test Case for a Lukan Perspective on the Miracles of Jesus', *CBQ* 51 (1989), pp. 643-54.

—*The Theology of the Gospel of Luke* (Cambridge: Cambridge University Press, 1995).

Green, M., *I Believe in the Holy Spirit* (London: Hodder & Stoughton, 1975).

—*Matthew for Today* (London: Hodder & Stoughton, 1988).

—*I Believe in Satan's Downfall* (London: Hodder & Stoughton, 1995).

Grigsby, B., 'Washing in the Pool of Siloam - A Thematic Anticipation of the Johannine Cross', *NovT* 27 (1985), pp. 227-35.

Grimm, W., 'ἐπιτάσσω', *EDNT*, II, p. 41.

Grundmann, W., *Das Evangelium nach Lukas* (Berlin: Evangelische Verlagsanstalt, 1934).

—*Das Evangelium nach Markus* (Berlin: Evangelische Verlagsanstalt, 1968).

—'ἁμαρτάνω', *TDNT*, I, pp. 267-316.

Guelich, R.A., *Mark 1-8:26* (Dallas: Word Books, 1989).

Guilding, A., *The Fourth Gospel and Jewish Worship* (Oxford: Clarendon Press, 1960).

Gundry, R.H., *Soma in Biblical Theology* (Cambridge: Cambridge University Press, 1976).

—*Matthew: A Commentary on his Literary and Theological Art* (Grand Rapids: Eerdmans, 1982).

—*Mark: A Commentary on his Apology for the Cross* (Grand Rapids: Eerdmans, 1993).

Guthrie, D., *Galatians* (London: Nelson, 1969).

—*New Testament Introduction* (Downers Grove, IL: IVP, 1990).

Haenchen, E., *The Acts of the Apostles: A Commentary* (trans. B. Noble, G. Shinn, H. Anderson and R. McL. Wilson; Philadelphia: Westminster Press, 1971).

—*John*, I (trans. R.W. Funk; ed. R.W. Funk and U. Busse; Philadelphia: Fortress Press, 1984).

Hagner, D.A., *Matthew 1-13* (Dallas: Word Books, 1993).

Hamm, M.D., 'The Freeing of the Bent Woman and the Restoration of Israel: Luke 13:10-17 and Narrative Theology', *JSNT* 31 (1987), pp. 23-44.

Hamman, A., 'Prière et culte chez S. Jacques', *ETL* 34 (1958), pp. 35-47.

Hanson, A.T., *The Pastoral Epistles* (Grand Rapids: Eerdmans, 1982).

Hanson, R.P.C., *The Second Epistle to the Corinthians* (London: SCM Press, 1935).

Hansen, W., *Galatians* (Leicester: IVP, 1994).

Harder, G., 'Soul', *DNTT*, III, p. 684.

Hare, D.R.A., *Matthew* (Louisville: John Knox, 1993).

Harnack, A., *The Acts of the Apostles* (trans. J.R. Wilkinson; New York: Putnam's Sons, 1909).

Harrell, D., *Oral Roberts: An American Life* (San Francisco: Harper & Row, 1987).

Harrer, G.A., 'Saul Who Also Is Called Paul', *HTR* 33 (1940), pp. 19-34.

Harrington, D., *The Gospel of Matthew* (Collegeville, MN: Liturgical Press, 1991).

Harrington, W., *Mark* (Wilmington, DE: Michael Glazier, 1979).

Harrison, P.N., *The Problem of the Pastoral Epistles* (London: Oxford University Press, 1921).

Harrison, W.P., 'Faith-cure in the Light of Scripture', *Methodist Quarterly Review* 28 (1889), pp. 402-405.

Harrisville, R.A., *First Corinthians* (Minneapolis: Augsburg, 1987).

Harse, H., 'ἔνοχος', *TDNT*, II, p. 828.

Haufe, G., 'ὁμοθυμαδόν', *EDNT*, II, p. 511.

—'τυγχάνω', *EDNT*, III, p. 372.

Hawthorne, G.F., *Philippians* (Waco, TX: Word Books, 1983).

Hay, L.S., 'The Son of Man in Mark 2:10 and 2:28', *JBL* 89 (1970), pp. 69-75.

Hayden, R., 'Calling the Elders to Pray', *BibSac* 138 (1981), pp. 258-86.

Heading, J., *Second Epistle to the Corinthians* (London: A. & C. Black, 1973).

Heitmuller, W., *Im Namen Jesus* (Gottingen: Vandenhoeck & Ruprecht, 1903).

Held, H.J., 'Matthew as Interpreter of the Miracle Stories', in G. Bornkamm, G. Barth and H.J. Held (eds.), *Tradition and Interpretation in Matthew* (trans. P. Scott; Philadelphia: Westminster Press, 1963), pp. 52-57.

Hendricksen, W., *The Gospel of Mark* (Grand Rapids: Baker Book House, 1975).

Hengel, M., *The Johannine Question* (Philadelphia: Trinity Press International, 1989).

Hengstenberg, E.W., *Commentary on the Gospel of John*, I (Edinburgh: T. & T. Clark, 1865).

Hennecke, E., *New Testament Apocrypha*, I (ed. W. Schneemelcher; Philadelphia: Westminster Press, 1963).

Herdan, G., 'The Authorship of the Pastorals in the Light of Statistical Linguistics' *NTS* 6 (1959-60), pp. 1-15.

Héring, J., *The First Epistle of Saint Paul to the Corinthians* (trans. A.W. Heathcote and P.J. Allrock; London: Epworth Press, 1962).

—*The Second Epistle of Saint Paul to the Corinthians* (trans. A.W. Heathcote and P.J. Allcock; London: Epworth Press, 1967).

Hiebert, D.E., *Mark: A Portrait of a Servant* (Chicago: Moody Press, 1974).

—'An Exposition of 3 John 1-4', *BibSac* 144 (1987), pp. 53-65.

Higgins, A.J.B., *The Lord's Supper* in *the New Testament* (London: SCM Press, 1952).

Hill, D., *The Gospel of Matthew* (Grand Rapids: Eerdmans, 1981).

Hobart, W.K., *The Medical Language of St. Luke* (London: Longmans, Green & Co., 1882).

Hodge, C., *An Exposition of the Second Epistle to the Corinthians* (Grand Rapids: Eerdmans, 1953).

Hodges, Z.C., 'The Angel at Bethesda-John 5:4', *BibSac* 136 (1979), pp. 25-39.

Hofius, O., 'βλασφημία', *EDNT*, I, pp. 219-21.

Holmes, B.T., 'Luke's Description of John Mark', *JBL* 54 (1935), pp. 63-72.

Holmes-Gore, VA, 'St. Paul's Thorn in the Flesh', *Theology* 32 (1936), pp. 111-12.

Holtz, G., *Die Pastoralbriefe* (Berlin: Evangelische Verlagsanstalt, 1965).

Hooker, M.D., *The Gospel According to St Mark* (London: A. & C. Black, 1991).

Horst, P.W. van der, 'Peter's Shadow: The Religio-Historical Background of Acts V. 15', *NTS* 23 (1976-77), pp. 204-12.

—'Hellenistic Parallels to Acts (Chapters 3 and 4)', *JSNT* 35 (1989), pp. 37-46.

Hoskyns, E.C., *The Fourth Gospel* (ed. F.M. Davey; London: Faber & Faber, 1956).

Houlden, J.L., *A Commentary on the Johannine Epistles* (London: A. & C. Black, 1973).

Howard, J.K., 'New Testament Exorcism and its Significance Today', *ExpTim* 96 (1984-85), pp. 105-109.

Huby, J., *Evangile selon Saint Marc* (Paris: Beauchesne, 1948).

Hudson, R.L., 'Sin and Sickness', *Journal of Pastoral Care* 13 (1956), pp. 65-75.

Hughes, P.E., *Paul's Second Epistle to the Corinthians* (London: Marshall, Morgan & Scott, 1962).
Hull, J.H.E., *The Holy Spirit in the Acts of the Apostles* (London: Lutterworth Press, 1967).
Hull, J.M., *Hellenistic Magic and the Synoptic Tradition* (Naperville, IL: SCM Press, 1974).
Hunter, A.M., *According to John* (London: SCM Press, 1968).
Hurtado, L.W., *Mark* (New York: Harper & Row, 1983).
Huther, J.E., *Handbuch über die drei Briefe des Apostel Johannes* (Göttingen: Vandenhoeck & Ruprecht, 1880).
Jackman, D., *The Message of John's Letters* (Leicester: IVP, 1988).
Jacquier, E., *Les Actes des Apôtres* (Paris: J. Gabalda, 1926).
Jahnow, H., 'Das Abdecken des Daches Mc 2:4 Lc 5:19', *ZNW* 24 (1925), pp. 155-58.
Jaubert, A., *Approches de L'Evangile de Jean* (Paris: Editions du Seuil, 1976).
Jeremias, J., *The Rediscovery of Bethesda* (Louisville: Southern Baptist Theological Seminary, 1966).
Jervell, J., *Luke and the People of God* (Minneapolis: Augsburg, 1972).
—*The Theology of the Acts of the Apostles* (Cambridge: Cambridge University Press, 1996).
Johnes, A., *The Gospel According to St Mark* (London: Chapman, 1965).
Johnson, E.A., 'St. Paul's Infirmity', *ExpTim* 39 (1927-28), pp. 428-29.
Johnson, L.T., *The Gospel of Luke* (Collegeville, MN: Michael Glazier, 1991).
—*The Acts of the Apostles* (Collegeville, MN: Liturgical Press, 1992).
—*The Letter of James* (New York: Doubleday, 1995).
Johnson, S.E., *A Commentary on the Gospel According to Mark* (London: A. & C. Black, 1960).
Johnstone, R., *Lectures on the Book of Philippians* (Minneapolis: Klock & Klock, 1977).
Jones, A., *The Gospel According to St Mark* (London: Chapman, 1963).
Jones, P.R., 'Exegesis of Galatians 3 and 4', *RevExp* 69 (1972), pp. 471-82.
Jones, W.H.S. (trans.), *Pliny: Natural History,* VI (London: Heinemann, 1961).
Juel, D.H., *Mark* (Minneapolis: Augsburg, 1990).
Käsemann, E., *Essays on New Testament Themes* (trans. W.J. Montague; London: SCM Press, 1964).
Keller, W.E., 'The Authority of Jesus as Reflected in Mk 2:1-3:6: A Contribution to the History of Interpretation' (PhD thesis, Cambridge University, 1967-68).
Kelly, J.N.D., *A Commentary on the Pastoral Epistles* (Grand Rapids: Baker Book House, 1981).
Kernaghan, R., 'History and Redaction in the Controversy Stories in Mark 2:1-3:6', *Studia Biblica et Theologica* 9 (1979), pp. 23-47.
Kertelge, K., 'Die Vollmacht des Menschensohnes zur Sündenvergebung (Mk 2, 10)', in P. Hoffmann *et al.* (eds.), *Orientierung an Jesus* (Freiburg: Herder, 1973), pp. 205-13.
—'δικαιοσύνη', *EDNT,* I, pp. 325-30.
Kingsbury, J.D., 'Observations on the "Miracle Chapters" of Matthew 8-9', *CBQ* 40 (1978), pp. 559-73.
—'The Verb akolouthein ("To Follow") as an Index of Matthew's View of his Community', *JBL* 97 (1978), pp. 56-73.
Klausner, J., *From Jesus to Paul* (London: George Allen & Unwin, 1944).
—*From Jesus to Paul* (New York: Menorah, 1979).
Klostermann, E., *Das Lukasevangelium* (Tübingen: J.C.B. Mohr [Paul Siebeck], 1975).
Knight, G.W., *The Pastoral Epistles* (Grand Rapids: Eerdmans, 1992).
Knox, E.M., *The Acts of the Apostles* (London: Macmillan, 1908).
Kodell, I., 'Luke's Use of *Laos,* "People", Especially in the Jerusalem Narrative (Lk. 19,28-24,53)', *CBQ* 31 (1969), pp. 327-43.
Kratz, R., 'ἔνοχος', *EDNT,* I, p. 457.
Kremer, J., *2 Korintherbrief* (Stuttgart: Katholisches Bibelwerk, 1990).
Krentz, E., *Galatians* (Minneapolis: Augsburg, 1985).

Krodel, G.A., *Acts* (Minneapolis: Augsburg, 1986).

Kruse, C., *2 Corinthians* (Grand Rapids: Eerdmans, 1987).

Kugelman, R., *James* (Wilmington, DE: Michael Glazier, 1980).

Kummel, W.G., *Promise and Fulfillment: The Eschatological Message of Jesus* (trans. D.M. Barton; London: SCM Press, 1961).

Kuthirakkattel, S., *The Beginning of Jesus' Ministry According to Mark's Gospel (1,14-3,6): A Redaction Critical Study* (Rome: Pontifical Biblical Institute, 1990).

Kydd, R.A.N., *Charismatic Gifts in the Early Church* (Peabody, MA: Hendrickson, 1984).

—'Jesus, Saints, and Relics: Approaching the Early Church through Healing', *JPT 2* (1993), pp. 91-104.

Kysar, R., *John* (Minneapolis: Augsburg, 1986).

—*I, II, III John* (Minneapolis: Augsburg, 1986).

Lagrange, M.-J., *Evangile selon Saint Jean* (Paris: J. Gabalda, 1936).

—*Evangile selon Saint Marc* (Paris: J. Gabalda, 1947).

—*Evangile selon Saint Luc* (Paris: J. Gabalda, 1948).

—*Evangile selon Saint Matthieu* (Paris: J. Gabalda, 1948).

—*Saint Paul épître aux Galates* (Paris: J. Gabalda, 1950).

Lambrecht, J., 'ἐξίστημι', *EDNT*, II, pp. 7-8.

Lampe, G.W.H., 'Miracles in the Acts of the Apostles', in C.F.D. Moule (ed.), *Miracles: Cambridge Studies in their Philosophy and History* (London: Mowbray, 1965), pp. 163-78.

—'Church Discipline in the Epistle to the Corinthians', in W.R. Farmer, C.F.D. Moule and R.R. Niebuhr (eds.), *Christian History and Interpretation: Studies Presented to John Knox* (Cambridge: Cambridge University Press, 1967), pp. 337-61.

Land, S.J., *Pentecostal Spirituality: A Passion for the Kingdom* (JPTSup 1; Sheffield: Sheffield Academic Press, 1994).

Lane, W.L., *The Gospel According to Mark* (Grand Rapids: Eerdmans, 1974).

Larkin, W.J., Jr., *Acts* (Leicester: IVP, 1995).

Latourelle, R., *Miracles de Jésus et théologie du miracle* (Paris: Cerf, 1986).

Lattey, C., 'A Suggestion on Acts xix. 16', *ExpTim* 36 (1924-25), pp. 381-87.

LaVerdiere, E., *Luke* (Collegeville, MN: Michael Glazier, 1980).

Laws, S., *The Epistle of James* (New York: Harper & Row, 1980).

Lea, T.D., *1, 2 Timothy* (Nashville: Broadman Press, 1992).

Leaney, A.R.C., *The Gospel According to St. Luke* (Peabody, MA: Hendrickson, 1988).

Leary, T.J., 'The Aprons of St. Paul–Acts 19:12', *JTS* 41 (1990), pp. 527-29.

—' "A Thorn in the Flesh"–2 Corinthians 12:7', *JTS* 43 (1992), pp. 520-22.

Lee, J.A., 'Some Features of the Speech of Jesus in Mark's Gospel', *NovT* 27 (1985), pp. 1-26.

Leon-Dufour, X., 'La guérison de la belle-mere de Simon-Pierre', *EstBib* 24 (1965), pp. 193-216.

—*Le partage du pain eucharistique selon le Nouveau Testament* (Paris: Editions du Seuil, 1982).

Leroy, H., *Rätsel und Missverständnis: Ein Beitrag zur Formgeschichte des Johannesevangeliums* (Bonn: Hanstein, 1966).

Lietzmann, D.H., *An die Galater* (Tübingen: J.C.B. Mohr [Paul Siebeck], 1923).

—*Korinther I-II* (Tübingen: J.C.B. Mohr [Paul Siebeck], 1923).

Lieu, J. *The Second and Third Epistles of John* (Edinburgh: T. & T. Clark, 1986).

Lightfoot, J.B., *Saint Paul's Epistle to the Galatians* (London: Macmillan, 1896).

—*St. Paul's Epistle to the Philippians* (Grand Rapids: Zondervan, 12th edn, 1953).

Lindars, B., *The Gospel of John* (London: Oliphants, 1972).

Link, H.-G. 'Weakness', *DNTT*, III, pp. 996-99.

Loader, W., *The Johannine Epistles* (London: Epworth Press, 1992).

Loader, W.R.G., 'Son of David, Blindness, Possession, and Duality in Matthew', *CBQ 44* (1982), pp. 570-85.

Lock, W., *The Pastoral Epistles* (Edinburgh: T. & T. Clark, 1936).

Lods, A., 'Les idées des Israélites sur la maladie', in K. Budde (ed.), *Vom Alten Testament* (Giessen: Alfred Töpelmann, 1925), pp. 181-93.

Lohmeyer, E., *Das Evangelium des Markus* (Göttingen: Vandenhoeck & Ruprecht, 1953).

Loisy, A., *L'Epître aux Galates* (Paris: Nourry, 1916).

—*Le quatrième evangilé* (Paris: Emile Nourry, 1921).

Longenecker, R.N., *Galatians* (Dallas: Word Books, 1990).

Loos, H. van der, *The Miracles of Jesus* (Leiden: E.J. Brill, 1965).

Lührmann, D., *Das Markusevangelium* (Tübingen: J.C.B. Mohr [Paul Siebeck], 1987).

Luz, U., *Matthew 1-7* (trans. W.C. Linss; Minneapolis: Augsburg, 1989).

Lys, D., 'L'onction dans la Bible', *ETR* 29 (1954), pp. 3-54.

Macchia, F.D., 'Is Footwashing the Neglected Sacrament? A Theological Response to John Christopher Thomas', *Pneuma* 19 (1997), pp. 239-47.

MacGregor, G.H.C., *The Gospel of John* (London: Hodder & Stoughton, 1928).

Mackay, B.S., 'Further Thoughts on Philippians', *NTS* 7 (1961), pp. 161-70.

MacMullen, R., *Christianizing the Roman Empire A.D. 100-400* (New Haven: Yale University Press, 1984).

Maddox, R., *The Purpose of Luke-Acts* (Edinburgh: T. & T. Clark, 1982).

Maier, G., *Matthäus-Evangelium*, I (Neuhausen-Stuttgart: Hänssler-Verlag, 1979).

Maisch, I., *Die Heilung des Gelähmten: Eine exegetisch-traditiongeschichtliche Untersuchung zu Mk 2,1-12* (SBS, 52; Stuttgart: KBW Verlag, 1971).

Malina, B.J., and J.H. Neyrey, *Calling Jesus Names: The Social Value of Labels in Matthew* (Sonoma, CA: Polebridge Press, 1988).

Mangan, EA, 'Was Paul an Invalid?', *CBQ* 5 (1943), pp. 68-72.

Mann, C.S., *Mark* (Garden City, NY: Doubleday, 1986).

Manns, F., 'Confessez vos péchés les uns aux autres', *RSR* 58 (1984), pp. 233-41.

Manson, W., *The Gospel of Luke* (London: Hodder & Stoughton, 1930).

T. Manton, *An Exposition on the Epistle of James* (London: Banner of Truth Trust, 1962).

Marguerat, D., 'La mort d'Ananias et Saphira (Ac 5.1-11) dans la stratégie narrative de Luc', *NTS* 39 (1993), pp. 209-26.

Marshall, I.H., *Commentary on Luke* (Grand Rapids: Eerdmans, 1978).

—*The Epistles of John* (Grand Rapids: Eerdmans, 1978).

—*Last Supper and Lord's Supper* (Exeter: Paternoster Press, 1980).

—*The Acts of the Apostles* (Grand Rapids: Eerdmans, 1980).

Marshall, P., 'A Metaphor of Social Shame: ΘΡΙΑΜΒΕΥΕΙΝ in 2 Cor. 2:14', *NovT* 25 (1983), pp. 302-17.

Martin, R.P., *The Spirit and the Congregation: Studies in 1 Corinthians 12-15* (Grand Rapids: Eerdmans, 1984).

—*2 Corinthians* (Dallas: Word Books, 1986).

—*James* (Waco, TX: Word Books, 1988).

Marty, J., *L'Epître de Jacques* (Paris: Librairie Felix Alcan, 1935).

Martyn, J.L., *History and Theology in the Fourth Gospel* (New York: Harper & Row, 1968).

Massebieau, L., 'L'Epître de Jacques, est-elle l'oeuvre d'un chretien?', *RHR* 32 (1895), pp. 249-83.

Mastin, B.A., 'Scaeva the Chief Priest', *JTS* 27 (1976), pp. 405-12.

May, E., '... for Power Went forth from Him', *CBQ* 14 (1952), pp. 93-103.

Mayor, J.B., *The Epistle of James* (Minneapolis: Klock & Klock, 1977).

McCant, J.W., 'Paul's Thorn of Rejected Apostleship', *NTS* 34 (1988), pp. 550-72.

McNeile, A.H., *The Gospel According to St. Matthew* (London: Macmillan, 1915).

Mead, R.T., 'The Healing of the Paralytic – A Unit?', *JBL* 80 (1961), pp. 348-54.

Meecharn, H.G. 'Acts 19.16', *ExpTim* 36 (1924-25), pp. 477-78.

Mees, M., 'Die Heilung des Kranken vom Bethesdateich aus Joh 5:1-18', *NTS* 32 (1986), pp. 596-608.

Meier, J.P., *Matthew* (Wilmington, DE: Michael Glazier, 1980).

Menoud, P.H., 'La Mort d'Ananias et de Saphira (Actes 5.1-11)', in *Aux sources de la tradition chrétienne: Mélanges offerts a M. Maurice Goguel* (Neuchâtel & Paris: Delachaux & Niestlé, 1950), pp. 146-54.

—'L'echarde et l'ange satanique (2 Cor. 12.7)', in J.N. Sevenster and W.C. van Unnik (eds.), *Studia Paulina* (Haarlem: Bohn, 1953), pp. 163-71.

Merkel, H., *Die Pastoralbriefe* (Göttingen and Zürich: Vandenhoeck & Ruprecht, 1991).

Merrins, E.M., 'St. Paul's Thorn in the Flesh', *BibSac* 64 (1907), pp. 661-92.

Metzger, B.M., 'A Reconsideration of Certain Arguments Against the Pauline Authorship of the Pastoral Epistles', *ExpTim* 70 (1958), pp. 91-101.

—*A Textual Commentary on the Greek New Testament* (London: UBS, 1971).

Meyer, A., *Das Rätsel des Jacobusbriefes* (Giessen: Alfred Topelmann, 1930).

Meyers, C., *Binding the Strong Man: A Political reading of Mark's Story of Jesus* (Maryknoll, NY: Orbis Books, 1988).

Michael, J.H., *The Epistle of Paul to the Philippians* (London: Hodder & Stoughton, 1928).

Michaels, J.R., *John* (Peabody, MA: Hendrickson, 1984).

Miller, D.G. *Saint Luke* (London: SCM Press, 1959).

Miller, P.D., *Sin and Judgment in the Prophets* (Chico, CA: Scholars Press, 1982).

Minn, H.R., *The Thorn that Remained or St. Paul's Thorn in the Flesh* (Auckland: G.W. Moore, 1972).

Mitton, C.L., *The Epistle of James* (Grand Rapids: Eerdmans, 1966).

Mlakuzhyil, G., *The Christocentric Literary Structure of the Fourth Gospel* (Rome: Pontifical Biblical Institute, 1987).

Moffatt, J., 'Philippians II. 26 and 2 Tim. IV. 13', *JTS* 18 (1917), pp. 311-12.

—*The General Epistles James, Peter and Jude* (London: Harper & Brothers, 1928).

Moo, D.J., *James* (Grand Rapids: Eerdmans, 1985).

Morris, L., 'The Punishment of Sin in the Old Testament', *AusBR* 6 (1958), pp. 63-83.

—*The Gospel According to John* (Grand Rapids: Eerdmans, 1971).

—*The Gospel According to St. Luke* (Grand Rapids: Eerdmans, 1974).

—*1 Corinthians* (Leicester: IVP, 1985).

—*The Gospel According to Matthew* (Grand Rapids: Eerdmans, 1992).

Morton, J.R., 'Christ's Diagnosis of Disease at Bethesda', *ExpTim* 33 (1921-22), pp. 424-25.

—*1 Corinthians* (Leicester: IVP, 1985).

Motyer, A., *The Message of James* (Downers Grove, IL: IVP, 1985).

Moule, H.C.G., *The Epistle to the Philippians* (Cambridge: Cambridge University Press, 1897).

—*The Gospel According to Mark* (Cambridge: Cambridge University Press, 1965).

—*Studies in Philippians* (Grand Rapids: Kregel, 1977).

Mounce, R.H., *Matthew* (Peabody, MA: Hendrickson, 1991).

Mowvley, H., 'Health and Salvation in the Old Testament', *The Baptist Quarterly* 22 (1967), pp. 100-13.

Müller, J.H., *The Epistles of Paul to the Philippians and to Philemon* (Grand Rapids: Eerdmans, 1955).

Mullins, T.Y., 'Paul's Thorn in the Flesh', *JBL* 74(1957), pp. 299-303.

Munck, J., *The Acts of the Apostles* (New York: Doubleday, 1967).

Murphy-O'Conner, J., 'Péché et communauté dans le Nouveau Testament', *RB* 74 (1967), pp. 161-93.

—*The Theology of the Second Letter to the Corinthians* (Cambridge: Cambridge University Press, 1991).

Mussner, F., *Der Jakobusbrief* (Freiburg: Herder, 1964).

Neil, W., *The Letter of Paul to the Galatians* (Cambridge: Cambridge University Press, 1967).

—*The Acts of the Apostles* (Grand Rapids: Eerdrnans, 1981).

Nestle, E., 'Luke vi. 19', *ExpTim* 17 (1905-1906), p. 431.

Nicol, W., *The Semeia in the Fourth Gospel* (Leiden: E.J. Brill, 1972).

Nicole, A., *La marche dans l'obeissance et dans l'amour: commentaire sur les trios épîtres de Jean* (Vevey: Editions des Groupes Missionaries, 1961).

Nineham, D.E., *The Gospel of St Mark* (London: A. & C. Black, 1963).

—*Saint Mark* (Baltimore: Penguin Books, 1963).

Nisbet, P., 'The Thorn in the Flesh', *ExpTim* 80 (1969), p. 126.

Nock, A.D., *Early Gentile Christianity and its Hellenistic Background* (New York: Harper Torch Books, 1964).

Nolland, J., *Luke 1-9:20* and *9:21-18:34* (Dallas: Word Books, 1989, 1993).

Noorda, S.J., 'Scene and Summary: A Proposal for Reading Acts 4,32-5,16', in J. Kremer (ed.), *Les Actes des Apôtres* (Paris-Gembloux: Duculot, 1979), pp. 475-83.

Nyberg, H.S., 'Zum grammatischen Verstandnis von Matth. 12, 44f.', *ConNT* 13 (1949), pp. 1-11.

Oberlinner, L., 'δόλος', *EDNT*, I, pp. 343-44.

O'Brien, P.T., *Philippians* (Grand Rapids: Eerdmans, 1991).

O'Collins, G.G., 'Power Made Perfect in Weakness: 2 Cor. 12:9-10', *CBQ* 33 (1971), pp. 528-37.

O'Connell, D.C., 'Is Mental Illness a Result of Sin?', *Lumen Vitae* 15 (1960), pp. 233-43.

Oepke, A., 'νόσος', *TDNT*, IV, pp. 1091-98.

Omanson, R.L., 'The Certainty of Judgment and the Power of Prayer', *RevExp* 83 (1986), pp. 427-38.

Orr, W.F., and J.A. Walther, *1 Corinthians* (Garden City, NY: Doubleday, 1976).

O'Toole, R.F., 'Some Exegetical Reflections on Luke 13, 10-17', *Bib* 73 (1992), pp. 84-107.

Packer, J.W., *Acts of the Apostles* (Cambridge: Cambridge University Press, 1966).

Page, S.B., 'Some further Observations on Sin and Sickness', *Journal of Pastoral Care* 13 (1959), pp. 144-54.

Page, S.H.T., *Powers of Evil: A Biblical Study of Satan & Demons* (Grand Rapids: Baker Book House, 1995).

Painter, J., 'John 9 and the Interpretation of the Fourth Gospel', *JSNT* 28 (1986), pp. 31-61.

—'Text and Context in John 5', *AusBR* 35 (1987), pp. 28-34.

Park, D.M., 'Paul's σκόλοψ τῇ σαρκί: Thorn or Stake?' (2 Cor. XII. 7)', *NovT* 32 (1980), pp. 179-83.

Patte, D., *The Gospel According to Matthew* (Philadelphia: Fortress Press, 1987).

Peterson, S., 'εὐοδόω', *EDNT*, II, p. 81.

Pesch, R., *Das Markusevangelium* (2 vols.; Freiburg: Herder, 1976).

—*Die Apostelgeschichte* (2 vols.; Zürich: Benziger Verlag, 1986).

Pelts, D., 'Healing and the Atonement', *EPTA* 12 (1993), pp. 23-37.

Pickar, C., 'Is Anyone Sick among You?', *CBQ* 7 (1945), pp. 165-74.

Plummer, A., *The General Epistles of St. James, St. Jude and St. Peter* (New York: Funk & Wagnell, 1900).

—*The Gospel According to S. Luke* (Edinburgh: T. & T. Clark, 1901).

—*The Second Epistle of Saint Paul to the Corinthians* (Edinburgh: T. & T. Clark, 1915).

—*A Commentary on St. Paul's Epistle to the Philippians* (London: R.S. Roxburghe House, 1919).

Polhill, J.B., 'An Analysis of II and III John', *RevExp* 67 (1970), pp. 461-71.

—*Acts*. (Nashville: Broadman, 1992).

Porter, C.L., 'An Interpretation of Paul's Lord's Supper Text in 1 Corinthians 10:14-22 and 11:17-34', *Encounter* 50 (1989), pp. 29-45.

Powell, T., 'Anointing with Oil', *DPCM*, p. 11.

Price, R.M., 'Punished in Paradise (An Exegetical Theory on II Corinthians 12:1-10)', *JSNT* 7 (1980), pp. 33-40.

Prior, D., *The Message of 1 Corinthians* (Leicester: IVP, 1985).

Rackham, R.B., *The Acts of the Apostles* (London: Methuen, 1901).

Rad, G. von, *Old Testament Theology* (2 vols.; trans. D.M.G. Stalker; New York: Harper & Row, 1962).

Rahtjen, B.J., 'The Three Letters of Paul to the Philippians', *NTS* 6 (1960), pp. 167-73.

Ramsay, W.M., *Historical Commentary on the Galatians* (London: Hodder & Stoughton, 1900).

—*The Bearing of Recent Discovery on the Trustworthiness of the New Testament* (London: Hodder & Stoughton, 1915).

Reicke, B., *The Epistles of James, Peter and Jude* (Garden City, NY: Doubleday, 1964).

—'L'onction des malades d'après Saint Jacques', *La Maison-Dieu* 113 (1973), pp. 50-56.

Rengstorf, K.H., *Das Evangelium nach Lukas* (Göttingen: Vandenhoeck & Ruprecht, 1962).

Resseguie, J.L., 'John 9: A Literary-Critical Analysis', in K.R.R. Gros Louis (ed.), *Literary Interpretations of Biblical Narratives*, II (Nashville: Abingdon Press, 1982), pp. 295-303.

Reumann, J., *Variety and Unity in New Testament Thought* (Oxford: Oxford University Press, 1991).

Ridderbos, H.N., *The Epistle of Paul to the Churches of Galatia* (Grand Rapids: Eerdmans, 1956).

Riesenfeld, H., 'Sabbat et jour du seigneur', in A.J.B. Higgins (ed.), *New Testament Essays: Studies in Memory of Thomas Walter Manson* (Manchester: Manchester University Press, 1959), pp. 210-17.

Rieu, C.H., *Saint Luke: The Acts of the Apostles* (Edinburgh: Penguin, 1957).

Robertson, A.T., *A Grammar of the Greek New Testament* (New York: Hodder & Stoughton, 1919).

—*Paul's Joy in Christ* (Grand Rapids: Baker Book House, 1970).

Robertson, A.T., and A. Plummer, *First Epistle of St. Paul to the Corinthians* (Edinburgh: T. & T. Clark, 1929).

Robinson, J.A.T., *Redating the New Testament* (Philadelphia: Westminster Press, 1976).

—*The Priority of John* (London: SCM Press, 1985).

Rogge, L.P., 'The Relationship between the Sacrament of Anointing the Sick and the Charism of Healing within the Catholic Charismatic Renewal' (PhD Dissertation, Union Theological Seminary, 1984).

Roloff, J., *Die Apostelgeschichte* (Göttingen: Vandenhoeck & Ruprecht, 1981).

—*Der erste Brief an Timotheus* (Zürich: Benziger, 1988).

Roos, J.M., 'Epileptic or Moonstruck?', *Bible Translator* 29 (1978), pp. 126-28.

Ropes, J.H., *The Epistle of James* (Edinburgh: T. & T. Clark, 1961).

Rowley, H.H., *The Faith of Israel* (London: SCM Press, 1956).

Ruef, J., *Paul's First Letter to Corinth* (Baltimore: Penguin, 1971).

Runacher, C., *Croyants incrédules: La guérison de l'épileptique Marc 9, 14-29* (Paris: Cerf, 1994).

Sabourin, L., *L'Evangile de Luc: Introduction et commentaire* (Rome: Editrice Pontificia Universita Gregoriana, 1987).

Sanders, J.N., *A Commentary on the Gospel According to St. John* (ed. B.A. Mastin; London: A. & C. Black, 1968).

Scaer, D.P., *James the Apostle of Faith* (St Louis: Concordia, 1983).

Schatzmann, S., *A Pauline Theology of the Charismata* (Peabody, MA: Hendrickson, 1987).

Schenke, L., *Die Wundererzählungen des Markusevangeliums* (Stuttgart: Katholisches Bibelwerk, 1974).

Schlier, H., *Der Brief an die Galater* (Gottingen: Vandenhoeck & Ruprecht, 1949).

—'ἐκπτύω', *TDNT*, II, pp. 448-49.

Schnackenburg, R., *Matthäusevangelium I, 1-16,20* (Würzburg: Echter Verlag, 1985).

—*The Gospel According to St. John*, II (trans. C. Hastings; New York: Crossroads, 1987).

—*The Johannine Epistles* (trans. R. and I. Fuller; London: Burns & Oates, 1992).

Schneider, G., *Die Apostelgeschichte* (2 vols.; Freiburg: Herder, 1980, 1982).

Schürer, E., *The History of the Jewish People in the Age of Christ*, II (eds. G. Vermes, F. Millar and M. Black; Edinburgh: T. & T. Clark, 1979).

Schürmann, H., *Das Lukasevangelium*, I (Freiburg: Herder, 1969).

Schwartz, D.R., 'Non-Joining Sympathizers (Acts 5,13-14)', *Bib* 64 (1983), pp. 550-55.

Schweizer, E., *Church Order in the New Testament* (trans. F. Clarke; London: SCM Press, 1961).

—*The Good News According to Mark* (Richmond, VA: John Knox, 1970).

—*The Good News According to Matthew* (trans. D. Green; London: SPCK, 1975).

—'ψυχή', *TDNT*, IX, pp. 608-60.

—*The Good News According to Luke* (trans. D.E. Green; Atlanta: John Knox, 1984).

Scott, E.F., *The Pastoral Epistles* (London: Hodder & Stoughton, 1936).

Seim, T.K., *The Double Message: Patterns of Gender in Luke-Acts* (Edinburgh: T. & T. Clark, 1994).

Senft, C., *La première épitre de Saint Paul aux Corinthiens* (Paris: Delachaux & Niestlé, 1979).

Senior, D., *Invitation to Matthew* (Garden City, NY: Image Books, 1966).

Shelton, J.B., *Mighty in Word and Deed* (Peabody, MA: Hendrickson, 1991).

Shogren, G.S., 'Will God Heal Us – A Re-examination of James 5:14-16a', *EvQ* 61 (1989), pp. 99-108.

Sidebottom, E.M., *James, Jude, 2 Peter* (Grand Rapids: Eerdmans, 1971).

Smalley, S.S., *1, 2, 3 John* (Waco, TX: Word Books, 1984).

Smith, D.M., *First, Second, Third John* (Louisville: John Knox, 1991).

Smith, M., *Jesus the Magician* (San Francisco: Harper & Row, 1978).

Smith, N.G., 'The Thorn that Stayed: An Exposition of II Corinthians 12:7-9', *Int* 13 (1959), pp. 409-16.

Smith, R.H., *Matthew* (Minneapolis: Augsburg, 1989).

Southard, S., 'Sin or Sickness?' *Pastoral Psychology* 11 (May 1960), pp. 31-34.

—'Demonizing and Mental Illness (2): The Problem of Assessment: Los Angeles', *Pastoral Psychology* 34 (1986), pp. 264-87.

Spencer, F.S., *The Portrait of Philip in Acts* (JSNTSup 67; Sheffield: JSOT Press, 1992).

Spencer, W.H., 'John ix. 3', *ExpTim* 55 (1943-44), p. 110.

Spicq, C., *Les Epitres pastorales* (Paris: J. Gabalda, 1947).

Spitta, F., 'Der Brief des Jacobus untersucht', *Zur Geschichte und Literatur des Urchristentums* 2 (1896), pp. 1-239.

Spittler, R.P. 'The Limits of Ecstasy: An Exegesis of 2 Corinthians 12:1-10', in *Current Issues in Biblical and Patristic Interpretation* (Grand Rapids: Eerdmans, 1975), pp. 259-66.

Squires, J.T., *The Plan of God in Luke-Acts* (Cambridge: Cambridge University Press, 1993).

Stählin, G., 'ἀσθενής', *TDNT*, I, pp. 490-93.

—*Die Apostelgeschichte* (Göttingen: Vandenhoeck & Ruprecht, 1966).

Staley, J.F., 'Stumbling in the Dark, Reaching for the Light: Reading Character in John 5 and 9', *Semeia* 53 (1991), pp. 55-80.

Standaert, B., *L'Evangile selon Marc: Composition et littéraire* (Brugge: Zevenkerken, 1978).

Stanton, G.H., *A Gospel for a New People: Studies in Matthew* (Edinburgh: T. & T. Clark, 1992).

Stein, R.H., *Luke* (Nashville, TN: Broadman, 1992).

Stevenson, H.F., *James Speaks for Today* (London: Marshall, Morgan & Scott, 1986), pp. 96-97.

Stoger, A., *The Gospel According to St. Luke* (trans. B. Fahy; London: Burns & Oates, 1969).

Stokes, G.T., *The Acts of the Apostles* (2 vols.; New York: A.C. Armstrong & Son, 1891).

Stoll, J.R.W., *The Message of Galatians* (Leicester: IVP, 1986).

—*The Message of Acts* (Leicester: IVP, 1990).

Strachan, R.H., *The Second Epistle of Paul to the Corinthians* (London: Hodder & Stoughton, 1935).

Strathmann, H. *Das Evangelium nach Johannes* (Göttingen: Vandenhoeck & Ruprecht, 1955.

Strecker, G., *Die Johannesbriefe* (Göttingen: Vandenhoeck & Ruprecht, 1989).

Strom, M.R., 'An Old Testament Background to Acts 12.20-23', *NTS* 32 (1986), pp. 289-92.

Swete, H.B., *The Gospel According to St Mark* (London: Macmillan, 1909).

Talbert, C.H., *Reading Luke: A Literary and Theological Commentary on the Third Gospel* (New York: Crossroad, 1984).

—*Reading Corinthians* (London: SPCK, 1987).

Tannehill. R.C., *The Narrative Unity of Luke-Acts: A Literary Interpretation Volume One: The Gospel According to Luke* (Minneapolis: Fortress Press, 1990).

—*The Narrative Unity of Luke-Acts: A Literary Interpretation Volume Two: The Acts of the Apostles* (Minneapolis: Fortress Press, 1990).

Tasker, R.V.G., *The General Epistle of James* (Grand Rapids: Eerdmans, 1957).

—*II Corinthians* (London: Tyndale Press, 1958).

—*The Gospel According to St. Matthew* (London: Tyndale Press, 1961).

—*The Gospel According to St. John* (Grand Rapids: Eerdmans, 1965).

Taylor, B.E. 'Acts xix. 14', *ExpTim* 57 (1945-46), p. 222.

Taylor. R.O.P., 'The Ministry of Mark', *ExpTim* 54 (1942-43), pp. 136-38.

Taylor, V., *The Gospel According to St. Mark* (London: Macmillan, 1952).

—*The Gospel According to St Mark* (Grand Rapids: Baker Book House, 1981).

Tenney, M.C., *John: The Gospel of Belief* (London: Marshall, Morgan & Scott, 1948).

Thackeray, H.S.J., *Josephus,* II (Cambridge, MA; Harvard University Press, 1939).

Thiele, F., 'ἔνοχος', *DNTT,* II, pp. 142-43.

Thierry. J.J., 'Der Dorn im Fleische (2 Kor. xii 7-9)', *NovT* 5 (1962), pp. 301- 10.

Thissen, W., *Erzählung der Befreiung: Eine exegetische Untersuchung zu Mk 2,1-3.6* (Wurzburg: Echter Verlag, 1976).

Thomas, J.C., 'A Reconsideration of the Ending of Mark', *JETS* 26 (1983), pp. 407-19.

—'Discipleship in Mark's Gospel', in P. Elbert (ed.), *Faces of Renewal* (Peabody, MA: Hendrickson, 1988), pp. 64-80.

—'εὐχή' in T. Gilbrant (ed.). *The Complete Bible Library: The New Testament Greek-English Dictionary-Delta-Epsilon* (Springfield, MO: Complete Biblical Library, 1990), pp. 658-59.

—*Footwashing in John 13 and the Johannine Community* (JSNTSup, 61; Sheffield: JSOT Press, 1991).

—'The Fourth Gospel and Rabbinic Judaism', *ZNW* 82 (1991), pp. 159-82.

Thompson, G.H.P., *The Gospel According to Luke* (Oxford: Clarendon Press, 1972).

Thompson, M.M., *1-3 John* (Downers Grove. IL; IVP, 1992).

Thompson, W.G., 'Reflections on the Composition of Mt. 8:1-9:34', *CBQ* 33 (1971), pp. 365-88.

Thrall, M.E., *I and II Corinthians* (Cambridge: Cambridge University Press, 1965).

Thurneysen, E., *La Foi et les oeuvres* (trans. C. Pittet; Paris: Delachaux & Niestle, 1959).

Thyen, R., *Der Stil der jüdisch-hellenistichen Homile* (Göttingen: Vandenhoeck & Ruprecht, 1935).

Tiede, D.L., *Luke* (Minneapolis: Augsburg, 1988).

Tilborg, S. van, *Imaginative Love in John* (Leiden: E.J. Brill, 1993).

Tinsley, E.J., *The Gospel According to Luke* (Cambridge: Cambridge University Press, 1965).

Tipei, J., 'Laying on of Hands in the New Testament' (PhD thesis, University of Sheffield, 2000).

Torrance, T., 'The Giving of Sight to the Man Born Blind', *EvQ* 9 (1937), pp. 74-82.

Trémel, B., 'A propos d'Actes 20,7-12: Puissance du thaumaturge ou du témoin?', *RTP* 112 (1980), pp. 359-69.

Trilling, W., *The Gospel According to Matthew* (London: Sheed & Ward, 1969).

Turner, M., *The Holy Spirit and Spiritual Gifts: Then and Now* (Carlisle: Paternoster Press, 1996).

—*Power from on High: The Spirit in Israel's Restoration and Witness in Luke-Acts* (JPTSup, 9; Sheffield: Sheffield Academic Press, 1996).

Twelftree, G., *Christ Triumphant: Exorcism Then and Now* (London: Hodder & Stoughton, 1985).

—*Jesus the Exorcist: A Contribution to the Study of the Historical Jesus* (Peabody, MA: Hendrickson, 1993).

Van Elderen, B., 'Some Archaeological Observations on Paul's First Missionary Journey', in W. Gasque and R.P. Martin (eds.), *Apostolic History and the Gospel* (London: Paternoster Press, 1970), pp. 151-61.

Venerable Bede, *Commentary on the Seven Catholic Epistles* (trans. D. Hurst; Kalamazoo: Cistercian Publishing, 1985).

Vermes, G., *The Dead Sea Scrolls in English* (London: Penguin, 1987).

Vincent, M.R., *Critical and Exegetical Commentary on the Epistles to the Philippians and to Philemon* (Edinburgh: T. & T. Clark, 1897).

Voigt, G., *Die Kraft des Schwacher* (Göttingen: Vandenhoeck & Ruprecht, 1990).

Vouga, F., 'Jacques 5/13-18', *ETR* 53 (1977), pp. 103-109.

—*L' Epître de Saint Jacques* (Geneva: Labor et Fides, 1984).

Waetjen, H.C., *A Reordering of Power: A Socio-Political Reading of Mark's Gospel* (Minneapolis: Fortress Press, 1989).

Wahlde, U.C. von, 'The Johannine "Jews": A Critical Survey', *NTS* 28 (1982), pp. 33-60.

Ward, R.A., *1 & 2 Timothy & Titus* (Waco, TX: Word Books, 1974).

Warrington, K., 'Some Observations on James 5:13-18', *EPTA* 8 (1989), pp. 160-77.

—'The Significance of Elijah in James 5:13-18', *EvQ* 66 (1994), pp. 217-27.

Watson, D., 'A Rhetorical Analysis of 3 John: A Study in Epistolary Rhetoric', *CBQ* 51 (1989), pp. 479-501.

Watson, N., *The First Epistle to the Corinthians* (London: Epworth Press, 1992).

Weiser, A., *Die Apostelgeschichte* (2 vols.; Würzburg: Gütersloh and Echter Verlag, 1981).

Weiss, D.E., *Das Johannes-Evangelium* (Göttingen: Vandenhoeck & Ruprecht, 1902).

Weiss, J., *Der Erste Korintherbrief* (Göttingen: Vandenhoeck & Ruprecht. 1910).

Wells, C.R., 'Theology of Prayer in James', *CTR* 1 (1986), pp. 85-112.

Wengst, K., *Der erste, zweite und dritte Brief des Johannes* (Würzburg: Gutersloher, 1978).

Wesley, J., *Explanatory Notes upon the New Testament* (Salem, OH: Schmul, n.d.).

Westcott, B.F., *The Epistles of St John* (Grand Rapids: Eerdmans, 1966).

—*The Gospel According to St. John* (London: Murray, 1881).

Wieand, D.J., 'John 5:2 and the Pool of Bethseda', *NTS* 12 (1966), pp. 392-404.

Wiesinger, A., *St Paul's Epistles to the Philippians, to Titus, and the First to Timothy* (trans. J. Fulton and A.M. Garvald; Edinburgh: T. & T. Clark, 1851).

Wilkinson, J., 'Healing in the Fourth Gospel', *SJT* 20 (1967), pp. 442-61.

—'The Case of the Epileptic Boy', *ExpTim* 79 (1967-68), pp. 39-42.

—'Healing in the Epistle of James', *SJT* 24 (1971), pp. 326-45.

—'The Case of the Bent Woman in Luke 13:10-17', *EvQ* 49 (1977), pp. 195-205.

—*Health and Healing: Studies in New Testament Principles and Practice* (Edinburgh: Handsel, 1980).

Wilkinson, W., *The Good News in Luke* (Glasgow: Collins, 1974).

Williams, C.S.C., *The Acts of the Apostles* (London: A. & C. Black, 1964).

Williams, D.J., *Acts* (Peabody, MA: Hendrickson, 1990).

Williams, J.F., *Other Followers of Jesus: Minor Characters as Major Figures in Mark's Gospel* (JSNTSup, 102; Sheffield: JSOT Press, 1994).

Wilson, E.M., 'The Anointing of the Sick in the Epistle of James, and its Bearing on the Use of Means in Sickness', *PTR* 19 (1921), pp. 64-95.

Wink, W., 'Mark 2:1-12', *Int* 36 (1982), pp. 58-63.

Winn, A.C., *The Acts of the Apostles* (Richmond, VA: John Knox, 1960).

Witkamp, L.T., 'The Use of Traditions in John 5:1-18', *JSNT* 25 (1985), pp. 19-47.

Wood, H.G., 'Interpreting this Time', *NTS* 2 (1955-56), pp. 262-66.

Woods, L., 'Opposition to a Man and His Message: Paul's "Thorn in the Flesh" (2 Cor. 12:7)', *AusBR* 39 (1991), pp. 44-53.

Wright, J.S., 'Satan', *DNTT*, III, pp. 468-77.

Yamauchi, E., 'Magic or Miracle? Diseases, Demons, and Exorcisms', in D. Wenham and C. Blomberg (eds.), *Gospel Perspectives: The Miracles of Jesus*, VI (Sheffield: JSOT Press, 1986), pp. 89-183.

Yaure, L., 'Elymas-Nehelamite-Pethor', *JBL* 79 (1960), pp. 297-314.

Young, F.W., 'Luke 13:1-9', *Int* 31 (1977), pp. 59-63.

Zmijewski, I., 'ἀσθένεια', *EDNT*, I, pp. 170-71.

Zwaan, J. de, 'Gal 4, 14 aus dem Neugriechischen erklärt', *ZNW* 10 (1909), pp. 246-50.

INDEX OF REFERENCES

21.15	267, 269	2.13	83-84, 91	5.8	90
21.36	280	2.18	91	5.9-13	83, 91-93
22.3	228	2.20	91	5.9	89-91, 94
22.19	282	2.22	81	5.10	89, 91
22.23	257	2.23-25	81	5.11	92, 94
22.25	254	2.25	88	5.12	92
22.31	228	3.1-15	81	5.13	89, 93
22.45-46	284	3.1-10	88	5.14	40, 83, 93-97,
22-49-50	258	3.1	91		106, 113, 294,
22.53	200	3.2	102		301
22.56	269	3.3	89	5.15	83, 97-98
22.59	212	3.5	85	5.16-18	83
23.2	268	3.9	81	5.16	98
23.6	212	3.14	91	5.17	99
23.49	194, 240	3.19-21	109	5.19-47	83
23.55	194, 240	3.23	85	5.23	108
24.10	240	3.26	102	5.24	108
24.14-15	285	4	246	5.30	108
24.19	264	4.1	100	5.37	108
24.25	264	4.2	85	6.1-8.59	98-99
24.27	264	4.9-15	85	6.5	88
24.30	282	4.9	91	6.6	88
24.33	200	4.10	89	6.25	102
24.35	282	4.16-19	88	6.29	99, 107
24.38	231	4.25	97	6.37	99
24.44	189, 264	4.27-30	81	6.38-40	108
24.49	222	4.31-38	108	6.44	108
		4.31	102	6.59	99
John		4.34	108	6.60-71	101
1-12	81	4.39-42	81	7.1	99
1-4	82, 98	4.46-53	95, 98	7.3	102
1.4-5	109	4.47	89	7.7	99
1.7-9	109	4.50-53	81	7.11	99
1.19-4.54	81	5-12	83, 98	7.13	99
1.19-34	94	5-11	82	7.14	99
1.19	91-92	5	98, 102, 111,	7.16	108
1.21	92		130, 137, 309	7.18	108
1.25-28	85	5.1-18	83	7.20	81, 99
1.25	92	5.1-16	81-98	7.23	89, 94
1.29	94-95	5.1-5	82-87	7.25	99
1.33	85	5.1	83-84, 91, 93	7.28	108
1.35-51	81	5.2	84-85	7.32	99
1.35-39	94	5.3	85, 87	7.33	108
1.39	102	5.3b-4	86	7.37-40	99
1.47-51	94	5.4	86, 88, 90	7.37-39	85
1.47-50	88	5.5	86-87	7.44	99
1.50	102	5.5-9a	83	7.45-52	99
2.1-11	85	5.6-18	83	8	99, 101
2.5	91, 110	5.6-15	93	8.12	109
2.6	91	5.6-9a	87-91	8.16	108
2.11	81	5.6	87-89, 93	8.18	108
2.13-20	81	5.7	86, 89-90	8.20	99-100

AUTHOR INDEX

Other Books from CPT Press
http://www.cptpress.com

R. Hollis Gause, *Living in the Spirit: The Way of Salvation* (2009). ISBN 9780981965109

Kenneth J. Archer, *A Pentecostal Hermeneutic: Spirit, Scripture and Community* (2009). ISBN 9780981965116

Larry McQueen, *Joel and the Spirit: The Cry of a Prophetic Hermeneutic* (2009). ISBN 9780981965123

Lee Roy Martin, *Introduction to Biblical Hebrew* (2009). ISBN 9780981965154

Lee Roy Martin, *Answer Key to Introduction to Biblical Hebrew* (2009). ISBN 9780981965161

Lee Roy Martin, *Workbook for Introduction to Biblical Hebrew* (2010). ISBN 9780981965185

Martin William Mittelstadt, *Reading Luke–Acts in the Pentecostal Tradition* (2010). ISBN 9780981965178

Roger Stronstad, *The Prophethood of All Believers* (2010). ISBN 9780981965130

Kristen Dayle Welch, *'Women with the Good News': The Rhetorical Heritage of Pentecostal Holiness Women Preachers* (2010). ISBN 9780981965192

Steven Jack Land, *Pentecostal Spirituality: A Passion for the Kingdom* (2010). ISBN 9780981965147

John Christopher Thomas (ed.), *Toward a Pentecostal Ecclesiology: The Church and the Fivefold Gospel* (2010). ISBN 9781935931003

Robert P. Menzies, *The Language of the Spirit: Interpreting and Translating Charismatic Terms* (2010). ISBN 9781935931010

Most of these books are available for the iPad.

81227126R00205

Made in the USA
Middletown, DE
22 July 2018